TEACH YO

THE
100 BEST
COMPANIES
TO WORK FOR
IN THE UK

THE
100
BEST
COMPANIES
TO WORK FOR IN THE UK

Nightingale Multimedia

TEACH YOURSELF BOOKS

A catalogue record for this title is available from The British Library

ISBN 0 340 68347 3

First published 1997
Impression number   10 9 8 7 6 5 4 3 2
Year   2002 2001 2000 1999 1998 1997

Typeset by Transet Limited, Coventry, England.
Printed in Great Britain for Hodder & Stoughton Educational, a division of Hodder Headline
Plc, 338 Euston Road, London NW1 3BH by Cox & Wyman, Reading, Berks.

Dedication

To Ben and Verity
To Bob
To my mother and father
To Peggy

Contents

Contents

Acknowledgements

There are many people whom I would like to thank who have given freely of their time and insights. Kevin Delany at Coopers & Lybrand was enormously helpful in refining our guidelines for the project. Equally Robin Linnecar who is always so kind. His list of credits is extensive but suffice to say he has worked with Arthur Andersen, Shell, Deloitte, Coopers & Lybrand and KPMG, and is now a director of The Change Partnership. Chris Kiddy, our industrial psychologist, gave us some useful guidance and wrote a splendidly thought-provoking article for this book. May we also say thank you to Mary Chapman, chief executive of Investors in People, for a splendid piece and also the tremendous support IIP has given us with this book. A special thank you to Richard Medley and his colleagues at Countrywide, to Simon Jones at Havard Public Relations, to contacts at the *FT*, *The Economist*, *EIU* and various regional newspapers who offered help and guidance. We have spoken to many careers advisors in the universities, and to all you grateful thanks. To everyone at Hodders, especially Brian Steven, Tim Gregson-Williams and Sue Hart. To Stephen Whybrow at Cameron McKenna. To Mark Taylor, whose insightful comments and research were always welcome. To Shirley Smith for your tireless and always accurate typing. A grateful thank you to Dennis at Chantry Office Supplies and to John at Prontaprint Beckenham.

Journalists

Kay Reynolds editor
Managing Director of Nightingale MultiMedia. Former editor of *Bankers Digest International, Pan-European Handbook*, author *Financial Times Management Reports* and manager *The 100 Best Companies To Work For In The UK*

Mark Taylor
Freelance journalist, including *Financial Times Management Reports*. Chartered accountant and former stockbroking analyst

Peter Welbourn
Freelance journalist. Former *Daily Express* parliamentary and business writer

Frazer Wright
Former business editor *Sheffield Telegraph*. Freelance journalist for *Financial Times* and *Yorkshire Post*

Chris Mellor
Respected IT journalist. Writes for national newspapers and magazines on IT

Helen Elias
Freelance journalist for a range of national newspapers and magazines

Nick Hills
Former business editor *Vancouver Sun*, director London House

Keith Walker
Former business editor of several regional newspapers. Writer on business for the COI

Guy Campos
Business journalist, freelance after long spell at Haymarket

Liz Unsworth
Freelance journalist for a range of national newspapers and magazines

Bridget Mellor
Freelance journalist, formerly with the DTI

Introduction

Kay Reynolds

This is the second edition of *The 100 Best Companies To Work For In The UK*. It is eight years since the original was published and almost ten since we began researching that edition. In a decade, the whole ethos of corporate life has changed. Ours was the first book of its nature and it was the first time that such an extensive weight of research has been done to identify Britain's leading employers. In February 1989 – at publication date – the idea of being a good employer was a realm of something desirable but not essential. If any one aspect of corporate life has shifted beyond compare, then this is it. Today most businesses accept that they must respect, honour and value their workers. Their motivation is rarely altruism – it is purely commercial. The markets for most sectors have become fiercely competitive and worldwide in their scope. The quality of service provided to the customer has become paramount and therefore the relationship between employer and employed has had to change.

The scope of this change has been widespread. Hierarchy has – for most companies – gone through the door to be replaced by flatter structures providing more opportunities for project-based work and that most invaluable of 1990s skills – networking. In some companies – as you will see through these pages – that project alignment now operates on a global basis. National businesses have been replaced by vertical product or service divisions and people work in global teams, spending much of their time on the telephone, on e-mail or on planes. The global marketplace has also emphasised the individual above the group and while teamworking is the preferred method by most businesses, the objectives and aspirations of the individual employee are much more to the fore than at any stage in the past. Companies now say that the individual is responsible for their career and the business provides help and advice – and a framework.

There is much talk about employability – providing someone with the skill to be selective in their career options. In practice, this is a phenomenon of the disappearance of the job for life. In order to attract and keep highly talented people companies now have to offer something in return and superior level training is certainly what most undergraduates look for in their initial assignments.

In putting together this latest edition of *The 100 Best Companies To Work For* we have been conscious of the fact, through initiatives such as Investors In People, that the general level of employment practice has risen substantially in the last decade. There are more good employers in the UK than at any stage in the past. Therefore the standards to enter this book are much higher than they were ten years ago. The task of locating the best has been made no easier, though. As one commentator remarked, defining what constitutes the best employers is also a hard task. He said 'There are great companies to have on your cv and nice places to work'.

1

Introduction

In practice we have some of both. By most reliable measures good employers should offer a stimulating career and a pleasant working environment. Some, like the trading floor of securities houses, should be exciting for a short while but then people often move to calmer waters.

The companies which win highest praise in our assessment are those which offer good all-round benefits, a stimulating work environment, good training and reward packages and which treat employees as individuals.

Trust, Learning and Community: A Realistic Approach

Robin Linnecar

'Ten years ago I was making lending decisions which now I have to refer. I had autonomy before but now I am only an account manager. In the name of empowerment, there is more control because we're just lean and hungry. There isn't the loyalty or trust any more – it's just fear management and it's affecting results.' So said a friend of mine working at a senior level in financial services. It seems that the only place he finds the word encouragement is in the dictionary. This attitude raises some serious issues about the goals of a business, the atmosphere within it and what personnel or human resources functions inside businesses can do about it.

At its core the future of any function lies in the goals which the business has set itself. The human resource (HR) function has professionals who are dedicated to serving the goals or needs of the business in respect of its people. So what does this mean in practice?

The goal is to build trust

The goal and purpose of HR and those responsible for it (which includes the entire management team in an organisation) has been and always will be to build trust between people. People are customers, employees, shareholders, local residents, suppliers and any other stakeholders one can name, either directly or indirectly involved in the business. This network of interwoven interests can be seen as amazingly complex. But viewing it as a network for people for whom the goal is to build trusting relationships, it becomes a simple task for the business to focus on, led by the HR director. Let's take three examples which will have a major impact in the future:

ROLE IN THE COMMUNITY

Whether large or small, companies are concerned to be visible in their markets. Since their market is diverse, global very often and certainly public, they should not just be concerned to be seen, but seen to be concerned. Businesses are part of their communities and how employees are perceived or perceive themselves will matter considerably. The HR director will be concerned with links with education, secondments and exchanges with strategic alliance partners to the business, those who are outsourced from the business but are *employed* by the business because of the contribution made, and other areas of community affairs where the employees can play a direct role.

CREATING A COMMUNICATING ORGANISATION

The nature of organisational change means that traditional control and direct methods of management are inadequate. There will be some need for such traditions but alongside the networked organisation is the need for indirect control, influence, involvement and communication on a wider scale than ever before. While emphasising self-development and self-management of careers in the new world of work, employers have to provide the infrastructure and support of a community to help individuals further their self-reliance.

For fear of being politically incorrect allow me to misquote a famous saying – 'no person is an island!' We all need to have links or bridges between our islands so that there is some concept of the mainland. Those many people who have taken up self-employment in recent years know only too well the need to develop their own business networks. Those operating within structures in organisations that have seen several layers removed, now realise that they have to make linkages and network across the organisation in order to get things done. Individuals coming from hierarchical backgrounds aren't used to operating in this different way and so need every support from their employer.

Building trust is the key.

PROVIDING A LEARNING ENVIRONMENT

Enabling employees to develop learning skills and to become self-reliant to manage all that the workplace and economy, international or otherwise, can throw at them requires an atmosphere of trust: trust between employer and recruit, between employee and employee, between manager and managed, and between department and department. Such trust enables sound employment practices to be adopted, teambuilding, project cooperation, development and training opportunities and intra-organisational movement of people. All of these are key requirements of the future.

The strategy and tactics

If the end is to build trust then there are several key elements which will make that possible, if it is ever to be fully achieved at all (but that's why goals are worth striving for).

Firstly, there is the establishment of **mutual respect**. This means that nomenclature and job titles will need to change – indeed the words *job title* need to change to *work title* anyway, since we need flexibility of opportunity and not compartmentalisation of employees. HR directors must be instrumental in identifying ways in which status is not implied in discipline – because I am a manager does not mean I am better than a clerk, it means I do a different job of work, with both activities of manager and clerk contributing to the organisation.

Secondly, there needs to be a **mutuality of service**. The HR function should lead the way in demonstrating how the maximum productivity is gained from people when they are both led and directed but also supported and encouraged. This means an active role in teamwork, relationships, selecting and developing people and facilitation skills at the highest level on the part of HR.

With these two mutualities of service and respect will come the tactics of:

- eliminating discrimination – employees treated equally;
- increasing participation – employees sharing in the business;
- emphasising cooperation – employees having mutual understanding and mutual responsibilities.

Perennial issues to be tackled

Ever since I started paid employment nearly 30 years ago there have been some issues lodged as seemingly permanent fixtures for the personnel and HR activity. Seen in the context and new perspective of building trust and seeking mutual service and respect, these issues must be first on any HR agenda to be tackled.

- People are often promoted on technical merit into positions of managing others and have immense difficulty in adapting. HR needs to gain respect itself and earn the right to comment as well as create a mutual service culture.
- The business is always focused on tasks but needs to think strategically. HR needs to take time out for strategy and building well.
- How can HR people influence without direct authority? HR must know the business backwards.
- Will the administrative tasks (systems of appraisal, pay, contracts of employment, etc) in HR balance the development areas (training, organisation review, internal consulting, etc)? HR needs to become efficient,

effective and focused on building trust.

- Firefighting problems have always gained HR an indispensability which has given the discipline its *raison d'être*. In doing so it often becomes a blocker to change because change means a change in role. HR needs to get to the roots of problems and change the processes and thus gain a role as a people process engineer (it sounds marginally better than business process re-engineering in any event.)
- 'Appraisal systems don't fit the pay structure'; 'authorisation procedures run counter to quicker lines of communication'; 'meetings are too many and mismanaged'. All of these concerns hit the issue that systems (HR in particular) are divorced from the required behaviours. HR's finger on the business culture pulse must ensure the balance is obtained.

People are the key to the operation and potential of a business. We need to connect the individual islands and develop self-reliance within a broad base of support. This is founded on the belief that the best and most successful businesses are those that employ people who can be trusted to operate in the wider community: *all round people* who are not only specialists and skilled but know what it means to be in a team and to communicate and relate to all levels in society.

This is intensely practical and not an intellectual nicety – otherwise we end up in the shaky thinking of the Peanuts cartoon 'Mankind I love... it's people I can't stand!' and act accordingly.

Surviving in a Post Modern World

Chris Kiddy

I have drawn largely on the work and ideas of my colleague, Dr Brian Baxter, in preparing this article.

Virtue brings its own rewards

I was brought up to believe that a combination of hard work, integrity and clear goals would result in success. Once in the business world this was refined such that:

VIRTUE
equals
Be clear about what is expected of you
Work hard
Demonstrate integrity
Be professionally competent
Plan and organise yourself
equals
SUCCESS

Armed with these simple truisms I embarked on a career as an occupational psychologist, secure in the view that my prime contributions would involve:

- **individual assessment** in which, through psychometric tests and skilful interviewing, I would be able to establish the essential essence of individuals and predict their success in given jobs
- **job design** aimed at creating stable, unambiguous structures and roles in which there would be minimal conflict. Within a given type of business there would be a perfect solution to be found such that business demands and human capabilities would be in harmony
- **team-building** in which the differing beliefs and values of the team members would be reconciled in order to achieve a common goal to which all subscribed. Team-working would include clarity and buy-in to the long-term goals and a set of strategies and plans which would bring about the achievement of the goal
- **skills training** in which the *right* way to interview, coach, negotiate, resolve conflict and appraise performance was established and each skill broken down into its sequential parts which could be practised until competent, skilled, consistent behaviour resulted.

Having spent the first half of my career becoming expert in my profession, the second half is becoming devoted to unlearning or - at best – relearning those things that seemed the most certain.

Help! – Someone has changed the rules (did I say rules? Clearly still caught in a moderist time-warp).

During my working life spanning some 35 years so far, the philosophies underpinning our view of the world have undergone fundamental changes – and I thought existentialism was sufficiently avant-garde to sustain a reputation for radicalism!

SUCCESS FOR A CHILD OF THE 1940S

Belief Systems Under-pinning Modernity

Meaning and facts are defined in relation to each other. There are fundamental laws, theories and causality 'waiting' to be discovered

Life, society and *ultimate* purpose is part of a progression towards something better (greater order, clarity, the collective good)

It is possible to abstract from the turmoil of life the essences and deep structure of things to find their *real* meaning and value

We all have an inner true self which we should try to fulfil and grow

Modernism starts from an assumption of a single moral code and a single way of seeing the world based on the belief that there *is* a real world out there

The modernist *quest* is for mastery, control, consistency, purity, abstract elegance

As a young psychologist the idea that intelligence might not be something fixed (and hence measurable) but developable was both exciting and political dynamite.

SUCCESS FOR THE NEW MILLENIUM

Belief Systems Under-pinning Post-modernity

Meaning, facts and theories are only temporarily pinned down and are always constructed through language, culturally determined constraints and personal assumptions and beliefs

Life and purpose is the consequence of managing the paradoxes in life – autonomy/community; controlled/controlling; order/disorder; self/others; survival/death

There are no true meanings – they exist because we have learnt to see the world in that way in order to provide ourselves with the basis for decisions or actions

Our inner selves are the reference points we form to reassure ourselves that we exist and which come from integrating with other people and from reflection and introspection

Post modernism accepts a diversity of ways of seeing and interpreting the world and hence believes in the greater utilitarian good rather than a moral good

The post modern *quest* is for connection, recognition, flexibility, richness, diversity, action, functionality

The implications of post modernism for some of our most cherished business beliefs

WHAT ACCEPTING POST MODERN BELIEFS MAY REQUIRE

Organisation culture

- An atmosphere where transformations are **revolutionary** in result but **evolutionary** in execution
- A necessary belief that all processes, products and services are **experiments**
- Organisations will be clear about their own distinctive purpose but not impose a single set of values – each company will have its own brand personality which will form the basis of all its relationships
- An environment of continuous learning – learn fast to change fast
- A focus on inspiring people to attain new levels of skills (yes, inspirational leadership is enjoying a new life)
- A culture that acknowledges transcendent values (quality of life, community, self-fulfilment, self-expression, and spirituality)
- All relationships are reciprocal and value-adding, rather than power-based and controlling

Business goals and strategies

- Business **vision** is out – business **foresight** is in – to create competitive space based on insights into trends in technology, demographics, regulations, lifestyles
- Business will recognise the need to measure and communicate its performance in **all its relationships** – both through subjective assessment and objective criteria
- Businesses will need to develop an 'inclusive' approach towards success measures, e.g. bottom-line **and** customer delight **and** shareholder return **and** employee development
- The need to create a sense of mutually beneficial destinies with customers suppliers, investors and employees
- The growth of **relationship investing** as a source of capital
- The expansion of **partnership sourcing**
- Quality is seen simply as a basic price of market entry and not as a competitive differentiator
- Move from re-engineering hard processes to **regenerating** soft processes to ensure survival and growth
- Globalization – performance on a par with the world's best – to **succeed**, yet balanced with a regional and local focus to make things **happen**
- Benchmarking, via market intelligence, which is targeted at customer-related information, competitor activity, process, organisation, finance, personnel and suppliers
- Leaders/managers will identify the underlying **processes** of the business that create value and sustainable performance for the company – and from these create an understanding of the linkages between the key stake-holders and the main business drivers.

Jobs

- Jobs are **either** 'whole jobs', i.e. people work as business people and are expected to think as 'owners' and empowered as such, **or** 'McJobs', i.e. 'quick hire, quick fire do as you are told' jobs

- Accordingly, management will be less about creating structures and procedures and more about developing hard and soft processes that **integrate** people
- Focus is on developing relationship-based competencies and building strategic networks
- Jobs are likely to be much more complex, more measurable in their results, yet more ephemeral in their definition – job descriptions are out
- From fixed jobs to project-based activities
- Managing people will be more about managing feelings and interactions
- Leading people is about organising meaning: i.e. giving life to seemingly disparate events and processes
- Organisations (and the jobs therein) are sites where individuals make meaning for themselves and have their meanings shaped (the psychological ecosystem)
- The senior management of a company will be expected to set appropriate performance targets, not just for people's objective achievement, but also to clarify the working relationships. Cross-functional team targets will predominate
- Jobs will constantly need to have their boundaries reframed in terms of time, function, technical expertise and professional know-how.

Careers/development
- Continuing education and retraining (away from training and development into **learning** and **useful performance**)
- Employability security (rather than job security) is the philosophy underlying personal learning

- Self-help with guidance and resource availability will determine career development
- Personal development will need, as a basic requirement, to strengthen the qualities of:
  – balancing paradoxes
  – trusting process over structure
  – valuing differences
  – managing changes
  – seeking life-long learning
  –driving for the bigger, broader picture

Overall working life in the next century will have a greater sense of optimism than perhaps we have experienced this century. But it will be optimism based on a deep sense of realism rather than the quicksands of idealism. In the post modern world, 'Virtue brings its own rewards' is replaced by a new adage, 'Practicality means nothing'.

Achieving Success in Business: The Human Dimension

Mary Chapman

The authors of this book argue that the top 100 companies to work for are also some of the most successful commercially. Why is that true, and why are poor companies to work for so often some of the UK's poorest performers? The most common answers always focus on: good or bad strategies; the right or wrong product; innovation or lack of it; or the amount of investment in new technology. But the common factor behind all of these is the human dimension.

The human factor remains the blindspot in discussions about business success in the UK. Yet it is a factor that has kept the UK lagging behind many of its competitors when it comes to developing and exploiting this asset. This may be one of the reasons that the recent World Competitiveness Report (produced by the World Competitiveness Forum) shows the UK in 19th position out of 40, lagging behind Chile, Switzerland and Norway. It comments that 'the United Kingdom does not perform well in management (23rd) or people (27th). It seems that despite improvement in other areas, the UK is unable to make the best of what is its most important asset – people. All the analysis of world class companies points to one thing – that the people dimension is the critical factor for success.

A report commissioned jointly by Coopers & Lybrand and Investors in People UK at the end of 1995 – called *Making People Your Business* – provides graphic evidence that there is plenty of room for improvement in the performance of many British companies. Although chief executives are reporting considerable efforts to put into practice their stated belief that investment in people is vital for competitive success, a number of key elements are preventing these efforts from bearing fruit.

The Investors in People standard was developed specifically as a framework to help to improve the competitiveness of enterprises in the UK and is proving a powerful instrument in raising performance. The standard enjoys widespread backing from all sides of the British industrial and political scene. The number of organisations becoming involved with the standard is testament to the benefits which it produces. Already almost 4,200 organisations have been recognised as meeting the Investors in People standard and there are a further 20,500 committed to doing so. In total they cover 27 per cent of the UK workforce. The results for companies involved with the standard all impact the bottom line – from reductions in absenteeism and staff turnover to rises in productivity, customer satisfaction and profit levels.

The standard is also increasingly being used to build discussion and collaboration between employer and unions. It is supported by the TUC, which is itself a recognised organisation. The City is also beginning to recognise the vital strategic importance of HR policies in the building of successful businesses. Kleinwort Benson has taken this one step further. It has made Investors in People commitment a key reference point in its investment selection for its new Tomorrow's Company Unit Trust, giving a high value and positive rating to those companies using the standard.

This reflects perhaps a general trend in the way forward-thinking organisations operate with people, viewing them as a resource and with recognition of the need to maintain their skills and motivation. Companies which have achieved sustainable success create a culture which promotes involvement, accountability, responsibility, high performance and the achievement of business goals. They *walk the talk* and display the real commitment required to ensure that people policies and development are not reduced to fine slogans and little action.

What we are seeing is a gap between the best intentions of employers and what is happening in practice. These failures are because the initiatives introduced by employers are not being coordinated effectively; nor are they in line with the real needs of the organisation. Only a third of companies have a budget attached to their people strategy. The links between their people and business strategies are often unclear with the result that investments in people are often not based on a clear assessment of the business benefits those investments will bring, and companies are not good at tracking the returns they get from them.

What is essentially missing between employees and companies is involvement. The *involvement gap* is caused as a result of employees not knowing the direction of

the businesses in which they work, or the role that they play within it. This leaves many employees insufficiently engaged with their organisation, and the result is that they feel undervalued and demotivated.

In addition there is a *performance gap*, where the management skills of employers are inadequate to motivate and develop the workforce to improve performance, and processes to support this are failing. Meanwhile skill shortages act as a brake on business success with the result that many enterprises cannot take full advantage of the UK's competitive advantage in terms of wage levels and labour market flexibility.

The organisations that seem to succeed in getting the best from their people are those with the right combination of three ingredients:

- the infrastructure of systems and processes
- the management skills to use the infrastructure effectively
- the commitment to make the phrase *people are our greatest asset* really live in the culture of the organisation.

UK business will need to tie people management more closely into business strategies to ensure that what investment they make will help achieve the goals of the organisation. It is only then that the issue of developing people will rise to the top of the corporate agenda – and turn the well-meaning intentions of employers into a force for business success.

It is this commitment and this integrity which has a direct impact on how people feel about their work and why companies which achieve these things are the companies for which people want to work.

Achieving Success in Business: The Human Dimension

The challenges faced by UK business are manifold: global competition, rapid technological change and an education system not yet providing the skills required in the workforce of the next century. If we are to meet the challenges ahead, we must put people at the top of the agenda for UK business. Only then will there be more successful companies (and by definition, good companies to work for) which will enable the UK to improve its overall competitiveness.

THE 100 BEST COMPANIES TO WORK FOR IN THE UK

A–Z Listing

ABB

In 1996, for the third year running, ABB (Asea Brown Boveri) was voted the most admired company in Europe in a survey conducted by the *Financial Times*. Led by President and Chief Executive Goran Lindahl, the company, which is the world's largest electrical engineering group, combines a global presence with highly autonomous local operations and is noted in particular for its capacity to react quickly to changing market conditions. ABB's emphasis on career development and its willingness to delegate responsibility to the lowest possible level are reflected in another of the categories in the *FT* survey which ABB also won – the company which maximises the potential of its employees.

ABB at a glance

Employees: 220,000 worldwide, 13,100 UK
Annual staff attrition rate: 3–4 per cent
Key locations: London (HQ),
  22 manufacturing and more than
  100 customer service centres around
  the UK
Av. annual graduate recruitment: 30
Annual intake: 450

An inside view

Founded in 1988 from the merger of Sweden's ASEA AB and Swiss-owned BBC Brown Boveri (in what was then the biggest cross-border merger ever), ABB is a global engineering group, with annual revenues in excess of $35 billion. Worldwide, the group is structured into five business segments – power generation, power transmission and distribution, industrial and building systems, transportation (which is run as a joint venture with Daimler-Benz) and financial services – which are then subdivided into around 50 specific business areas. This structure is then overlaid with a network of country-based reporting in order to create ABB's famous matrix management system.

Much of the respect for ABB from its peer group derives from the company's distinctive management style. In particular, the group is highly decentralised. Accountabilities are broken down into 5,000 small profit centres operating within 1,000 companies – typically each profit centre contains only 40 people, deals directly with customers and is focused on specific products. All profit centre leaders are responsible for their own profit and loss results. There is an absolute minimum of corporate bureaucracy; the UK headquarters, for example, has a staff of only 17 to look after more than 13,000 employees. This style of management allows individual units the freedom and motivation to run their own businesses, while still being able to take advantage of the global presence and economies of scale conferred by ABB's size.

A defining characteristic of ABB is the importance it places on constantly raising productivity, which it believes is essential to sustaining the company's competitive advantage in the long-term. To achieve this, ABB invests substantially in management training. The company strongly believes that most companies utterly fail to exploit the full potential of their workforce – he has been quoted as saying that 90 per cent of an employee's capabilities are unused. ABB avoids this trap by involving as many of its employees as possible in the decision-making process and encouraging the transfer of know-how across borders and businesses.

ABB is a highly flexible and fast-moving company. Its streamlined management structure allows its young managers a miniature business of their own in which to develop their entrepreneurial flair, while also contributing to the group's undoubted success in managing changing business conditions. Unlike some other business leaders, Barnevik does not see continuous change as a threat, but rather as a security – if you stand still, in reality you go backwards.

How does ABB rate?

Pay:	good
Benefits:	good
Communications:	good
Training:	excellent
Career development:	very good
Morale:	excellent

People and personnel policies

ABB's commitment to stimulating and empowering its employees is one of the principal reasons for the strength of its management team. This is then supplemented by an extensive investment in formal training and career development. As well as the (largely technical) training which is conducted at a local level, programmes are also organised by business areas and at a corporate level. These latter programmes generally take the form of management workshops at which attendees are assigned a particular project to complete. At more senior levels still, managers attend courses organised by the London Business School, sometimes run in conjunction with other leading international companies. However, on-the-job training continues to be regarded as the most valuable. Individuals learn best when they have the scope to succeed or fail.

The group does not operate a central graduate recruitment policy in the UK but, consistent with its philosophy of decentralisation, leaves this as a matter for individual companies. Nevertheless, potential high-flyers are tracked from an early stage in their career and the outstanding ones are given an early exposure to international assignments. A database is maintained centrally of high-performing employees around the world.

Not surprisingly, given ABB's global presence, international experience is a valuable asset. ABB is known for its teams of global managers who are parachuted into situations at short notice as part of a trouble-shooting assignment. However, product knowledge is considered equally important. One of ABB's competitive advantages is its closeness to its customers and it is unwilling to jeopardise this by introducing staff who are unfamiliar with the product concerned. For this reason, movements between product areas are relatively unusual.

Remuneration is primarily the responsibility of the country head. However, in the UK, the general policy is that salary should be set at the median level, with incentive payments based on performance increasing total remuneration to the upper quartile. Similarly to many other leading companies, ABB is moving to a structure where incentive payments for good performance are increasingly important and typically in some companies all employees are part of a business-wide incentive scheme. In the UK, the company has an excellent pension plan, but there are no share option schemes.

Like many engineering companies, ABB has a paucity of women at senior levels. Most of its recruits tend to be men and, although many of the constituent parts of the group are tolerant of flexible working arrangements, ABB does not believe in pursuing a policy of positive discrimination. Racially, however, the group is much more diverse. This is due not least to its somewhat complex ownership structure, which means that ABB is not particularly identified with any one set of national characteristics.

In common with remuneration, communications are also a matter for local management, although the group does produce regular internal newsletters. Barnevik believes that the firm's highly decentralised structure significantly aids communication within the organisation. Decisions made by phone and e-mail impact immediately when there are only two levels between country manager and company shop floor.

The speed of communication is further enhanced by the fact that 50,000 ABB staff worldwide are plugged into Lotus Notes. In terms of community action, ABB focuses specifically on the environment and on health and safety issues. For example, as part of its internal consultancy practice, two ABB employees are dedicated entirely to assisting small firms with a range of environmental initiatives.

Contact address

Mr Paul Upton,
Group Personnel Manager,
ABB Asea Brown Boveri Limited,
Orion House, 5 Upper St Martin's Lane,
London WC2H 9EA.
Telephone: 0171 753 2000.
Fax: 0171 753 0205.

Allied Dunbar Assurance plc

Allied Dunbar Assurance is the UK's largest unit-linked life assurance, investment and pension company. A wide range of financial services is marketed through a direct sales force of nearly 3,700 and several thousand more independent financial advisors. The head office in Swindon employs more than 2,100 people, and there are further offices and sales branches spread across the country – impressive proof of growth for a relatively young company. Allied Dunbar was first launched only 25 years ago in 1971, as a subsidiary of BAT Industries. This business attracts organised, motivated and resourceful people. Graduates from all fields of study are drawn to Allied Dunbar not least because of the excellent long-term career prospects, staff facilities and excellent pay and benefits package.

Allied Dunbar at a glance

Employees: 2,197, with a further 3,700 self employed
Annual staff attrition rate: 16 per cent
Key locations: Swindon (HQ), plus offices and sales branches across the UK
Av. annual graduate recruitment: 20–25
Annual intake: 200

An inside view

Allied Dunbar designs, sells and manages pensions, investments, life and health assurance products and provides mortgages, commercial loans, corporate banking and international financial services. It is an impressive package in a demanding and highly competitive commercial sector. Changes in the insurance industry have driven new business figures down, but the business environment is improving. Allied Dunbar is determined to emerge from the new business trough faster than its competitors, and early indications point to the organisation being well placed to meet this target.

Indeed, the company's growth from the eighth largest life office in the UK in 1993 to the third largest in 1995, as measured by UK individual new business premiums, demonstrates that the right strategies are in place to succeed. In 1995 pre-tax profits at £153 million were 28 per cent lower than the previous year, while post-tax profits were 24 per cent lower at £114 million – a result of a 32 per cent reduction in single premium business due to consumer misgivings about the investment markets. Funds under management rose by more than £17 billion in 1996.

Annual graduate intake, usually numbering 20–25 people each year, is from a broad range of disciplines. Academic success is important (2.1 or a 1st), but equally those who succeed will be highly motivated; with energy and initiative, they'll be able to communicate well both verbally and in writing, with an analytical mind, and, just as important, an ability to flexibly adapt to an ever changing business environment. With a very high long-service record, and a substantial investment in training new staff, the company is looking for people able to make a long-term commitment. The graduates must be capable of rising to middle and senior management positions in the future.

How does Allied Dunbar rate?

Pay:	very good
Benefits:	good
Communications:	very good
Training:	excellent
Career development:	very good
Morale:	very good

People and personnel policies

Operating successfully within a service industry calls for people with tact, diplomacy, and integrity in all the main Allied Dunbar recognised graduate career entry paths: actuarial, accountancy, information technology and client services. Each trainee position carries a healthy starting salary – in 1996 £17,000 for actuaries, £15,500 for other departments, including a 15 per cent profit-related pay scheme. Salary progression is performance related. Graduate entrants are assured relevant professional training within their field, and monitored career progression to step them up to management levels at early opportunities. Staff are positively encouraged to achieve professional accreditation and membership of professional institutes. The training programme lasts two years, with the exception of actuaries who have between three and five years of training ahead of them.

Other starting attractions include non-contributory pension cover, a life assurance package, generous holiday allowances and the promise of a company car usually within the first two to three years. All in all, a pretty good first job deal for those who sparkle enough to meet the exacting entry criteria. On top of these benefits, facilities at the Swindon offices are excellent, with a subsidised staff restaurant, a company-owned sports and leisure centre, and a superb high technology custom-built state-of-the-art learning resources centre.

The corporate graduate development programme is supplemented by individually tailored training within the department, as part of the professional progression scheme. After a comprehensive graduate induction programme, Allied Dunbar continues to offer career development, especially training courses and on the job projects where theory is quickly put into practice. Those who apply to work at Allied Dunbar must be confident of their communication skills and ability to grasp and understand information quickly.

The company culture is very results orientated, with extra focus put upon getting it right and adhering to correct practice at all times; and within this framework, graduates are given real responsibility from their first day. Assessment is an on-going process, completed mutually by graduate and manager. The training culture embraces establishing skills to achieve the job in hand, while developing competencies for the future.

Allied Dunbar is evolving as a company. As the financial services market becomes ever more competitive, and highly regulated, it is deliberately focusing upon the market and the consumer, becoming a market-led, not product-driven organisation as a result. Internally, a flatter management structure is taking shape, reducing bureaucracy and layers of management hierarchy.

Fast communication is essential, with IT, team meetings, management briefings and cascade briefings used to disseminate clear messages. Feedback is a two-way process, with an annual employees' views and values monitor evaluating company culture, management, and communications. Frankly, Allied Dunbar is under-represented by women in more senior management positions, but women are well represented at middle management and sales force level.

All in all, the consistent striving to attain excellence that permeates Allied Dunbar's culture identifies this organisation as one with a future both for the corporate body, and for the individuals in its employ.

Contact address

Mr Peter Campbell,
Director of Personnel and Organisation
Allied Dunbar Assurance plc,
Allied Dunbar Centre,
Swindon SN1 1EL.
Telephone: 01793 514514.
Fax: 01793 502611.

Andersen Consulting

Part of the Arthur Andersen worldwide group of professional services firms, Andersen Consulting is the world's largest business and technology consultancy. It is currently growing at an annual rate of more than 20 per cent and its success has been founded on offering the highest levels of client service. In addition to recruiting the best and brightest of the country's graduates, the company is increasingly looking for experienced professionals with particular industry and technical expertise. With its record of consistent growth and a commitment to demanding standards, Andersen can offer a challenging and highly rewarding career.

Andersen Consulting at a glance

Employees: 2,200 UK*
Annual staff attrition rate: 12 per cent
Key locations: London (HQ), offices
throughout main cities in UK
Av. annual graduate recruitment: 250
Annual intake: 350
*excluding employees under outsourcing
arrangements

An inside view

Andersen Consulting is consistently rated top of the UK and European league tables of management consultants. Even through the recession, it managed to increase market share and the company is now growing at an annual rate of more than 20 per cent. Structured around five competencies – strategy, technology, change management, process and practice management – Andersen sees its role as helping clients solve their business problems, harnessing the power of technology and implementing solutions. In recent years, it has become increasingly involved in outsourcing, whereby it takes wide-ranging responsibility for the operation and management of client processes and facilities.

Despite the industry's rapid growth, management consultancy is a highly competitive business and Andersen's success has been based on providing the highest level of client service and measuring up 100 per cent to the client's (often rigorous) expectations. In order to achieve this level of client satisfaction, it is essential that Andersen attracts the best people in the market. This means not only individuals who are academically well qualified, but also those who have strong interpersonal skills, and in the case of experienced recruits, relevant industry or technical expertise. The ability to communicate effectively and work well in teams is very important.

Another critical attribute is integrity – an Andersen consultant is expected to exercise a fine level of judgement and be able to deal with difficult and demanding situations.

Given that Andersen Consulting is in the business of change, it must be able to respond quickly and efficiently to changing demands and circumstances in its own markets. Andersen is not, therefore, a hierarchical organisation and individuals can typically be handed responsibility at a very early stage in their career. It is also a highly entrepreneurial organisation, particularly at higher levels. Marketing the firm and its services becomes an increasingly important part of the job specification.

Some observers comment that Andersen is regarded by many in its industry as aggressive and somewhat arrogant. This does not mean that the firm is unfriendly. According to Liz Hopkins, Andersen's human resources director, Andersen can actually be a very supportive environment. Nevertheless, she will acknowledge that it is a challenging one and the constant pressure to perform will not necessarily suit everybody.

How does Andersen Consulting rate?

Pay:	excellent
Benefits:	good
Communications:	good
Training:	superb
Career development:	excellent
Morale:	good

People and personnel policies

Andersen Consulting's philosophy of providing the highest quality of service to its clients inevitably translates into its attitude to the workforce. As a matter of policy, it seeks to recruit the most talented and driven individuals in the market. Andersen Consulting is a meritocratic organisation, in which individual achievement is both recognised and well rewarded. Although graduate entry remains important to the firm, a recent trend in its personnel policy has been the increasing recruitment of experienced professional staff with established and valuable skills.

One of the principal ways in which Andersen retains its competitive edge over its rivals is through the excellence of the training which it provides. Andersen regards training as a career-long commitment, and the company currently spends more than \$400 million per year on dedicated training centres in Chicago, London, Sofia and Eindhoven. For most graduate recruits, training commences with an intensive three-week course in London, focusing on IT and its role in the modern world. Those who join its strategy area will attend a tailored business course which focuses on developing commercial awareness and analytical skills. This is followed by a second three-week course held near Chicago, which is renowned (some might say infamous!) for the sustained demands it puts on the individual's intellect and stamina. At higher levels, training courses are specially structured and all staff have a specifically devised training plan throughout their time at Andersen.

Andersen Consulting employees spend at least 15 weeks in core skills training during their first four years within the firm. The continuing development of personal and professional skills is seen as an essential complement to on-the-job learning, and the process never ceases. Right up to the most senior levels, time is set aside for the individual to acquire new skills and knowledge. All employees are assigned a career counsellor, who is charged with monitoring an individual's career. Regular performance appraisals are also held where particular development needs are identified.

Not surprisingly given the demands placed upon them, Andersen Consulting employees tend to be very well remunerated. In benchmarking remuneration for lower-level professional staff, Andersen's policy is to target itself at the upper quartile. On the road to partnership – the ultimate goal – there are two significant milestones, manager and associate partner. At both these levels, there will be further step increases in compensation although it should be noted that an associate partner does not receive a share of the profits. However, it is at full partnership level that the riches are really on offer.

Andersen Consulting is working hard to promote women in the workforce. Prior to joining the firm, it holds special seminars at universities to educate women about Andersen, and for those who have joined, networks have been established to share experiences and provide mutual support. In recruitment interviews, the company always attempts to include a woman in the interview process. Andersen also offers female employees who have had children a two-year career break and

encourages flexible and part-time working arrangements.

Andersen Consulting is keen to provide a supportive and participative culture to encourage its employees to balance their work and personal lives. One particularly innovative initiative for all staff is the creation of help desks designed to take some of the hassle away from their busy working lives. It includes services ranging from house-sitting, organising theatre tickets, providing emergency nanny services and dry cleaning to purchasing gifts.

With the majority of professional staff regularly working on client sites, communication within the organisation can be a challenge. In response, therefore, the firm organises a series of regular communication days to inform staff about what is going on and listen to them. There is also an employee newsletter. Andersen has also created focus groups of junior staff to obtain feedback on the workforce's moods and aspirations. Social activities are also encouraged.

Contact address

Ms Elizabeth Mills,
Director of Resource Management,
Andersen Consulting,
2 Arundel Street,
London WC2R 3LT.
Telephone: 0171 438 5000.
Fax: 0171 831 1133.

Asda

Five years ago, Asda was down and out. The company had lost its way. As the business publication *Management Today* put it 'Customers were dwindling, the share price was plummeting, stores were falling into disrepair and the staff into despair'. Or as a current senior executive of the reborn Asda says 'Five years ago the business was basically bust. But it concentrated our minds and gave us momentum and vision'. Today, the supermarket chain employs 75,000 people, and rising; with a £6 billion plus turnover and 5.4 million customers going through the stores every week.

Asda at a glance

Employees: 75,000
Annual staff attrition rate: 18 per cent
Key locations: Leeds (HQ); 210 stores nationwide
Av. annual graduate recruitment: 100
Annual intake: n/a

An inside view

While most companies would prefer to play down the cult of personality and performance, there is no doubt that the coming of Archie Norman saved Asda. He had already played a transforming role at Woolworths, and was established as working under the banner of effecting 'major change in substantial companies'. Asda, from the outside at least, still appeared substantial, through the building of a major edifice of a head office at Leeds, Asda House. As Jan Shaw, the company's manager of human resources, puts it 'We built ourselves a fancy office building seven years ago, but the moment a company builds itself a fancy headquarters, you know it's time to get out, we're spending money on the wrong things'.

Norman immediately engaged in a reversal of direction which resulted in a reversal of fortune. He turned the new headquarters from an all-powerful, domineering bureaucratic centre of administration into a simple support office for all the Asda stores out there in the real world. Archie, as everyone calls him, has made each Asda store the centre of his food world; decentralised profit centres whose success depends on the talents of individual managers and workers.

A one-off as an executive manager, he has turned Asda around by making the company work internally and externally. Customers now view Asda as their own champion in more ways than one. They know it provides good, cheap food but they are also aware – as are those who shop at its main competitors – that Asda Man is out there battling on other fronts. He has led the protests against government threat to the tax-free share options of Asda check-out operators; almost single-handedly broken the Net Book Agreement to bring down the price of books, and is now at work on the same consortium price issue involving a whole range of non-prescription medicines. Through all this, Archie Norman and his Asda have become known as the customer's friend. His strategy based on permanently low prices for food, plus a wide range of clothes, books and records, continues to produce flourishing financial performance, with the latest year's figures showing taxable profits up 15 per cent at £160 million.

The turnaround in the company has been centred on its people and the way they have been allowed freedom to run Asda in a decentralised fashion. Five years ago, as Shaw puts it 'There was no investment, particularly on the people side. There were no trainees. We were doing it cheap and what we could get away with. Across the spectrum, from checkout to management, the company was in a permanent holding mode. Archie came and put in the vision, proper controls and gave us all a direction and meaning. He established the stores and their managers as the centre of the Asda world instead of the headquarters head office.'

How does Asda rate ?

Pay:	good
Benefits:	good
Communications:	good
Training:	very good
Career development:	very good
Morale:	excellent

People and personnel policies

In some ways, the company has gone from one extreme to the other. The old corporate culture of layers of management which empowered itself out of head office has become what is called a seamless system in which everyone helps everyone else. At Christmas, for example, more than 1,000 employees at Asda House go out and help in the stores. Asda is egalitarian. Norman does not sit in a spacious office. Often, he is to be found in a lumberjack shirt, blue jeans and black boots. On Fridays, of course, everyone at Asda House turns out in clothes from the George Davies collection, one mark of the Asda differential, which means that it is 'Thank George, It's Friday' Day. Everyone is a colleague in this company. The hierarchy is obviously still clear in the annual report, but in essence the structure is extremely flat.

'There are no private offices for the directors,' says Shaw. 'Secretaries are shared, there is no reserved parking for anyone, and there is no directors' dining room. We are very anxious about how we behave on the people side of the operation. There is a direct connection, we believe, between our own people policy here and how we treat our own customers. We are always looking to employ people who love to interact, and are on the front foot with others – with a positive, engaging approach. These qualities transfer naturally into the selling mode which, of course, is what Asda is all about.'

The company provides a basic, but above-average, benefits package which might not in itself make headlines, in any human resource manual. It is the little things that count, little things that are actually big things to those who work for this company. 'We have a very flat structure,' says Shaw. 'We don't like organisational charts, or job definitions and grading. This puts people in boxes. This is partly reflected in our broad bands of pay. There are no pyramids. In the stores, you have a manager and the rest are all on one level. From checkout to chief executive, there are not more than four or five layers of hierarchy, or responsibility.'

Norman is in his stores every weekend, and he knows all the managers by name. The stores, the managers and their staff are now the power in this company – and he makes this clear by his visits. 'We work hard on creating and sustaining a community where everyone knows each other,' says Shaw. No one denies that Asda was in bad shape and that it needed bringing back to life with outside talent. In the period of rejuvenation, the company recruited 250 managers from outside. But having brought the company back to life partly through outside people recruitment, Asda is now investing heavily in internal training. '1996 is the year in which we have begun to reinvest and redevelop our training skills across the business,' says Norman. 'We believe that many of the old-fashioned craft skills that have disappeared from British retailing in the last decade need to be brought back. We are therefore recreating training schemes for master bakers and butchers, produce and clothing managers.'

Because the company operates a flatter structure in its organisation than most of its competitors, argues Norman, it must rely upon the quality of its skilled craftsmen and managers to make the business work.

'Service is the new battleground in food retailing,' he says. 'Whereas many of our competitors see this as issuing manuals and national television advertising, we believe that service comes from the heart. Only by recruiting the right people, creating the right workplace community and motivating colleagues well, will we achieve our objective: *service and personality*. We believe in colleague involvement and motivation. If we express a sense of fun, and personality in the way we manage the business, this will help colleagues to do the same for our customers.'

Norman admits that Asda's style of trading is very demanding and depends critically on the enthusiasm and motivation of the company's employees at all levels. 'Our approach to colleague motivation and the extension of our single status principles is something we continue to believe in strongly. We aim to create a single status company of employee owners in which everyone's contribution is valued.' Perhaps the most signal achievement of Norman's revolution is the workers' ownership of his company. It now has the biggest share ownership workforce in the United Kingdom. The share options scheme is offered to all employees on the same terms as top executives. It has been taken up by more than 50 per cent of the workforce.

Contact address

Mr Jan Shaw, Human Resources Manager, Asda,
Asda House, Southbank,
Great Wilson Street,
Leeds LS11 5AD.
Telephone: 0113 243 5435.
Fax: 0113 241 8636.

Astra Pharmaceuticals

A stra is an international pharmaceutical company which ranks among the largest in the world. Currently in a rapid phase of growth, it focuses on areas of disease in which its proficiency in research can satisfy important medical needs. Research and development activities are the responsibility of five research units in Sweden and the UK. Marketing is carried out through subsidiaries in about 40 countries and through agents and licensees in a large number of additional countries. Employees total approximately 17,000 worldwide. More than 1,700 people are employed in the UK within research, manufacturing and other functions.

Astra at a glance

Employees: 1,750 UK
Annual staff attrition rate: n/a
Key locations: Kings Langley,
    Loughborough, Corby, Edinburgh
Av. annual graduate recruitment: n/a
Annual intake: n/a

An inside view

The pharmaceutical industry is currently encountering one of its greatest periods of sustained international competition. The process of globalisation, apparent in many business sectors, is one of the key determinants in the healthcare spectrum which is simultaneously undergoing rapid growth. The implications for pharma companies are stark. They must compete on a worldwide basis or they will be outstripped. This means heavy, ongoing and long-term investment in drug discovery and development, effective distribution and capable sales and marketing. Implicitly it also places demands on the leading players in the industry to locate, attract, develop and keep talented people. In any pharmaceuticals multinational with ambitions to compete at the top table, constructing fruitful client and partner relationships is everything. And the people who succeed will be the innovators who can communicate and network to great business effect. New standards of achievement in research, production, and delivery are now expected as normal practice by clients.

Major international drug companies are engaged in a vigorous battle for market share and only the degree of their determination to be leaders in target markets will ensure their future prosperity. Among the most impressive is the Swedish-owned company Astra Pharmaceuticals. Astra currently has 8.8 per cent of the UK market, with 19 per cent growth between 1995 and 1996. Sales have risen from $50 million in 1990 to $330 million in 1995. The company began operations in Sweden in 1913 and many of its values remain fundamentally the same today as they were at the outset. These include commitment to technological excellence and safety, a strong belief in research, an enterprising, innovative spirit, an emphasis on hard work and a respect for the individual. In common with many other global pharmaceutical companies, Astra has produced a defined corporate vision. This is to stay one step ahead of market developments; to expand its global influence; to be better where Astra is already good and to acknowledge that individual performance is the key to long-term success.

The operation in the UK has grown rapidly in the last decade, inspired by these beliefs. It is highly decentralised – a core concept at Astra worldwide. This means that the corporate values may be incorporated into its operations in different ways but the core policies at the sites are the same. Key developments during 1995 included the acquisition from Fisons of its research and development operation, where more than 60 per cent of employees are graduates or hold PhDs. Current research work covers respiratory disease (asthma), cardiovascular disease (thrombosis), and diseases of the central nervous system (epilepsy).

How does Astra rate?

Pay:	very good
Benefits:	very good
Communications:	excellent
Training:	very good
Career development:	excellent
Morale:	very good

People and personnel policies

Mike Mitchell, director of Astra's clinical research unit in Edinburgh, ACRU, says that the global success of Astra is the result of many years of investment in research, production and marketing. He comments that this longer term perspective is a key factor in the Astra approach to business and that even in an industry where R&D programmes can last a decade or more, Astra is firmly committed to the long-term.

He emphasises the importance of valuing the individual in the company's quest for success. 'Our culture is summed up in our statement *The Astra Way* which describes the values and ways of working that make Astra special. People are our most important resource. A high degree of autonomy is built into the company culture which puts responsibility onto the individual to grow to their personal potential,' he says.

Each of the company's locations in the UK devises its own business and human resources approaches which fit with the spirit of the international targets and values of the group. Mitchell says that the factors which motivate individuals in research and in sales will often be different. Equally, the competencies needed to work effectively in these disciplines will vary considerably. So, many HR issues are decided at the local level which is generally the most effective in meeting business and personal demand. However, formal policies and procedures are standarised across the sites in the UK.

Astra aims to be competitive in a well-paid market place and performance-related payments can boost individual take-home salary to the best in the industry. A profit-sharing scheme, a pension scheme and comprehensive health insurance plans are available.

'We don't have a highly structured system for career development. Self-motivation is important. Employees must be very good at their current job in order to progress in the business. We are essentially an informal company – communication and networking are all-important. We are team driven, particularly in our research facility offices in Edinburgh. We do not believe in a rigid functional structure. We believe strongly in management by culture, which means applying a framework of core principles to local operational procedures.'

The overall structure of Astra is described as a matrix although within individual operating units there will be line or line and project structures. Employees throughout the company are encouraged to spend time working abroad. International opportunities are advertised locally and any employee from secretary to middle and upper management can apply to work overseas. Careers are based on Astra's business objectives, focused on skills and the development of competencies. Individual line managers are especially active in career development and scope exists in the company as a whole for career opportunities.

Training is seen as an essential part of both a successful career and a successful company. 'We must have highly qualified people within Astra. Training priorities are worked into our business objectives and human resources policies are aligned with business performance. This is in line with the Investors in People programme

which the Edinburgh unit has recently committed to,' explains Mitchell. The company runs an internal learning centre but external trainers are also brought into Astra to run structured courses. On-the-job training is seen as vitally important. International and local communications within Astra are strong. Staff are provided with annual company reports and briefing sessions are held to ensure that all the employees are aware of the Astra financial picture as well as current projects and planned developments. Quarterly reports and an international internal magazine, *Astra Digest*, are made available to employees worldwide. Individual UK sites also produce their own newsletters when appropriate giving information on company performance, organisational changes, new appointments and particular activities related to the business.

Contact address

Government and Public Affairs,
Astra Pharmaceuticals Limited,
Home Park,
Kings Langley,
Herts WD4 8DH.
Telephone: 01923 266191.
Fax: 01923 260431.

AT&T

A T&T is the world's second largest telecommunications company, providing services in more than 200 countries worldwide. The company has been active in the UK since the late 1980s and is now busily expanding its product and service portfolio. AT&T's strategy is focused around building long-term relationships with customers and constantly seeking to use innovation to exploit business opportunities. Its UK operation is firmly at the centre of a rapidly developing industry and can offer a range of stimulating and rewarding careers.

AT&T at a glance

Employees: 200,000 worldwide, 2,500 UK
Annual staff attrition rate: 8 per cent
Key locations: five offices in the UK –
    Central London, Redditch, Ealing,
    Slough and Edinburgh
Av. annual graduate recruitment: 25
Annual intake: 550

An inside view

Advances in technology, combined with the effects of industry deregulation, have made the global telecommunications market an extremely competitive environment over the last few years. One of the keys to AT&T's success during this period has been its ability to retain a clear business focus and adapt quickly to changing circumstances. This is best manifested by its decision in September 1995 to demerge its Lucent Technologies (communications systems and technology) and NCR (computer services and systems) subsidiaries in order to concentrate on its core strengths of communications services. This restructuring was finally completed in December 1996.

The new AT&T is now the world's second largest telecommunications company. Its worldwide network provides services to more than 200 countries and carries more than 210 million voice, data, video and facsimile messages every business day. AT&T first became active in the UK in the late 1980s with the acquisition of Istel, an on-line data processing company serving electronic trading communities. Encouraged by market research which showed that many telecommunications managers were disappointed by the cost and quality of service offered by existing telecoms providers, AT&T has been steadily expanding the range of services it provides and the company was awarded a UK public telephone operator's licence in December 1994.

AT&T's corporate philosophy is built around a *common bond* of core values designed to establish worldwide standards of excellence. It is mandatory that all employees sign up to this common bond when they join AT&T. One of these core values emphasises the importance of customer service in differentiating AT&T from its competitors. Another concerns respect for the individual. AT&T believes in giving its workforce the authority to use their capabilities to the fullest extent and in creating an environment which supports personal growth and continuous learning. A third underlines the importance of employees having the highest standards of integrity and professional behaviour in their business dealings. The final two values – innovation and teamwork – are a reflection of how AT&T believes it can maintain its competitive advantage in a rapidly changing marketplace.

Not least as a consequence of market conditions, AT&T can sometimes represent a demanding working environment and the group announced major job losses in the US in January 1996. However, the UK operation was not affected by this restructuring – on the contrary, AT&T (UK) has been growing rapidly – and continues to offer a wide range of exciting opportunities for those individuals who are prepared to invest their career in the company.

How does AT&T rate?

Pay:	good
Benefits:	good
Communications:	very good
Training:	very good
Career development:	good
Morale:	good

People and personnel policies

Unlike some companies where the commitment to the employee is effectively little more than a platitude, AT&T is keen to ensure that its own personnel policies translate into everyday action. To this end, it undertakes regular, detailed surveys of staff attitudes. Moreover, these surveys are managed by an outside agency in order to maintain confidentiality. The results of these surveys show that AT&T remains highly rated in terms of management and internal communications. Over recent years, the competitive nature of the telecoms industry has caused AT&T to examine the way in which it is managed with the result that the group has now put in place a much flatter management structure. One consequence of this is that teamwork has become increasingly important and the company has started to operate and deploy cross-functional teams very successfully.

Not surprisingly, AT&T is heavily committed to ongoing training and career development within its workforce. Its basic approach is to attempt to put the responsibility on the individual for identifying their own development needs. For those who wish to progress within the organisation, there is a variety of options. A wide range of courses – covering both technical and personal development issues – is available. AT&T sponsors adult education and professional education where this is thought to be appropriate. The company has also established a series of 20 Open Learning Centres around the country, where staff can go – either during work time or their own free time – to develop their PC-based skills. In addition, technical and management training is provided through AT&T's own Intranet.

At more senior levels, leadership programmes are being built into AT&T on a global basis. For example, executives – as well as others – can attend the AT&T School of Business & Technology based in New Jersey. Movement within the business is encouraged although, to date, relatively few international movements have taken place, mainly due to the expanding number of opportunities within the UK. Further opportunities are provided through the number of joint venture operations into which AT&T has entered.

In terms of remuneration, AT&T's strategy is to offer a total package which will place the company at the upper quartile of earnings. Although base pay is set around the median level, AT&T uses a series of incentive payments (determined by business, team and individual performance) to increase total remuneration. With the UK operation having grown largely by acquisition, one of the company's key objectives for 1997 is to move towards a single set of employment conditions. One of the primary benefits of this consolidation will be to make movement within the business much easier.

Like other progressive US-based corporations, the company also takes a strong view on improving gender and racial diversity within its workforce. As mentioned earlier, one of AT&T's core values is respect for the individual and the company is absolutely intolerant of any breaches of this rule. To improve the participation of women in the workforce, AT&T is supportive of flexible working arrangements for women returners and has introduced incentive payments to encourage women to return to work following maternity leave. However, it is important to recognise that AT&T's primary responsibility is to the customer and flexibility can only be sanctioned where it does not conflict with the customer's service requirements.

In the US, AT&T has always been recognised as a good corporate citizen and the company is determined to replicate this image in the UK. To date, this has taken the form of the company getting involved in a series of community involvement programmes and sponsorship schemes – such as The Almeida Theatre in London and the Proms in the Park – designed to raise corporate awareness. AT&T (UK) will also launch a matched-giving programme under which charitable donations raised by staff are matched by the company.

Contact address

Ms Lynda Shattlock,
Resourcing Manager,
AT&T (UK),
Norfolk House,
31 St James's Square,
London SW1Y 4JR.
Telephone: 0171 925 8340.
Fax: 0171 925 8341.

BAA plc

BAA (formerly the British Airports Authority) is the world's largest commercial operator of airports. It owns and operates seven major airports in the UK, including all three London airports, and is now starting to develop a greater international presence. The company's strategy, which focuses on providing the highest possible level of customer service (whether the customers concerned are airlines or passengers), has been successfully translated into a progressive approach to continuous learning and employee empowerment.

BAA at a glance

Employees: 8,250 worldwide, 8,100 UK
Annual staff attrition rate: n/a
Key locations: some seven airports in the UK, with corporate HQ in Central London
Av. annual graduate recruitment: n/a
Annual intake: n/a

An inside view

Since its privatisation in 1987, BAA has developed into the world's largest commercial operator of airports. It dominates the UK airport industry, currently owning and operating seven UK airports – Heathrow, Gatwick, Stansted, Glasgow, Edinburgh, Aberdeen and Southampton – which between them handle 71 per cent of UK passenger traffic and 81 per cent of air cargo. In addition to its airport management activities, the company has developed acknowledged skills in retailing (which now accounts for 45 per cent of its revenue) and property

management. BAA has recently started to export its expertise overseas. It already manages the Indianapolis airport system and the shops and facilities at Pittsburgh airport, and is actively looking at opportunities in a number of other countries.

The company has changed significantly since its privatisation in 1987. Much of this change has been achieved under the leadership of John Egan, who joined the group as chief executive in 1990 and has been primarily responsible for instilling a more commercial culture into the organisation. This has been manifested in an increasingly customer-focused approach throughout BAA's activities. In addition, the company has spent heavily on information technology, particularly with regard to security issues following the Lockerbie bombing. One of the key issues facing BAA at the moment is its proposed fifth terminal at London Heathrow. This project, which the company believes is essential to maintaining Heathrow's standing as the world's busiest international airport, is currently the subject of a public enquiry which will not be completed until 1998.

BAA's objective is to become the most successful airport company in the world. In order to achieve this, it has adopted a philosophy of encouraging – and rewarding – continuous improvement in all its processes and services. Inherent in this approach is the need for all employees to feel that they can make a contribution to the business and, accordingly, BAA has taken a series of initiatives to empower its employees. One of the most important of these is its *Freedom to Manage* programme which is specifically designed to allow every individual the opportunity to maximise the contribution which they make. In particular, it enables front-line staff, who are best equipped to understand customer's needs, to improve service at the point of delivery. Moreover, by streamlining its management structure, BAA has been able to eliminate a variety of unnecessary controls and administrative hurdles, thus significantly improving communication between senior management and front-line staff. Another important element of BAA's culture is the importance it places on ethical behaviour – the company is one of the few PLCs to have established an ethics committee.

Air travel continues to be one of the fastest-growing industries in the world, and BAA is firmly at the centre of the UK aviation industry. The company is involved in a wide range of projects, including Terminal 5 and the Heathrow Express rail link, which can offer a variety of exciting and challenging opportunities.

How does BAA rate?

Pay:	good
Benefits:	good
Communications:	very good
Training:	very good
Career development:	very good
Morale:	good

People and personnel policies

Through its progressive personnel policies, BAA seeks to align the success of the individual with the success of the company. This is manifested not only by its *Freedom to Manage* programme, but also through an increasing focus on teamwork, simpler structures and functional leadership which is provided through centres of excellence as well as airport level management. Although more than 80 per cent of the workforce is unionised, the company has not lost a single day due to industrial action.

BAA is increasingly investing in the training and career development needs of its workforce and it is currently estimated that 5 per cent of the company's payroll costs are spent on training. In recent years, the company has launched a series of new training programmes. For example, all BAA's managers have taken part in a week-long *Sharing the Vision* programme which is designed to educate them about the company's mission. This has been followed by further courses on *Growing the Business* and *Creating Successful Teams*. Other training initiatives include a new career development programme for middle managers and tailored programmes for managers in key business areas such as projects, retail and property. The company has formed an alliance with Surrey University to develop management skills and has established a residential training centre. Experience of different aspects of BAA's business is becoming an increasingly important pre-requisite for career progression within the company.

Another area in which the company has devoted considerable resources is communications. In addition to the benefits generated by a more streamlined management structure, the company believes that its philosophy of making its managers walk the floor has further improved communication. BAA has also instituted an annual staff meeting at which the chief executive invites questions from the floor and encourages a no-holds barred attitude. This is supplemented by a regular series of roadshows fronted by senior management. Openness within the company is also fostered by making the annual performance review process subject to 360 degree feedback.

Remuneration within the company is set on a competitive basis by relation to comparable functions in other leading companies. BAA offers a standard range of benefits and encourages its employees to share in the development of the business by participating in approved Sharesave and share option schemes. All members of the workforce receive an annual bonus and it is currently estimated that 90 per cent of staff have shares in the company.

Given the nature of its activities, it is not surprising that BAA is very conscious of environmental concerns. Accordingly, it is determined to fulfil its commitment to be an environmentally responsible neighbour and to achieve a balance between the interests of the growing number of people who want to fly and those who live close to its airports. To improve relations with local communities in the Heathrow area, it opened a purpose-built visitor centre in 1995, and also has supported a range of other community relations programmes. In addition, BAA sets itself annual environmental performance targets and publishes its progress in annual performance reports. The company's environmental credentials were improved significantly by the recent appointment of noted environmental campaigner Des Wilson as director of corporate and public affairs.

Contact address

Mr John Mills,
Personnel Director,
BAA plc,
130 Wilton Road,
London SW1V 1LQ.
Telephone: 0171 834 9449.
Fax: 0171 932 6699.

Bass plc

Bass is one of the UK's largest brewers and operators of leisure facilities. It operates in hotels, pubs, betting shops, greyhound tracks and runs more than 63,000 electronic entertainment machines. In 1996, the company reported £5.1 billion in turnover and £671 million in pre-tax profits. The company has experienced widespread change in the 1990s which has enhanced the profitability of the group, especially its hotels, pubs and brewing divisions.

Bass at a glance

Employees: 67,500 UK, 85,000 worldwide
Attrition rate: n/a
Key locations: London (HQ) plus outlets across the UK
Graduate recruitment: 50
Annual intake: n/a

An inside view

Bass is one of the UK's traditional brewing companies. It has a history which goes back over many decades, synonymous with pubs and beer. But the Bass of 1997 is a remarkably different organisation from that even of the early 1980s. It now spans hotels, taverns, leisure, brewing and soft drinks. The group is the fifteenth largest employer in the UK with 67,500 people in the UK – and 85,000 worldwide.

It owns 2,249 hotels in the Holiday Inn Worldwide chain which means it manages 387,000 guest rooms. In the Bass Taverns portfolio are 2,778 managed pubs and 1,443 leased and tenanted pubs. Bass Leisure has an even more widespread group of activities. It runs 136 Gala Clubs (bingo establishments) in the UK and seven in Spain. The company operates 15 Hollywood Bowl Ten Pin establishments and one Charrington Bowl. Bass Leisure also has one multi-entertainment complex and 911 Coral retail betting shops. In addition it has two Coral greyhound stadia and more than 53,000 electronic entertainment machines. Bass Brewers owns eight breweries and two maltings. Another division, Bass International Brewers, has opened brewing operations in the Czech Republic and in China. In addition it exports to more than 60 countries worldwide.

The operational management of Bass is in the hands of the directors of the subsidiary companies. The group provides a framework, including financial targets, which subsidiary managers must follow but much of the management philosophy and direction is left to company MDs to interpret. The Bass board believes that it gets best value from its businesses by devolving as much authority as possible to their managers.

The central strategy has been to move away from a concentration on brewing into hospitality, food, drink and electronic entertainment. Sir Ian Prosser, group chairman, says 'We aim to build and develop leading positions in each of the inter-related segments of the market in which we operate. We do this by continuing to improve the hotel and leisure retailing properties; by driving forward our brands in retailing and drinks, thus gaining marketing economies of scale; by reducing costs and by acquiring assets and businesses which assist in these aims'.

How does Bass rate?

Pay:	very good
Benefits:	good
Communications:	good
Training:	good
Career development:	very good
Morale:	good

People and personnel policies

The strong commitment to devolution in management extends to wide areas of human resources policy. The group is largely contained by a determination that people will be respected, that they will be remunerated and treated fairly, that training will be given, that equal opportunities will be observed and that certain specific issues will be handled on a groupwide basis. These include graduate recruitment, certain aspects of training, and management selection and development.

Virtually every other aspect of human resources policy within the group is dealt with at operating company level – and the conditions which determine this policy will vary from company to company, sector to sector and location to location. There is a recognition that in a business which comes into contact so strongly with the public there is a need to motivate, encourage and develop its people.

In a report to shareholders the company places great stress on the recent reaccreditation of Bass Taverns and Gala under the Investors in People scheme. 'Taverns recorded its highest ever assessment, a success borne out by the fact that 70 per cent of assistant pub managers go on to become managers. Holiday Inn will use the Investors in People standard from the UK as a model throughout Europe, the Middle East and Africa region. All our UK businesses are working towards the achievement of the IIP standard,' says Sir Ian.

He adds that the company has made great efforts to develop its people – for the mutual benefit of the employees and the business. Also it has boosted the quality of internal communications to inform and to receive feedback. 'Managers are responsible for ensuring that good communications and open feedback channels are in place, and that employees are encouraged to use them. We have created groupwide structures for communicating on corporate issues, and local information and consultation procedures to meet the needs of each division.' He points to an electronic suggestion box for innovative ideas which has been established at group level, and employees at Bass Brewers are using the company's IT network to circulate news and information.

A Bass European Forum has brought

together senior representatives of group management with 30 elected employee representatives from ten European Union companies for information and discussion on groupwide themes. As well as developing existing communication channels, the forum complies with the remit of the European Commission's directive on works councils by involving all UK employees.

Pay and benefits are set in accordance with the standards in each sector and according to local variables. Nevertheless, the company aims to provide a pay package which is at least as good as the industry norm. Most benefits are designed to fit with the overall strategy for the specific business and employment conditions in that sector. There are, however, a number of benefits which are common to more than one Division. In particular, these include pension provision and opportunities to participate in share ownership. These are in keeping with a general philosopy of ensuring employees have an interest in the business and a secure future.

Two specific policies within operating companies which the group is keen to identify is the launch of a personal performance programme at Britvic which clarifies the personal objectives for each individual and sets out criteria against which performance will be evaluated. In the US and Canada, Holiday Inn has created an online communications and training system providing high quality training to employees and franchisees through the company's IT network. At a group level, Bass has initiated the appointment – in each division – of equal opportunity champions to raise awareness and facilitate good practice.

Contact address

Human resources,
Bass plc,
20 North Audley Street,
London W1Y 1WE.
Telephone: 0171 409 1919.
Fax: 0171 409 8503.

Bettys and Taylors of Harrogate

A warded two of the Tea Council's awards of excellence in 1996 (the Oscars of the tea world) for its tearooms in Harrogate and Ilkley, Bettys is truly a grand day out for any beverage connoisseur or gastronome. People travel from all over the world to Harrogate, not to take the waters, but to visit one of the best café-tearooms in the world. Behind a Victorian facade of glass and hanging baskets there is a traditional English tearoom which is also totally European. The secret of this family-run company's success is its commitment to the highest standards of service and quality that were brought to England from Switzerland in the early 1900s by founder Frederick Belmont. His family have continued the tradition ever since.

Bettys and Taylors at a glance

Employees: 620
Annual staff attrition rate: n/a
Key locations: Harrogate (HQ) and café-tearooms and shops throughout Yorkshire
Av. annual graduate recruitment: n/a
Annual intake: 60

An inside view

The Swiss confectioner Frederick Belmont arrived in Yorkshire by mistake after boarding the wrong train. But soon after his arrival in Bradford, he realised that the city was home to more millionaires within one square mile than anywhere else outside London. He also discovered fashionable Harrogate, opening the first Bettys Café Tea Rooms there in 1919. With gleaming silver, flowers, music and tea served to perfection, it became a safe haven for townswomen who were limited in where they could respectably and comfortably meet.

Today, Bettys offers the same splendour and respectability. In its shop window, local delicacies such as Yorkshire Fat Rascals and curd tarts are displayed next to continental stollens and ciabattas. In the Tea Room, the speciality of the house is Bettys Rarebit or, for the more adventurous, Swiss Rosti, grated, fried potatoes with a selection of mouth-watering toppings. The merger between Yorkshire-but-Swiss Bettys Café Tea Rooms and another Yorkshire institution, Taylors of Harrogate, tea and coffee merchants, has created a £35 million business which is now one of the county's main employers.

HR manager Sue Symington says the culture and business approach can be summarised simply. 'We strive continuously to be the best; we treat people as we would wish to be treated ourselves; we actively involve every single member of staff in how the business is run; and we share our success.' Above all, quality, the desire to be the best, sharing and mutual respect drives this intriguing company forward, as it has done for the past 75 years. It has a tightly controlled culture – its shared language and values are evident among staff in each of the company's tea rooms and manufacturing operations.

The company's business plan is totally integrated within the human resources plan. Bettys and Taylors was one of the first businesses to apply for the Investors In People (IIP) standard in 1991 which proved to be the catalyst for what has become a firm and clear management structure within the company. 'I needed the business plan to progress the IIP application,' says Symington. 'It was only when our managing director pulled it out of his desk that we both had a blinding realisation that only the eight directors were aware of its content and objectives.'

An annual staff questionnaire gives directors a fair idea of where Bettys and Taylors employees see strengths and weaknesses. This taken into account, the completed annual operational plan and strategic aims are displayed throughout the company. Each year has a strategic theme. 1997 is *Building on Success*, during which Bettys and Taylors will focus on teamwork, its customers, its budgets and training.

How does Bettys and Taylors rate?

Pay:	good
Benefits:	very good
Communications:	good
Training:	very good
Career development:	good
Morale:	very good

People and personnel policies

Each of the company's 620 employees contributes to the business plan through a matrix of 104 teams, consisting of not more than five or six people and a leader, trained in people management skills. Everyone who joins the company, irrespective of where they will eventually work, undertakes the same training. This includes how to handle food safely, look after themselves safely and how not to be a liability to others. In addition, trainees are given a group induction day to understand the company as a whole. And, occasionally, groups of high flyers will be given specific training for a year or so. All training is carried out in-house with the exception of professional certification which provides the opportunity to meet colleagues in other businesses.

Each month, staff teams demonstrate – to senior management – the results of benchmarking exercises where they have compared their activities with their competitors. Sometimes these examine new products, packaging and environments.

'There's a great sense of respect for others within our business,' Symington comments. 'There is so much to learn from other people. Our customers perceive Bettys as non-changing when, in fact, behind the scenes, it changes all the time.'

There is no formal policy regarding graduate recruitment but due to Bettys and Taylors' popularity among the Yorkshire working population, graduates apply to Bettys and Taylors sometimes having already had several years' experience. During 1996, four management trainees were recruited, 'but it can be more if we find people who interest us'. The company involves local schools on a regular basis, being an active member of the North Yorkshire Business & Education Partnership.

Potential staff are 'those with a ready smile and a desire to please. We need people who can work hard for the company with grace and commitment'. Once on board, employees each receive their own skills training booklet and are assigned to a team. During their employment, the booklet is a record of competence in core skills for their specific job, extra training for first aid or fire officer duties, and a comprehensive tasting list – everyone is expected to know and have experience of the products produced by Bettys and Taylors. Personal appraisals are carried out quarterly and give staff the chance to discuss career progression. If new blood is needed, they may be seconded to other areas of the business. The sharing culture extends to an attractive employee bonus scheme, paid out tax- free, quarterly. After 2 years, employees are provided with free health insurance. And, on top of staff restaurant facilities and discounted products, every member of staff receives a Christmas present of £100 for a personal gift for themselves.

Socially, staff are active in fundraising for a specific charity, elected each year. In 1996, they raised £10,000 which was then matched by the directors. As one would expect in such a people conscious and locally focused firm, community relations figure highly. Among the company's community activities is a mentoring project with local schools where pupils with learning disabilities are paired with company staff. It encourages the children to develop valuable job skills while experiencing the joys of working with culinary materials. Another is the Trees for Life appeal which is still going strong after six years. The aim is to plant one million trees by the year 2000. By February 1996, through this on-going promotion, Yorkshire tea drinkers had helped to fund 750,000 trees worldwide in places such as Africa, India, Brazil and in Britain. Over the years this has been carried out with leading environmental charities including: Oxfam; the British Trust for Conservation Volunteers; World Vision; and The National Trust.

Contact address

Ms Susan Symington,
Human Resources Manager,
Bettys and Taylors Limited,
Pagoda House,
Prospect Road,
Harrogate,
North Yorkshire HG2 7NX.
Telephone: 01423 889822.
Fax: 01423 881083.

Black & Decker

I n 1910, two young entrepreneurs, S Duncan Black and Alonzo G Decker, founded a small machine shop in Baltimore, Maryland. They called it Black & Decker Manufacturing Company. Even in their wildest dreams, they could not possibly have imagined what they had started. Their shop has grown beyond all hopes and expectations. Today, Black & Decker is a global marketer and manufacturer of quality products that have become famous for their application in the home and factory. Spreading its wings in a business environment that cried out for diversification, Black & Decker has also become a major supplier of information systems and services to government and commercial clients around the world. Its products are marketed in more than 100 countries.

Black & Decker at a glance

Employees: 4,700 Europe, 2,000 UK
Annual staff attrition rate: 5 per cent
Key locations: European HQ: Slough,
    Manufacturing at Spennymoor,
    Country Durham
Av. annual graduate recruitment: 10–20
Annual intake: 70–100

An inside view

Black & Decker is the world's largest producer of power tools, power tool accessories and security hardware. It is also a worldwide leader in golf club shafts and glass container-making equipment, and suppliers of fastening systems. Its success has been built on the widest range of products and marketing strengths, and B&D enjoys a particular reputation for quality, innovation, design and value.

Seventy years of growth ended in the early 1980s but by the middle of that decade the company had revitalised itself and was performing strongly again, emphasising new products and speed to market. B&D has created a product development process which gives the company a significant competitive advantage in consumer and commercial markets around the world. It has also become known for its computer-aided design systems, which allow for modelling in realistic, three-dimensional images.

Its philosophy today is predicated on business improvement through quality, using what it accepts as the enormous people potential at Black & Decker. The company's mission statement says 'We know that there is enormous people potential within our business - intelligence, commitment, loyalty, innovation, motivation, creativity, initiative – we will harness this fantastic power and apply it in a single forward direction, towards our customers. As a result, our customers will be satisfied, market share gains will be made, profits will be increased, employees will be fulfilled and our shareholders will be satisfied because our performance will be superb. We are dedicated to exceeding the expectations of all our customers with uncompromising integrity. In a teamwork environment of continuous improvement, our commitment is to satisfy our customers by continuously providing error-free products and value-added services at the right price. Total quality is the most important drive of our business. We will be consistently focused on the customer, and the subsequent recognition and success will be the main contributor to employee satisfaction.'

In 1994, Black & Decker's retuned operating philosophy began to bite, 'displaying the level of superior performance that our strong market positions, technical expertise, financial discipline and talented workforce are capable of achieving,' reported Nolan Archibald, chief executive officer of Black & Decker. In 1995, 'we improved on that beginning. Our total return to stockholders was more than 50 per cent, marking the second consecutive year that our return has significantly exceeded that of the Standard and Poor's Industrials.'

Revenues from continuing operations set a new record, increasing 9 per cent in 1995 over 1994, while operating income rose by 21 per cent. The impact on profits of new products, cost reductions, and productivity gains is apparent in every one of the company's businesses. Worldwide sales of Black & Decker now total more than \$5 billion, with the European

operations contributing a fifth; and the UK contributing a fifth of that – at \$200 million. Europe drives 10 per cent of total sales, with an operational budget of \$1 billion, with net profit close to 10 per cent. The UK provides the company's main consumer base with the production of everyday consumer items such as lawnmowers and power drills. The plant at Spennymoor in County Durham manufactures 14 million units a year.

How does Black and Decker rate?

Pay:	very good
Benefits:	excellent
Communications:	good
Training:	good
Career development:	very good
Morale:	very good

People and personnel policies

Black & Decker's employee policies have grown out of visits that senior executives made to study Japanese industry a decade ago, and they are very apparent at Spennymoor. They had gone to that country with the belief that the Japanese won on technology, but came back with the conclusion that what the Japanese did so well was get its employees to believe in, indeed, become obsessed by, success. Black & Decker already had good employee relations, partly because it had made the commitment to put roots down in the uninviting northeast part of the country. Today, Black & Decker is well known in industry for looking after its people. In 12 of 14 professional categories, it rates above average – and in particular it is noted for a generous pension allocation. Someone who has worked for the company for 30 years, with a final salary of £30,000, and retired at age 55, will command a pension of £20,000. In many companies, you would have to have worked another ten years to obtain that kind of pension reward. All employees, after one year's service, are provided with permanent health insurance.

In particular, over the past ten years, the company has made a determined attempt to implement progressive practices that are closely aligned to business objectives and needs. 'We do not have human resource people policies that are separate from the other objectives of the company,' says Dave Douglas, human resources director. 'They are tied in with the whole business plan. HR plays a pivotal role in the running of the whole business.'

The company, with its dominating headquarters in Baltimore, Maryland, is obviously still very American; but serious efforts have been made to distil a mixture of philosophies into its human resource policy. 'We have always been interested in what people do, but now we are interested in how they do it. Some years back all we cared about was selling our products. Now, we have to support and help our customers in order to do the selling. We send Black & Decker people into the stores to demonstrate the products. We work in partnership with our customers, believing they are business partners.'

'The consumer needs to be helped to get a feel for the product; and this is how we try and differentiate ourselves from our competitors.' The message from this is that Black & Decker is developing a supportive relationship with the customer through having a supportive relationship with the company's employees. 'Our human resource policy is full, rounded, progressive and business aligned,' he says. 'We have a very supportive culture, quite paternal. If we lose people – or have to lose people – we pay redundancy that is far in excess of any statutory requirements. We are renowned for the support we give in outplacement. You are not thrown on the scrap heap, you are looked after – and psychologically, as well.'

While the company, with its American heritage, is extremely profit driven, the workforce has deliberately been given its own empowerment. 'We are not hierarchical any longer,' says Douglas. 'Management levels have been reduced and we are continuously giving more responsibility to the employees to use their initiative and apply their knowledge. There is nowhere near the same number of managers as ten years ago. We are customer focused, not focused internally. One major layer of management has gone, which provides a much more direct path to our managing director, Richard Sanderson.'

Contact address

Mr Dave Douglas,
Director of Human Resources,
Black & Decker,
210 Bath Road,
Slough, Berkshire SL1 3YD.
Telephone: 01753 500722.
Fax: 01753 576811.

The BOC Group

The BOC Group, best known as one of the world's major suppliers of industrial gases, is one of the small number of British industrial companies which can truly be described as being global in both its scale and ambition. Its activities, which also include healthcare, vacuum technology and distribution services, are technology-driven, and the group estimates that it patents new inventions at the rate of one every four days. BOC provides a professional, yet relaxed, working environment in which creativity and lateral thinking are encouraged and rewarded.

The BOC Group at a glance

Employees: 41,000 worldwide, 15,000 Europe
Annual staff attrition rate: 3 per cent
Key locations: Windlesham (HQ), centres around the UK and throughout the world
Av. annual graduate recruitment: 200 globally
Annual intake: 1500

An inside view

The BOC Group is one of the largest industrial concerns in the UK, with an annual turnover in excess of £4 billion. Although it is divided into four operating divisions – industrial gases and related products, healthcare, vacuum technology and distribution services – the group continues to be dominated by its industrial gases activities, which contribute more than 70 per cent of both sales and operating profit. In recent years, BOC has developed an extremely strong international presence and now has manufacturing operations in more than 60 countries worldwide. Moreover, the group occupies a leading position in many of its key markets, and the sheer scale of its operations gives it the technical, commercial and financial muscle to exploit new business opportunities.

Many of BOC's operations are managed on a global basis. In the industrial gases division, for example, global management teams have been created to focus on specific customer sectors such as electronics, chemicals and petroleum, and metals. This not only allows BOC to deliver consistent standards of product service and quality throughout the world, but also facilitates the rapid transfer of technology and the export of commercial expertise. BOC's global representation has also been important in creating a strong sense of cultural diversity within the group. This is manifested at senior levels within the organisation; seven different nationalities are represented in BOC's top 30 management positions. Another facet of its management team is its length of service with the company. Many of its senior executives have been with the company for many years and this level of experience lies behind BOC's reputation for providing a highly professional service.

In order to empower local management and engender a more relaxed working environment, the group employs a relatively flat management structure. Within this context, managers are expected to have a broad base of business understanding so they can identify potential new business opportunities. Innovation is another quality which BOC perceives to be vital in its workforce. Despite its leading position in many of its markets, BOC will only continue to prosper by offering higher quality products and services than its competitors. As a consequence, it needs individuals who can think laterally and devise radical solutions to complex problems.

Intelligence and a required level of technical competence are not of themselves sufficient, however. The ability to work effectively in teams and network within the organisation is becoming increasingly important – BOC is not a command and control environment. Furthermore, in common with other successful companies, BOC remains achievement-oriented. Its most productive employees will be those who can satisfy its customers', often highly-demanding, expectations.

How does The BOC Group rate?

Pay:	good
Benefits:	very good
Communications:	very good
Training:	excellent
Career development:	very good
Morale:	good

People and personnel policies

BOC recognises that, in order to achieve the required levels of technical excellence and commercial creativity, its workforce must possess the necessary skills and attitudes. Historically, the group has been extremely successful in developing a cadre of senior business managers, with more than three-quarters of the group's senior appointments currently promotions from within the group. This leaves what the company believes is the right amount of scope to bring in new people, with different experience and fresh thinking.

BOC's philosophy clearly demonstrates the importance of effective training and continuous professional development. All companies within the BOC Group believe in delegating responsibility at an early stage in an individual's career. The emphasis is then on planned development, with training programmes designed to ensure that employees gain experience of all the areas within their chosen sphere. On-the-job training is supplemented with specialist product and skills training. These courses may be in-house or external and will cover a diverse range of subjects. Programmes in 1996 included strategic marketing, the development of leaders for the next millennium and an innovation workshop designed to stimulate and promote innovation and creativity among technical and non-technical managers.

At senior levels, the company has created a series of management programmes with faculties of major universities around the world. One particularly innovative initiative is the establishment of a BOC Management School in China. This is a unique cooperative venture with a local university aimed at upgrading the skills of its Chinese managers. The group felt that creating its own MBA-style programme was preferable to sending Chinese managers to business schools abroad because of the high costs involved and the language problems entailed, and the school underlines BOC's commitment to management development. Perhaps not surprisingly within a company with such a strong international presence, the movement of executives between countries is encouraged. It is extremely rare for an executive to get very far within BOC without having at least some international experience.

The group promotes a culture of excellence and recognises and rewards outstanding performances by both teams and individuals. Indeed, the company is moving towards a much more performance-driven philosophy with regard to remuneration setting throughout the organisation. At senior levels, it is common for between 20 and 30 per cent of the total remuneration package to be bonus-driven. Lower down the group, employee involvement is encouraged through a variety of schemes which include profit sharing, productivity schemes and employee share schemes.

Formal communication programmes include videos, management magazines and other publications, briefing and personal appraisal sessions. BOC's in-house magazines, *BOC World* and *BOC Technology*, are recognised as being two of the most sophisticated company magazines produced. In 1996, the company established a European Forum, comprising representatives from the workforce of the group's European businesses. BOC aims to work collaboratively with trade unions and embraces those collective arrangements which it regards as sensible. At more senior levels, the company has found that the most effective form of communication is to bring people together and, consequently, the senior management team meets every six weeks.

The BOC Group has a long history of corporate giving and believes that contributing to the communities in which it operates is an integral part of responsible corporate citizenship. It was a founder member of The Per Cent Club, whose members agree to contribute no less than half a per cent of the UK pre-tax profits, or 1 per cent of dividends, to the community. The BOC Foundation for the Environment has been established to provide funding for projects which aim to demonstrate in a practical way how pollution can be reduced in the UK. Other support is provided by way of a matched-giving scheme, while the group's healthcare businesses also fund academic research projects.

Contact address

Mr Don Beattie, Chief Executive – Personnel,
The BOC Group plc,
Chertsey Road, Windlesham,
Surrey GU20 6HJ.
Telephone: 01276 477222.
Fax: 01276 471333.

The Body Shop International

A *passionate and caring* commercial enterprise was launched in 1976 when Anita Roddick opened a small shop in Brighton, selling naturally based skin and hair care products. Today The Body Shop is a globally operated multi-local business, with franchisees running their own businesses and thousands of people working towards common goals in 46 countries worldwide. The Body Shop has 1,451 shops throughout the Americas, Europe and Asia and sells over 580 different products backed by a similar number of accessory items. Headquarters are based in Littlehampton, Sussex, with three manufacturing sites in the UK and one in the US. The company has approximately 3,849 staff.

The Body Shop at a glance

Employees: 3,849
Annual staff attrition rate: 28 per cent (incl. seasonal workers)
Key locations: HQ at Littlehampton, Sussex; manufacturing at Wick, Sussex and Easterhouse, Scotland; design in London; also at North Carolina, US and Singapore
Av. annual graduate recruitment: not recorded
Annual intake: 926

An inside view

The Body Shop is one of the most distinctive retail operators in the UK. Its success among its key customer base is due to its principled stand on ethical issues and its finely honed commercial skills supplying its clientele with competitively priced and attractive merchandise. Such is the degree of its achievement that, on average, a new branch of The Body Shop opens every two and a half days. Franchising is the key to the rapid growth of the company, and commitment to customer service, animal care, environmental protection and human rights are at the philosophical core of The Body Shop trading policy. When announcing latest interim results its chairman Gordon Roddick said 'Our focus continues to be long-term, balanced growth. Our challenges remain clear, our plans are underway and there are many signs that we are on track'.

Financial results for the first six months of 1996 demonstrate the pattern of growth of The Body Shop and the diversity and strength of the international operation. Pre-tax profit increased by 30 per cent to £11.8 million – an improvement reflecting turnover growth of 11 per cent to £117.1 million. Business is strong in Asian markets and signs of regeneration in its Australian outlets are healthy. The 46th country to join The Body Shop stable is the Philippines with the opening of two stores in early 1996. There are plans to open in Korea in 1997. Of its 1,450 shops worldwide, 1,269 are franchised and 182 are directly company owned. The structure of the company is flat rather than hierarchical. Within the UK is a supply division, a corporate division with support services and a UK retail division. Within the retail division are a number of company shops which are directly owned by The Body Shop International and act very much as image makers for the other 1,269 franchised outlets.

The company's human resources policy has evolved from one central mission: 'To create and sustain a successful community of individuals actively committed to meeting each other's needs'. Within that creed is a recognition that by being successful the company achieves its business goals both in profit and values; that a community has a common purpose in which there must be a sense of belonging and security; that individuals are not only accepted but encouraged to contribute their own qualities and aspirations; and that by meeting others' needs, objectives are achieved and an environment of mutual trust and respect created which ultimately sustains a successful community.

How does The Body Shop rate?

Pay:	good
Benefits:	excellent
Communications:	superb
Training:	good
Career development:	very good
Morale:	excellent

People and personnel policies

Monica Newton, The Body Shop's working practices manager, says that the company aims to 'enable a diversity of people to succeed within their key capabilities. We look for people who are hardworking, energetic, who agree with our values and, obviously, who have the right qualifications. We have a policy of informal dress throughout the organisation and an atmosphere which is open, honest and friendly'.

She emphasises that The Body Shop is values not technology driven, innovative but not aggressive and generally supportive in all its policies which are maintained throughout its different locations. Recruitment policy within The Body Shop is a key feature of its human resources strategy. The company does not have a graduate recruitment programme but commits itself to selection on ability and merit and measures which are clearly relevant to individual job demands. Its recruitment policy statement promises that policies will be fair and ensure equality of opportunity; will aim to ensure recruitment of the best person for the job; and will select on ability and merit only.

Newton believes that the company's culture promotes a sense of responsibility within employees to develop their own careers. Career counselling is available to all and sponsorship is available through the company's further education and professional qualifications policy. The company's training policy encourages individuals into further education job-related study programmes and financial and personal support is given to those who successfully apply for these programmes. Personal careers are not linked to unit or national objectives and Newton says that as The Body Shop organisation is still comparatively young, a job for life culture is not yet applicable within the structure.

The Body Shop boasts a total renumeration package for each part of the business, which it places in the medium and upper quartile against similar businesses. There are seven salary bands within the pay structure and all jobs are evaluated against these bands. Annual pay reviews are based on the contribution made by an employee over a year and there are appeal procedures in place. *Choices* is the name given to the company's flexible benefits system – it offers employees a degree of choice over some of the benefits provided. The aim of the scheme is to recognise the individual needs and priorities of employees. For instance, within the company pension scheme employees are able to buy extra contributions from the company up to a certain level or sell back to the company provided that their minimum contribution is 5 per cent. A similar scheme applies to holiday entitlement – employees can buy or sell up to five days' holiday per year according to their personal requirements. Other benefits include private medical insurance and a contributory health scheme.

The marketing communications department is regularly in touch with all of The Body Shop's 46 countries through a monthly dispatch box system. A special information pack is sent to each individual country containing news, videos, and product information, and a response mechanism is in place so that a two-way exchange of information goes between each country and headquarters. International franchisee meetings are held periodically as well as regional meetings between those based in Europe, those in Asia and franchisees in the Americas.

The Body Shop's social statement is now available on the company's internet site and is summarised in its publication, *Our Agenda*. This is an attempt to produce a public statement of the company's social performance with input from employees, franchisees, customers and suppliers, gained from a series of focus groups conducted internationally. Women do well within The Body Shop. Sixty-six per cent of the entire workforce are female and in the middle to upper management bracket, 57 per cent are female. Womens' issues are actively promoted, including an excellent maternity package which is linked to length of service. Ten days' paternity leave is also granted to fathers. An on-site nursery, after school care and holiday camp facilities are all available at headquarters. A family care scheme for pre-school children provides vouchers towards child care for all employees with over one year's service.

Contact address

Mrs Monica Newton,
Working Practices Manager,
The Body Shop International PLC,
Watersmead, Littlehampton,
West Sussex BN17 6LS.
Telephone: 01903 731500.
Fax: 01903 726250.
Web address: http//www.the-body-shop.com.
e-mail: info@bodyshop.co.uk.

The Boots Company plc

Boots is one of the most well-known names in the high street. It is the UK's leading chain of chemist shops, and the group also includes Halfords, Do It All, Boots Opticians, A G Stanley, Boots Healthcare International, Boots Contract Manufacturing and Boots Properties. The company employs 84,000 people – the vast majority of them in its shops around the UK. It has a long tradition as a thoughtful and active employer which seeks to attract high calibre people, and has some of the highest numbers of employees who have been through National Vocational Qualification schemes. In 1995 the company received the Investors in People award and Boots The Chemists spends at least £25 million on training. In 1996 the company reported sales of £4.1 billion with an operational profit of £443 million.

Boots at a glance

Employees: 84,000
Annual staff attrition rate: n/a
Key locations: 400+
Annual graduate recruitment: n/a
Annual intakes: n/a

An inside view

Boots The Chemists is one of the best-known names in the UK high street. Most people will be familiar with it, if not daily shoppers in the company's chemist stores. It is also highly regarded by the City, giving the fourth highest shareholder return in the period to March 1996. Its share prices appreciated accordingly, and during the period from April 1995 to March 1996 it rose 120p on its then level of 500p. Chairman Sir Michael Angus says

'We continue to maintain a high level of investment focused on our existing operations and directed to maximising long-term value. Increasing focus on core businesses is a common theme across the group. Boots The Chemists is concentrating space and product development on healthcare and beauty products. Halfords is shifting its emphasis from high street branches to superstores, and increasing its own brand ranges. Boots Opticians continues to build its own brand business. A G Stanley is scaling down Fads to a core of more profitable high street stores, or focusing Homestyle on retail parks. Do It All is differentiating itself in an overcrowded market by concentrating on product-focused display format and expert DIY advice. Boots Healthcare International is building and extending its strong brands internationally in the self-medication market. Boots

Contract Manufacturing is expanding internationally in Europe to meet growing demand there. Boots Properties, our second largest business, continues to expand the property portfolio by selective purchases and development ends.' In the last few years, Boots has expanded from being a UK business into certain acquisitions around the world. In Europe in particular Boots Contract Manufacturing has acquired a series of companies and its customers now include major retailers from France, Spain, the Netherlands and Portugal. In December 1995 Boots acquired Crodar International's cosmetics and toiletries manufacturing businesses in France and Germany.

Boots measures its performance in terms of total shareholder returns. The key driver is the long-term cash flows generated by high levels of investment throughout the group. In 1996 the company reinvested more than £200 million in capital expenditure in its various businesses. The biggest net beneficiary was Boots The Chemists itself and also Boots Properties. Boots The Chemists has 1,226 stores, Halfords 404 stores, Boots Opticians 263 practices, Homestyle 369 stores, Do It All – a joint venture with W H Smith – 178 outlets, Boots Healthcare International has 14 businesses operating around the world, Contract Manufacturing runs five factories and one major development laboratory, and Boots Properties holds 933 UK properties. The largest number of employees is in Boots The Chemists where it has 53,577 employees, the nearest largest being Halfords which has a little over 9,000. Boots The Chemists accounts for £3.1 billion of the group's £4.1 billion sales. It is clearly the largest

part of the enterprise and continues to expand, reporting a profit increase of 10 per cent. Dispensing sales are the heart of the business. The authority of its pharmacists and their expert advice secure the trust and authority which Boots demands. The pharmacists attract customers, bringing additional sales, and giving BTC clear differentiation from the supermarkets. Over-the-counter medicines and general chemist sales rose rapidly in 1996 and beauty and personal care products are also continuing to grow. Its strategy focuses on powerful own brands, a strong customer relationship, a quality property portfolio, motivated and trained people, vertical integration giving control over rapid product development, manufacturing distribution and retailing, and innovative information systems.

How does Boots rate?

Pay:	very good
Benefits:	very good
Communications:	good
Training:	excellent
Career development:	very good
Morale:	very good

People and personnel policies

Boots has a long-standing reputation as a forward-thinking employer. This helps the company to attract the best people and enables its managers to demand high standards of performance encouraged by incentives and strong rewards. In 1995/96 three of its businesses were accredited by Investors in People and a fourth was reaccredited. It is one of the largest participants in the National Vocational Qualifications scheme, and some 21,000 staff are currently working for NVQs. It has a policy of actively encouraging people to transfer between its businesses, and its management development programme is aimed to give them broad experience and perspective and to aid the spread of ideas and best practice throughout the group.

Commenting on the reward packages available with Boots, chairman Sir Michael Angus said, 'We are motivating our staff through the organisation to recognise and build shareholder value. In all of our business units, bonus schemes are based on the achievement of targets related more closely than ever to value creation. Our short-term bonus scheme for some 200 senior managers continues to evolve and now includes an option to convert half of bonus payments into longer-term share-based schemes. We have ended awards of executive share options for directors and our most senior managers, which are being replaced by a long-term incentive scheme.' Half of each bonus earned is paid immediately with the balance due in the form of shares after three years' continued employment. 'These schemes relate executive directors and senior managers' rewards closely to the benefits they deliver to shareholders and put us in the forefront of businesses working to tie incentives to the achievement of strategic objectives, and have been well received by our major shareholders.' Within the chemist chain BTC continues to improve staff training and development. The company believes

these are vital to differentiate Boots' service to its customers from those of its competitors. 'In 1995 it launched its *Selling the Boots Experience* programme, which involves all staff in annual customer service training. BTC's excellent training and development was recognised in 1995 when it became the largest organisation to be recertified under the Investors in People scheme, three years after its original assignment.

The recruitment of high quality people is vital for Boots as the company trades on the quality and excellence of its advice. Particularly in Boots The Chemists in its pharmaceutical operations and Boots Opticians, it makes high demands on the quality of the people that it recruits. Boots is increasingly successful in retraining its skill base. Investment in training leads to reduced staff turnover. In Boots The Chemists three-quarters of store staff who had taken maternity leave returned to work. The company supports staff retention through a variety of family friendly policies, including flexible working, term-time working, job shares and career breaks.

One of the most important strategic aims is to maximise the affiliation benefits that each business gains from being part of the wider group. The transfer of people is one of the most effective ways of disseminating ideas and best practice from business to business, creating more rounded managers and enriching their careers in the process. The company is working to increase the number of transfers. During 1995/96 more than 70 senior managers transferred between businesses, roughly a third on secondment and two-thirds in permanent career moves, up to and including business unit managing director level. These represented almost 9 per cent of available senior managers compared with 3 per cent two years earlier. The company argues that another valuable way to build and share managers' experience is through participation in multi-business project groups. Almost 16 per cent of senior managers took part in these in the last year compared with under 2 per cent three years earlier.

Clear and consistent two-way communication is a priority through the organisation. To monitor its effectiveness MORI was commissioned to conduct the first group-wide employee attitude survey in November 1995. The results guide future personnel activity and provide benchmarks for subsequent research. Significantly, MORI found that the proportion of staff claiming to understand the business and objectives was exceptionally high compared with other organisations. As well as communicating through line management and award-winning staff news magazines and videos, the company has a well-established formal structure of staff councils. This complements the relationships with trade unions and is a key for good industrial relations. During 1995/96 the company updated the constitutions of several councils to reflect business and employee needs more effectively.

Contact address

The Boots Group Personnel Company plc, Group Headquarters Nottingham, NG2 3AA.
Telephone 0115 9506111.
Fax: 0115 9592280.

The British Petroleum Company plc

BP is one of the world's largest oil, gas and chemical companies, operating in 100 countries across the globe. For long seen as one of the better companies to work for, BP has in recent years become even more focused on gaining superior performance from all its assets and employees. The company maintains high standards of integrity and respect for health, safety and the environment. It is also a believer in partnership with customers, communities and the environment. BP is a major recruiter of graduates, offering early development and the opportunity to build world-class careers in business and technology.

BP at a glance

Employees: 53,000
Annual staff attrition rate: n/a
Key locations: Head Office in London with several sites across the UK; BP also operates in 100 countries across six continents.
Av. annual graduate recruitment: 150
Annual intake: n/a

An inside view

BP is a different enterprise from a decade ago. In fact it is a much tighter, clearer-sighted and logical company. Its business focus and a performance-driven culture have contributed to a much greater effectiveness throughout.

Like many large companies it has had to lay off staff, ending the tradition of a job for life. BP now only employs half the workforce it did towards the end of the 1980s. Of the people who have left, around a half went with the sale of non-core activities to other companies; many, for instance, left the BP fold when the company sold its nutrition interests. A further quarter would have left through early retirement programmes. Of those made redundant some 80 per cent who could be contacted had found another job within 12 months – a reflection on the marketability of the skills and experience they had acquired at BP.

BP is now clearly focused into three divisions: exploration and production; refining and marketing; and chemicals. The divisions operate separate career paths although they have common personnel policies and the company recognises that it is seen as a whole rather than three different entities by the outside world.

As a result of a major new emphasis on

performance, each of the company's assets is now required to be in the top quarter of a comparison group drawn from competing companies. If an asset has not achieved this degree of excellence, BP will first look to improve it. It is for example putting a number of refineries through a 'pacesetter' programme to bring the standard of the poorest-performing up to that of the top quarter of the industry. But if the asset cannot attain this target, it will be sold to another party for whom it might be more appropriate.

Openness is another value that has come to the fore in recent years. Much of BP's business is carried out in partnership with governments and joint venture operators and good relationships with them are essential. BP believes that being open about its health, safety and environmental record and the steps it needs to take to improve and maintain standards in these areas helps to build trust. Likewise, the company is trying to extend the same approach to its suppliers, and it has developed closer relationships with them.

The desire for good relationships extends to a large community programme, and BP employees are encouraged to give of their time and skills to the community in which they work. The company will match employees' private donations to good causes and it offers grants to groups supported by BP employees. In 1996 BP invested more than £18.4 million in community programmes, with £6.2 million being spent in the UK. A BP scheme to aid small businesses in Colombia has won the praise of the World Bank while the company has contributed to the teaching of science in 40 countries across the world.

How does BP rate?

Pay:	good
Benefits:	very good
Communications:	good
Training:	excellent
Career development:	excellent
Morale:	very good

People and personnel policies

Anyone looking to work for a good company who cannot work as part of a team should not consider applying to BP. 'If they can't work in a team, then that does not mean they are not a super person or that they will not get a Nobel prize but they're just not right for BP,' says a company spokesman.

After technical competence demonstrated through an academic discipline, the potential to be a good teamworker is one of the qualities sought in recruits. There is now a much more explicit emphasis on interpersonal skills in recruitment as the company is looking for employees who can show leadership potential with people as well as showing leadership in a particular technological or business discipline. Even in the case of technical knowledge, single-subject excellence is not enough as employees need to gain breadth as well as depth of knowledge and experience.

BP now has a policy of recruiting between 100 and 200 graduates a year worldwide, after a dip in graduate recruitment in the early 1990s. It hopes these employees will become the principal feedstock for the company's leadership in

The British Petroleum Company plc

the years ahead. Graduates are in general expected to be mobile, and there is a European recruitment programme specifically for people who want to work in marketing across Europe.

Graduates undergo a training programme and are assigned to one of the company's three business streams but are brought together again after about two years in a ten-day group induction course held regularly around the world. There is also a programme for people who have shown exceptional promise in the three business streams who are given all-round development to prepare them for the company's group leadership.

There is now quite explicit encouragement for BP employees to draw up their own career strategy, called a personal development plan, and to consider how they can fulfil their ambitions within the company. Those who are told they have the potential to go far are also told that this is in itself only potential that needs to be demonstrated through achievement. The company aims to be realistic, recognising that not everyone is suited to or wants jobs that can place huge demands on time and require lots of travelling, which can be in conflict with family life. 'It is better to get this out in the open,' a spokesman says. 'You may or may not be able to fulfil your ambitions at BP but if you are open about this you are more likely to find an outcome that benefits both the employee and the company.'

The changes that the company has made to flatten its organisational structure in recent years to encourage more efficient working are also to be reflected in corporate communications. The company's stable of employees'

newspapers is to be complemented by an intranet, linking computers in the 100 countries where BP operates into a single network, enabling faster and easier sharing of information with and among employees.

Meanwhile, at BP pay is linked to performance. Basic pay is generally at a median level in comparison with competitor companies but performance pay can bring salaries into the top quarter of the industry range. Staff can gain bonuses that are usually linked to the performance of a team or asset. There are, for instance, a lot of gain-sharing schemes in the exploration division, in which employees can earn a portion of the benefits of good performance or a cost-cutting programme. There are also employee share-ownership schemes and a long-term performance plan which links the rewards of top executives to the performance of the company over a long period.

Contact address

The British Petroleum Company plc, Britannic House, 1 Finsbury Circus, London EC2M 7BA.
Telephone: 0171 496 4000.
Fax: 0171 496 4630.

Brann Limited

There are few direct marketing companies which enjoy the reputation of Brann. Its stated objective is to help its clients to create loyal customers through more effective contact. The company is positioned at the higher quality end of the direct marketing industry, moving increasingly towards consultancy and integrated project work. In a sector where people management is given a low priority, Brann is exceptional. Since its inception in the mid-1960s, it has distinguished itself as a business which recognises the importance of its people and built upon this policy to create a company which is highly employee-focused. The benefits have been legion.

Brann at a glance

Employees: 695
Annual staff attrition rate: 10 per cent
Key locations: Cirencester,
    Gloucestershire, Bristol and London
Active graduate recruitment: 10
Annual intake: 100

An inside view

It seems obvious that a sector which depends wholly on its people, their expertise and commitment should acknowledge and develop their role. But the direct marketing industry has one of the poorest reputations in the UK economy for its recognition of the contribution of employees in winning and delivering client assignments. Direct marketing is a pure service discipline – and the quality of the service which is delivered to clients is the key reason why businesses are successful. There are two main reasons why Brann stands head and shoulders above other companies in the market: it has, long since, understood the relationship between excellent client service and dedicated employees, and its human resources policies are designed to equate with those of the UK's top employers.

'Life is more complex than going out with a sales message in whatever medium and then hoping that the customer will order. Companies need to think through all of the ingredients. There are aspects which organisations cover internally – sales material, staff information and training – which equip them to be knowledgeable at the point of customer contact. We help in some of these activities with our clients. Then there is Interactive and Telephone which are direct contact points, where we also assist clients and, crucially, we work with them to plan and execute advertising and response promotions where we draw the customer into the contact zone,' says CEO Chris Gater. 'Everything we do is focused on when our clients and their customers come together. That positions us very differently from providing direct mail or telephone sales packages in isolation. We help the client work out how this entire process works.

'Traditional direct marketing – mail order advertising – has been about customer behaviour rather than increasing an impression of the client and its values. We work with advertising agencies. They are often briefed to create the brand image; we make it come true for the customer.' He says that this is a holistic process where Brann shapes the communication and defines the target markets. It collects the responses from customers and feeds this data back to influence the future development of the client's communications, products and services. Crucially, it also builds awareness of the client in the mind of the customer. At the outset of an assignment, Brann will identify with the client what the objective of the exercise is: an increased retention of customers, penetration of a new market sector, growing the value of a particular target group. Not all Brann clients take advantage of the full service and may enter its portfolio for a specific service but the aim of the company is to broaden the base of work for its core clients.

How does Brann rate?

Pay:	very good
Benefits:	very good
Communications:	superb
Training:	excellent
Career development:	very good
Morale:	very good

People and personnel policies

Personnel director Jon Parsons says 'We are outgoing people with a high degree of ideas and creativity. And one of the things which distinguishes the company is the low level of rules and regulations. It is clearly a meritocracy. We recognise that there are certain attributes and talents which tend to fit the type of work we do and the kind of clients we have. This is a very diverse organisation and our personnel policy reflects that diversity. Procedures, policies and methods can vary from area to area. We are low on rules, high on flexibility. We encourage people to contribute as much as possible.'

This is a truly open culture where ideas and debate are fostered. There is a vision which provides a framework for the commercial objectives of the business but the application of the vision will vary from department to department and team to team. The company has moved from a traditional structure to a flatter environment. There are six key disciplines – systems, printed communications, call centre, planning, creative and project management. These are all presented to clients through service teams. 'Increasingly we want to orientate ourselves along client team lines as well as by function. We have a board of about a dozen people who run this structure. A larger group called the operating board, which numbers about 40, is a way of involving more people in the thinking behind the strategy. I will not pretend that this is the executive forum but we try hard to involve people like this in the process.'

Parsons says that Brann is becoming

more cross-functional in its approach. 'This is easier in some functions than others. Making a shift from systems to creative is difficult but people from systems do move to planning and people from planning go to interactive. If someone does not fit in one department we will move them elsewhere. We tend to start from the premise that the role is wrong, rather than the person. We will try people out in other functions and sometimes this works very well.'

This is a highly literate workforce which reinforces the need for additional education and training where Brann excels. 'If you are, for example, an account manager in fund-raising, you will agree your training with your manager. This could be a fund-raising conference or one-day training which is organised by the function. Above that, the group personnel team will arrange several corporate programmes – technical, managerial and commercial. In 1996 we introduced the Brann Diploma which is a ten-month programme to develop people at the business and personal level.' Parsons says that as the company deals with bigger clients on larger assignments, more senior people at the client will question Brann people on the validity of certain strategies. So the company needs people who have deep experience and can move with great flexibility. One of the key ways that Brann creates experienced people is by skill development through moving around the business and gaining expertise in a variety of sectors.

In three years the complement of employees has grown by more than 40 per cent and although some are graduates, very few come as a direct result of active graduate recruitment. In 1994 and 1995, the years of large recruitment exercises,

some six to eight graduates were enlisted straight from university; in 1996 when the aim was to hold steady in staff numbers only two people entered as a first job after college. 'In client service and creative areas the emphasis is still on recruiting young talent from wherever but we have placed more stress on drawing from candidates who are at a more senior stage in their careers. We have grown the numbers of senior client managers and so we have engaged some very experienced people to meet this demand. Since July 1995 we have located 17 new people for our interactive function where we want new skills such as designers, authors, editors and project managers,' says Parsons.

Pay is high for the sector and is composed of basic pay and profit-related pay for all permanent staff. In addition there is a company pension scheme, which is 4 per cent contributory, and several incentive packages. The company also provides life assurance and a top notch healthcare plan for all members of the workforce. 'We have a discounted staff restaurant and a local sports centre at Cirencester which is used extensively and which we shamelessly advertise as a staff benefit.' Brann gives 25 days' annual holiday as standard.

Contact address

Mr Jon Parsons, Personnel Director,
Brann Limited,
Phoenix Way,
Cirencester,
Gloucestershire GL7 1RY.
Telephone: 01285 644744.
Fax: 01285 654952.
E-mail: jparsons@brann.co.uk.

British Airways plc

British Airways (BA) is the world's largest international passenger airline, and one of the UK's most respected companies. Its success has been built around a strategy of providing high quality customer service, combined with a strongly focused marketing effort. BA has also invested heavily in creating global alliances with other airlines operators, and is currently attempting to cement an alliance with American Airlines which would enhance its presence in the important North Atlantic market.

British Airways at a glance

Employees: 58,000 worldwide, 48,000 UK
Annual staff attrition rate: 2 per cent*
Key locations: Heathrow Airport (HQ),
    Gatwick Airport, London and various
    locations around the UK and the world
Av. annual graduate recruitment: n/a
Annual intake: n/a
*excluding restructuring

An inside view

Since its privatisation ten years ago, BA has been transformed into one of the world's most successful airlines. In the year to March 1996, the company carried a record 36.1 million passengers, and its scheduled route network is one of the most extensive in the world, serving some 175 destinations in 83 countries. Its fleet, of course, includes Concorde, the world's only supersonic passenger aircraft. BA's main base is London Heathrow Airport (the largest international airport in the world), but the company also operates an increasing number of services out of

London Gatwick Airport. In a 1996 *Financial Times* survey, BA was voted the second most respected company in Europe (after Swiss-Swedish engineering concern ABB).

British Airways argues that in many parts of the world the airline industry is still highly regulated. However, the trend is towards deregulation and where this has occurred, it has fostered competition between existing operators and by enabling easier market entry by new low-cost carriers. The overall effect is that in most developed markets there is strong competition and these competitive pressures are increasing. The airline says that one remaining problem is that many governments continue to keep unprofitable state-owned airlines in business through state subsidies, although, in Europe this is, strictly speaking, illegal. BA obviously cannot expect to be immune from increasing competition and in late 1996 it announced a four-year business efficiency programme which is designed to improve efficiency by £1 billion a year by 2000. It is important to understand that this programme consists of a wide range of measures designed to improve efficiency and is not simply a cost-cutting programme. (Neither, by the way, does it turn BA into a 'virtual airline', as some analysts have claimed.) BA fully expects to be employing as many staff at the turn of the century as it does now and some areas of the company, particularly those concerned with customer service, will see substantial recruitment.

BA's mission is to be the most successful company in the airline business. In order to achieve this, the company believes two factors are critical: firstly, the safety and security of passengers is of paramount importance; secondly, the quality of customer service provides BA with an important source of competitive advantage. In addition, BA is trying to create an atmosphere of greater openness and employee involvement within the company. It believes that this is especially important in the current trading environment which demands greater operational flexibility. Moreover, while BA is managed in a classic matrix management style, one of the principal effects of the emphasis on cost control over recent years has been to remove intermediate layers of management. As a result, business heads have now assumed much more operational autonomy.

It is undoubtedly true that competitive pressures within the airline industry will continue into the foreseeable future, and that these will be exacerbated by the next economic downturn. Nevertheless, most commentators would expect to see BA retain its market position (or, perhaps, even strengthen it as the industry consolidates and the strength of the company's global alliances becomes more important). In these circumstances, career opportunities within BA remain considerable.

How does British Airways rate?

Pay:	good
Benefits:	good
Communications:	very good
Training:	excellent
Career development:	very good
Morale:	average

People and personnel policies

BA has made a major investment in training and development since privatisation, and regards itself as being at the leading edge of training within the industry. Consistent with its policy of continuously improving customer service, many of the training initiatives are focused on this area – a new training programme for cabin crew, for example, was initiated around 18 months ago. Management training and leadership development programmes run alongside these technical courses. 400 of the company's leading executives have already passed through its leadership development programme, and a further 1,800 have been identified as future candidates. Open learning centres have also been established to provide employees with additional training and development opportunities through multi-media, including interactive video, computer-based training and an extensive business library.

In terms of career appraisal, sophisticated systems are already in place at management levels and these will be extended to all employees within the next three years. The philosophy behind these systems is that, by identifying and setting individual objectives, they should focus on achievement. The appraisal process is supplemented by encouraging 360 degree feedback.

BA believes that a major part of its success is a consequence of the motivation and commitment of its employees. This is rewarded through the airline's profit share scheme which for 1995/96 gave every eligible employee a bonus equivalent to nearly four weeks' pay. At senior levels, further incentive payments become an increasingly large element of total remuneration. Employee ownership in the company is encouraged and it is estimated that currently around 65 per cent of the workforce are shareholders.

BA has a comprehensive internal communications programme to ensure that employees are well informed about the business and the airline industry in general. As well as formal methods of communication, line managers are encouraged to regard communication as an integral part of their job and are assessed accordingly. A particularly innovative development is that the company has started to hold an annual business fair where employees can learn more about the company and question senior directors face-to-face. The staff newspaper, *BA News*, is produced weekly and the company has also recently launched its own TV channel. Electronic communication methods are also being improved.

One area which BA recognises requires further improvement is the diversity of its workforce. The airline is a champion member of Opportunity 2000 (a campaign working to improve the representation of women in management), while Robert Ayling, BA's chief executive, is also chairman of Race for Opportunity, which aims to encourage businesses to invest in the diversity of Britain's ethnic minority communities. BA has also established its own equal opportunities steering group. However, progress on this issue is slower than the company would like.

In an industry which can be linked in the public perception with the problems of noise, pollution and congestion, BA understands the importance of the need to consider the environment in all aspects of its business. The company sets itself annual environmental objectives (e.g. to reduce the number and frequency of noise infringements), with the results published in an annual environmental report.

Contact address

Mr Mervyn Walker,
Director of Human Resources,
British Airways plc,
Speedbird House, PO Box 100,
Heathrow Airport, Hounslow,
Middlesex TW6 2JA.
Telephone: 0181 759 5511.
Fax: 0181 513 3279.

British Steel plc

S ince its privatisation in 1988, British Steel has become one of the UK's major success stories. In the financial year 1995–96 it made a record pre-tax profit of £1.1 billion on sales of £8 billion. The company has 54,000 employees worldwide (20 per cent of them outside the UK) and is the largest steel producer in Europe – and the third largest in the world. It is consistently among the UK's top ten exporters. It aims to be the premier low-cost steel producer around the world.

British Steel at a glance

Employees: 54,000 worldwide, 44,000 UK
Annual staff attrition rate: n/a
Key locations: London (HQ), Llanwern, Port Talbot, Sheffield, Rotherham, Scunthorpe, Stockbridge, Teeside, Brinsworth, Corby, Dalzell, Ebbw Vale, Hartlepool, Shelton, Skinngrove, Templeborough, Trostre, Whitehead and Workington
Av. annual graduate recruitment: 200
Annual intake: n/a

An inside view

As British Steel delights in pointing out, steel is part of everything we buy, use, and consume. Even if a product does not contain steel, it will have been manufactured or processed with machines made of steel – or harvested with steel tools or equipment. If steel is not used in the packaging of a product, the packaging will have been produced with steel machinery. The product will have been distributed by transport made of steel. Even the buildings in which we live and work depend on different types of steel. Undoubtedly, the world as we know it could not exist without steel.

Some 70 per cent of the steels in use today have been generated within the last ten years and British Steel is at the forefront of this development. It has created three world-renowned technology centres, employing 1,000 scientists in research and development, including metallurgists, engineers, designers, physicists, chemists, mathematicians and computer scientists. These scientists develop products for diverse markets. The largest is the construction industry which accounts for 24 per cent of UK sales. Products include piling for foundations, tubes and sections for structural frames, plates for bridgework, metallic and organic coated steels for cladding, roofing and internal partitions, profiled sheets for cladding and roofing systems, and steel framing for domestic housing.

The second largest market is the automotive sector which accounts for 20 per cent of UK sales. As well as supplying flat rolled steel for car bodies, the company works closely with the automotive industry to produce finished, forged and machined components, from crankshafts and hubs to axle beams, brake parts, gears, transmission and suspension parts. British Steel is also a leading member of a world wide consortium of 33 steel companies which is developing technologies to reduce the weight of today's typical car body by over 24 per cent.

Twelve per cent of British Steel's output goes into industrial plant and some 10 per cent into packaging – from the thinnest of materials for the food trays used in microwave ovens to steels for giant 210 litre drums. The company says that four out of five cans of all types are made of steel and that every steel can contains 25 per cent of recycled metal.

With 55 per cent of its business outside the UK, distribution is vitally important for British Steel. The company has developed a network of more than 70 sales and distribution companies throughout Europe, North America, Asia Pacific, the Middle East, South Asia and Australasia. It also operates stock holding and further-processing services in Germany, France, Holland, Norway, Denmark and the Irish Republic. In the UK it has 45 Steel Service Centres.

Joint investments include 75 per cent of European Electrical Steels, 51 per cent of Avesta Sheffield AB, and 25 per cent of Trico Steel Company. Recently British Steel announced that it is to enter into overseas partnerships, the first being a £29 million investment in Jindal Iron and Steel in India to form a coatings joint venture.

How does British Steel rate?

Pay: very good
Benefits: excellent
Communications: very good
Training: excellent
Career development: very good
Morale: excellent

People and personnel policies

The culture of British Steel can be described as competitive, demanding, merit-based, product-orientated and with a high level of commitment. Nevertheless, the company recognises that as the leading player in the UK steel market it has few competitors from which to acquire staff and that it must encourage, train and nurture its own talent. Over the last five years it has spent an average of £45 million annually on the training and development of employees at all levels. This represents 1 per cent of the company's sales turnover and five per cent of its employment costs during this period. And by the end of 1995 it had won more training awards than any other UK company – 40 in total.

As George Spencer, manager of management development and selection says 'In the same way that we add value to our products, we are equally dedicated to adding value to our people through individually tailored career plans, supported by extensive management development systems. The aim of the company is to get the best out of people by making full use of their individual abilities, to develop senior managers for the future, and to provide fulfilling and challenging careers'. For graduates this means competitive pay and benefits, superior training, the opportunity of accelerated management development, the possibility of a business-school designed programme which includes the option of an in-company MBA, and an international management programme to equip managers with the necessary business skills to meet the increasingly international nature of British Steel's markets.

The international nature of British Steel needs to be emphasised. It has a growing requirement for its managers to understand the global business environment of which the company is a part. To aid this process it uses international business schools (such as INSEAD in France and IMD in Switzerland as well as schools in North America) and provides in-house language training facilities. The company stresses that it is keen to develop a culture where it is natural for every manager to speak at least one foreign language. 'We encourage early exposure to other countries and cultures,' says Spencer, 'and we operate an exchange scheme with a number of foreign steel producers. There are also opportunities for secondments, especially in commercial functions, to our businesses overseas.'

Other management development initiatives include two assessments, in the first four years, of the potential of each graduate, and regular performance appraisals – which provide the primary means of feedback within the organisation. In addition, as mentioned earlier, selected graduates also have the opportunity of an accelerated management development programme. Every year about 24 managers enter this intensive programme which allows those with high potential to broaden their existing management skills, and to acquire additional capabilities and perspectives at

a relatively early stage in their careers. The participants tend to be managers in their late twenties with about five or six years' experience within the company.

The first year of the programme is run in conjunction with Warwick Business School, with four separate modules being run at Ashborne Hill, British Steel's own management college. The second phase of the programme (now in its eighth year) offers the option of obtaining an MBA via Warwick's distance learning programme. These MBA graduates form what British Steel considers to be its corporate resources of the future. For the company is constantly aware that there is no lake of competitors' management that it can fish in. It must train its own successors to today's senior management. British Steel also gives high priority to professional qualifications and strongly encourages its graduates to gain membership of a relevant professional body. It gives the appropriate support, such as paid study leave or financial assistance, to enable graduates to do this as quickly as possible.

Contact address

Mr George Spencer, Manager,
Management Development and Selection,
British Steel plc,
9 Albert Embankment,
London SE1 7SN.
Telephone: 0171 735 7654.
Fax: 0171 735 0709.

BSkyB Broadcasting Group

British Sky Broadcasting Group plc – or BSkyB as it is known – is the world's largest and most successful pay-television, direct-to-home operator, with more than 6 million paying subscribers, and some 16 million viewers. In the seven years since the merge of British Satellite Broadcasting and Sky Television, it has undergone rapid growth and is now capitalised at more than £10 billion. This means it is one of the top 20 companies in the UK and top 200 listed businesses in the world. Watching television is the single most popular leisure activity in Britain and Sky has taken television programming into a new age. BSkyB currently owns and operates 12 television channels in the UK and is a joint venture partner in 13 other channels. The company's activities include the purchasing, production, packaging and promotion of programming; the operation of an extremely successful subscriber service in two centres in Scotland; the sale of advertising air time.

BSkyB at a glance

Employees: 4,200
Annual staff attrition rate: n/a
Key locations: Isleworth (HQ),
    Livingston, Dunfermline
Av. annual graduate recruitment: 10
Annual intake: 200

An inside view

As the world's biggest and most successful satellite television operator, BSkyB's phenomenal growth has transformed the television industry in this country, making it a world leader not only in programming but also in technology, new media development, as well as subscription management and satellite support systems. Its direct employment of industry professionals has grown from 500 in its first year of operation to more than 3,500 permanent employees – which represents more than 8 per cent of all those employed in the television industry in this country.

In 1989, there were only four television channels, with total employment estimated at 19,000. In 1997, there are more than 50, supporting some 42,000 jobs. This proliferation of channels means wider choice to those pursuing a career in television; and the resulting competition has brought salary levels closer to international standards, guaranteeing that this industry remains competitive by attracting the highest quality staff.

Since it was founded, Sky has invested more than £3 billion in developing a pay television infrastructure; and its success has made Britain a leading exporter of satellite television services, spurring on the development of a whole new industry. In 1995, consumer satellite companies generated revenue of more than $4.8 billion and employed around 17,000 in this country.

One of the fastest growth sectors in the high street in this decade has been the sale of satellite television equipment. More than 3,500 independent retailers, together with the major multiples such as Comet, Currys and Dixons, plus department stores and mail order houses, have all benefited from the Sky revolution.

In the cable sector, Sky has again had a major impact. In 1989, only 2,300 people were employed. By 1996, the number directly employed had risen to 17,000 with another 16,000 in temporary employment with contractors. That year, half a million new subscribers signed up, representing a growth rate of close to 40 per cent. The financial performance of the company in the past fiscal year has exceeded all market expectations. Turnover exceeded £1 billion as revenues rose by 30 per cent. Operating profit was up 39 per cent to £315 million; and pre-tax profit up 66 per cent to £257 million. From the beginning, BSkyB has been dedicated to delivering the highest standards of customer service.

How does BSkyB rate?

Pay:	good
Benefits:	good
Communications:	very good
Training:	good
Career development:	very good
Morale:	good

People and personnel policies

BSkyB operates the most advanced subscriber management system in the world. This is a real people business and its success is dependent on how these telephone operators are trained, and how they are treated by the company. The service's success speaks for itself. Customer service operators, as they are called, handle a million telephone calls a month at its two centres in Scotland, offering straightforward, easily understood advice on anything from billing details to up-to-the-minute programming information.

All operators are fully trained, and the company employs multi-lingual personnel. Viewers can call the subscriber management centres every day of the year from early morning until late at night. It takes less than 15 seconds to activate the smart card in a new subscriber's decoder so that they can receive new Sky programmes. The training of Sky employees is an awesome responsibility and lies at the heart of the company's human resource policy, particularly when it is realised that the subscriber management system was set up in Livingstone only eight years ago with a staff of 12.

Cynthia Guthrie, group head of personnel, spent most of her BskyB years in Scotland, right in the middle of explosive growth that set totally unparalleled challenges for dealing with a rapidly expanding workforce. 'In view of the great growth, recruitment policies were an absolute key to success. We had to be sure we had the right resource. This was the growing sunrise industry and we had to be innovative and creative in our recruitment. No one in the marketplace had had this experience, and no one had done what we were doing.'

What Sky is most proud of is that it went out into Scotland and found untrained people and turned them into skilled technician operators who could communicate with the subscriber. The company fully believes that its recruitment policies have had a substantial impact on unemployment in this part of the United Kingdom. The company has found people who turned out to have innate skills for this eclectic, diverse workforce. 'We are giving people the opportunity to show skills they would otherwise not have the opportunity to display.'

The culture of Sky is definitely customer-focused, on the leading edge, technology-driven and very heavily into teamwork. The company has entrepreneurial flat structures. 'This is a very lean organisation, there is no fat,' says Guthrie. 'A lot of older companies are now into delayering to reach a point where we are today.' 'We are not a bureaucracy. All the time, we are being self-critical and looking at how to be more flexible and efficient. We have a sound track record of growing our employees. There are lots of examples of them growing with, and in, the company, rising to management positions.'

The company's Scottish operations are the key to its success in human resources because the nature of the job means people are often hired as raw recruits. 'In Scotland,' says Guthrie, 'we are particularly looking at developing the needs of the individual; the training policy is one of continuous self-development. This is very much a learning culture.' Eighty per cent of Sky's workforce is in customer service. It is interesting what this produces: for example, half the senior managers in the Scottish operations are female, with an overall 60–40 per cent female to male ratio. 'Ethnic minorities represent more than 2 per cent and that is higher than the national average. The company is a truly equal opportunity employer. We practise this.'

Contact address

Ms Cynthia Guthrie, Head of Personnel
BSkyB,
Grant Way,
Isleworth,
Middlesex TW2 5QD.
Telephone: 0171 705 3000.
Fax: 0171 705 3435.

BT plc

BT is one of the world's largest telecommunications companies. It is – by far and away – the biggest telecoms provider in the UK, operating commercial and domestic services and running a vast network. The company has experienced massive change since its privatisation, transforming its reputation from slow and bureaucratic to an alert, innovative and efficiently managed operation. As part of this cathartic change, the company has substantially improved its standing as an employer. BT is now a highly attractive business for all grades of employee, especially graduates.

BT at a glance

Employees: 120,000
Staff attrition rate: 14 per cent
Key locations: Central London (HQ), plus every major city in the UK. It also has offices in a variety of cities worldwide
Active graduate recruitment: 250
Annual intake: 1,100

An inside view

The transformation of BT has been one of the great corporate success stories of the last decades. During the 1970s it was part of the Post Office monopoly and after demerger it became one of the early Thatcher government candidates for privatisation. In 1984 British Telecommunications plc was inaugurated. It was heralded as one of the former public sector businesses which did most to extend the shareholder franchise. More than 2 million small shareholders subscribed to the BT offer. BT is now one of two global telecommunications giants which lead the world in rapid, flexible and multi-level telecommunications services.

Today's BT is one of the top five companies in the UK by market capitalisation, worth in the region of £22.3 billion. But it is much smaller in employee terms than in its public sector days. The company has clinically removed whole sections of its management and workforce – a process which its senior directors said was necessary to be an effective competitor in world markets. The service which it now provides to its domestic customers is widely agreed to be manifoldly more effective, cheaper and diverse. The quality, cost effectiveness and responsiveness to which the customers of US telecoms companies have long been exposed is becoming a reality in the UK. Spurred by competition initially from Mercury and now from a range of operators in different market sectors, BT has enthusiastically embraced the challenge of high quality customer service.

It also aims to be a technology leader and is the largest business in the world to receive company-wide accreditation under the ISO9001 quality standard.

BT has also changed radically in structure and approach to staff. Much of the old-fashioned public sector culture has been removed – and although BT is probably more centrally directed than many modern businesses, the comparison between now and 15 years ago is light years apart. Possibly because BT had further to travel than many of its competitors in revolutionising the business, it remains a steely organisation with drive and determination. This is hardly an easy-going West Coast emergent-technology company basking in the Californian sunshine. It is a resolute, structured business which equips its people with the skills to take on the world's finest.

This is now a customer-orientated organisation, managed professionally, which emphasises quality and continuous improvement. It is a case study in how a major international corporation can be refashioned and redirected. *The New York Times* has been prompted to comment about BT 'Few companies have remade themselves so completely as BT. It has cut costs, shed its bureaucratic methods and claimed a place as a dominant force in the worldwide telecommunications industry'.

How does BT rate?

Pay:	very good
Benefits:	very good
Communications:	very good
Training:	superb
Career development:	very good
Morale:	good

People and personnel policies

One of BT's strongest achievements in recent years is its emergence as a management culture, respected globally for its tenacity and its capacity to build on its strengths as a business while moving relatively quickly to eliminate some of the handicaps which had held the company back. The fact that it is now a primary choice by undergraduates demonstrates how effective BT has been in introducing a positive, objective-orientated environment. In a survey conducted by employment specialists Pearn Kandola, BT emerged as the second most favoured choice for graduates, after long-term top selection ICI. The study also showed that the same group also enjoyed a detailed appreciation of the company's operations and business objectives. It ranked fourth best known business among the control group. Its dexterity in planning makes a key contribution to the corporate achievement and nowhere is this more apparent than in the field of human resources.

John Steele, group personnel director at BT, emphasises the care and attention that is given to selecting, retaining and developing a workforce which is robust, articulate and skilful. Two of its five corporate values focus on HR issues: 'we respect each other' and 'we work as a team'. In their entirety the values give a graphic snapshot of a business on the move. Steele says 'We have moved from a single, unitary company to a series of autonomous businesses which operate within a common framework. Each business has its own people requirements and recruits personnel to meet its own specific needs. The way in which people are employed in the separate businesses will vary and we have adopted a range of flexible contracts to suit the demands of the time.' BT used to be a job for life company but now Steele talks about improving the employability of its workforce. Many will be on assignment with the company for a limited period during which they will enhance their skills substantially to offer to other organisations after their BT work has been completed.

'BT will move progressively to even greater decentralisation,' he comments. The common feature in all the BT businesses is its attitude towards personnel and its management style. There is an increasing drive towards strengthening personal leadership talents. Steele sees BT people as leaders and coaches who work in teams to manage designated business areas, technical developments or customer initiatives. He places great store by the company's policy to create, and manage teams to address every key commercial, technical and administrative issue. Structurally, BT's companies are based on flexible teams which are made and remade in response to market conditions.

Each individual is set targets according to BT's corporate and divisional scorecards, and reward is based on performance, creativity, contribution to the team and considered risk-taking. It is therefore inherently personal in its value and scope. 'We place much emphasis on the importance of individual/team contribution through: reward/recognition

programmes, quality awards, bonus plans for managers and individual performance-related pay, share plans, personal objective setting and annual performance review. We also operate a profit-sharing scheme where annual rewards are made to everyone on an equal basis which works out at around £200 worth of shares a year.' BT employs around 6,000 middle and senior managers and each one will have a reward package which is tailored to personal performance.

The annual performance review process provides for a personal development review. In the first the individual is assessed against certain core and secondary competencies which determine training and development needs. Based on the performance in the current year, the targets for the next year are set. Strong two-way internal communications are also seen as important for informing personnel and stimulating debate within the business.

The company places a great deal of stress on its role in the community. One of the latest studies of the most admired corporations in the UK places BT top out of 250 on community and environmental responsibility. It is the largest corporate donor in Great Britain, making £15 million in cash and kind donations to a wide portfolio of charitable causes.

Contact address

Andrew Harley, Group Personnel, BT
81 Newgate Street,
London EC1A 7AJ.
Telephone: 0171 356 5000.

Burmah Castrol plc

Burmah Castrol is a large international company made up of many smaller companies. A major force in specialised lubricants and chemicals, it aims to operate as a premium business, extracting a premium performance from its staff. The company upholds a clear set of values and provides plenty of training in the softer, interpersonal skills for its employees. Decentralisation provides many opportunities for employees to develop satisfying careers, with regular reviews of performance and a chance to shape their own future.

Burmah Castrol at a glance

Employees: 21,500
Annual staff attrition rate: n/a
Key locations: Swindon (HQ). The
   company operates in 50 countries
   worldwide
Av. annual graduate recruitment: n/a
Annual intake: n/a

An inside view

Burmah Castrol combines a clear focus on two core areas of business with a high degree of decentralisation. A £3 billion turnover company in the mid-1990s, it received some £2 billion of its income from lubricants and around £1 billion from chemicals. Chief executive Jonathan Fry says 'We don't worship on the altar of 27 different businesses and we don't believe we should try and be a hero in 27 businesses either'. The company's lubricants division is based on the famous Castrol brand of motoring, industrial and marine oils. Its chemicals business supplies five different categories of products: metallurgical, construction and mining, screen printing inks, coatings and adhesives.

Each of these business streams is managed autonomously and the company has as many as 150 profit centres, reflecting the international reach and scale of its business. As well as operating subsidiary companies in more than 50 countries, its products are marketed to 150 in all. 'Many of our companies are quite small,' says Fry. 'We've a great many £5 million to £6 million companies and we even have £2 million companies. We're very decentralised, entrepreneurial and concentrated on what we do.' Burmah Castrol does however reject the advice of those business experts who tell companies to keep their head offices tiny. It believes that it can gain economies of scale by centralising key functions there and avoiding duplication. In the area of personnel, for instance, it operates a single human resources policy across the group and promulgates a single set of company values.

The company values statement has been translated into many languages and communicated to Burmah Castrol's companies overseas. 'We thought its use is a soft, touchy-feely thing which might not be completely applicable in areas with different cultures,' says Fry. 'It might even be regarded as highly offensive. But the values statement is often highly valued, particularly in the far-flung parts of the empire.' Burmah Castrol contributes to the communities in which it is based in a way it describes as balanced and practical. There is a Burmah Castrol appeals committee for charities, overseas companies are encouraged to make contributions locally, and the company will match donations that employees make to good causes.

But the company does not go overboard in this area. 'We do not subscribe to the modern, stakeholder theory of the company. Our main task is to make the best possible return for our shareholders,' says Fry.

How does Burmah Castrol rate?

Pay:	very good
Benefits:	very good
Communications:	good
Training:	very good
Career development:	very good
Morale:	very good

People and personnel policies

Burmah Castrol is looking for people who can demonstrate what were once, in a less politically correct age, called the three B's: brains, balance and balls. Brains are needed because business is becoming more and more intellectually demanding. Balance is needed as the entrepreneurial employees the company is looking for need to be able to show grace under pressure. 'It's no good having someone with extreme hangups, chips on their shoulder or worries about themself,' says Fry. 'They are going to be under pressure and they mustn't blow up or become peculiar.' There are also going to be a few occasions in an individual's career where they are going to have to stand up for something they believe in, and that takes courage. An international outlook is also necessary – the company is not a place for little Englanders.

Burmah Castrol does not have the kind of central graduate recruitment programme that is typical at other public limited companies, although in a bid to make sure it has the right international mix of management it is trying to gain agreement on a graduate programme with subsidiaries in Japan, India, Germany, Australia and America. In the UK, it finds it easier to recruit graduates for specific vacancies.

Once an employee has joined, there is no fixed career path. It is up to every individual to take responsibility for their own career and they are encouraged to write career direction letters setting out their aspirations. Higher up in the company, there are board level discussions about jobs where there are issues that need to be addressed and promising employees whose experience needs to be developed and broadened.

There are plenty of opportunities for international career moves, and Burmah

Castrol is keen to get its managers from America and Germany, where international moves are less common, to match the mobility shown by its British and Indian staff. International moves help to create trust and acceptance between companies in the group and those who gain a taste for international assignments can continue to take on new challenges abroad, if they so wish and it is right for the company. Top managers at Burmah Castrol are encouraged to set an example in the area of training and development by committing five days a year to personal development courses, as the softer, touchy-feely skills involved in teamwork and management are given as much weight as technological expertise.

The company places a great deal of emphasis on open communications. There are regular briefings at head office and for the chief executives of every Burmah Castrol company on the company's objectives and performance. Employees have a chance to feed their views upwards in their annual performance reviews and surveys are taken of employee opinion. Burmah Castrol firmly believes in separating management reviews from pay assessment to give employees and their managers a chance to talk openly about performance and areas for improvement.

Burmah Castrol aims to pay salaries that lie between the median and the upper quartile of a comparison group of companies. There are opportunities for managers to gain up to 50 per cent more than their base salary in incentive pay. In line with the separation of management reviews and salary discussions, incentive pay is linked to demonstrated financial performance rather than qualitative measures. There is an executive share option scheme for the top 350 managers in the company and a share-saving scheme for employees with a high take-up and a high rate of retention of shares.

The company's aim is to pay premium rates for premium performance. 'We don't cheesepare,' says Fry. 'Some companies make a religion of cost reduction and no frills. We're not like that. Our whole approach is designed to be of a premium nature.'

Contact address

Mr Jim Prophet,
Human Resources Director,
Burmah Castrol plc,
Burmah Castrol House,
Pipers Way,
Swindon SN3 1RE.
Telephone: 01793 511521.
Fax: 01793 488036.

Cadbury Schweppes

Over 200 years ago Jacob Schweppe began processing mineral water in Geneva. A little later John Cadbury began selling tea and coffee in Birmingham. The two operations finally merged in 1969 and Cadbury Schweppes began a programme of worldwide expansion. The acquisition of the US soft drinks company Dr Pepper/Seven-up in 1995 heralded the most substantial move for the group since its merger in the 1960s.

Cadbury Schweppes at a glance

Employees: 41,789 worldwide, 13,886 UK
Annual staff attrition rate: n/a
Key locations: Cadbury Ltd, Birmingham; Sodastream Ltd, Peterborough; Reading Scientific Services Ltd, Reading; Trebor Bassett Ltd, Maple Cross, Herts
Av. annual graduate recruitment: n/a
Annual intake: n/a

An inside view

The confectionery side of Cadbury Schweppes is a major global force in both chocolate and sugar confectionery, which produces a mix of international, regional and local brands. It has manufacturing plants in 24 countries and sales in a further 156. The beverages arm of the company has bottling and partnership operations in 14 countries and licenses its brands in a further 96 countries worldwide, of which Schweppes, Dr Pepper, Crush and Canada Dry are key products. In 1996 it reported sales of £5.1 billion and pre-tax profits of £592 million.

Just under 14,000 people are employed in the UK within sales, manufacturing, marketing and head office functions.

UK operations are divided into beverages and confectionery. On the confectionery side, Cadbury Ltd increased its market share in 1996 while Trebor Bassett Ltd held its overall position. The overall confectionery market fell in 1995, affected by the abnormally hot summer of that year.

The values system of Cadbury Schweppes was originally set out by Sir Adrian Cadbury, chairman from 1974–89. 'Cadbury Schweppes earns its living in a competitive world. It needs to do so successfully to meet its obligations to all those with a stake in the enterprise and to make the company one to which people are proud to belong,' he said. The main points made by Sir Adrian and relevant to current strategy include: the respect and appreciation of the loyalty of the consumer; the right of the consumer to expect quality of service and product; the continuing provision of a work environment which encourages employees to realise the potential of their own capabilities, the encouragement of innovation and the avoidance of complicated business structures; and the recognition that the way the company behaves within the community and in relation to the environment must be compatible with the values implicit in company products and brands. 'Our behaviour inside and outside the business will be characterised by integrity, open-mindedness, courtesy and a concern for the well-being of others,' said Sir Adrian.

The belief that achieving commercial objectives and meeting the needs of customers in a profitable and competitive manner is dependent on the contribution of all employees, is central to company philosophy. Employees are encouraged to develop their contribution to the business wherever they happen to work. Continuing programmes on quality and customer service are run in the UK and provide an opportunity for all employees to be involved in making improvements within their own operations. Employees are also encouraged to participate financially through a variety of share schemes which provide the employee with a direct stake in the growth and prosperity of the business.

The group saw a period of intense development activity in 1995 as manufacturing bases were extended into countries which had been previously closed to the business. Chairman Dominic Cadbury believes that the company's ability to sustain a competitive advantage over the long-term is dependent on the continuous development of the employees. 'The company is committed to providing an environment which values continuous learning and which provides learning and development opportunities within individual business units and across the entire group. Development is a shared

responsibility and employees for their part must possess the drive and initiative to take advantage of the available learning and development opportunities,' he says.

How does Cadbury Schweppes rate ?

Pay:	very good
Benefits:	very good
Communications:	excellent
Training:	very good
Career development:	excellent
Morale:	very good

People and personnel policies

Business units within the group provide the relevant systems and programmes to meet the differing development needs of employees which vary significantly from business to business. For instance National Vocational Qualifications have been adopted in the UK by Cadbury Ltd and Trebor Bassett in order to suit their individual business needs.

The company also operates several development initiatives for its most senior managers. The top 200 managers have undertaken a tailored executive development programme in the past three years which has enhanced strategic business skills, built international networks and exchanged best practice across the entire group. A new initiative *Leadership, Performance, Change* has just been launched to strengthen the ability of the company to cope with the constantly changing aspects of the marketplace. International assignments are also encouraged through an Accelerated Development Programme.

A special remuneration committee reviews and approves annual salaries, incentive arrangements, option grants, service agreements and other employment conditions for executive directors. In setting basic salaries for directors, the committee takes into account the pay practices of other companies and the performance of each individual director. Salaries are competitive with those of other similar companies which trade on a worldwide basis.

Cadbury Schweppes contributes actively to the communities in which it operates. In the UK corporate giving is channelled through the Cadbury Schweppes Foundation. Recent donations have included £60,000 to Business in the Community to fund a new initiative designed to demonstrate to companies the benefits of Cause Related Marketing, and £20,000 to Young Enterprise to set up a scheme enabling students to experience the running of their own businesses. Apart from financial support, community involvement also includes commercial sponsorship, the provision of facilities at a local level and the encouragement of direct involvement by Cadbury Schweppes' employees.

The company also plays an active role through the CBI and the Education Business Partnerships in promoting the importance of learning leading to employment and practical competences.

In 1995 Cadbury Schweppes was voted 'Britain's Most Admired Company' through a widely supported poll of peer companies. The criteria for the award included quality of management, quality of products/services, capacity to innovate, quality of marketing, community and environmental responsibility and financial soundness. In looking ahead, chairman Dominic Cadbury says '1995 was regarded as a landmark year for Cadbury Schweppes. It marks the year in which we became a major player in the mainstream beverages market and while we do not underestimate the strength of the competition, we now have the experience and equipment to compete globally.

Contact address

Human Resources Department,
Cadbury Schweppes,
25 Berkeley Square,
London W1X 6HT.
Telephone: 0171 409 1313.
Fax: 0171 830 5200.

Cap Gemini

I n almost 30 years, the Cap Gemini Group has grown to become the largest European provider of information technology and consulting services, and the third largest worldwide. The group is focused around a commitment to the highest levels of customer service – its strategy is to deliver on time and above customer expectations – and operates on a global basis through eight business sectors. Together with its consultancy and business transformation arm, Gemini Consulting, Cap Gemini has a consistent demand for talented and energetic people.

Cap Gemini at a glance

Employees: 27,000 worldwide, 4,700 UK
Annual staff attrition rate: 10 per cent
Key locations: London (HQ),
    and nine other offices in major cities
    around the UK
Av. annual graduate recruitment: 150+
Annual intake: 500+

An inside view

Initially formed just under 30 years ago, the Cap Gemini Group includes two separate, although increasingly convergent, businesses: Cap Gemini, which acts in a range of capacities – consultant, contractor, systems integrator or project manager – on complex IT assignments (generally for major corporations and government agencies), and Gemini Consulting, a consultancy specialising in business re-engineering. The group is increasingly focusing on developing its international presence, and early in 1996, dropped a number of long-standing local trading names (including Hoskyns) in order to adopt Cap Gemini as a single brand name globally.

Recognising that clients are becoming steadily more demanding in terms of their service requirements, Cap Gemini has chosen to focus on four global sectors: pharmaceuticals, insurance, telecommunications, and travel and transport, as well as other traditional local markets. Through a policy of convergence, it is also intended that Cap Gemini works more closely with Gemini Consulting. This creates the opportunity for the group to assist clients by transforming both businesses and their information systems concurrently.

It is significant that much of Cap Gemini's growth over recent years has come from winning outsourcing contracts. This is one of the main reasons why there is no single Cap Gemini culture: instead, it is more accurate to characterise the group as being an assimilation of different cultures. According to Robert Ingram, Cap Gemini's human resources director 'What is distinctive about our culture is our mix of people'. The group believes that this diversity is one of its principal strengths.

Unlike some of its competitors, Cap Gemini makes no attempt to clone its consultants and it has no desire to impose standard rules and operating procedures on businesses and people who join the group. Its philosophy is to decentralise decision-making as much as possible. (Another distinctive feature about Cap Gemini is that – unusually for the IT industry – it does not regard an employee over 30 as being over the hill.)

Within this context of different cultures, however, Cap Gemini has developed a set of core values which employees should espouse. These are defined as follows: courage, humour, energy, excellence, teamwork, openness and respect. Underpinning these values is a commitment to quality. In return, Cap Gemini offers a relaxed and informal working environment, working with blue-chip clients on the leading edge of technology.

How does Cap Gemini rate?

Pay:	good
Benefits:	good
Communications:	very good
Training:	excellent
Career development:	very good
Morale:	good

People and personnel policies

In order to retain its position in the marketplace, Cap Gemini knows it must maximise the development of its human resources. Throughout the group, special care is taken to ensure that employees have the skills, perform the jobs and receive the training best suited to the needs of the market. In an industry which is characterised by high staff turnover, Cap Gemini's capacity to retain a high percentage of the employees who come to the company under outsourcing arrangements or via an acquisition, is seen as proof of its success in providing an attractive working environment.

The group has a long-standing commitment to training and development needs. One of the company's primary training tools is its university, 50 kilometres outside Paris. This is regarded as the nerve centre of many of the technical and commercial initiatives undertaken by the company, but also plays an important part in fostering communication between people in different parts of the group. Cap Gemini is working hard at developing a multiplicity of skills in its workforce. Not only is a breadth of knowledge essential given the constant pace of change in the IT industry – those who cannot adapt are unlikely to survive – but it also makes life more interesting for employees by allowing them to work on different types of projects.

Cap Gemini also has a commitment to employees owning their own careers. It runs career workshops and has just published a career framework outlining the skills needed for specific jobs. In addition, all employees have a staff manager who acts as a counsellor or adviser, helping them to examine their career options. In order to help identify its business leaders of tomorrow, the company is also hoping to introduce a high-flier programme in the near future. All jobs and training opportunities are notified on Cap Gemini's Intranet facility, which went live in the middle of 1996.

It should be recognised that a willingness to be somewhat flexible remains a distinct advantage in terms of career development. While the company tries to recognise that its staff have a life outside the office, the constant turnover of contracts inevitably means that individuals can be subject to movement at very short notice. The importance of flexibility is one reason why females continue to be under-represented at senior levels in the company. Cap Gemini is attempting to address this issue by encouraging working practices that maximise flexibility.

The IT industry is acknowledged as one where employees can move between jobs extremely frequently. As a result, Cap Gemini knows it must be prepared to pay competitively to recruit and retain the right people. The company also operates a profit-related pay scheme for all staff, and has other incentive schemes at higher management levels. Other attractive benefits are available: the company has recently introduced interest-free loans for employees to purchase a PC at discount prices.

Nevertheless, Cap Gemini believes that intangible factors – such as the relaxed and informal working environment – are as significant as financial inducements in persuading employees to remain with the organisation. Given the difficulties that some of the company's competitors have had with integrating new people, its seems that its strategy has been successful.

Contact address

Mr Robert Ingham,
Human Resources Director
Cap Gemini UK PLC,
Cap Gemini House,
130 Shaftesbury Avenue,
London W1V 8HH.
Telephone: 0171 434 2171.
Fax: 0171 437 6223.

CCSB

C CSB is Coca-Cola & Schweppes Beverages Limited – the largest soft drinks maker in the UK. Founded in 1987 by Cadbury Schweppes and Coca-Cola, it dominates cola sales with between 50 and 60 per cent of all British colas bought. Its total share of all soft drinks in this market is probably around 25 per cent. Both figures demonstrate why it is No 1 and Pulling Ahead. In less than ten years it has established a formidable operation which refuses to be tied to a limiting description of its scope as a business and is distinctly different from the cultures of its founding parents.

CCSB at a glance

Employees: 3,000
Staff attrition: 4 per cent
Key locations: Uxbridge, Milton Keynes, Huddersfield
Annual graduate recruitment: n/a
Annual intake: 200

An inside view

Language is important at CCSB. In a competitive world where change is a daily and multiple reality, the words which define the company and its approach are deliberately chosen to minimise the risk of perceptual restriction and the introduction of psychological boundaries. This is meant to be a free-flowing business. There are fixed points inside the company but they serve to emphasise the freedom with which individuals and teams can operate. CCSB does not, for example, have a culture. Instead, the atmosphere within the organisation is described as a climate which suggests impermanence, movement and changing values. This is not the recognition and acceptance of change as can be seen in other corporate cultures but a business which is an expression of change itself.

CCSB was formed in the late 1980s from its parents Coca-Cola and Cadbury Schweppes. The company produces such soft drinks favourites as Coke and all its varieties, Fanta, Lilt, Schweppes Tonic, Appletise, Sunkist, Kia-Ora, Perrier and Gini. It is the market leader in the vast majority of its sectors in the UK and it is home to the UK's largest bottling and canning operations. The company employs more than 3,000 people in Britain and sells more than 2 billion litres of its products each year. The company emphasises its logo which is 'No 1 and pulling ahead'. This is a central and guiding philosophy for CCSB. It runs through its sales, production and training initiatives and it characterises an approach to its business which is that of the winner.

In February1997, the European Commission gave its go-ahead to the founding owners of the business to sell their shares entirely to the largest Coca-Cola canner and bottler worldwide. To a certain extent this will favour the influence of the Coke approach and methodology, although since the outset CCSB has been a lusty and vocal infant and it has carved its own, original mark.

How does CCSB rate?

Pay:	excellent
Benefits:	superb
Communications:	good
Training:	excellent
Career development:	superb
Morale:	very good

People and personnel policies

Personnel director Keith Dennis comments that the creation of a completely new business was an opportunity to fashion something fresh. The degree of personal responsibility and independence which is the hallmark of CCSB's atmosphere is not reflected in the more collective approach of its founders.

CCSB genuinely believes in certain core values which define the nature of the company. First there are few barriers within the business. The organisation is completely open and direct; honesty is essential. Second is that change is current. It is not enough to appreciate that change is an ongoing factor in business but rather the company professes

to live change. As an entirely pragmatic company, this means total flexibility and a ready acceptance of new ideas as they emerge.

Third, responsibility is given to the individual to shape and plan their career. Many companies profess to give greater responsibility to the individual for career management but at CCSB if the employee does not take responsibility for their career, they probably will not have one. As counterpoint to this rather direct appreciation, skill, training for the job in hand is thorough and ongoing. There is complete fluidity between roles, so an employee who is not performing well in sales but who has a stated preference and the appropriate skills for a role, say, in marketing will usually be given the chance to prove themself.

'We work so hard at the recruitment and assessment processes that we tend to assume that if someone is not performing in one assignment then the company – not the individual – is to blame. We try to find the employee in question a more appropriate role but the process is not endless.' Dennis says. There is great stress in CCSB on providing the most effective support for people to succeed. Its training approach is typical, offering a wide variety of courses, but finely targeted to the best benefit of the company and the staff member.

One highly original piece of thinking is evident in an innovative recruitment initiative. CCSB is sponsoring individuals through a four-year course at the University of London for a degree in management. This is available to bright, energetic youngsters with good grades at A level. What makes it different is that it combines a degree course with paid employment. Candidates join CCSB as employees and London University as students simultaneously. They complete a 35-hour week at CCSB as well as 20 hours' study at the university. And students are able to use their experience at CCSB as part of project work on the course.

CCSB is also at the leading edge in the reward package. Almost everyone has one variable element to their pay, although clearly senior management and sales people will have a larger proportion which is not fixed. Where CCSB is out in front is cafeteria benefits. It is one of very few companies which offers full cafeteria facilities. This idea sets out certain benefits which are standard such as pension, life insurance, sick pay and holidays but then puts a value, according to grade and performance, on the remainder of an individual's entitlement. The employee can then choose from several options to draw up their own benefits package. Dennis says that the take-up of cafeteria has been greatest in the bottling and canning plants but slowly sales and marketing personnel are warming to the concept.

To make the package more understandable the business has produced a CD-ROM which is available to all employees; it explains the system and allows them to select between various options for themselves. Among the options available is to take lower basic pay and redistribute the difference into benefits. In that way an employee can often get much better value for money. As it is CCSB is extremely generous with its catalogue of benefits, and the implementation of a full cafeteria approach is a typical evocation of wanting to make the best use of resources.

Contact address

Keith Dennis,
Personnel Director,
CCSB,
Charter Place,
Uxbridge,
Middlesex UB8 1EZ.
Telephone: 01785 400400.
Fax: 01785 400300.

CMG

CMG plc is one of Europe's leading information technology services groups, founded in 1964 but now operating in more than 30 countries from bases in the UK, the Netherlands and Germany. It supplies systems development, management consultancy and advanced technology services to the finance, transport, trade and industry, energy, telecommunications and public sectors. It specialises particularly in providing information solutions to help customers achieve their business objectives. The company has developed many long-term relationships with commercial and government organisations; its clients range from London Underground to BUPA and bankers Dresdner Kleinwort Benson. It is renowned for a unique human resource culture developed around a strong employee share ownership policy.

CMG at a glance

Employees: 3,500
Attrition rate: -10 per cent
Key locations: London
Annual graduate recruitment: 100
Annual intake: 1,000 in the group

An inside view

CMG has never made a loss since it was established, largely because it recognised early on that the company and its clients were operating in a world where the only constant was change, and that the rate of change – particularly in this decade – would only increase, providing enormous challenge for commercial and government organisations alike.

All have faced competitive pressure and the need to reduce costs and grow at the same time. Companies have realised that as well as meeting the needs of global customers, they must meet economies of scale that global markets provide, and the flexibility and potential cost savings afforded by using suppliers and resources all over the world. They have delayered their management structures and increased local autonomy so that customer service is optimised at local level while global contracts can still be secured.

In recognising this sea change of almost constant upheaval, CMG has concentrated its strategy on long-term relations with large companies which must satisfy three basic criteria: fast growth, sharply changing business environment, and sufficient size. It is particularly known for work with the banking sector and its development of risk management systems and software packages for central bank reporting.

From the start, CMG's founders intended to build their company by staying close to their customers, doing exactly what their customers wanted of them and growing as their customers grew. 'We knew that by helping to make customers more successful, the company would become more successful,' says Cor Stutterheim, chairman of CMG. 'Over a period of time, we would build a relationship that would develop into a partnership and mutual trust difficult to break.'

This apparently simple business philosophy has been the cornerstone of over 32 years of profitable growth. The group's growth has been largely organic although a number of strategic acquisitions have been made mainly to gain access to individual software packages or to enhance CMG's position in certain geographical markets.

Its work with leading banks throughout Europe has become a company trademark. It works for the leading banks in each of the Netherlands, the UK and Germany, for eight of the top ten international oil companies, 27 European telecom operators, ten of Europe's leading transport companies, and 18 government departments in the Netherlands and the UK. Recent projects range from developing an early warning system to prevent flooding in the Rotterdam port area to developing a mobile data gathering system for British Gas. It has developed world class products in areas such as mobile telephony, central bank reporting and direct insurance.

The company's year end results for 1996 reflect outstanding performance, with pre-tax profits up 37% to £20.1 million, and the 25% growth in group turnover to £245.2 million being virtually all organic. Improvement in CMG's performance in the UK stands out, with profits up 69%. The company now employs 3,500, which is an increase of 26% on the same period last year.

How does CMG rate ?

Pay:	very good
Benefits:	very good
Communications:	good
Training:	very good
Career development:	excellent
Morale:	very good

People and personnel policies

The most important facet of CMG, which was established from its founding and has continued to this day, is the involvement and commitment of its employees – this is remarked upon by outside business observers as much as those who work for the company. The founders felt strongly that all employees should share in the success of the company, be involved in decisions about the company, and also be shareholders. Until its public flotation in December 1995, CMG was primarily owned by its directors and employees. Today, more than 2,600 of its 3,500 employees have an equity interest in CMG, either through direct shareholdings or share options. Furthermore, all CMG employees reaching the first level of management are required to hold CMG shares equal to the value of one half of their annual salary. Higher levels of management are required to hold a year's salary in shares.

The company believes that such a considerable investment in its future makes its workforce, particularly management, more focused on its success and profitability. This cornerstone of employee share ownership has been a key factor in developing a culture of shared success in the group, and has helped foster a high level of employee commitment and loyalty which have contributed to its long record of profitable growth. Since the early 1980s, the group has produced compound annual growth in sales of 18.5 per cent and 25 per cent compound annual growth in pre-tax profits.

Barbara Ward, group director for human resources, says that CMG is run on a family basis, but it's a family that no one joins by accident. 'It's very difficult to get in. The company wants to be convinced that anyone who wants to work at CMG is a CMG person. Unlike many other companies, we want people to come here for the duration.' But once inside, an employee discovers a work place quite different, if not unique. There are, for example, no offices – and there are also no pay-slip envelopes. CMG operates in 'open plan' that embraces all aspects of the work environment. The monthly salary slip is left on everyone's desk in a totally open plan physical environment. 'Everyone knows what everyone else earns. Traditionally, you know another person's grade by the size of their desk or their chair. Everyone has the same size desk and the same type of chair,' she says. 'And there is no kowtowing to rank, either. This is a can-do company in which everyone is encouraged to have a go. And if you don't do well in your job, you are not fired but demoted. We have an overt concern for our people. The person who was promoted and didn't do well in the new position obviously did well in the previous position, otherwise they wouldn't have been promoted. So, this is our fault as much as anyone's.'

At CMG, anyone can hear their manager's telephone calls. That is just one way that the truth gets out. 'Openness is self-correcting,' says Cor Stutterheim. 'When people ask questions directly of their managers in this kind of environment, they have to tell the truth; and in an open environment, they all find out whether it is good or bad news. It is definitely self-correcting in the way it works.'

There are five sectors of the CMG Group, in three countries, and the company's board of directors visits each sector twice a year. This is extremely time consuming, but essential to the culture of openness. The directors always have lunch with the people who have just joined the company. 'We try and spend as much time on staff matters as on business matters,' says Barbara Ward. 'This all comes from the belief that you treat people as you would wish to be treated. Our balance sheet is filled with people, not buildings, and they earn the company's living.'

CMG has only one work contract, from directors down to graduates; and there is no one employed part-time. 'We want people who live to work, not people who work to live,' says Stutterheim, 'and full-time people deliver better quality work.'

The benefits package is among the top in the industry, and there is no variable or performance-related pay. 'We don't want our people to worry about their annual income; we want them to know what they will be getting – we only want them to worry about doing the job properly.'

Contact address

B L Ward, Group Director, CMG, Telford House, Tothill Street, London SW1H 9NB. Telephone: 0171 233 0288. Fax: 0171 799 3435.

Coats Viyella

Coats Viyella is the UK's largest textiles and clothing group. Its strategy is based on building long-term relationships with both customers and suppliers, as well as investing heavily in new technology. Although the company has not been immune from the severe competitive pressures afflicting the textile sector in recent years, it has still managed to develop a strong international presence and has retained a dominant position in many of its markets. Indeed, the changing nature of the businesses in which Coats Viyella operates can provide a range of challenging and rewarding career opportunities.

Coats Viyella at a glance

Employees: 65,000 worldwide, 24,000 UK
Annual staff attrition rate: n/a*
Key locations: London (HQ),
  various sites around the UK
Av. annual graduate recruitment: 30–40
Annual intake: n/a*
  *Current figures for staff attrition and
  total annual recruitment are distorted
  by the company's restructuring
  programme

An inside view

Coats Viyella is the largest textiles and clothing group in the UK, with annual sales of more than £2 billion. In common with the majority of the textile industry, it has encountered very difficult market conditions over the last two years, principally as a result of low-cost competition from the Far East and eastern Europe. This has necessitated a considerable amount of business restructuring – its latest programme, announced in April 1996, involved the loss of 2,700 jobs in the UK and India – and the disposal of a number of non-core activities. It is now structured into five divisions: thread (which is easily the largest), clothing, home furnishings, precision engineering, and fashion retail.

In an industry where the trend is towards companies reducing the number of their business partners, Coats Viyella is determined to retain its market position by developing strong, long-term relationships with both customers and suppliers. Furthermore, the company's facility to make a wide range of products makes them particularly attractive as a one stop shop partner for high street retailers. For example, it maintains a dedicated 94-strong design team for Marks & Spencer, responsible for the manufacture of 27 different garment categories. Coats Viyella is also determined to continue to build its overseas presence, with an increasing amount of production now being located overseas.

The company's business philosophy is to delegate as much authority as possible, with the central management team based in London concerning itself primarily with questions of strategy. Given the highly international nature of the company's operations, there is a great deal of cultural diversity within the group and the retention of this is actively encouraged. However, although all Coats' divisions operate with a high degree of autonomy, they also take advantage of the opportunities to share expertise, improve manufacturing processes and improve customer service that come with being part of a large, international grouping.

Although the style of management and the nature of operations vary considerably throughout the world, Coats Viyella is keen that all its employees unite behind a common set of values. Central among these are commitments to compete on quality, service and value, and to encourage a policy of openness. Also critical, especially given current market conditions, is a pledge to take advantage of change.

How does Coats Viyella rate?

Pay:	good
Benefits:	good
Communications:	good
Training:	very good
Career development:	very good
Morale:	average

People and personnel policies

Another of the company's core values is a commitment to its employees. Coats Viyella believes that people should know what is expected of them and should be given help to meet those expectations. Accordingly, it invests heavily in the development of its workforce. Another of the company's key personnel policies is the promotion of a meritocratic culture within the organisation. All appointments in Coats Viyella are made solely on the basis of an individual's ability to meet job requirements. This is manifested in the increasing diversity at senior levels in the company.

Textiles, historically, has been an industry which, although it has attracted significant numbers of female workers, has generally employed them in low-level, production functions. Coats Viyella has gone some way to rectifying this and women are now increasingly represented at middle and senior mangement positions within the group; indeed, one of the five divisional heads is a female.

In addition, women are well represented in the graduate intake. Furthermore, the growth of Coats' overseas activities has led to increasing numbers of non-UK staff being promoted within the organisation. For example, some outstanding managers are now being produced by the company's Indian operation.

Responsibility for training and development is largely held by the operating divisions. However, there is a group management training scheme, which has been developed in association with the London Business School, whose purpose is to develop high-fliers for senior management positions. Of the top 500 executives within Coats Viyella, it is estimated that more than 75 per cent will have been through this training programme. The graduate programme developed in the UK has now been extended to a number of other countries overseas.

At other levels, all staff undergo an annual appraisal. Fourteen UK companies within the group have now attained the Investors in People Award and others are preparing for assessment. In order to assess the effectiveness of its human resources management policies and practices, the group has also developed an employment practices audit, which allows individual operating companies to monitor their progress.

Another historical characteristic of the textiles industry is that it has been very poorly paid. Recognising that it must pay attractively to attract management talent, Coats Viyella has been in the vanguard of making salaries in the industry much more competitive. Remuneration typically falls into three categories: salaries, an annual bonus scheme (measured against defined criteria); and a share option scheme. There is also a pension scheme for UK staff, although overseas this is generally a matter for local management.

An increasingly important source of recruitment is from the pool of older, more experienced employees, who are recruited into the company at more senior levels. Consistent with the company's growing international presence, overseas experience is increasingly regarded as a pre-requisite for promotion within the organisation. The company believes that it is vital that senior managers understand the different cultures within the group in order for them to be able to manage successfully.

Communication is focused on local needs and the methods which are employed vary throughout the group. However, all managers are assessed on their ability to communicate with subordinates. In order to improve its group-wide communication, the company is making increasing use of electronic mail. In Europe, one of the most important forms of communication is the works council. These take the form of regular meetings where employee representatives and senior divisional management meet to discuss key issues and future developments for the business.

Contact address

Mr Bill Shardlow,
Group Personnel Director,
Coats Viyella plc,
28 Savile Row,
London W1X 2DD.
Telephone: 0171 292 9200.
Fax: 0171 437 6839.

Coopers & Lybrand

oopers & Lybrand is one of the world's leading professional services
organisations. Structured in five businesses - business assurance,
business recovery and insolvency, corporate finance, management
consulting and tax and human resource advice - the UK firm currently has
more than 9,500 employees and has annual UK revenues of £700 million.
The Coopers & Lybrand organisation worldwide has some 70,000 people
and global fee income of around US$7 billion. The demanding and
constantly changing business environment in which the firm and its
clients operate means that Coopers & Lybrand's demand for flexible and
talented people is considerable.

Coopers & Lybrand at a glance

Employees: 9,500 UK
Annual staff attrition rate: 17 per cent
Key locations: HQ in London,
   35 UK offices in total
Av. annual graduate recruitment: 700
Av. non-graduate recruitment: 400

An inside view

Coopers & Lybrand is one of the largest
professional services firms in the UK and
the Coopers & Lybrand organisation
services clients in 140 countries. In an
increasingly competitive and global
marketplace, the firm recognises that it
can maintain its pre-eminent position
only by constantly refining and updating
the services which it offers its clients.

A key part of its business strategy
involves the development of specialist
skills. Companies are now much more
discriminating about the quality of the
service they require from their business
advisers. To address this, Coopers &
Lybrand has recently restructured itself
into five specialist lines of business. These
are: business assurance which includes
audit, forensic accounting and risk
management; business recovery and
insolvency, focusing on advice and
assistance to troubled businesses;
corporate finance, which provides advice
on acquisitions and disposals;
management consulting, which works with
clients to improve business performance;
and taxation and human resource
advisory, an integrated and
comprehensive range of expert tax, legal
and human resource consultancy services.

The culture of flexibility and
responsiveness to client requirements is
an essential element of the Coopers &
Lybrand ethos and is instilled in each
member of the workforce from day one.
Another important quality is integrity. In
addition to its statutory and legal

obligations, Coopers & Lybrand realises that its reputation for providing expert and independent advice is central to its commercial success. Employees must be astute enough to detect wrongdoing and be prepared to report it, even if the situation is uncomfortable.

Two other drivers in the firm's success are performance and competitiveness. To develop these qualities among its people, Coopers & Lybrand has tried to create an innovative environment, in which people are encouraged to take responsibility early and are rewarded for stretching themselves. This is manifested in the firm's Fit for Business programme which is designed to broaden individuals' skills at an early stage, whether they wish to continue their career at Coopers & Lybrand or leave after obtaining their professional qualification. As part of this strategy, all graduate joiners complete an immediate development programme within their first 14 months and are then encouraged to put their learning into effect as soon as possible as team leaders on client assignments.

How does Coopers & Lybrand rate ?

Pay:	very good
Benefits:	good
Communications:	very good
Training:	excellent
Career development:	excellent
Morale:	good

People and personnel policies

The competitive nature of the professional services market demands that Coopers & Lybrand employs high quality people and that their skills are continually improved and updated. In recruiting staff, great emphasis is placed on non-academic selection criteria, such as communication and team skills. The firm's objective is to ensure that it is regarded by potential recruits as the employer of choice. It is also worth noting that recruitment is not simply taken from the graduate market. As part of its policy of engendering specialist skills, Coopers & Lybrand is also interested in attracting experienced managers with particular industry expertise.

Coopers & Lybrand's performance review process is designed to link people's objectives and contribution clearly to its strategy. While the firm's overall benchmark is to set remuneration based on the top quartile of industry earnings, within this context there is considerable flexibility to reward people based on performance. A relatively flat management structure also means that work is allocated to people according to their skills rather than their grade. This approach also tends to mean that promotion is regarded as an achievement rather than an automatic progression.

To ensure that its people offer the best service in the industry, Coopers & Lybrand invests heavily in training and development. The objective is to integrate training and career development into a package which gives its employees a competitive edge over its rivals', and this approach is continued all the way up the firm - up to and including partnership level. Training is provided not only on professional and technical issues, but also on personal development skills. To monitor performance, all employees undergo an annual appraisal at which their progress is reviewed and objectives for the following year are agreed. The firm has also started a mentoring programme to help staff plan their long-term career development over three to five years, looking at opportunties both inside and outside the firm.

Movement within the organisation and on secondment to clients or overseas is a key component in the firm's overall business strategy. This serves two purposes. First, there is a need in Coopers & Lybrand to move specialist resources quickly to respond to client demands. Secondly, as far as employees are concerned, it helps to provide new challenges to meet their career aspirations. The prospects in terms of job movement (in both activity and geographically) for those staff who remain with the firm are considerable. International secondments are a key part of the strategy for providing clients with global support.

Given that the majority of Coopers & Lybrand's employees spend most of their time at clients' premises, and hence are only occasionally in the office, the firm has devoted considerable resources to keeping them informed about the firm's strategy and progress. As well as publishing a regular series of internal newsletters, it also encourages its managers to disseminate information by holding regular briefings for employees. Furthermore, in order to promote feedback from staff, it undertakes an annual business attitude survey which is designed to act as a firm-wide barometer of employee expectations and attitudes.

With the accountancy and professional services market becoming increasingly attractive to women, Coopers & Lybrand actively encourages the development of female employees inside the firm. Currently around half of its annual intake is women, and the proportion of women who are partners is steadily rising. In order to assist the re-entry of women into the firm after childbirth, Coopers & Lybrand provides generous maternity arrangements. There is also a career break scheme to enable staff to take periods of time out for family care or personal development reasons.

The firm has realised that the world of professional services is changing rapidly. The days of 'ticking and bashing' are long gone. Today, as non-audit work becomes increasingly important, the emphasis has shifted to identifying and providing value-added services to clients. Employees must be flexible and responsive in the face of fast-changing business environments. They must be prepared to work closely with clients to discover the best solutions to their problems. However, for those individuals who have the requisite skills and adaptability, the professional training and business background which Coopers & Lybrand can provide is without equal.

Contact address

Mr Tony Allen, Head of Human Resources,
Coopers & Lybrand,
1 Embankment Place,
London WC2N 6NN.
Telephone: 0171 583 5000.
Fax: 0171 822 4652.

The Corporate Services Group plc

The Corporate Services Group is the largest employer of contract labour in the UK. It was started in 1987 and it has thousands of people on assignment with a range of businesses at any one time. Most of its clients are blue chip organisations, companies or public sector bodies. The company's estimated sales in 1997 will be £300 million, which is a dramatic rise from £42 million in 1993. The business has grown through capable acquisition and remarkable organic performance.

The Corporate Services Group at a glance

Employees: 2,600 (40–50,000 on assignment)
Staff attrition rate: n/a
Key locations: London (HQ), Glaston (Leicestershire) and many other locations round the UK
Graduate intake: 50
Total intake: Not available

An inside view

The Corporate Services Group is unlike any other employer in the UK. It employs people on behalf of other companies. The business has recognised a growing trend in industry. This method of staffing companies accounts for 20 per cent of all employees in France and as many as 18 per cent in Germany and 15 per cent in the US. As might be expected, the Corporate Services Group is the strongest advocate in the UK for the use of contract labour, and believes it can be applied to almost every industrial situation.

Chairman and chief executive Jeffrey Fowler says the demand for contract labour will grow rapidly in the years up to the millennium. There are certain circumstances, he says, where contract labour does not work, but in those circumstances where it applies it works exceedingly well.

The group employs 2,600 people in the UK but it has between 40,000 and 50,000 suppliers, that is to say individual employees who are on contract working with client companies at any one time. The group takes care of the pay, benefits and pension arrangements of those individuals who are contracted to work for the group but are employed elsewhere. It has grown to four wholly owned autonomous divisions: Industrial Contract Services, which is the contract labour division providing technical and industrial contractors; Blue Arrow, supplying office and catering contract staff, and Medacs which provides contractors to the healthcare market including NHS Trusts and local authorities. A fourth division comprising the group's external training arm is the largest provider of National Vocational Qualifications in the UK. Group services such as finance, property, human resources and internal training are provided centrally by the group which is now based in Glaston in Leicestershire. The rapid growth in the Corporate Services Group has been due to its articulate and sustained advocacy of the concept of contract labour and its capacity to convince major employers that this is a cost-effective and reliable way for them to employ staff. During the last five years in particular, many well-known blue chip companies have taken Corporate Services Group people to fulfil major functions. An example is BT. The telecoms giant employs only half of its own engineering staff. The rest come from contracts supplied by the Corporate Services Group. A famous example of a smaller type of company which is often cited by Fowler is the food sector companies which will have seasonal peaks. The Corporate Services Groups guarantees to meet any seasonal variation in demand.

'We can supply as many or as few people as an employer requires. Some clients source all their work from us, other have a handful.' Fowler says that not only blue chip companies but also government agencies and scientific establishments with limited budgets use the industry regularly. 'A company may need a group of research scientists for a fixed term, a three-year research contract for example, and we will find the most appropriate people with precisely the right scientific background.'

The company operates across the industrial landscape. It sources doctors worldwide and places them in hospitals. In the UK through its network of 210 locations, CSG is active in the catering, healthcare, telecommunications, manufacturing, railways, aeronautics, distribution and retail sectors. Some 60 per cent of its revenue is derived from the industrial sector, a further 20 per cent from technical, 15 per cent from healthcare and 5 per cent from commercial. The acquision of the Blue Arrow businesses in 1996 has shifted these figures and emphasises catering as the key element.

The divisional structure of CSG gives greater autonomy to the divisional chairman and managing directors. It holds monthly board meetings with each chairman who attends in addition to the holding company directors which provide a forum for clear lines of communication and direction. Each division has a series of monthly management meetings for directors and senior management in which information is commuted down to staff and up to directors. The group's training and quality assurance director is responsible for organising regular and effective internal communications throughout the group and uses such media as newsletters, circulars and information sheets.

How does Corporate Services Group rate?

Pay:	very good
Benefits:	excellent
Communications:	good
Training:	superb
Career development:	excellent
Morale:	excellent

People and personnel policies

The low uptake on contract labour in the

UK means that the Corporate Services Groups faces a potentially exciting future. It has added coherently to its group of companies and has built an organisation which is resilient and represents increasing depth in the marketplace. For individuals who are recruited by the Corporate Services Group, and who are effectively on assignment for the organisation, this means that the wealth of opportunities available to them will expand. Typically, an individual may approach the Corporate Services Group through one of its agencies such as Blue Arrow in order to find a particular assignment. As they are taken on by the group and not by the client company, their pay and benefits are assured and are also continuous through the length of time that they stay with the CSG. It also means that if a particular assignment doesn't work out from the perspective of the client or the employee, then another assignment can be found somewhere else.

In terms of career development CSG is an excellent option. Its approach means that for all the clients who work for the Corporate Services Group there are a range of opportunities which allow an individual scientist or skilled worker to elect a particular career path. The coherence of the CSG vision has direct implications for each individual employee. Its central management understands its clients extremely well and has concentrated wholly and precisely on their employment needs. This means that the group appreciates particular needs and the types of individuals who would work well in particular circumstances. From the other perspective – that of the employee – its trade personnel work diligently to understand the particular skills and the

development and training needs of the raw material on its books.

All employees are rated on a set of agreed performance criteria. This enables them to increase their earnings by up to one-third for on-target performance. In addition all senior management participate in a profit-related bonus scheme and enjoy healthcare cover and contributory pension arrangements. Fowler says, 'The group has a policy of promoting from within. Most of the senior management team have on average a length of service well in excess of five years. The group's rapid expansion and the changing market in which it operates continually provides opportunity for career advancement for talented and hard-working individuals.' He points to the detailed training needs analysis which is used to identify the strengths and weaknesses in the capabilities and competencies of individuals who work for the group. This is combined with structured training programmes to groom staff for assuming greater responsibility and achieving greater success in their careers. Training assumes a high priority within the group. It provides specific in-house training for all staff under a structured training programme from inductions through to selling skills or management development courses. It expects its staff to be committed, professional, flexible, willing to learn and to take on new responsibilities and to respond to changes in markets and client requirements.

It operates a graduate recruitment scheme where annually some 50 newly qualified graduates enter various operations throughout the country as recruitment consultants. This programme is designed to teach graduates the basic skills of a successful recruitment consultant, which then lead them on to junior or senior management opportunities throughout the group. It also has its own dedicated in-house training centres. Every employee attends these as part of the induction training and further career development programmes at a later stage.

This is a very commercially aware organisation. Corporate Services Group expects its people to work hard and make a definite contribution towards the business through serving clients at a very high level. The 40,000 who are on assignment at any one time – which can rise up to 50,000 – will be permanent employees of the Corporate Services Group and their careers will be managed by the consultants who work within the Corporate Services Group divisions. The business itself is expected to do extremely well in the next three to four years, which means that the level of opportunity for people entering the business will be much stronger. The acquisition of Blue Arrow in 1996 was a major step forward for the organisation because it extended the base of its clients. Analysts expect that the group will continue to grow and that its skilful central management and its policy of corporate acquisition and growth through organic means will make it a key contributor to the UK economy and a baseline stock.

Contact address

Human Resources Department,
Corporate Services Group PLC,
Alexandra House,
7 Alexandra Road,
Hemel Hempstead, HP2 5BS.
Telephone: 01442 247697.
Fax: 01442 254979.
Internet: http://www.corpserv.co.uk.

De La Rue plc

Best known for the fact that it almost certainly printed the cheque book in your pocket, De La Rue is in fact involved in a wide range of activities other than security printing. The company has grown strongly over recent years and has developed an extensive international presence, with more than 87 per cent of its turnover arising from overseas sales. The nature of its activities necessarily means that De La Rue's ethos is one of integrity and technical excellence, while the diversity of its operations offers considerable potential for career movement and development.

De La Rue at a glance

Employees: 10,000 worldwide, 4,000 UK
Annual staff attrition rate: 7 per cent
Key locations: London (HQ),
  16 centres in total around the UK
Av. annual graduate recruitment: 30
Annual management intake: 100

An inside view

Despite the fact De La Rue's products and systems are encountered during our daily lives, the company is surprisingly little known. Its background is in security printing and the company is currently split into three strongly focused divisions: the security paper and print division is the world's leading commercial supplier of banknotes and banknote paper, as well as being involved in a wide range of security documents including passports, cheques and bonds; the cash system division provides security and cash handling equipment to a variety of industries; and the transaction systems division provides magnetic stripe cards and smart cards, transaction terminals and complete solutions for payment and identification markets worldwide. De La Rue is also a member of the consortium which owns Camelot, the operator of the UK National Lottery.

Although the company has faced difficult trading conditions in certain of its markets over the last 18 months, it has continued to grow strongly, not least through a series of strategic acquisitions designed to strengthen its position in key activities and develop its international presence. As a result of this expansion, 87 per cent of the company's sales are now made outside the UK. Another strategic imperative for De La Rue has been to derive greater synergies in its business (both within and between divisions). One consequence of this strategy has been a greater movement of executives around the group.

Given De La Rue's background in security printing, it is scarcely surprising that one of the company's core values is integrity. De La Rue can only be successful as long as its clients have complete faith in the company, and its workforce, to deliver products and services securely. In addition to integrity, quality and technical excellence are also considered an integral part of the company's ethos. Accordingly, De La Rue's intention is always to employ high quality people worldwide. Finally, and in part reflecting the highly competitive environment in which the company now operates, the company is increasingly looking for innovation and creative skills amongst its workforce.

Despite its low profile, the attractions of De La Rue as an employer are demonstrated by the fact that the company has been extremely successful in retaining its graduate recruits – more than 50 per cent of those who joined the company as graduates over the last 15 years are still with the company. De La Rue's strong position in growth markets worldwide can offer a range of challenging and rewarding opportunities and, as its business develops, the company will in particular be seeking to recruit those with strong language skills and information technology capabilities.

How does De La Rue rate ?

Pay:	good
Benefits:	good
Communications:	good
Training:	excellent
Career development:	excellent
Morale:	good

People and personnel policies

De La Rue is determined to build a high quality management team that reflects the international nature of its markets, and is investing heavily in employee development as a way to achieve this objective. As one example of this, it has set up a process in order to match employee aspirations with available positions within the group. It is now company policy to advertise all vacancies internally both on noticeboards and using the e-mail system. Through the internal advertising of jobs, more than 150 managers have secured promotion or transfer within the group over the past two years.

The company's investment in training has also improved significantly. In 1996, it launched a major new training initiative for senior executives designed to ensure that the company has the quality of leadership to take it into the next century. This leadership development programme will be extended to cover the top 75 executives worldwide during the next 12 months, and complements the existing middle and junior management courses through which more than 250 individuals have already passed. Another benefit of this suite of training programmes is that it brings together employees from many different parts of the group. In terms of graduate recruitment, the majority of graduates are recruited directly into one of the operating businesses, although a small cadre enter a formal 16-month management development programme, during which they will be exposed to many different areas of the business.

De La Rue plc

De La Rue acknowledges that, in the past, it has not always been successful in exploiting the full potential of its workforce. It has therefore recently introduced a personal development review system. As part of this process, all executives are invited to specify their ambitions and aspirations within the company. Furthermore, De La Rue realises that this system will only be successful as long as both the company and the individual are honest with each other – a policy of openness is therefore encouraged. As well as exploring personal development issues, a separate annual cycle of performance appraisal is performed.

The company's remuneration policy is based on benchmarking against a series of competitor companies. To encourage a performance-driven culture, basic salary is then overlaid by a network of bonus payments, which are based on the company's financial performance. For senior employees, the maximum bonus is set at 50 per cent of basic salary and this can only be achieved if the financial results significantly exceed the target. All UK employees may join a savings-related share option scheme, which engenders share ownership by employees.

De La Rue is keen to improve the ethnic and sexual composition of its workforce at all levels. It is also keen to ensure that international experience is not simply a case of moving UK managers abroad to run overseas offices – it is also interested in moving and promoting executives who have come up through overseas operations. The company has also recently reviewed its policies on maternity leave and related working practices in order to foster the development of women managers – currently only 13 per cent of its management population is female, although this is increasing. In terms of community involvement, De La Rue focuses in particular on environmental matters and has established an environment group to sponsor a series of initiatives.

Contact address

Mr John Gilkes,
Director of Human Resources,
De La Rue plc,
6 Agar Street,
London WC2N 4DE.
Telephone: 0171 836 8383.
Fax: 0171 240 4224.

Dell Computer Corporation Ltd

The Dell Computer Corporation began life in 1984 from Michael Dell's dormitory room at the University of Texas. Today the business reports global sales of $5.3 billion. Dell employs more than 8,000 people worldwide and it is growing at an average 35 per cent a year. In some territories it is expanding at more than 100 per cent annually. The UK business employs 250 people in Bracknell in sales and support, and 300 people in Dublin at a telesales centre. The Europe, Middle East and Africa HQ is also based in Bracknell, embracing operations in 15 European countries including a manufacturing plant in Limerick, Ireland.

Dell at a glance

Employees: 550
Annual staff attrition rate: 20 per cent
Key locations: Bracknell (HQ), Dublin
Av. annual graduate recruitment: 10
Annual intake: 100

An inside view

Michael Dell is the computer entrepreneur personified. At the age of 19, when he was studying at the University of Texas, his PC broke down and he attempted to get it serviced. He was so unimpressed by the quality of the service he received that he thought he could do better himself. Dell set up a computer service company from his dormitory bedroom which expanded into the multi-billion dollar enterprise of today. Only 12 years after his initial idea, Dell employs more than 8,000 worldwide and the business is growing at an average 35 per cent a year.

He started as a service provider but after a short while moved into manufacturing. 'In the same spirit which prompted Dell to get into computer service, he looked at the composition of the modern PC and thought that he could do better than what was already on offer.' says one leading IT journalist. One of Dell's key principles was to remove third parties from the sales equation. 'He has always sold directly to corporate customers and never, as an article of faith, uses resellers.' The direct sales approach has won Dell many friends and enabled the business to experience rapid and sustained growth. In 1995, the global corporation reported sales up 52 per cent to $5.3 billion and operating income up 82 per cent to $272 million. The UK operation is a central part of the Europe, Middle East and Africa (EMEA) region, with headquarters for both Britain and EMEA in Bracknell. Europe is the most developed area in the EMEA region – there are Dell offices in 15 countries and clients in every European country.

The financial success of the company has set industry records. Dell has the highest earnings per share growth of any business in its sector. It is top in unit growth – up 57 per cent and market leader in asset management with a 68 per cent improvement year on year. The company has the lowest cash conversion cycle of any business in the Fortune 250. This demonstrates that Dell is a tightly managed ship with heavy emphasis on performance and returns. Resilience is an essential personal quality for people who want to do well in the business.

Lisa Farthing, UK human resource manager, says that Dell in the UK is composed of a sales and support operation in Bracknell which employs 250 people, and a telesales facility in Dublin where a further 300 are on site. Although Dublin is clearly not in the UK, the office there is regarded for Dell purposes as part of the UK operation. The European headquarters is also based in Bracknell, covering Dell staff in 15 countries and a manufacturing plant in Limerick.

How does Dell rate?

Pay:	good
Benefits:	very good
Communications:	very good
Training:	excellent
Career development:	very good
Morale:	very good

People and personnel policies

Dell looks for a mixture of personal qualities in candidates who seek employment in the business. Many companies stress teamworking as a key attribute, other prefer self-starters who take personal responsibility at an early stage. Dell wants both in equal measure. The company is heavily customer-led and many of the roles in the UK business are customer-facing. Farthing talks about hardiness as a characteristic which defines the business and its people. This is the personal and corporate strength that lies at the heart of the Dell culture.

The company likes people who like a challenge and are sufficiently flexible to move as the nature of the business changes. Mario Tribello, European head of training, says that the UK personnel policies derive directly from the global corporate goals of the Dell Corporation. He says that the European region has established a core of HR policies based on the worldwide personnel philosophy. Employees are assessed annually in a formal appraisal process which is updated quarterly and sometimes monthly. 'We manage by objectives. We have created a management leadership model which identifies 24 competencies which are key to the success of our managers.' These competencies are rated within a model of four quadrants dealing with the internal and the external customer.

Farthing says that each new employee goes through an induction course. The length of the course will depend on the extent of training needed to fulfil the role, for example in finance the induction lasts one week whereas in sales it lasts three weeks. There is a generic element which outlines the business, its philosophy and how it operates and then the remainder is technical training. Tribello says that generally there is a mix of on-the-job training and courses which cover specific managerial skills which are conducted in classroom environments.

Reward is structured in a typical package of pay and benefits. 'We aim to pay at the market rate but given the sales-orientation of the business almost everyone receives commission which means that take-home pay is high,' says Farthing. Inevitably there is a large variable element in the pay package, some of which is profit-related. One of the key incentives is the share purchase plan which extends to all employees and has been very lucrative for employee stockholders who began purchases at the outset of the UK operation. Michael Dell says that there is a group of volunteer workers who now have no immediate financial need but who come to work because they enjoy it so much.

Even recent subscribers to the plan have seen their stock rise faster than many other sector shares. So there are many Dell employees who have benefited handsomely from their share plans. The company also offers a range of other standard benefits including pensions, life insurance and healthcare cover.

Careers in a company like Dell in the UK can be very rewarding provided people can keep pace with the ever-changing technological demands and the search for more demanding sales targets. But for those who can keep pace, this is an exciting environment in which to work.

Contact address

Lisa Farthing,
Human Resources Department,
Dell UK,
Milbanke House,
Western Road,
Bracknell,
Berks RG12 1RE.
Telephone: 01344 860456.
Fax: 01344 860187.

Dresdner Kleinwort Benson

Dresdner Kleinwort Benson is an investment bank that combines the traditional strengths of an old City institution with the financial muscle of a new German owner, the Dresdner Bank. A leader in mergers and acquisitions advice and in equity finance and trading, it aims to grow both functionally and internationally with the added opportunities arising out of its purchase by the Dresdner bank. The company, which has historically been a stable employer, is a meritocracy offering exceptionally high incomes in return for the highest standards of service to clients.

Dresdner Kleinwort Benson at a glance

Employees: UK 2,307; 3,109 global
Annual staff attrition rate: 15 per cent
Key locations: Fenchurch Street, London, New York, Tokyo, Hong Kong and Frankfurt
Annual graduate recruitment: 35
Annual intake: 600 worldwide

An inside view

Dresdner Bank bought Kleinwort Benson, a prominent merchant bank whose origins lay in family-owned banking houses that dated back two centuries. The German bank brought to the City firm a stronger credit rating and a branch network covering more than 60 countries.

The British firm was enjoying one of its best years ever. It was ranked as the largest adviser by value to UK companies on overseas mergers. The combined Dresdner Bank-Kleinwort Benson equity operations were also ranked as the number one global coordinator of international equity issues and they were named as the European Equity House of the Year.

Corporate finance including mergers and acquisitions advice and equities are the provinces of just two of the operating divisions of the company – Dresdner Kleinwort Benson also operates global specialist financing and treasury divisions.

Employees on the equities and treasury side of the business can expect to work the same hours as the stock market – a typical day running from 7.30 a.m. to 5.30 p.m. The equities side of the business researches more than 1,900 companies worldwide, deals in the shares of more than 1,500 UK and international companies, and acts as a corporate broker for more than 130 UK clients. The treasury operations deal with government and non-government debt, foreign exchange, financial futures and derivatives.

Dresdner Kleinwort Benson employees are noted for their client ethos – a determination that the client must be served properly which permeates the business – and for their work ethic. Staff tend not to be self-aggrandising or to engage in lots of personal PR. For this reason they are trusted to offer clients the best advice.

How does Dresdner Kleinwort Benson rate?

Pay:	excellent
Benefits:	very good
Communications:	good
Training:	excellent
Career development:	good
Morale:	good

People and personnel policies

In an era when the City of London has been subject to rapid change, Dresdner Kleinwort Benson has managed to preserve some of the feel of a family-run firm. There is among its staff the feeling of stability found at long-standing institutions and this has persisted even after the company's incorporation into the Dresdner Bank Group.

This particular ambience is translated into an approach to employment issues that focuses on looking after people. 'We do care about our staff,' says personnel director David Henderson. 'We are not a hire-and-fire place.

Dresdner Kleinwort Benson targets a number of UK, European, Asian and US universities when recruiting and looks for teamworking ability, presentation skills, creativity, numeracy, verbal reasoning and leadership qualities. Graduate recruits are sent on a three-month induction programme where they are taught the basics of investment banking. The training programme covers a wide range of skills: effective presentation, understanding people's different styles of working, adding value and career management, together with the essential technical background in accounting, financial analysis, the capital markets and corporate finance. It also includes an exam to become an SFA-registered representative – a regulatory requirement for advising the firm's clients.

Training thereafter can lead to professional qualifications, with each of the firm's divisions having its own review, appraisal and training programmes. In Corporate Finance, for example, junior employees are regularly rotated between teams to broaden their experience.

In all divisions gradutes work closely with the managers to ensure that they continue learning and developing. This process often includes secondments overseas.

Like other major companies, Dresdner Kleinwort Benson is encouraging its employees to manage their own career plans. Discussions about an individual's ambitions need not be limited to their immediate boss: useful mentors often work in other departments. At the higher levels in the bank, there is careful succession planning for key posts and employees.

As an investment bank, Dresdner Kleinwort Benson operates in an exceptionally well-paid industry and it keeps a close eye on surveys of pay and benefits throughout the sector. Basic salaries are boosted in some cases by formula-driven bonus arrangements but for the most part bonuses are worked out on a discretionary basis. These bonuses are increasingly being linked to annual appraisals. Alongside the impressive salaries which Dresdner Kleinwort Benson provides, a comprehensive package of employee benefits is on offer. This can include healthcare programmes, cars or car allowances, mortgage subsidy and subscribed gym memshipship.

Employee turnover at Dresdner Kleinwort Benson runs at around 15 per cent a year due to the high pace of change in the industry. High turnover is a feature for all City firms, partly because not everyone who aspires to the high salaries on offer in the City is suited to the demands of the work. Dresdner Kleinwort Benson's recruitment assessment procedures are designed to identify those who will make it.

David Henderson sums it up as this 'We want to combine being fair to our staff with providing the best possible service to our clients.'

Contact address

Personnel Department,
Dresdner Kleinwort Benson Ltd,
20 Fenchurch Street,
London EC3P 3DB.
Telephone: 0171 623 8000.
Fax: 0171 956 5801.

Electronic Data Systems (EDS)

From the moment of its founding in Dallas in 1962, EDS blazed a different kind of trail. It did not make any product in the traditional sense. There were no factories and no distribution chains. Yet it broke ground with every developmental step. Today, it stands at the top of the information mountain, shaping how information is created, distributed, shared, enjoyed and applied for the benefit of enterprises and people worldwide. EDS employs more than 9,000 people in its UK operations, out of a global workforce of 95,000. Its human resource policies have a universal reputation, and the company is particularly proud that people from more than 25 other UK companies have transferred to EDS.

EDS at a glance

Employees: more than 9,000 UK
Annual staff attrition rate: 9 per cent
Key locations: UK headquarters at Stockley Park; Fleet/Hook, Milton Keynes, Bristol, Telford, Derby, Cheadle, Lytham, Washington, Aberdeen
Av. annual graduate recruitment: 300
Annual intake: 1100

An inside view

A subsidiary of General Motors for 12 years, this strategic alliance was so successful that EDS's turnover hit $10 billion in 1994. But as it grew within the company of the automotive giant, its reliance actually became less. Shortly after the acquisition, GM work accounted for 75 per cent of EDS sales. As time went by, the absolute revenues from GM remained constant, but the percentage share fell steadily to 31 per cent. In June 1996, EDS split off from GM and became a publicly owned company listed on the New York and London stock exchanges.

The world leader in information technology services, EDS offers a complete portfolio of IT-based services ranging from management consulting through systems development, integration and management, to process management. In leading the market in IT outsourcing, EDS effectively operates by taking over the responsibility for development and delivery of another company's information services.

EDS has offices in 42 countries worldwide meeting the needs of governments, businesses and people. Global sales in 1995 increased by 25 per cent to $12.5 billion drawn from such clients as GM and Xerox. The UK operation is part of the Europe, Middle East and Africa (EMEA) region, representing 19 per cent of global sales. EMEA has major contracts with Norway's largest bank, Den norske Bank, one of Spain's biggest construction companies,

Agroman, the UK's Department of Social Security, and Rolls-Royce Aerospace. The company plays a major role in public events and was technology supplier to the Barcelona Olympics, the World Cup 1994 Football Tournament in the United States and the US Indy Car Championship Races.

If there is any central belief upon which the phenomenal success of EDS has been built it is that imagination – particularly the unencumbered mind of the child – is the key to unlocking the door of technology. Chairman and CEO Lester Alberthal Jr says Children are unencumbered by the past – they have no limits to their creativity. What if we all retained a childlike imagination - one that takes in information and creates something new and wonderful? Well, that's how we describe EDS people. Our people look at things from a brand new perspective, like a child, with imagination and innovation. We then apply our innovation in ways that provide value for our customers.'

How does EDS rate?

Pay:	good
Benefits:	very good
Communications:	very good
Training:	excellent
Career development:	very good
Morale:	very good

People and personnel policies

The American founding fathers and 95,000 employees in 42 different countries have a profound effect on how EDS's human resources policy has evolved and how it continues to develop in the face of changing commercial imperatives. 'While the basis of our human resources policy is in principle set by the corporation, there is a very high degree of adaptation to each local environment,' says Graeme Simms, the UK company's human resources director. A key EDS principle is to think global and act local. 'Our policies are global because our clients operate on a worldwide basis and our business solutions need to reflect the global orientation of the commercial system. We apply a common EDS approach to everything we do but this general framework allows us great freedom at a local level to respond to market conditions and to locate innovative solutions for particular clients.

EDS lives by three corporate values which centre on 'Our people, our customers and our business'. These values represent the three stakeholders – the customer, the shareholder and the employee. Simms describes them as the corporate glue which keeps EDS together, and they are recognised in every sphere of the EDS operation where they are adapted to the local culture. From these values, employment policy is focused on business ethics, compensation, equality, an open-door communications commitment and a promotions policy which is aimed at moving people upward, promoting and appointing from inside the company.

'People are our most important asset,' comments Simms. 'We strive to hire and retain the best people by providing an exciting and rewarding place to work; and to promote from within.' Special emphasis is placed on the individual and rewards are based on performance, creativity and contribution. The company emphasises teamwork, and is proud of its commitment to open internal communications, even though it recognises that it still has more to do in this area. One illustration of this approach is the absence of a corporate culture. 'The idea of a monoculture is anathema because of the diversity of our customers and our business,' says Simms.

In structure, EDS is relatively flat, with a high degree of mobility of employees between industry groups and centres of competency. The focus of groups inside the business is through the account management structure of the customer. There are few organisational barriers to mobility and that includes the movement of EDS people between countries. In the UK, more than 75 per cent of EDS people have joined from other blue chip organisations; and they have spent their formative years in strong cultures. The people approach in the company is to blend their experience synergistically. The pay-for-performance policy reflects a belief that reward should be based on individual and team contributions which add value to customers' business. It focuses on four aspects: contribution, customer, added value and teamwork. Remuneration is split into: salary, bonus, recognition (non-cash compensation) and benefits. Salary increases can occur at any time, and bonuses can be fired by exceptional circumstances, ranging between 3 and 25 per cent. Leaders administer the programme, and they, as senior managers, are themselves subject to a variable pay system. This is based on a balanced scorecard of achievement covering the three core areas of people, customers and business.

A commitment to equality is underlined by the fact that the company's health scheme is the same for a starter as for the managing director. Flexibility is also evident in the company's attitude towards maternity leave which can be adapted to meet a degree of personal need. Employee attitude and customer service surveys are conducted annually to ensure that EDS knows what is going on internally and externally. Training is a major priority and is ongoing, aimed at employees fulfilling their job requirements and maximising their potential. This encompasses on-the-job training, on-line and off-line computer training, self-study packages and formal classroom work.

EDS launched the Jason project in 1989. The brainchild of Dr Robert Ballard, discoverer of the wreckage of the Titanic, this project was based on the voyages of Jason and the Argonauts who set out to locate the Golden Fleece. Since its inception the Jason project has taken 2 million teachers and students to the floor of the Mediterranean, the rain forests of Belize, the Galapagos Islands and the Sea of Cortez. But these are virtual trips, conducted through EDS technology, rather than physical visits to the locations concerned.

Contact address

Mr Graeme Simms,
UK Human Resources Director,
EDS Ltd, 4 Roundwood Avenue,
Stockley Park, Uxbridge,
Middlesex UB11 1BQ.
Telephone: 0181 754 4261.
Fax: 0181 754 4811.

Eli Lilly and Company Ltd

L illy is part of Eli Lilly, one of the world's leading pharmaceutical companies. Best known for Prozac, its anti-depressant drug, the company has recently been restructured to focus on five major disease categories and offer customers a more solutions-based approach to healthcare through integrated disease prevention and management programmes. Lilly has recognised that, in order to maintain its position in a rapidly changing healthcare environment worldwide, the innovation and technical excellence of its workforce is critical. It has won industry awards for the quality of its performance on key human resources issues.

Lilly at a glance

Employees: 24,000 worldwide, 1,800 UK
Annual staff attrition rate: 3-4 per cent
Key locations: three in the UK –
　　Basingstoke (HQ manufacturing)
　　Liverpool (manufacturing),
　　Windlesham (R&D)
Av. annual graduate recruitment: 90
Annual intake: 125

An inside view

Throughout the world, pharmaceutical and healthcare industries are undergoing galvanising and wide-reaching change. Buyers of healthcare services, whether they are national governments, insurance companies or private individuals, are demanding much more from their providers and this means the marketplace has become intensely competitive. Lilly has responded to these pressures by developing an integrated, solutions-led approach to the provision of healthcare

services. As well as using its existing technologies and innovative skills to create life-saving drugs, Lilly is increasingly educating people about disease prevention and management. The company believes that it is this holistic attitude which is most likely to benefit the business – both clinically and financially – in the years to come.

Lilly has recently been restructured in order to concentrate on five disease categories – central nervous system, endocrine, infectious diseases, cardiovascular diseases and cancer. The company is now acknowledged as a world leader in the fields of diseases of the central nervous system – Prozac now generates annual sales of over $2 billion – and endocrine diseases.

A central element of the Lilly philosophy is the importance of innovation and creative thinking. Although its annual sales exceed $6 billion, Lilly is dwarfed by some of its competitors in the global pharmaceutical industry. To maintain its position, therefore, the company must continually strive to offer new, high-quality products and services: not only ensuring that there is a constant source of new drugs in the pipeline, but also that new ways of improving service to the customer are identified. The concept of technical excellence, supported by personal integrity and a respect for others in the organisation, defines the Lilly culture. In addition, the company's matrix management structure means that the capacity to work successfully in teams and communicate effectively are qualities which are similarly valued in employees.

Recognising the importance of its workforce as its primary asset, in late 1994 Lilly commissioned its first global opinion survey of employees. Its purpose was to give employees a chance to express their opinions about working for Lilly and, through those opinions, to identify areas of strength and opportunities for improvement. As a result of the survey, a number of measures, such as improvements to the current merit/appraisal process, are now being instituted.

How does Lilly rate?

Pay:	good
Benefits:	excellent
Communications:	good
Training:	excellent
Career development:	good
Morale:	very good

People and personnel policies

As Lilly's current chairman and chief executive officer, Randall Tobias, says, 'Research findings indicate very clearly and very convincingly that employee and customer satisfaction are strongly and positively linked'. Accordingly, the company takes a pro-active approach to the recruitment and development of its workforce. This is manifested in a whole series of initiatives ranging from the flexibility of working arrangements which it endorses to the deliberate policy of promotion from within.

Lilly sees the training and development of its workforce as part of a long-term – and ongoing – process. The company's philosophy is that experience is the best teacher and therefore the majority of training is provided on-the-job. However, the company also provides supplementary training programmes (run both in-house and externally). In the sales and marketing area, for instance, Lilly has established a development centre which offers technical and personal development courses for those individuals who have been identified as likely to progress within the organisation. In addition, it is common for individuals with general management potential also to spend a period of time in the market research or strategy and planning functions in order to get a wider view of the business. Lilly is moving towards a more individual approach to employee appraisal and development, as part of which specific objectives are set for each individual. It is hoped that, as a consequence of this process, employees will play a much greater part in identifying their own career aspirations. Movement within the company is also encouraged. As the sector becomes more global, international knowledge and experience is increasingly valuable. Lilly's UK operation has proved to be a highly successful training ground for executives who are later promoted to run offices overseas.

Also in recognition of the state of the industry as a whole, Lilly recognises that it must be prepared to pay competitively to recruit and retain high calibre people. The company regards remuneration from a total compensation point of view and there is an increasing tendency, particularly at senior levels within the firm, for bonuses and other incentives to comprise a significant element of the overall remuneration package. One of Lilly's most innovative (and attractive) benefits is its share option schemes. There are two. The first is the ShareSave scheme – a five-year savings plan providing a guaranteed rate of interest, which also carries an option to buy shares in the company. This is open to all employees within the company. Additionally, it has a programme called GlobalShares where all employees, worldwide, have received share option grants.

Lilly has a very enlightened attitude to the promotion of women within the workforce. One of the principal ways in which this is manifested is the company's WorkLife programme. This is a coordinated series of initiatives designed to promote alternative working practices. Arrangements such as job sharing, staggered start times and reduced hour working are available. Naturally, these prove to be particularly popular with female employees, and have been identified as a major factor in retaining women within the workforce. Lilly has recently won a coveted award (Employer of the Year from the Parents at Work Foundation) as best employer for parents. As part of its drive to create an

atmosphere of greater diversity, the company has also adopted a positive attitude to the recruitment of people from ethnic minorities.

This diversity adds to the complexity of communication with the workforce, and this is one area on which the company invests a great deal of effort. The company's aim is that communication with employees is one of the most important tasks of line management and so this is the primary method of dispensing news and information to the workforce (and managers are judged on their communication skills). Lilly also employs formal channels of communication such as newsletters, and is making increasing use of e-mail and video conferencing. In order to obtain feedback from the workforce, Lilly has established a EuroForum which includes employee representatives from the UK and other European countries. Involvement with the community is one of the company's core values. Financially, it supports organisations with which it has a common interest, especially those which are located in areas where Lilly is a major employer. Lilly is also keen to let its employees become involved in local affairs, and tries to facilitate this by providing financial or administrative support.

Contact address

Mr Greg Reynolds,
Personnel Director (UK),
Lilly Industries Limited, Dextra Court,
Chapel Hill, Basingstoke, Hants RG21 5SY.
Telephone: 01256 315000.
Fax: 01256 315858.

Esso & Exxon Group of Companies

The Exxon Corporation is one of the world's greatest companies. It is a key standard setter for the energy sector, enjoys a triple A financial rating and combines excellent technical and marketing skills. The UK business is composed largely of Esso, the oil refining and marketing company, and Exxon Chemical. Both provide long-term careers in a stable, challenging and diverse environment with a high emphasis on operational safety, quality, teamworking and innovation. Staff attrition is well below average and the pay/benefits package is among the best in industry.

Esso at a glance

Employees: 4,000
Annual staff attrition rate: 5 per cent
Key locations: 12 in Esso and 8 in Exxon Chemicals. Esso UK's HQ is in London with a purpose-built complex in Leatherhead and refinery at Fawley. The Exxon Chemical HQ is based at Fareham.
Av. annual graduate recruitment: 40–50
Annual intake: 100

An inside view

Exxon enjoys a commanding reputation among global businesses. One of the oldest and most impressive multinational corporations, it has consistently outperformed competitors while setting demanding standards for quality and excellence. In Britain, its principal manifestation is Esso UK which is composed of two major operations – Esso Exploration and Production, and Esso Petroleum Company. Its upstream company is one of the largest investors in UK offshore oil and gas, while the refinery operation processes 300,000 barrels a day of crude oil. Its sister company Exxon Chemical is the sixth largest chemicals business in the UK, manufacturing and distributing petrochemicals for a broad range of corporate users.

In the original report on Esso in the 1989 edition of this book, we commented on the high degree of distinction between the parent and the UK business. The core values of integrity, quality, safety and tight financial controls are replicated in the British operation but they are expressed in different ways. 'It is still predominately a national focus,' says Chris Fox, UK recruitment manager. 'Oil is a commodity which is expensive to ship and so most countries will have their own refineries and a marketing policy which is driven by the local culture.' Esso and Exxon Chemical derive benefits as key components of the

Exxon Corporation but they are also granted significant freedom to achieve financial and operational targets.

Despite an increasing international orientation away from long-term careers with a single employer (which Esso recognises), Esso is keen to recruit people for the duration of their working life. Fox says that the company experiences high retention rates with 50 per cent of graduate entrants staying for longer than ten years. Traditionally this has been a culture of science, engineering and technology graduates. The intake today comes from a broader range of disciplines but Esso is still a highly attractive career option for mechanical and chemical engineers. The careers of graduate managers are planned as part of job families - or disciplinary groups – within the UK businesses. An individual recruited to work in the refinery, for example, can expect assignments in the supply, planning, upstream, manufacturing or distribution departments.

Equally, someone who joins information technology may have opportunities in public affairs, human resources, purchasing, finance/accounting or the treasurer's department. These families are not rigidly enforced but they provide a vehicle for managing personal career expectations. 'We provide a greater range of career opportunities within the group than many people could find in the external world.

As a multinational, Esso offers international assignments and recruits often give overseas experience as a key reason for joining the company. For future senior managers, overseas engagements are an essential part of the package of experience which will equip them for later

responsibility. But for other grades of manager, international work is optional.

How does Esso rate ?

Pay:	good
Pensions:	good
Communications:	excellent
Training:	excellent
Career development:	excellent
Morale:	very good

People and personnel policies

Esso aims to be a quality employer which maximises the potential of its people to generate positive returns for the group. Exxon is strong on financial controls and it sees its people as chief among its resources for reaching its targets. In order to ensure that it fully understands what its employees and potential recruits regard as key issues, Esso conducts regular surveys among cross-sections of staff and undergraduates.

The feedback from these exercises shows that the single biggest issue for employees and potential recruits is training and development. The company has responded to this fact by extending and enhancing its continous learning processes. Esso has gone significantly further than many other leading businesses in devoting time and money to building its expertise in training. In September 1996 Esso started a course developed with the London Business School which will equip graduates with a broad package of skills.

Item number two on Esso's slate of issues which influence commitment to an employer is the provision of challenging work. The company says that its drive for superb performance in all areas of its operation means that its people are faced with key challenges on a daily basis. It also suggests that its activities are so diverse that individuals can move to a new discipline, take an assignment overseas or seek another posting elsewhere in the UK. People are also looking for long-term commitment by the business which reflects Esso's own desire to find individuals who are keen to have the option of staying with one employer.

Prospective employees are also concerned about the quality of the pay package and standing of the company in its communities. Although the industry as a whole may not always win plaudits for its approach to the environment, Esso has always taken its responsibilities as a petrochemical company seriously. Where problems have occured the company has acted ethically and won respect.

Esso has evolved since we first examined the company in the late 1980s. One of the major changes is the rise of women within the culture. As recently as 1985, there were few women chemical engineers emerging from universities. At that stage, Esso took a long-term decision to encourage young women to enter science, engineering and technology courses at university. Part of this process involved working with primary school teachers to adopt a positive attitude towards science and engineering. At the secondary stages active projects are in place to capitalise on a greater awareness of these disciplines and to foster interest among girls and boys. The strategy has paid off because in 1995 some 45 per cent of graduates recuited into Esso were women.

Another central human resources policy is communication. As befits a lean, quality-orientated engineering company, Esso's policy is to produce messages which are simple and direct. Its brochures, newsletters and reports are elegant but not ornate. They emphasise the contribution of its people. Fox says that Esso people are well qualified and literate, which means that all communications should be informative, well written and truthful.

The core beliefs of the company have remained unaltered for many years. It is personal, informal, team-led and multi-disciplinary. It is an organisation where numeracy is important. Figures control the business. Esso also creates an environment where people can innovate. It is popular among research scientists because they have both the resources and a supportive atmosphere in which to develop. The company also has a formidable commitment to safety, not only in exploration and refining but throughout the business. Above all else, Esso is a company where commitment to doing an excellent job – in every aspect of the business – is paramount.

Contact address

Mr Chris Fox, Recruitment Manager,
Esso & Exxon Group of Companies,
Recruitment Centre,
Administration Building,
Fawley, Southampton SO45 1TX.
Telephone: Freephone 0800 373 518.

Federal Express

Federal Express – or Fedex as it is more commonly known – is one of the great worldwide express carriers. It employs 140,000 people around the globe and turns in annual revenues of $10.3 billion. Throughout the world the company carries around 2.4 million packages daily. In a fiercely competitive market, customer service is at a premium and the contribution of employees is vital to commercial prosperity. The UK operation is smaller than it was a decade ago but the quality of the business has been considerably enhanced.

Fedex at a glance

Employees: 1,300 (3,500 in EMEA)
Annual staff attrition rate: 15 per cent
Key locations: Stansted, Prestwick, London, Nuneaton, Coventry, Leicester, Manchester, High Wycombe, Birmingham, Dublin
Active graduate recruitment: 3
Av. annual recruitment: 500

An inside view

As the world of business has become definitively faster, more intensely competitive and in all senses more demanding, the pressures on services which support commerce and industry have multiplied. One sector where this gathering drive is most evident is in the express carrier business. Four major international brand names battle for the accounts of the world's most prominent businesses and speed of delivery, efficiency and reliability are key players in the bid to capture new orders.

The giants in this market – perhaps more than in many other sectors – depend on the quality and commitment of their people to win and retain the accounts of key customers. This is not a complex business to understand but it is one where consistent reliability of service and an extraordinary willingness to find solutions to client delivery problems is the best way to keep customers. Fedex was the inspiration of its CEO, Fred Smith, from whom came the concept of a central hub based close to an air terminal and whose views on the structure of the enterprises – and importantly its human resources policies – still hold sway. Smith on founding the company in 1973 coined the phrase 'People Service Profit' and Fedex employees today still invest the phrase with mantric-like properties. 'If you look after your people well, they will provide a good service to the customer which should return a profit. This can then be reinvested back into the people and the business infrastructure,' says Helen Hutchins, senior UK personnel officer.

The UK operation was somewhat larger in the mid-1980s than it is today. 'In 1992 we went through a massive reorganisation,' she recalls. The UK and Ireland region is now starting to expand again and it is opening new depots outside London. The administration of the business is largely contained in the Midlands, while the hubs are at Stanstead in Essex and Prestwick near Glasgow. The workforce is divided 60–40 between operational and functional staff. Operations people are the couriers, the depot management and workers at the hubs. Functional staff include administration, finance and human resources but also the customer service personnel who answer the company's 0800 telephone lines. Between 1992 and 1996 the company stopped actively recruiting graduates and putting them through a graduate entry scheme. Hutchins says that since new opportunities are beginning to develop within the business a graduate entry policy may be revived during 1997 but it will take only a handful of people in the initial stages.

How does Fedex rate?

Pay:	good
Benefits:	good
Communications:	good
Training:	superb
Career development:	very good
Morale:	very good

People and personnel policies

Energy and drive are the basic materials of Fedex people. The core of the company's activities is not hard to appreciate but a combination of intelligence, commitment, a capacity to work with and inspire others, and determination goes a long way to career success in the company. Fred Smith put his people first in his business cycle and that recognition has never been lost.

There are two main streams of recruitment into Fedex. Much of it is entry level, for example to fill courier, customer service agent or handler positions, where little formal qualification is needed. 'They need to be numerate and literate and to show through the tests that we give that they have potential to do that job. Their communications and interpersonal skills will enable us to differentiate between candidates,' says Hutchins. 'In sales we will probably recruit people with some business experience and commercial understanding but not necessarily any formal qualification. For managers, it is desirable to have some academic achievements – maybe up to a degree – but we do not make this a pre-requisite. We are more interested in their personal qualities.'

The business environment is demanding and, if nothing else, Hutchins and her colleagues are looking for people who want to make a difference to the company. This is not only making a contribution to Fedex but, for example, wanting to take customer service to new standards of excellence or winning fresh customers who previously were a closed door. It is a blend of originality and vitality which distinguishes some of the best operators in Fedex. 'I cannot think of many people in the business who will not deal with customers at some time in their career, so we need people who are confident, cooperative and helpful,' she says.

All employees at entry level go through three weeks' mandatory training. Some is on-the-job but much is in the classroom. Recruits must pass this initial period of training to be able to take up their new roles. Very few actually fail because Fedex invests heavily in counselling during the sessions. Leadership is a quality much prized in the company and the US business has established its own Leadership Institute which devises appropriate courses for Fedex managers. The Institute was Fred Smith's personal vision and he regularly attends its courses today. These classes introduce managers to the values and approach of the corporation, the way Federal Express wants its managers to operate, the internal communications systems within the business and the strategy of the enterprise. Training is continuous and Fedex is good at preparing candidates directly for the challenges which they will face in the future.

Smith was a groundbreaker in the 1970s and 1980s for management techniques which are now widely accepted as concepts which progressive companies should adopt. Two examples are LEAP – a leadership evaluation programme – and Survey Feedback Action, an early and innovative employee awareness survey. LEAP was initiated in the States after Smith heard from staff groups that some managers were good at their operations role but less good at people management. 'You cannot be called a manager in Federal Express unless you actually have people to manage,' says Hutchins. He devised nine dimensions – or competencies – which people would need to excel in to be appointed managers. This became the basis of the development process for potential managers and literally anyone in Fedex can apply for this Management for Me workshop. The employee survey has consistently produced good results and as many as 97 per cent of the Fedex UK population completes the document. 1992 – the year of the reorganisation – produced an understandably poor overall performance rating for the company but since then it has matched and exceeded previous bests.

Communication is a great theme in the business. Global issues are communicated via informal feedback meetings and more formal presentations at key times during the year. There is a series of publications appearing at different times in the calendar. The reward package is focused on the market average. Human resources personnel are concentrating on critical roles where they know that in order to attract the best people they must offer attractive reward packages. In addition it has introduced so-called accelerated merit programmes and star awards for people who do exceptionally and deserve double rises.

Contact address

Helen Hutchins,
Human Resources Officer,
Federal Express,
Bond Gate, Nuneaton,
Warwickshire.
Telephone: 01203 343333.
Fax: 01203 642415.

F.I. GROUP plc

The F.I. Group is an outstanding organisation which started in the early 1960s and has become, under current CEO Hilary Cropper, one of the most able and active businesses providing outsourced IT services. In five years from 1992–1996, F.I. Group tripled its turnover to £78.82 million and over the same period increased pre-tax profit by a similar amount to £3.8 million. F.I. Group is remarkable in many ways but in particular in its high degree of workforce ownership which is a distinguishing factor for the business.

F.I. Group at a glance

Employees: 1,000 salaried plus 900 associate suppliers
Staff attrition: 10 per cent
Key locations: Hemel Hempstead (HQ) and around the UK
Annual graduate recruitment: 100
Annual salaried intake: 400

An inside view

F.I. Group is in the information technology and outsourcing businesses – two disciplines which regularly experience high levels of employee attrition. But not this company. The F.I. Group workforce is woven into the fabric of the business, the vast majority are stockholders in the group and view the company as their business. Despite the fact that it is now a thriving PLC with substantial external shareholdings, it remains for the workforce the company which they have created. The workforce is actively consulted on key management issues and is a natural and vigorous part of the decision-making process.

Hilary Cropper explains that employees are consulted as workers in the business but also as shareholders, Indeed, before its flotation on the stock market, the workforce was asked to vote on whether they wanted the listing to go ahead. The company has always attracted lively minded, articulate and intelligent individuals and a culture where debate is commonplace has been the consequence.

The company's marketplace is applications management for blue chip institutions. It has profound expertise in banking and credit card systems, live retail systems such as supply chain management and customer loyalty systems, and customer information and billing. Among its client list are BT, Barclays Bank, Tesco, Lloyds, TSB, Granada, Waitrose, Whitbread, Royal & Sun Alliance and Standard Life.

F.I. Group is UK market leader in applications management – an area which is experiencing sustained growth. According to the market specialist Richard Holway, the applications management sector was worth £70 million in 1991. This rose to £315 million in 1995 and is projected to grow to £730 million by 1999. As a strategic imperative, the group has made this market its home and used it as a basis to develop longer-term and broader outsourcing contracts. In some cases there has been a transfer of undertakings where the workforce of a client company has been absorbed by F.I. Group.

The employee structure of the company is unusual. It employs around 1,000 salaried members of staff. In addition to this group is a band of around another 400 so-called associate suppliers who work either full-time or part-time for F.I. Group usually on freelance contracts. These are mainly specialists who are brought in for particular assignments. There are also another 200 people who are supplied by F.I.'s contractorarm F.I. recruitment.

How does F.I. Group rate?

Pay:	very good
Benefits:	excellent
Communications:	superb
Training:	very good
Career development:	good
Morale:	superb

People and personnel policies

The company majors on quality and expertise which is recognised in the copious endorsements from leading clients. Locating able personnel is, self-evidently, a key activity for the group. People who do well in the company are not necessarily IT specialists but alert and intelligent people with familiarity with IT concepts. The capacity to communicate, to think and to interact with others is vital. The strength of the business is in its ability to understand clients, their IT and applications management issues, and to translate solutions into efficient management.

In recent years F.I Group has been awarded a series of long-term outsourcing contracts – five to seven years is typical. The company enjoys the flexibility of having a balance between full-time salaried employees and contractors, some of whom are associates. This gives F.I. Group a core resource which can be more than doubled as projects and assignments demand. The company also emphasises the exposure which its people get to many new methodologies and systems by delivering services to such a range of top drawer clients.

BT, another company selected for this book, says 'We rate FI's people very highly. They are experienced, highly professional and committed and they obviously come from a quality culture which emphasises ownership and pride in their work.'

The business offers a three-dimensional career path which includes IT consultancy, project management and technical expertise. People work in a flexible environment but generally teams remain highly stable. FI has a long-term vision of its relationships with its clients and wants people, if possible, to stay with an assignment for its duration. The group invests heavily in training, some of which is handled by its own training company, F.I. Training.

The benefits package is highly attractive. Everyone takes part in a profit-share scheme, as well as the dividend which more than 80 per cent of the workforce receive as shareholders. And there are schemes under which employees can buy shares in the company's share option scheme. In addition, FI has one of the most attractive pension plans in its sector.

IT and outsourcing are demanding marketplaces for pay and the company aims to be competitive. It has taken an understanding view about people who transfer to the group from client companies and has guaranteed their existing benefit arrangements while they have breathing space to consider whether to switch to the FI plan.

In fact, the FI approach is an increasingly personal one because the company has introduced flexible benefits, which give employees the chance to select between various benefit possibilities, according to which suit their personal situation. It is a scheme which attracts widespread enthusiasm within the company, because it includes preferences in pensions and healthcare, and holidays and life assurance.

In 1995, the group introduced personal development planning which provided a coordinated and coherent system for appraising employees and initiating individual developmental programmes. This represented a further step forward for the group in the consolidation of a human resources framework which at once allows greatest personal flexibility combined with meeting the needs of a growing, demanding and challenging business.

Contact address

Human resources department,
F.I. Group plc,
Campus 300,
Maylands Avenue,
Hemel Hempstead,
Herts HP2 7TQ.
Telephone: 01442 233339.
Fax: 01442 238400.

Finelist Group plc

Finelist Group is one of the most impressive businesses to have emerged in the West Midlands in the last decade. In early 1997 the company became the largest independent distributor of motor vehicle parts in the UK. Based in William Shakespeare's town, Finelist has grown by acquisition and organically to provide a national network through such brands as Autela Components, Edmunds Walker, Motor World and Charlie Browns. With sales of £300 million and pre-tax profits of £24 million, Finelist now employs 4,300 in around 700 sites.

Finelist at a glance

Employees: 4,300
Annual staff attrition rate: 15 per cent
Key locations: Stratford-upon-Avon (HQ), heavy concentration in West Midlands, Yorkshire, North West and the North East but now effectively a national network
Active graduate recruitment: 20
Average annual recruitment: 500

An inside view

The idea of the Finelist Group emerged after a management buyout at Autela Components in 1988. One of the leaders of the MBO – Chris Swan – bought out his partners three years later and, with some help from venture capitalists, began the initiative which has created the most innovative group of automotive parts distributors in the UK. The sector has been characterised by thousands of small local operators whose business approach was largely untutored and in many cases

deeply inefficient. Swan realised at an early stage that a major group with critical mass could command preferential arrangements from suppliers and that an able, trained workforce should establish long-lasting and rewarding relationships with customers.

The purchase of Edmunds Walker was a milestone – it was three times bigger than Finelist but the integration was achieved successfully by early planning. Since then the company has made an on-going series of acquisitions, for example, Truckline, Engine Express, First Line, Ferraris Piston Service, AutoGem, Panther Products, Genex, Motec, Motor Store (Eire) and Maccess. 'The Motor World Group consists of seven companies – and 326 sites – including Motorworld, Charlie Browns and Autogem,' says Swan. Typically, Finelist buys up scores of small-scale operators with one, two or three outlets every year. But the latest series of acquisitions has been much larger and includes Ferraris Piston Services, Firstline and Maccess. 'Management are often very happy to sell,' he says. 'Margins for them are getting tighter and the level of competition makes their solo operation unattractive.'

A key part of the Finelist strategy has been to buy up collections of smaller operators and to impose the disciplines of a major group. The level of service which is offered to customers is now light years ahead of what it had been previously. The customers are private garages, retail customers, motor factors and accessory shops. The Finelist guarantee is that it will provide the parts within hours to customers inside a 50-mile radius. After its acquisition of Ferrais Piston Services in February 1997, Finelist has emerged as the largest independent distributor in the UK.

Swan and his colleagues have been able to exploit the hitherto indifferent standards of service to the customer in the sector and build commanding market advantage by being good at what they do. Necessarily, people are at the core of this achievement and have been since the outset.

How does Finelist rate?

Pay:	good
Benefits:	good
Communications:	very good
Training:	very good
Career development:	excellent
Morale:	superb

People and personnel policies

At the outset Chris Swan realised that Finelist would need to locate natural enthusiasm in its people and build upon

that quality to achieve constantly improving standards of customer service. In many ways Finelist has certain values in common with TNT, which is based in North Warwickshire. Both TNT's managing director Alan Jones and Chris Swan recognise that with sufficient support and incentive employees can regularly achieve challenging standards of personal achievement.

Finelist's human resources manager Jerry Hayes says that from the outset the directors understood that distribution is intrinsically a people business. It is about personal relationships between customers and employees. To construct lasting customer relationships, Finelist invested heavily in motivating, training and communicating with its people.

In a business which moves as far and fast as Finelist, these have become essential qualities. Finelist on one level is growing rapidly by acquisition and on another it is seeking new ways each day to refine the service to the customers.

A high degree of attention is focused on the managers of the branches. They give on-the-job training and informal counselling on the progress of individuals in their charge. But this is not a highly structured human resources approach. Instead, the group provides a framework and great emphasis is placed on the manager to encourage and prepare employees for their roles.

Finelist is very selective about which individuals it recruits. The company devotes time and effort to locating people who will succeed in its friendly but driven culture. Whenever the company advertises the volume of applications is high and it can afford to be choosy. Picking the right entrants has copious spin-off benefits.

Aside from finding suitably ambitious and enthusiastic staff, Finelist is also looking for managers of the future. It is a business which believes strongly in promotion from within and should never have long-distance succession planning problems.

To be a manager in the company, individuals must demonstrate able people management skills, a capacity to win and retain new business and to organise their operations successfully. It is a big leap from shop floor to branch management, and the company identifies prospective managers at an early stage in their careers. For a company of its size, Finelist has a pragmatic but committed view of training. For general employees training is largely on-the-job but for managers there are core training sessions in a wide array of management disciplines.

The business is also keen that its junior staff add to their personal qualifications and it encourages them to take NVQs to broaden the base of their work. There is no active graduate recruitment scheme but there are many graduates in the company. It is an organisation which decidedly believes in promotion on merit rather than background, and so graduates have as much chance as anyone else to grow with the business. Given the extensive network of depots of different sizes and a nascent regional structure, the career development possibilities are extensive.

Finelist ensures that its people are well remunerated for their work and salaries and benefits compare well with the sector. At manager level an increasing amount of the package is performance related.

Contact address

Jerry Hayter,
Human resources manager,
Finelist Group plc,
Birmingham Road,
Stratford-upon-Avon,
Warwickshire.
Telephone: 01789 414545.
Fax: 01789 414526.

The Ford Motor Company Ltd

Ford in the UK is the biggest and longest established Ford subsidiary outside North America. It employs 30,000 people at 21 locations in the UK and it builds 420,000 vehicles a year and exports 23 per cent of that total. Ford argues that it is the largest automotive company in the UK, occupying the top three places in car sales and a leading position in commercial vehicles. It has led car sales for 19 years and commercial vehicle sales for 30 years. It sells half a million vehicles in this country every year and takes 21 per cent of the new car market.

Ford at a glance

Employees: 30,000
Annual intake: n/a
Key locations: Brentwood (HQ), Dagenham, Halewood and 18 other locations
Av. annual graduate recruitment: n/a
Annual intake: n/a

An inside view

In the week before the manuscript for this book was handed over to the publisher, Ford announced that it would be seeking help from the UK government to keep one of its significant sites in the UK open. According to the *Sunday Times*, the motor company wanted £75 million in aid to help finance a new vehicle project that would keep its Halewood factory open after Escort car production stops in the year 2000. Andrew Lorenz, the business editor, said 'If Ford does not get the cash for the new product, the Merseyside plant will almost certainly close with a loss of up to 2,500 direct jobs and many thousands more among its component and service suppliers. Ford will make a final decision on the project later this year. If the vehicle is not built at Halewood it would be made at Valencia in Spain, or in Poland or Hungary.'

Ford's plan to standardise Escort production at one location in Europe would have a devastating effect on morale in the UK. But nevertheless the Ford Motor Company has been selected for inclusion in this book for its innovative and far-sighted employment practices for those people who work for the company. Ford's Chairman, Alex Trotman, under his Ford 2000 principle, decided to eliminate effective duplication of resources and production. The analysis of the future of the Dagenham plant was much rosier and in fact it looks as strong as any motor industry production facility in the cut-throat environment of today's motor trade. Apart from the immediate strategic concern, Ford is guided by a company mission, values and guiding principles. Its mission is to be worldwide leader in automotive and financial products and services.

'Our mission is to improve continually our products and services to meet our customers' needs, allowing us to prosper as a business and to provide a reasonable return for our stockholders, the owners of the business.' Its values focus on three areas. First, people – Ford says that 'people are the source of our strength – they provide our corporate intelligence and determine our reputation of vitality. Involvement and teamwork are our core human values'. Second value, products – 'Our products are the end result of our efforts and they should be the best in serving customers worldwide'. And finally, profits – 'Profits are the ultimate measure of how Ford provide customers with the best products for their needs'. The company guiding principles include quality comes first, customers are the focus of everything we do, continuous improvement is essential to our success, employee involvement is our way of life, dealers and suppliers are our partners, and our integrity must never be compromised.

Ford 2000 is designed to turn Ford into a new global organisation where before there were regional operating companies making products for their own market. For example, in Europe or the US there are now five product divisions or vehicle programme centres, each with worldwide responsibility for designing, developing and producing a specific range of vehicles. Four of the centres are located in the US. The European vehicle centre, comprising research and engineering at Dunton in the UK and in Germany, will create small- and medium-sized front wheel cars such as the Fiesta, the Escort and the Mondeo. While these vehicles are global products, details of styling and specification are tailored to reaching all markets. Computer networks and video links allow engineers and executives throughout the world to discuss and work on the same vehicle. The result is real time 24 hours a day global dialogue.

Ford management says the globalisation is more than just a redrawing of the organisation chart. It is a fundamental reinterpretation of what the organisation should be. The old rules at Ford no longer apply. There is no point in using new technology to automate the past or overlay outdated manual processes. The prime purpose of organisational refreshment is to disseminate knowledge throughout the organisation to harness and channel the intelligence and capability of its people. Ford has abandoned its traditional organisational hierarchy and introduced a matrix. This relies on multidisciplinary teamwork and promotes cross-fertilisation of ideas. Designers, engineers and production people work on products in integrated teams. Individuals have more decision-making authority than at any stage in the company's history. Information and experience is shared to promote innovation and establish best practice.

How does Ford rate?

Pay:	good
Benefits:	superb
Communications:	excellent
Training:	very good
Career development:	very good
Morale:	good

People and personnel policies

The Ford 2000 project has recorded the qualities and personal capacities that Ford is looking for in its people of the future. One of the company's personnel managers said 'It is the strategy of a leader rather than a follower and as such it calls for people who thrive on calculated risk and unconventional thinking, those who understand the importance of individual flexibility and initiative, and also those who recognise its shared vision and values are essential to the success of any business team. We look for more than just average ability. We seek the best graduates of their generation, individuals with character, confidence and creativity, to make the most of a professional development programme that will transform them into the business and technical leaders of tomorrow.'

Ford is one of the remaining companies to attend the milk round at universities and provide regional interviews for prospective graduate entries. It also operates a graduate recruitment scheme, and every phase of training and development in the company is integrated into this approach. It begins with an induction course that introduces new entrants to the company and the way it works. It involves up to 30 new graduates and the course allows individuals to develop a network of contacts across functions. In addition graduates will attend a one-week development programme covering everything from problem solving and decision making to communications, team building and personal development. A manager will then set the goals of the graduate entrant, objectives and future training requirements. The ongoing development will reflect personal need and ambitions. It will also allow a new recruit to embark on a seamless process of learning that focuses strongly on practical experience and real responsibility.

Operational goals are also achieved under a pressure of deadlines and the company is keen that as well as meeting commercial targets, individuals should have the opportunity to pursue professional qualifications and accreditation with relevant professional institutions, to take further degrees, to undertake just in time training to deal with new challenges and contingencies, and to take advantage of its innovative Employee Development and Assistance Programme (EDAP). EDAP allows individuals to study anything from Open University, foreign languages, Tai Chi and horse riding. The company's innovative approach also embraces new dual career paths for graduates in engineering, vehicle manufacturing, product development and IT. The personnel manager says 'Until recently these graduates reached a point in their careers where a move into man management was the only way to achieve promotion. We have now opened an equally prestigious technical route for graduates called the Technical Specialist Programme. This will allow people the resources and opportunities to become a recognised expert in one or more specifically designed fields of technology. In common with its broader enthusiasm for networking, the Technical Specialist Programme will allow individuals to establish links with academic institutions, attend professional seminars and contribute to technology exchange forums throughout the world. This expertise will then be developed in a range of technological initiatives and the management of their flow into mainstream activities.

Ford is very keen on early responsibility and that responsibility is increasingly international in its scope. The company aims to send new graduates to places as diverse as Vietnam, China, Egypt and Chile in their first years of working for the company. 'They may work with very little back-up and in relatively harsh conditions to build effective relationships with potential customers and partners in cultural and business practices which are entirely different from their own. This will involve meeting challenges for which no textbook can prepare them. It means learning new rules and new ways of seeing things, and venturing into new territories.' In this sense Ford is a practical application of a learning culture.

The reward package in Ford is diverse depending on location, grade and status. Graduates have extensive sports and social facilities, they are allowed to buy up to three new cars every nine months at 25 per cent below retail price, and they have enhanced salary levels for relevant new qualifications and experience. Graduates tend to start at between £18,190 including bonus and rising to £20,808 after 18 months. The company also pays relocation expenses and will help to find accommodation near to the place of work. The majority of graduates begin work in the UK. Those in engineering, finance and resources may be based in Essex but could also go to Leamington, South Wales, Merseyside or Southampton. Marketing and sales graduates often join district offices in Edinburgh, Harrogate, Daventry, Bristol or Basildon.

With a company which is so innovation-led, it's not unsurprising to see innovation expanding through to other areas of the business. Communication in particular within Ford is inspired. Ford was the first company in the UK to set up an in-house television service purely for communicating messages to its employees, and its raft of publications and briefing meetings show the determination with which Ford management wants to communicate with its workforce and to get as much feedback as possible.

Contact address

The Recruitment Manager,
1/360X Ford Motor Company Limited,
Eagle Way,
Brentwood,
Essex CM13 3BW.
Telephone: 01277 253000.
Fax: 01277 253349.

Glaxo Wellcome plc

Glaxo Wellcome is the world's largest pharmaceutical company. In its present combination, it was formed in mid-year 1995 from the merger of Glaxo, which was already the foremost company in its sector, and Wellcome plc, another major player which was conducting some groundbreaking research. In March 1997, the company reported sales of £8.34 billion and pre-tax profits of £2.96 billion for 1996. The company is consistently among the top three UK companies by market capitalisation. Glaxo has traditionally been at the top table among Britain's best employers as a standard bearer for training and development in its sector. For many years it has been a premier choice for Britain's graduates as it scores highly in a wide catalogue of employment criteria.

Glaxo Wellcome at a glance

Employees: 55,000 worldwide, 14,000 UK
Annual staff attrition rate: +/– 5 per cent
Key locations: some 11 in the UK; HQ is in central London. The British operation includes manufacturing (7,500 people), R&D (4,500) sales and marketing (1,200) and corporate (800)
Av. annual graduate recruitment: 25
Annual intake: 200

An inside view

The 1990s have witnessed widespread change in the pharmaceutical sector. Formerly bound by national conventions and market ambitions, the industry has become increasingly global in orientation. Competition has multiplied, regulation has tightened, cost pressures have intensified and the transfer of knowledge from previously discrete functions is growing in every area of the sector. This means companies operating in the pharmaceutical industry have encountered a degree of ongoing change which has never been experienced at any earlier stage. Glaxo's management realised that in order to capitalise on these trends it needed to add critical mass, especially in certain key disciplines.

This thinking prompted its £9 billion acquisition of Wellcome plc. At the time it was the largest takeover in UK corporate history. The first year of combined Glaxo Wellcome was devoted to integrating the business developing a new strategy to be the number one pharmaceuticals company in the world. As deputy chairman and chief executive Sir Richard Sykes told shareholders in May 1996 'New technologies resulting from advances in cellular biology and molecular genetics create the potential for tremendous improvements but at a cost. A highly fragmented industry began to restructure and consolidate. Glaxo resolved to be at the head of the process. The successful pharmaceutical company of the future must have scale and strength in R&D, sales, product range and research. Wellcome was a good fit for us, with a similar culture based on science, sound research, a complementary range of products and high quality staff.' The result is a full service business which provides healthcare solutions in continuous dialogue with sector professionals and prescribers. It operates in discovery, development, manufacturing and marketing of pharmaceutical products. The new company has moved from a reliance on one major product – the remarkably successful anti-ulcerant Zantac – into a broad portfolio of treatments.

Latest company results show that sales of central nervous system drugs, including Imigran, rose by 47 per cent to £724 million, and respiratory drugs, mostly for asthma, grew 11 per cent to £1.76 billion.

Each business within the company is run as an autonomous unit with its managing director reporting to a main board member of Glaxo Wellcome plc. The priorities of the individual businesses will be different and although each operates to a global agenda, the factors which dictate the running of each will vary. For example, the R&D discipline has bases in the UK, US, Canada, Australia, Switzerland, Italy, Spain and France. It is run as a global entity and each location is viewed as a single piece in the total R&D jigsaw. Manufacturing is highly competitive and Glaxo Wellcome has concentrated on those areas in which it enjoys commanding success. It has formed alliances with those agencies which are also world leaders in their own specialisms. The commercial division of the business will, inevitably, be more nationally specific, working with customers to find solutions to local healthcare issues.

How does Glaxo Wellcome rate?

Pay:	very good
Benefits:	excellent
Communications:	good
Training:	superb
Personal development:	excellent
Morale:	very good

People and personnel policies

The focus on a family of businesses – each with its own HR requirements – is the basis of the Glaxo Wellcome personnel policy. A cross-functional team, emphasising the needs of the separate businesses, was created as part of a radical review of the company's operations to examine the reward structure. Tim Miller, director of human resources and UK coordination, says 'We are a company which rewards competitively according to the criteria of each marketplace. Our whole approach is to recruit highly motivated, highly intelligent and well-skilled employees and we recognise that talented people demand top rate remuneration.'

The reward approach taken with scientists in R&D is very different from that employed with sales people in the commercial division. A scientist is not necessarily motivated by individual performance in the same way as a marketing manager with personal targets. 'Our employee relations strategy is very clear: we intend to build the strongest possible relationships between the employee and the company. This is not a paternalistic relationship, but a realistic approach based on individual responsibility and flexibility where we re-negotiate the emotional – unwritten – and social contracts with our people.' An example is a new flexible approach to pension planning where employees can choose between various elements in their plans to suit their individual needs.

The Glaxo Wellcome pension plan, which is non-contributory in its basic form, is among the best in the UK and is benchmarked against those of the leading employers. The car policy is another case where an employee can have a car or cash or a car and cash up to individual limits. The company provides comprehensive healthcare facilities for all employees. Senior employees also have cover for their families and junior members of staff can buy in their immediate families. The employee appraisal programmes are being restructured to put the emphasis on self-development. Miller says that the traditional model fails to take account of new demands and a more interactive scheme is in preparation. 'We believe that it is the responsibility of the individual to develop career plans but the company will help employees. We wish to help individual's contribution to the company. The company believes that selecting and developing the best people – whatever their background – will lead to a truly diverse workforce which reflects the diverse nature of its customers and the population as a whole.'

One of the greatest challenges for Glaxo Wellcome's personnel team is to create cross-functional opportunities for employees who have succeeded in one area and then wish to apply their expertise in other sectors of the business. Given its highly educated, articulate and talented workforce, the company is aware that to retain and motivate its people it must redouble its efforts here.

Team-based project assignments are being used to broaden individual skills and to give greater exposure to fresh challenges. 'We have a fundamental belief in talent. We believe that talented people are flexible, adaptable, highly motivated, instinctively creative and better able to handle change and ambiguity more easily. Our aim is to recruit intelligent, positive individuals who can take on high levels of personal responsibility. These are people who do not walk away from problems. We aim to select as many of these individuals as we can and to develop them.

Contact address

Mr Tim Miller,
Director of Human Resources and
UK Coordination,
Glaxo Wellcome PLC,
Lansdowne House, Berkeley Square,
London W1X 6BQ.
Telephone: 0171 493 4060.
Fax: 0171 408 0228.

Green Flag Limited

Green Flag Limited is the emergency assistance service arm of the Green Flag Group – a wholly owned subsidiary of NCP. This is the youngster on a block where the famous names of the AA and RAC have been around for more than a century. Green Flag has established itself as a high-value, highly efficient and no frills service. The company reported sales of more than £100 million in 1995–96 and its directors say that it has grown annually by 10-15 per cent compound in turnover, pre-tax profits, staff numbers and members since 1990. Green Flag is strongest in the North and Midlands and at the end of 1996 it had achieved 3.5 million subscribers as opposed to the 4.5 of the RAC and 8 million of the AA. The business employs 1,000 people.

Green Flag at a glance

Employees: 1,000 (plus an extra 10 per cent at seasonal peaks)
Staff attrition rate: 18 per cent call centre staff, 5 per cent management
Key locations: Now concentrated at a single, purpose-built HQ building at Pudsey, Leeds in Yorkshire
Active graduate recruitment: 10
Annual intake: 100+

An inside view

When the National Breakdown Recovery Club was launched in 1971 as the first UK motoring organisation to offer a recovery service for stranded motorists, it was dismissed by some as an insignificant walnut between the mighty crackers of the RAC and the AA, which, until then, had dominated the market. Twenty-five years on that company, now Green Flag, spans medical assistance and repatriation, car and truck rescue and recovery, domestic breakdown and emergencies, a pan-European motoring service and comparable operations in the US. It now has more than 3 million members. Quite a walnut. The three businesses which comprise Green Flag all provide assistance to customers, whenever and wherever it is needed, 24 hours a day and 365 days a year.

Such round the clock operation places enormous emphasis on reliable telephone communications. Green Flag also handles recruitment by telephone. It employs no repair or recovery subsidiaries of its own, so all implementation of member services is dealt with by telephone. Green Flag is then, irrespective of its core activities, one of Britain's most intensive telephone user businesses. When the company was founded, it represented something unique for motorists. Then, contemporary motoring organisations provided only what was called a roadside repair service. If it were impossible to fix a car on the spot, then the motorist had to sort out the problems for himself. The prime rescue function of Green Flag has been widely copied since those days, as have such innovations premiered by the company as motorway assistance and freephone numbers. In 1996, the group, now the sponsor of the England football team, instituted a major reorganisation to shape a single company spanning all activities, based in a single modern headquarters on the outskirts of Leeds. This now services all calls from customers seeking motoring or domestic assistance; their only interface with the company is the Green Flag telephone operator, trained to elicit essential details of the problem. These operators have immediate access to computerised lists of some 1,500 independent garages available to carry out work on the company's behalf.

Green Flag insists that its emphasis on total information technology, as opposed to conventional systems of uniformed patrol officers and an extensive – and expensive – vehicle fleet, allows the company to pass on handsome system cost savings to customers yet still offer a professional, speedy service in breakdown or other emergencies. All emergency assistance services are handled by its independent network of contractors. There is a well-rehearsed determination to be distinctive and friendly that extends throughout Green Flag.

On average the Green Flag control room handles approximately 5,000 calls a day: in poor weather conditions this figure can rise dramatically. The single busiest time of the day is the morning rush hour, between 8a.m. and 9a.m., and the main pressure days are Monday morning in winter and Friday afternoon in summer. Green Flag called out service operators to over 1 million cars in 1995 and around 80 per cent of these breakdowns were fixed by the roadside. Most cars requiring attention failed to start because of electrical problems. A parallel Green Flag venture provides immediate attention to domestic problems in such areas as plumbing, electricity, glazing, roofing, heating, drainage, and security. This is aimed at both domestic customers and business users, such as utility companies, banks, building societies, insurance companies and housing authorities.

How does Green Flag rate?

Pay:	good
Benefits:	average
Communications:	excellent
Training:	very good
Career development:	good
Morale:	very good

People and personnel policies

Green Flag stands or falls on the quality and efficiency of its employees. They make the crucial link with the customer, whether the problem is on the road, in the home or while on holiday abroad. At first glance then, this might imply that Green Flag's recruitment policy should be far from problematical: simply a question of hiring the region's most experienced call centre personnel. But during the last decade, the Leeds/Bradford area has exploded into one of Europe's prime call centre regions. More than 10,000 people are employed in the broader call centre business, so expertise, even experience, in effective handling of this specialised form of communication is at a premium. The reasons for this astonishing growth are many and varied. All of which has not made life easy for Green Flag. When it set up operations 25 years ago, it was the only such local telephone operation of its kind. Today, it faces competition for employees from many other businesses ranging from Direct Line and N&P to Empire Stores and other catalogue companies. Green Flag knows that many of these rival operations, particularly the newer ventures, invariably use it to benchmark their call centre procedures – and often target some of its trained staff.

This means that Green Flag needs to offer a competitive reward package as well as an attractive environment in which to work. Human resources director Beverley Proctor says 'Green Flag is a standard-setter in call centre management. We put in place many of the systems and policy approaches at an early stage. This means that our professional environment is highly attractive to people who want to work in a call centre environment. We accept that some people move on, but many return, having broadened their expertise and competence. Having worked in different call centres, and been able to look at things through different eyes, there is no reason why they should not make a further contribution to our organisation'. This flexible approach is unavoidable in the Leeds telesales hothouse, argues Proctor. She sees a new shape of career development emerging which embraces cross-functional experience and a broader knowledge/experience base as increasingly important elements. She is blunt about Green Flag's role. We don't go out and mend cars or fix leaks. We are a call centre, a communications complex needing, above all, people with telephone skills.' So it makes recruitment sense, for instance, to have all initial job applications made by telephone. In training, emphasis is placed on keying and listening skills – the two vital areas of expertise for call centre staff – often by simulating the different types of calls and watching the reaction of the trainee.

The reward package is market-driven. Proctor says that as in most sales and call centre driven operations, pay contains a sizeable variable – or performance-related – element. This proportion of the pay increases with seniority. Green Flag's benefits portfolio includes pension, life insurance, health insurance, subsidised restaurant facilities and free membership of the company's assistance services.

The onus for career development within the company lies firmly with the individual. Formal review will take place with the manager annually but Green Flag expects its people to seize opportunities for themselves and to apply for assignments as they become available.

Contact address

Beverley Proctor,
Human Resources Director,
Green Flag Limited,
PO Box 300,
Leeds LS99 2LZ.
Telephone: 01132 393666.
Fax: 01274 658 164.

Guinness PLC

Guinness is a highly successful international drinks company which is based in the United Kingdom. Its portfolio of alcoholic drinks includes some of the world's most distinctive brands such as Johnnie Walker, Bell's and Dewar's Scotch whiskies, Gordon's and Tanqueray gins and the famous Guinness stout. Demand for Guinness PLC products across the globe is growing – the company reported sales of £4.7 billion and pre-tax profits of £876 million in 1995. The group includes Guinness Brewing Worldwide which employs 12,500 people, and United Distillers which has staff of 9,000.

Guinness at a glance

Employees: 25,000 worldwide, 6,000 UK
Annual staff attrition rate: 6 per cent
Key locations: London (HQ), Edinburgh, Runcorn, various distilling, brewing and distribution locations in the UK
Av. annual graduate recruitment: 30 (UK)
Annual intake: n/a

An inside view

Guinness is one of the world's most famous brand names. The distinctive creamy stout, first brewed on the banks of the River Liffey in Dublin, has become an archetype of Irish romantic imagery. It is also one of greatest commercial success stories in world brewing. Today Guinness products are brewed in 49 countries and drunk in more than 140 territories worldwide. Customer demand is thriving as the stout finds new advocates – and fresh business partners – around the globe.

But thirst for the group's products extends beyond the Guinness range of beers and lagers to its other core sector: Scotch whiskies. In 1987 the group created United Distillers (UD) to house a range of world class Scotch whiskies, Bourbons, gins, vodkas, rums and brandies. Guinness has also taken a 34 per cent shareholding in the highly respected French wines and spirits house Moet Hennessy. UD now operates 15 joint ventures with Moet Hennessy in expanding markets in Asia, the US, central America and Europe. The focus of group effort now comes in building volume and market share in mature, generally low inflation, territories and making significant investment in emerging markets, often with outstanding local partners. According to chairman Anthony Greener, Guinness needs to capitalise on its understanding of its consumers and to enhance the efficiency of its total business system to create greater success for the company.

Human resources director John de Leeuw says that the group sees brewing and spirits as a single consumer market where growth will largely be achieved by organic means. 'Essentially our playing field is alcoholic drinks and our goal is to be the best in that sector.' Within the two principal divisions – beer and spirits – the structure has changed radically in the last few years. In United Distillers, for example, although the business has adopted a flatter structure the number of regions has grown from four to six and the tally of direct reports to the MD has risen from eight to 12. The PLC is not an anonymous holding company but rather the strategic heart of the business which guides and directs the divisions. But nonetheless UD and Guinness Brewing Worldwide enjoy considerable operational freedom to develop local and international markets. Both divisions are market leaders in their own sectors, generating the highest profitability in each industry.

How does Guinness rate?

Pay:	superb
Benefits:	excellent
Communications:	good
Training:	superb
Career development:	excellent
Morale:	excellent

People and personnel policies

Recent changes to the Guinness graduate recruitment programme reflect, in part, how the strategic imperatives of the business have shifted in the 1990s. The graduate programme was an extensive affair – based largely on the UK and Ireland – where hundreds of candidates were interviewed. In 1996 the orientation of the initiative was substantially amended to take account of more global priorities in the company and to translate anticipated future recruitment forecasts into concrete targets. De Leeuw comments that each of the regions develops a business plan for the following five years which demonstrates the likely requirement in terms of skills and personnel. This is absorbed by human resources in London into a groupwide plan.

He says that one of the key commercial drivers has been market excellence. So, from a human resources perspective, Guinness needs to find superb people and to support them with suitable training and reward packages. The company focuses on constantly upgrading the quality of its people, putting in place proper processes to continuously assess performance, spending time at cross-functional forums of senior executives to achieve a shared judgement of who the high potential people are and then introducing a much more structured career development programme, and linking career development to future organisational structures.

Traditionally there has been an induction programme for new entrants to the company. A course of four core modules would have been completed during the first two years. This approach is currently being revised. In future new recruits will spend six months in post before an assessment is made of their training needs. Then a course is tailor-made to suit their particular requirements. Some entrants will have certain needs in common and so a modular approach will be appropriate here. 'Within our training portfolio we intend to be more flexible than we have been in the past.' Training used to be decentralised but recently the training plans of the divisions have been supplemented by a group initiative which will be implemented in the next two to three years and will focus on the management culture. Lower level training is also a high priority and a lot of work has been done with Investors in People.

De Leeuw is adamant that people should not be restricted to small pools inside operational groups. 'People are a group resource. I do not like the parochicalism which says, for example, this person is extremely talented but belongs to Latin America and should stay there. People who have the potential to be future general managers should be able to move between functions and regions for career development. We have already started to make an impact on cross-functional thinking. If you look at our executive group of 500 managers, and compare three years ago with today to see how many cross-functional job changes there have been, it is a significant improvement. Within Guinness, traditionally it has not been necessary to have cross-functional moves to succeed, but if there are opportunities available there should be no barriers to exploiting them. The starting point is what do we need from a commercial point of view and then what is best for the individual. Then I do not want any barriers.'

Guinness is a great innovator in terms of the reward package. The company sees reward as a spur to the right behaviour for commercial success. Some 20 workshops were held among senior executives across the world to identify new ways of rewarding people for appropriate

behaviour. Now the process has been extended to lower level employees and is generating equally novel ideas. Among the ideas put forward are profit-shares which kick in for everyone, shares in operating companies for local employees and the abolition of narrow pay bands in favour of flexibility in broad bands.

One of the key threads of the Guinness employment philosophy is its policy of active communication with the workforce. Almost every mechanism of effective dialogue is used. At results time, for example, the centre prepares a team briefing for the entire workforce which includes a video from the managing director, face-to-face presentations by local managers and a feedback approach which goes through line managers to the top of the company. The group invests heavily in employee communications through sophisticated publications, regular departmental briefings and videos, and bi-annual employee attitude surveys.

In Summer 1997, Guinness announced that it was in merger negotiations with Grand Metropolitan.

Contact address

Human resources department, Guinness PLC, 39 Portman Square, London W1H 0EE.
Telephone: 0171 486 0288.
Fax: 0171 486 4968.

Halifax Building Society

The Halifax is best known as Britain's – indeed the world's – largest building society. In June 1997 this tag will become irrelevant as it prepares to launch as a stock market quoted public company, following a merger with the Leeds. The Halifax plc will be among the top 25 FTSE quoted companies and operate in a much broader market than solely savings and loans. The new Halifax, which in the past has long been regarded as among the best employers in its sector, will have a total workforce of 36,000.

Halifax at a glance

Employees: 36,000
Annual staff attrition rate: 10 per cent
Key locations: Halifax (HQ), and sites
    throughout the UK
Av. annual graduate recruitment: 100
Annual intake: n/a

An inside view

The Halifax stands on the verge of a major leap forward. As this book is published it converts from its mutual tradition to a broadly-based financial services company. Central to the success of the corporate launch will be its people policy. The Halifax – as the UK's number one building society – is often regarded as a thorough, understanding but purposeful employer. Its new identiy will inject unrivalled employment opportunities.

The Halifax Building Society has – for many years – been the standard-bearer of its market sector. It has been in the vanguard of the customer service revolution and the introduction of new products in the financial services arena.

But the society's managers have not been slow to realise that the pace of change in financial services requires new forms and fresh organisational structures. The merger with the Leeds – another heavyweight player – and the planned conversion will radically change the way in which the new group will do business.

'The term *building society* locks into people's minds thoughts of just mortgages and savings. Today, the Halifax is more, much more, than that. When we convert, we will be in the top 25 of FTSE companies. Immediately,' says John Lee, its human resources director. Operations extend from housing – mortgages and estate agents; short-term loan and credit facilities such as savings, loans and credit cards; cash transactions – bank services with a checking account; long-term savings, which mean financial service in its broadest sense; general insurance to protect property and the family, right through to a fully fledged treasury business. The 1997 Halifax is a multi-faceted financial services group closely focused on the individual and his or her family, as opposed to a commercial financier providing credit for industry or mega loans to the Third World. The total payroll is about 36,000, including part-time employees. After flotation the Halifax will be one of the largest plc companies headquartered outside London/South East.

In its headquarters conurbation in Halifax and Leeds, West Yorkshire, it employs 5,000. As a business which will stand or fall by its ability to respond to public need, public scrutiny and public service, it has to be, indeed wants to be, a company with a reputation for providing quality employment on whatever level within the organisation you choose to focus.

But how does the Halifax define quality employment? For Lee it means that each individual has an interesting and absorbing job, be it senior or junior. 'If you are a cashier in a branch, you are doing work that is more, much more than just a question of sitting there and pressing buttons.' The Halifax wants to invest in each employee as an individual. So it has to constantly monitor personal development – and work to shape each employee's skills, thus enabling them to do more effective work within the organisation. It must provide real scope for the employee to maintain this growth in abilities, and, recognising the breadth of the company's operations and the increasing likelihood of career changes by the individual, to see that this covers a range of jobs.

How does Halifax rate ?

Pay:	very good
Benefits:	good
Communications:	good
Training:	very good
Career deveopment:	excellent
Morale:	good

People and personnel policies

The Halifax, as the sector's standard-setter, wants to create an environment which is alert to individual choice and achievement. It has steadily introduced advanced HR techniques to offer an unparalleled employment package.

The jobs for life concept is now generally regarded as outmoded – both employer and employee relish freedom of choice above such a formal long-term commitment. Yet there is still much the employer can do to ensure that staff are fully equipped for the job market if they – or the business – feel the need to part company. Lee says that the Halifax is a strong advocate of employability – giving employees, through the best possible training, career guidance and intellectual opportunity, the chance to ensure that they will reach a standard in the financial sector that makes alternative employers ready, even anxious, to take them on. This is not, he insists, a smokescreen for downsizing. Rather, it recognises that for whatever reason – domestic change, marital development, ambition or restlessness – an employee may need to leave. Equipping them for success in the outside job market is a logical extension of training them for the tasks they do in the company.

'Once an employee has settled in, we then provide considerable scope for them to achieve, through work and merit, a salary well beyond the average rate for the sector. This gives us actual pay practice which is ahead of the median,' he says. Salary reviews are made annually on performance and merit. There are obvious fringe benefits but in the current tax regime, having an employers' mortgage is of less importance than can sometimes be the case. The benefits package is much broader than this, of course, covering access to all products at preferential rates – tax man permitting – and a strongly-funded, highly regarded pensions package as well as, at relevant levels of seniority, healthcare and company car schemes.

It is a reflection of this patiently developed employment policy, and the quality of staff that it has trained and retained, that the Halifax is able to convert to a plc without a major recruitment programme. The inner strength and skills base was already in place. 'This was a big organisation performing well before the decision to convert. It did not have to first go for a brain transplant and then undertake a fitness course,' Lee remarks.

Training extends across three levels: product training and familiarisation with the equipment needed to do the job; managing the best possible customer service; and selling skills. These all contribute to the personal development of an individual, help career development and place them in line for internal promotion. 'We run a system of very carefully planned appointments throughout the company. We are continually thinking about the jobs in which we want to place people so management has to spend a fair bit of its time planning and developing careers.' He continues 'We are very clear that in this business, which has been remodelled back

from the customer, it is the individual who gives you the added value and makes a difference to the bottom line'.'

The Halifax with 20 million individual customers, nearly 9 million of whom will soon qualify as shareholders, is about to undertake the largest ever share flotation in UK history.

Contact address

Mr D G Thornbarrow,
General Manager,
Group Personnel,
Halifax Building Society,
Trinity Road, Halifax,
West Yorkshire HX1 2RG.
Telephone: 01422 333333.
Fax: 01422 333000.

Hewlett-Packard Limited

One of the world's most impressive and successful multinationals, Hewlett-Packard is widely praised for its innovation, originality, production quality, effective organisation, marketing capacities and people management. It was chosen as the corporate performer of the year in 1995 by *Forbes* magazine. The company has multiplied in size and scope since its foundation in 1938 but it remains true to its core values which is part of the reason for its outstanding performance. As an employer, H-P is among the very best, providing superb reward packages, substantial freedom of operation, leading edge projects to which individuals can make major contributions and a degree of openness rarely found elsewhere.

Hewlett-Packard at a glance

Employees: 110,000 worldwide, 5,300 UK
Annual staff attrition rate: 3 per cent
Key locations: 19 in the UK. HQ –
  Bracknell; H-P labs/computer
  peripherals – Bristol; telecom
  systems/microwave – South
  Queensferry; fibre optics – Ipswich;
  messaging/components marketing –
  Wokingham
Annual graduate recruitment: 100
Annual intake: 500

An inside view

Hewlett-Packard continues to astonish. This remarkable enterprise – in the teeth of relentless competition and accelerating technological advance – has set the standard for innovation and excellence in its industries against which others must perform. In five years H-P has doubled the size of its business by all reliable measures – sales, earnings per share, return on shareholder equity. In 1996 the company increased its net earnings by 8 per cent to $2.58 billion. Turnover was up, in the same period, by 16 per cent to $38.4 billion. At the same time the influential *Forbes* magazine named H-P as its corporate performer of the year against stiff competition from General Electric, Intel, Johnson & Johnson and Wells Fargo. The scale of the Hewlett-Packard achievement can be seen in the number of employees which it has added worldwide in the last decade. Computer companies reduced their workforces dramatically in the late 1980s and early 1990s but HP now employs 20,000 people more than it did in 1986. *Forbes* comments that IBM shed half its employee numbers in the same period.

The story of the company started in 1938 when Bill Hewlett and David Packard began working on measurement equipment part-time, with only $538 in the bank. Their oscillators impressed Walt

Disney which ordered eight units for production on its film *Fantasia*. In 1939 Hewlett tossed a coin to see whether his name or Packard's would go first in the Hewlett-Packard company name; in 1940 H-P reported revenues of $34,000. Today global sales stand at $31.5 billion, the company employs 105,000 people, it is the second largest American shipper of PCs and the world market leader in laser printers. H-P is active in PCs, laser and ink jet printers, UNIX machines, information storage, test and measurement, wireless communication, chemical analysis and healthcare. The company is ranked as the tenth most admired corporation in the US as assessed by *Fortune* magazine and operates the fifth most valuable brand name in the world. Above all else, H-P is respected for its vision. It invests $2 billion annually in research and development, a third of which comes to the UK. The British business is regarded by corporate chiefs as the primary role model for an H-P national subsidiary.

The company looks at least a decade into the future and identifies projected commercial and personal needs in electronics. Among its current projects based at H-P labs in Bristol is the home communications configuration of 2010. This suggests a single screen which will be the source of interactive television, telecommunications, video and computing. Users will have a small terminal with a keyboard which will allow them to order goods, pay bills, select films or music choices, hold multi-level telephone conversations and access computer networks. This is one of only nine futuristic projects in which H-P is currently engaged. Key to understanding the rationale for all of them is that they

will provide a platform for H-P's medium and long-term commercial interests. These are decidedly not altruistic investigations into the possible pattern of electronics in the future. They are hard-nosed business initiatives to locate novel sources of profits in the new century. It is this degree of commitment which distinguishes H-P from many of its direct competitors.

Lew Platt, global CEO, told directors of the company that despite its major successes in a range of product areas and geographical regions H-P should not rest on its laurels. This was barely a year after the business had improved profits by 135 per cent. This is a pragmatic organisation where a complacent attitude is strongly discouraged. H-P is also marked by the high degree of integrity of its people.

How does Hewlett-Packard rate?

Pay:	excellent
Benefits:	superb
Communications:	very good
Training:	excellent
Career development:	excellent
Morale:	excellent

People and personnel policies

For 20 years or more H-P has been esteemed as an employer. Its people work extremely hard but they enjoy outstanding benefits. This is a remarkably generous and far-sighted organisation which recruits able and talented people to create the innovative new products of the next generation. An atmosphere of achievement is present in all Hewlett-Packard operations and its new recruits are generally positive people who embrace business challenges.

The company focuses on small manageable teams which are linked directly to a product or service. In the early 1990s when H-P was the first of the sector companies to experience downturn, Hewlett and Packard were recalled to active duty. Their analysis of the company's difficulties was clear cut. H-P should stop acting like a big company and instead embody the speed of operation and decision-making, flexibility and vitality of a small company. Clearly a business employing more than 100,000 people needed to make radical changes. The outcome was that units of no more than 30 people became the structural core of the organisation. Each would concentrate on a particular product or service and the style of H-P would be heavily teamwork-orientated.

To understand how Hewlett-Packard operates, it is important to appreciate the heavy emphasis placed on the team. Equally, H-P attracts people who are innovative in their approach regardless of whether they are in research, sales & marketing or administration. There is a direct line open to the main board in Palo Alto, California for any group which has an original idea. The laser printer story could never have happened in many other businesses. H-P successfully made heavy duty printers for the 3 per cent of the computer market where its existing market lay. In a deeply unfashionable part of the H-P infrastructure in urban Ohio, a

senior local director wanted to go for the 97 per cent of the printer sector. He reasoned that H-P could take Japanese motors and some distinctive Hewlett-Packard features. The immense global marketing muscle of the corporation could then be brought into play. H-P's board was convinced and within a couple of years, printers became the single largest element of the company's income.

Originality, insight, energy and capacity to work with people are fundamentals in this enterprise. And H-P expects to recruit from the top stratum of performers at university. For many years there has been a relationship between Bristol University's science functions and H-P Labs which are close at hand. Many students do work experience at H-P which gives the individual and the company an opportunity to assess each other. Demand for jobs at Hewlett-Packard outstrips capacity. For many alert and aware candidates it is an ideal option. The company has long institutionalised its attitude towards its employees in the renowned H-P Way. This speaks of H-P's belief in its people, respect for an individual's self-esteem, recognition of personal contribution, shared beliefs and responsibility, management by objectives, informality, a chance to learn by mistakes, and a structured approach to training.

This is a company which is among the best payers. H-P also provides one of the most comprehensive benefits packages in industry and the company has a formidable reputation for its training and development programmes. The business provides top notch maternity benefit packages and is highly flexible about return to work. It is almost compulsive about openness and managers speak with coherent frankness about the nature of work in progress, salary structures, H-P's standing in its industries and a whole range of other issues which would be a closed book in other cultures. Internal communications is a vital component in fostering well-founded understanding of the company's goals and project achievements. The management also places strong emphasis on the quality of dialogue provided at cascade meetings. H-P is a well-rounded employer which enjoys a positive rapport with its people, outstanding levels of employee morale and a remarkable name as one of Britain's top companies to work for.

Contact address

Ms Jane Keith,
Recruitment Specialist,
Hewlett-Packard Limited,
Cain Road, Bracknell,
Berks RG12 1HN.
Telephone: 01344 360000.
Fax: 01344 363344.

Hoseasons

In 1945 Hoseasons Holidays booked 200 people for boating trips on the Norfolk Broads. Today 1 million people holiday annually with the company and it sits among the top five employers in the seaside town of Lowestoft. Launched in 1944 by the recently retired harbourmaster, Wally Hoseason, the business has remained a family-run firm. There are still three members of the Hoseason's family actively involved in the business.

Hoseasons at a glance

Employees: 280
Annual staff attrition rate: 2 per cent
Location: Lowestoft, Suffolk
Av. annual graduate recruitment: 3
Annual intake: 30

An inside view

Two hundred and eighty people are employed in the Lowestoft-based £2.5 million headquarters which the company moved into three years ago. The purpose-built development includes state-of-the-art telecommunications and a bespoke reservations system. Hoseasons has a reputation for investment in IT and has led the market in developing a comprehensive web site based around its products. Ninety per cent of Hoseasons' employees are full-time; 75 per cent are in sales, 10 per cent in management, 5 per cent in technical sales, 5 per cent in marketing and 5 per cent in accounts.

The last few years has been a period of intense development. The company has increased its holiday business to include the All Canada Travel Holidays brochure and Hoseasons Country Cottages.

Launched in September 1996 with a budget of over £1 million, Hoseasons Country Cottages offers 250 cottages throughout England, Scotland and Wales. Other Hoseasons brochures include: Holidays in Britain, Boating in Britain and Cruising in France and Holland.

A further diversification within the group has been the development of Hoseasons Marketing Systems which provides a range of direct marketing services. The latest account to join an impressive range of clients is the Reader's Digest Group.

Hoseasons work with 4,250 UK travel agents and 30 overseas. Annual sales from holidays are approximately £65 million and £3 million weekly at peak time.

Richard Overy explained that the recent growth and diversification has altered the company from being mostly a part-time employer to an operation where a major percentage of the staff are now full-time. 'Our business used to be very seasonal but is now spread throughout the year. We now have the Investors In People standard and being a service company, we place an enormous amount of importance on the development of our staff as frontline representatives of Hoseasons.'

Recruitment throughout the group is done through an agency which uses a method of psychometric testing. All would-be employees are shortlisted through the agency and recruits go on to do their internal training within the company. 'We do not think that qualifications such as NVQs are appropriate within our training. We believe that our staff should be multi-disciplined. For instance, we expect that 80 percent of our employees are able to deal with 80 per cent of our telephone queries, whatever the subject. The only way we can be effective is by using the skills that people offer. We can only grow through our staff and we need a team which is service-orientated and also individually motivated. These are the sort of people who succeed at Hoseasons. As long as our sales people have a good basic education then the sky is the limit.'

Hoseasons has a board of five directors, a managing director and a chairman. This is a low attrition rate company. Richard Overy has been with Hoseasons for 18 years. He was previously a computer programmer within a government department. 'I have found that people are encouraged to take on as much as they can cope with. We encourage lots of responsibility and the progression of an employee is, to a great extent, in the individual's hands. People have the chance to move up through the company; not even all our directors have formal qualifications.'

Hoseasons are proud of their place in the travel business and have a number of 'firsts' which the company believes are worth talking about. It was: the first company to develop the use of tele-sales for holiday bookings; the first company to develop a dial-a-brochure service; the first in the business to use colour advertising in

the national and specialist press; the first company to develop an on-line 'real-time' computer booking service; and the first to establish a viewdata service for UK self-catering holidays. This enables agents in Britain and abroad to phone the Hoseasons computer, look for vacancies and make bookings by remote control.

The group has also won a series of awards over the years. Two gained in 1996-7 were 'Best Holidays Afloat Operator', awarded for the tenth time running by *Travel Weekly* magazine and 'Top Holidays Afloat Company' which was awarded to Hoseasons for the third consecutive year by co-sponsors American Express and the *Travel Trade Gazette*.

How does Hoseasons rate ?

Pay:	excellent
Benefits:	very good
Communications:	good
Training:	very good
Career development:	good
Morale:	very good

People and personnel policies

Pay conditions at Hoseasons are considered to be excellent. 'We have to pay well to keep the best employees available and if necessary we will up our pay to stay ahead of the market', Richard Overy explains.

Holiday entitlement is between four and five weeks a year. Statutory sickness pay conditions are as normal but after one year's employment, the company will pay full salary for six weeks, followed by half salary for a further six weeks. The position after this is reviewed according to circumstances.

A free medical examination and eye test are available after one year's employment and staff are also eligible to join the BUPA company scheme after their first 12 months with Hoseasons.

Hoseasons run a standard contributory pension scheme which also provides life assurance and disability benefits which are paid for by the company. A recent change in policy has resulted in part-time staff benefiting from the same employment conditions as full-time staff. 'This has been done as a commitment by the company to ensure our part-time staff a guaranteed level of income annually. At the same time we expect a commitment back which guarantees agreed work rotas and set targets,' Overy says.

A Training for All policy is part of the philosophy behind the running of Hoseasons. Internal training is available at all levels and external trainers are brought in to run a series of courses throughout each year. For instance, skill development sessions for 1997 examine areas such as the use of your voice, developing quality relationships, and persuading people to buy.

A bi-monthly newsletter keeps staff informed of the latest news and developments within the company. There are also twice yearly 'calls to arms' sessions where the chairman, James Hoseason, takes the opportunity of telling staff how the company is doing and gives projections for the following few months. Monthly Board Meetings also provide feedback for the staff. Richard Overy explains that with the flat structure of the

company word passes quickly around. 'We don't have many levels within the company and communication is fortunately fast and informal.'

Ninety per cent of all Hoseason's staff are women. Yvonne Borg, Travel Trade Director sits on the Board and three out of five managers are women. 'Seventy-five per cent of staff are in sales and this is a job which is particularly attractive to women with families, as a rota system can fit around schools and holidays.'

Hoseasons staff are rightly proud of their premises in Lowestoft. The building looks good and has improved the area it is in. The company believes in supporting the local community and is involved in various local charities. One involvement is in Lowestoft 2000 and Futura which are both initiatives which work in areas of social deprivation.

Hoseasons is very aware of the important role it plays, not just as a provider of quality holidays but as a major employer in an area of high unemployment.

Contact address

Richard Overy,
Hoseasons Holidays,
Sunway House,
Raglan Road,
Lowestoft,
Suffolk, NR32 2LW.
Telephone: 01502 500505.
Fax: 01502 584962.

Howell Henry Chaldecott Lury and Partners

HHCL was always going to be different because of the particular period in which it was launched, the October of 1987, when the stock markets fell to earth. Although based from the beginning on sound business principles, there couldn't have been a tougher birthday for a new advertising agency. But run strictly on commercial lines, it has managed to combine a hard-nosed money attitude with extraordinary creativity to become unique in its industry. Like so many really successful companies which continually break new ground, it takes the same attitude towards its employees as it customers: an holistic approach in which the whole is greater than the sum of the parts.

HHCL at a glance

Employees: 160
Annual staff attrition rate: 1 per cent
Key locations: London
Av. annual graduate recruitment: n/a
Annual intake: 10% (driven by growth)

An inside view

The key to HHCL's extraordinary success is the way it treats its own people and its clients. The advertising business has generally centred on a commission-payment basis. There are no concessions paid in this company. Everyone from the janitor to the managing director receives a salary, plus 10 per cent of the profits, which are shared equally. HHCL works as a team and every client is regarded as special, but equal.

Brief but brilliant, would be one way of describing the history of HHCL. Only a year after its own launch, industry competitors were looking with awe at its campaigns for *Marie Claire* magazine and Molson Canadian Lager. In 1989, only two years old, it was named as Agency of the Year. Its clients today include the AA, Britvic, Martini, National Savings, and Guinness Ireland. It continues to win pitch after pitch but sometimes – as with Allied Domecq's Tequila brand, it is simply handed the business because of the company's performance. HHCL has been self-financed and profitable since start up and annual turnover is now more than £10 million.

Robin Azis, who is managing director of HHCL and Partners, without actually having the title (which is typical of the human resource attitude), says that working for the company is like receiving a complete education in the advertising industry.

When the world changes fundamentally, survival depends on fundamental change; and this company brought fundamental change to the industry. Change is a six-letter word, easy to talk about, easy even to identify but very hard to do. The company's statement of intent says that advertising agencies must not only change how and what they do, but 'must also change how they see. More conventional marketing is no longer the answer, we need a different marketing, a new approach, a new way of seeing'.

How does HHCL rate?

Pay:	very good
Benefits:	good
Communications:	excellent
Training:	very good
Career development:	good
Morale:	very good

People and personnel policies

HHCL was different from the beginning, and the way the company was run internally, as well as externally, showed just that. In almost every way, it treats employees differently. From the first day as a new employee, there is equality and this philosophy applies from top to bottom. There are 20 partners in the company but being a partner does not necessarily equate to the skills that are usually found in the advertising business. 'It all depends on your overall contribution to the company as a whole,' says Azis. As an example, one employee

became a partner in recognition of the great contribution made to HHCL in the area of work environment.

'It's attitude that counts here in making you a partner.' That attitude is cemented in the company's performance and development review policy. 'We are committed to becoming a learning organisation where people develop and grow in a positive way and within which everyone's potential is nurtured. We want an environment where everyone's contribution to achieving the company's objectives is recognised, fairly evaluated and valued.' HHCL is direct in the way it talks to its employees. 'We will try to meet your development needs, but you need to drive the process,' it says.

The success of the system cannot be measured in norms. In some ways, this company is a contradiction, and certainly there are those who would say it is contrary. It may be difficult to accept that a modern dynamo of the advertising sector does not provide any form of pensionary compensation for its employees. But that is fact, and admitted openly. As Robin Azis puts it bluntly 'We do not give people pensions. There is no company pension plan. At the outset, most employees had private pension arrangements but as we have grown, younger people have come in and I think we are now moving to having our own pension plan.'

If having no company pension plan is unusual, then so is the rest of the operation. 'Most advertising agencies are very departmentalised and very categorised. They work in set ways. There are no departments in this company. Everything is mixed up. We all come into contact with different disciplines.'

Wonderful communications, within a

corporate entity, are based almost entirely on teamwork, in the view of HHCL and it definitely practises what it preaches. For example, the annual self-assessment exercise is a democratic team effort, with the assessors being chosen by the person being assessed. Every six months, all the employees are physically moved around. 'This is to avoid creating cliques. It broadens the mind,' says Azis. There is a company ban on internal memorandums, written in traditional fashion. Working and communicating in this company comes from the next generation, or at least the way HHCL sees that generation evolving. On the last Thursday of each month, the company holds a communications meeting at a club, away from the office. 'Everyone turns up,' says Azis. 'We talk about what we are producing for our clients, company issues, new business, personnel matters – this is a complete, open meeting, an exchange of information. There are no holds barred – and everyone is treated the same.'

One of the most unusual aspects of this entire operational philosophy is that everyone employed at HHCL talks about everything – inside the office. The advertising business is traditionally gossip-ridden, and much of the gossip takes place in homes, health clubs, bars and restaurants. Keeping secrets is very important. Giving away information about clients and campaigns can be destructive. 'Our philosophy is that if you want to keep a secret, you tell everyone about it and then there are no secrets. But this is based on the total commitment that nothing is said outside the office.'

Training is supremely important because HHCL represents a unique culture. 'When people come into this company from the outside, they don't understand our systems because we are completely different from anyone else.' They are inducted into HHCL through a thorough series of instructional courses that cover the operating and management structures of the company. The company believes in collaboration, teamwork and individualism at the same time – a definite mix. Each employee has a mobile phone with a stated number. If they want to work at home, on the train, at a traditional desk, or sitting on a bean bag in an office corridor – whatever – it happens here. 'Everyone is an adult,' says Azis. 'If you trust, treat and empower them, you'll get it back in return. There is no time clock environment.'

The advertising industry is always talking about various products being really different. HHCL thinks that its performance speaks for itself. To mark the company's birthday, the staff traditionally take a day out, mostly to enjoy themselves and celebrate another year of a remarkable organisation.

Contact address

Robin Azis,
HHCL and Partners,
Kent House, 14–17 Market Place,
Great Titchfield Street,
London W1N 7AJ.
Tel: 0171 436 3333.
Fax: 0171 436 2677.

IBM UK Holdings Limited

The IBM story is one of the most remarkable in corporate history – and no part of its progress has been more enlightening than its transformation in the 1990s. The archetypal US multinational weathered heavy storms in the early part of this decade. Many thought the unthinkable – that IBM might not emerge from the other side of its horrendous difficulties. The resilience of the world's leading computer company was thoroughly tested. Today it has won the plaudits of industry worldwide by creating a new business out of the old. Though it remains true to its traditional values, it has recognised the imperatives of new market conditions and fashioned new approaches and products to meet that demand.

IBM at a glance

Employees: 15,000 in the UK (fixed-term, short-term contracts and students) plus several thousand people supplied by contractors

Staff attrition rate: 2.5–3 per cent

Key locations: Portsmouth (HQ), London and Greenock plus offices in major cities

Active graduate recruitment: 100

Annual intake: c.500

An inside view

IBM is a company of superlatives. Stretching back to its foundation as a business which made and marketed accounting machines, IBM has dominated. The largest business in its market sectors, it has commanded a global portfolio of clients which is breathtaking. IBM became the industry standard. No CEO was ever fired for buying the company's kit. Its international power was legendary as one of the world's most potent multinationals; countries queued to invite IBM to set up operations in their territories. The status of global market leader in the computer industry bred a certain degree of detachment, aloofness and outright arrogance which served Big Blue for decades. Businesses global and local, government departments and international public sector bodies actively needed IBM's powerhouse mainframes to function – and no other systems were nearly as acceptable.

The company was a shining example of international commercialism, paying great attention to the servicing of clients and the development of its technology. But in the 1980s the plot began to unravel. The company made two fundamental mistakes which were born out of its egocentric worldview. First it initially dismissed the PC (personal computer) as irrelevant to its mainstream business. Looking back this seems incredible but since IBM's core business was selling big boxes to big companies, the PC appeared a distraction. The next major failure was to misread market trends which suggested that software applications would become more important than the hardware. Since IBM was a company which sold machines rather than customer solutions again the error is predictable. But the penalty for these two crucial errors was the first financial losses in the global business's career.

Given IBM's tradition of never doing anything in a small way, the corporate losses were staggering. Critics and commentators forecast that if IBM were to emerge from this period, it would be a much smaller company without the capacity to compete with the big players. But they reckoned without its capacity to reinvent itself. A key to IBM's recovery was a genuine commitment to learn from its mistakes. Previously, the core of all decision making was its management committee in the corporate headquarters. While rivals devolved power down the line, IBM reinforced the authority of top executives. This was changed in line with prevailing management philosophy and had an immediate effect in releasing the talent and ambition of able IBM managers. The catharsis of going deeply into the red knocked off some of the arrogance which had restricted an assessment of changing market conditions.

Another crucial change was the business approach. The aim was no longer solely to sell its hardware into clients. It moved to a greater consultancy role – understanding customer business issues and locating appropriate solutions. Heavy investment has gone into developing new technology and establishing relationships with a much wider range of expert suppliers. As a telling sign of the new orthodoxy, IBM has also launched a series of joint ventures with rivals to share the costs of investment in new products and establishing common industry standards which are not purely IBM-driven. This is all a far cry from ten years ago. The result can be seen in its figures which are back where they belong.

How does IBM rate?

Pay:	good
Benefits:	excellent
Communications:	very good
Training:	excellent
Career development:	very good
Morale:	good

People and personnel policies

The UK companies of IBM have always been much more nimble than some of the parent's other national subsidiaries. Today, IBM employs around 15,000 people throughout the United Kingdom – the two largest sites being the headquarters at North Harbour, Portsmouth and IBM's manufacturing facility in Greenock on the banks of the Clyde. These people are engaged in manufacturing, sales, marketing, customer service, technical and administration.

Human resources director Ann Grinstead says 'Qualification is not the most important priority in recruitment.

We still recruit a high percentage of arts graduates rather than science or computer science students. Personal qualities are more relevant to us. We want candidates to be able to demonstrate some degree of achievement in their studies or their outside interests. IBM looks for people who have width in their activities, are articulate, mature in their thinking, and perform well in teams. Most graduates today are computer literate to some degree.'

Once inside the company, training is intensive. IBM majors on the quality of the expertise which it provides in extensive periods of detailed formal as well as on-the-job training. All employees are regularly updated on the IBM commitments (to win in the marketplace, to execute with urgency and to teamwork), its strategic imperatives, its principles and its vision. The IBM vision is to be the most successful and important information technology company by helping its customers to apply extraordinary technology, and for IBM to be the basic source for most of what is new in the industry. Its eight principles embrace its market focus, standards for success and commitment to teamwork, its people and its communities.

In the past, people who reached the top in IBM had started at the bottom and worked their way up the organisation. The company is now more flexible about recruiting from outside to fill more senior posts and using fixed-term contracts. 'We say to potential recruits: come and take advantage of our world class training and the exposure to our business groups. Once they join us most want to stay.'

Some of the credit for IBM's recent success is due to a change in organisation. 'Like many large companies, we have moved to a much flatter structure. Today, you would rarely see more than four levels between the general manager and the shop floor. We are also organised in a number of vertical crossborder business units rather than strict country functions. Many of our organisations are now wholly global which has cut reporting lines. It is important that people feel that they are close enough to the top so that decisions can be taken quickly and also that systems are sufficiently in common to create efficiencies.' In the last year IBM has invested in creating a 'common currency' in its people, so that when the global general manager looks down his unit he will find common approaches to pay, rewards, appraisal, training and appeals.

Increasingly, IBM is expanding the variable aspect of the pay package. This rewards individuals for their personal performance and, importantly, contribution to the team. For employees up to 10 per cent of pay is linked to the performance of both the unit and IBM UK. The pay of senior managers is also linked to the performance of IBM Europe. In the future the variable element will be linked mainly to the business unit and IBM corporate, and less to national companies. All regular employees are given private health insurance and are covered by the company's pension scheme.

Contact address

Ann Grinstead,
Human Resources Director,
IBM UK Limited, North Harbour,
Portsmouth PO6 3AU.
Telephone: 01705 561000.
Fax: 01705 388914.

Iceland

Iceland is Britain's leading specialist frozen food retailer, operating a nationwide chain of 770 stores, which offer the widest choice of frozen foods. Opened on a shoestring with one store in Shropshire in 1970 by two deputy managers from Woolworths, the initial investment of co-founders Malcolm Walker and Peter Hincliffe was £60. The Oswestry store took £90 in its first day and £320 in the first three days. The partners worked out their profits on the back of an envelope and discovered they had achieved gross margins of 30 per cent. Woolworths didn't like this little job on the side and Walker and Hincliffe were sacked. From one store has come 25 years of consistent growth. Iceland is one of only 14 UK growth companies to increase equity earnings year in year out over the past decade.

Iceland at a glance

Employees: 6,000 full-time,
11,000 part-time
Attrition rate (full time): 5 per cent
Key locations: HQ: Deeside; Distribution depots: Milton Keynes, Swindon, Stratford
Graduate recruitment: 20
Annual intake: 600

An inside view

Malcolm Walker, co-founder and currently chairman and chief executive of Iceland, is a persuasive man of considerable conviction who has confounded the traditional market sages, particularly those in the City, by proving through his company's extraordinary success over a quarter of a century, that frozen food can be marketed head-on against fresh food as being more healthy – and win. 'We will continue to educate consumers,' he says, 'that if they want it fresh, buy it frozen'.

His unremitting message has been that 'fresh is frozen'. Walker, the most senior member of the food industry, has been a radical thinker from the beginning, espousing the environmental causes of Greenpeace, and leading the attack on genetically engineered foods.

Like most companies trading in the 1970s, Iceland faced a roller coaster ride of a British economy that was unstable, to say the least. But this instability actually benefited the company. Consumers were nervous and looking for bargains, and frozen food came at prices that seemed reasonable.

By 1979, Iceland had acquired, through takeover and expansion, 28 freezer centres, mainly in the northwest of the country. After further expansion, Iceland went public in 1984, and its flotation on the London Stock Exchange was oversubscribed 113 times – a record for any flotation. Four years after that, it bought out its main competitor, Bejam, adding 270 stores. Today, it has expanded into Northern Ireland. With 770 stores in total and another 20 to 30 additional openings planned in 1997, Iceland's aim to trade nationwide is close to being met. Pre-tax profits for the latest reported year increased by 3.4 per cent to £72.6 million and earnings per share were up almost 2 per cent.

The company's current strong position is largely a result of a major strategic review that took place in 1994 identifying five objectives for future business – strengthening management, enhancing strategic focus, improving store profitability, attacking the cost base and continuing expansion. Says Walker 'We see a great future for Iceland as the leading specialist in frozen food. This is where we have built our business for 25 years, and the market potential remains huge. Training and development have continued to receive the greatest emphasis, as we have sought to involve every single member of staff in our drive to enhance customer service, sales, and profitability.'

In 1996, Iceland were proud to receive Investors in People accreditation.

How does Iceland rate?

Pay:	average
Benefits:	good
Communications:	very good
Training:	very good
Career development:	very good
Morale:	very good

People and personnel policies

'Human resource policy leads where the company is going, it does not follow,' says Jill McWilliams, head of corporate affairs. 'People are the most important part of this organisation. They are cared about, they are not just a number in the 17,000 workforce. We have an unusual attitude for the retail sector. Others find it very refreshing to be treated as individuals.' This attitude comes straight from the heart of the man who co-founded the company, and is still there all these years later. 'The culture of this organisation is quite different from the norm, because it is still led by the person who was there at the beginning. We are very entrepreneurial, but we reflect the spirit of Malcolm Walker. He's a very gutsy retailer and his personality is imprinted on Iceland,' she says.

He identifies himself with crusades as they relate to his business of frozen foods and what he believes is the common good; and that is reflected in how he treats his staff, and how they perform. Controversially, he publicly equates frozen foods with better health and has signed Iceland up to be a leading corporate supporter of the Cancer Research Campaign to encourage Britain, which languishes at the bottom of the Western European league table for vegetable intake, to think again about frozen vegetables as a healthy alternative to fresh. 'Clearly, much needs to be done to encourage people to eat more frozen vegetables,' Walker says.

The Cancer Research Campaign is one of several agencies currently undertaking a nine-nation pan-European study of the connection between diet and cancer, researching the eating habits of more than 400,000 healthy middle-aged men and women; and Iceland, through Malcolm Walker, has already raised more than £100,000 for cancer research by donating a percentage of the price of every pack of frozen vegetables bought from an Iceland store.

Whether this be genuine philanthropy or smart marketing it marks the personality of the man who, more than 25 years on from moonlighting strawberries on the side from his serious Woolworth's job, is still dedicated to being different; particularly as far as his employees are concerned. 'He does not pull any punches,' says McWilliam. 'He makes judgments, and his personality is the most motivating factor in the organisation. He attends a lot of staff training sessions. He is passionate about the company and he conveys this to all employees. They all know, through him, what Iceland is about. He gives the company a lot of purpose, a lot of excitement and a lot of fun. Iceland is a fun company to work for and Malcolm expects very hard work. We get the best out of people by providing an environment in which work is enjoyable – and this largely comes through his personality which cascades down through the organisation.'

Janet Marsden, personnel director, says the employee atmosphere is so different that one visitor reckoned there was something magic going into the staff coffee machine. One of the advantages is fast growth. When she joined in 1980, there was a staff of just 192. Now, there are 17,000 and that means promotion can come pretty quickly. Last year, more than 50 were promoted to the position of trainee store manager. Trainee managers regularly become deputy

managers and deputy managers become store managers.

Iceland is particularly sensitive about not enough women rising to managerial positions in a retail business that should naturally, through its marketplace, be dominated by women. 'We have a very fair policy on promotion,' says McWilliam, 'which centres on the right person, whether male or female, being given the job.' But the trickle-up effect has not so far worked. There is only one female on the nine-member board of directors. 'Females,' she says, 'do not necessarily want to be high flyers. Home life is important and we encourage balancing a career with home life. There are lots of flexi hours here, and part-time work, with very good maternity leave provisions.'

Currently, the company has 65 female store managers and 51 female deputy managers. The key to the future may be seen in the fact that there are currently 38 female trainee managers, which is 23 per cent of the total. The company wants to grow its own female managers, and it has set itself a target of having a quarter of its stores managed by women in two years' time. Store managers are powerful people at Iceland. They are free to talk to whom they want. 'There is a free human resource culture,' says McWilliam. 'There are no barriers and this is not abused either. Along with freedom has come a sense of responsibility.'

Contact address

Janet Marsden, Personnel Director, Iceland Frozen Foods, Second Avenue, Deeside Industrial Park, Deeside, Flintshire CH5 2NW.
Telephone: 01244 830100.
Fax: 01244 814531.

ICI

Imperial Chemical Industries (ICI) is a great industrial powerhouse. Almost since its inception in a great merger of 1926, ICI has been a standard-bearer of corporate Britain and an evocation of many of the qualities which inspire the better UK businesses. Its high emphasis on quality in production, research, marketing and also in the recruitment and development of its people is a hallmark of this business. In 1993 it demerged those interests which now constitute Zeneca but ICI continues to thrive. In 1996 global sales rose by two per cent to £10.5 billion and pre-tax profits were £603 million. ICI employs 64,000 people worldwide.

ICI at a glance

Employees: 64,000 worldwide, 17,700 UK
Staff attrition rate: 5 per cent
Key locations: London (HQ), Billingham, Runcorn, Wilton, Northwich, Ardeer, Slough
Av. annual graduate recruitment: 100
Annual intake: 350

An inside view

Ask any literate undergraduate to name a major British-owned industrial or commercial company and it will not be long before ICI is mentioned. ICI – for decades the epitome of a highly esteemed UK enterprise – remains among the most attractive choices for people leaving university. Its reputation as a quality producer is matched by its standing as a company which provides excellent careers for able people. The company was formed in 1926 by the merger of industrial giants Brunner, Mond, Nobel Industries, United Alkali, and British Dyestuffs. This was the era when many of the great global businesses were forged.

The depth and quality of the founding partners ensured the nascent conglomerate would be a strong international success. But ICI encountered a difficult start – partly prompted by the Wall Street Crash and also because some of the intended moneyspinners did not bear fruit. Growth came, paradoxically, from products which had failed to ignite great hope within the business. Its aggressive management ensured that ICI moved ahead and within a few years, ICI was a dominating force in the global chemical industry. The company was greatly assisted in its cultural development by a progressive industrial relations legacy which it had inherited from Brunner, Mond. In the post-Second World War period ICI extended its product and geographical remit and added further to its reputation as a formidable operation. ICI adopted different strategic and market approaches during the decades which followed but by the early 1990s the business was taking a radical review of its operations. Shortly after it announced major changes to the portfolio of businesses, Lord Hanson bought shares in ICI which led to speculation about a possible takeover. During the Hanson intervention, ICI's chairman asked its merchant bank to provide a lateral thinker to come up with new ideas for the future of ICI. In 1993 this led to the demerger of the highly profitable pharmaceuticals, agrochemicals and biological business which was named Zeneca. The new ICI would concentrate on chemicals with long term potential. Today ICI has eight divisions: paints, acrylics, polyurethanes, explosives, polyester, performance chemicals, chemicals & polymers, and Tioxide, and regional businesses, which consist of operations covering specific territories but outside the scope of the global products.

ICI seeks outstanding performance in every area of its operation through market leadership, technological edge and a world competitive cost base. The strategy of the company is to move into dominant market positions by the quality of its people and products, by market-driven innovation and focusing on quality growth markets worldwide.

How does ICI rate?

Pay:	very good
Benefits:	excellent
Communications:	very good
Training:	superb
Career development:	very good
Morale:	very good

People and personnel policies

ICI has always been a thoroughly attractive option for graduates. Over the decades, ICI's graduate recruitment has fluctuated wildly and in the comparatively recent past the company has brought in many hundreds of people through this route. Today, ICI tends to stick at an annual graduate intake of around 100. One ICI director has described its earlier approach as scatter-gun, whereas now it focuses most of its efforts on a dozen or so universities. To stimulate interest among students at these universities ICI runs a scholarship scheme, and also offers vacation assignments within the business. 'We are still very active among the graduate recruitment networks and we distribute our published material very widely,' says John Watt, general manager, personnel. Given that ICI is science-led, a technical qualification is important in selecting entrants for specific appointments. Beyond that, the company tends to recruit enthusiastic, self-starting individuals who are good communicators. Leadership qualities and a results-orientation are characteristics which ICI's recruiters hope to identify in candidates.

In previous years ICI was the contemporary model of an efficient company. Then a high-performing hierarchy was regarded as the best format for corporate structure. Times have moved on and companies are delayering at a formidable pace. Discrete units have been dissolved in favour of a more flexible environment within the global strands of business. ICI is moving towards a much flatter organisation which derives a great deal of benefit from cross-functional synergies.

There are two strands in the business for training: the on-going skills training which people need for the completion of their daily tasks, and the development programmes and activities which are in place to help people achieve their career potential. The first set of skills training includes subjects as basic as computer techniques, the operation of plant sites and elemental information on each particular task. Everyone will undertake developmental training but graduates in particular will go through a focused programme lasting four to five years. During this period ICI wants graduates to have the opportunity to achieve four key disciplines in a core development programme: personal effectiveness (understanding learning techniques, communication skills), professional effectiveness (how to be more effective in the chosen role), business effectiveness (understanding how the business operates), and managerial effectiveness (how to be a capable manager in ICI).

As the employee moves through this programme other on-going initiatives will be available to meet individual and business need. ICI is keen that its managers learn from the latest developments in management theory and people are regularly sent to the most prestigious business schools to attend leading-edge courses. Graduates will typically attend up to ten full training days a year in addition to on-the-job training. 'We have done a lot of work over the years on what an ideal chief executive looks like in terms of skills, experience and qualities. One of the critical areas of experience is that we would want them to have substantial cross-functional backgrounds

and to have worked in at least two other countries in a senior position,' says Watt. 'We have a facility called career groups where we look at people's progression through functional careers and across sites, and at a senior level across countries, functions and businesses. This helps the individual to locate the right sort of experience for progression through management. Strong leaders emerge from experience across functions and this is an essential requirement for future senior directors of the business.'

Chief executive Charles Miller Smith has determined that the business will be much more global by the early years of the next century and this definition of the essential component factors of future leaders will play a key part in realising his objective. ICI has targeted the Far East, Latin America and South America as sources for new business and great new ICI talent. At present some 40 per cent of all graduate recruits are female. Pay is high but not exceptional but is complemented by a profit-related pay scheme. Benefits, however, are top notch, including a final salary pension scheme. There is a range of other blue chip company benefits and regular employee surveys reveal great workforce pride in the company and satisfaction with its approach.

Contact address

Mr Martin Woods,
ICI Education and Recruitment Manager,
PO Box 90, Wilton, Middlesborough,
Cleveland TS90 8JE.
Telephone: 01642 454144.
Fax: 01642 432444.
Internet: http://www.demon.co.uk/ici/

The Intel Corporation

Intel is one of the great commercial success stories of the last two decades. The company designs and manufactures microprocessors for major computer companies. It has established an outstanding reputation for the excellent quality and commercial applicability of its products. The logos Intel® Inside and Pentium® Processor have become synonymous with leading edge technology and high processing power. In the UK the company has grown in around ten years to a significant force in the international organisation as the base for all its northern European operations. It is a demanding employer with an engineering-led culture and is among the top in its sector for pay, benefits and training.

Intel at a glance

Employees: 600 (UK) + 150 contractors
Annual staff attrition rate: n/a
Key locations: HQ at Swindon, Wiltshire
Average graduate recruitment: 20
Annual intake: 70

An inside view

The information technology revolution has created many new corporate stars. Businesses which started in a small workshop, a university laboratory or even on the dining room table have blossomed into multinationals. Some of the stalwarts of the *Fortune 500* of 20 years ago have fallen by the wayside to be replaced by innovative new companies which brought new ways of doing business, as well as an exceptional range of groundbreaking products and services. Intel is one of these remarkable newcomers. Microprocessors fueled the personal

computer paradigm shift in industry. These minute but vital components, engineered to exquisite degrees of detail, gave the PC its clout. Intel is one of the world's leaders in microprocessor technology – its trademarks *Intel® Inside* and *Pentium® Processor* are famous. Leading computer manufacturers badge their latest machines with these brands to emphasise the quality and innovative nature of the technology on offer.

The culture of these novel enterprises has been a major factor influencing their rapid growth. Most businesses in this sector are either quintessentially Californian in their laid back but creative approach or they are highly driven, commercial and sales-orientated companies. Intel is different again. The heart of this organisation is its engineering and technical excellence. It underpins the personality of the business and gives Intel its distinctive market focus.

Two apparently divergent cultural traditions – personal informality but demanding professional and technical standards – combine in a unique blend to define the Intel approach. The company advocates constructive confrontation – a policy where ideas but not the individuals who champion them are regularly challenged. Meetings are conducted on an adversarial basis and those people who argue most convincingly and passionately regularly win the day. Given Intel's engineering bias, the company also depends heavily on data and it respects well-researched and well-argued proposals.

The UK is the headquarters for its northern European activities. Its people work largely in sales, and customer support and service mainly from its site in Swindon but also it employs a small percentage of its total complement in teleworking from their homes. Intel is propelled by a series of values which include: discipline, results-orientation, risk-taking, providing a great place to work, customer orientation and quality.

How does Intel rate?

Pay:	very good
Benefits:	very good
Communications:	superb
Training:	very good
Career development:	very good
Morale:	very good

People and personnel policies

Intel people are a distinctive group. This is not a normal computer industry company. There are some similarities with the great hardware makers, for example, high emphasis on quality, customer service and product innovation. But the engineering focus creates a more questioning and analytical framework. In the past there has been a tendency to draw from exclusively engineering and computer science graduates but Intel now seeks a broader range of talents and trawls the principal business colleges across the continent. 'We are looking for people who have an adventurous view of the work environment; people who can take the initiative or even risks. They must have an international outlook because we are operating, more and more, in a global market. The willingness to be adaptable is central. Not only to be adaptable in oneself but also to make things change,' says Patrick Bigand, director of human resources. Travel is a key facet of any job in Intel: either because employees are expected to travel on a day-to-day basis or because international assignments are an essential feature of long-term careers with the company.

Intel's value system plays a crucial role in the operational lives of its employees. This is not an amorphous set of statements but a framework within which everyone works. In the first six months every new employee takes a series of courses which introduces them to the way in which the company thinks. 'These sessions cover the way we expect people to behave in Intel. These are typically taught by senior managers and cover such subjects as values, ethics, the way to behave with clients, and constructive confrontation. It can be a little difficult when you are not used to Intel's environment to understand the way in which we do business. These courses show new recruits how we approach relationships both within and outside the business and we make extensive use of role play and case studies.'

These classes are compulsory and form a key part of the early career. From day one, the entrant will be given a line job and teamed up with someone more senior. A formal development plan is sketched out in terms of broad areas of activity which will be given more substance as experience is gained. Once a month there will be one-to-one discussions including performance review and career development discussions. 'Our performance management system requires the one-to-one meetings to be held monthly for it to work effectively,' he says.

Most people work in a given team but increasingly Intel is building cross-functional groups on specific projects. Such taskforces are not based on rank within a group but are more loosely centred and a hierarchy develops on the competence of individual members. The team leader would be responsible for the running of the team and at the end of the project they disband with individuals moving back into their original groups. All training is also done on a completely cross-functional basis, partly to reinforce networks within the company.

Communication is open and direct, and the company uses a variety of techniques to ensure that its messages are disseminated and that employee feedback is actively heard. If individual staff members believe that they are not being treated fairly by their immediate manager they can take any concerns to the most senior level in the company. In some organisations this exists as a policy but once an employee attempts to exercise it,

then they find that their career collapses. In Intel it is a tenet of faith that this mechanism should work well and that no one should be penalised in any way for resorting to its use.

'The philosophy behind pay is that a sizeable proportion of our package is tied into our results. The goal is clearly to be among the top employers. When the company's results are good – and that has been the case for some time now – we are among the very best payers. Pay is related to both individual and corporate performance. If you and the company are doing well your take home pay is going to be much larger than average.

'We also have a stock purchase plan where employees can buy Intel shares at a substantial discount. That is also valuable since the stocks of Intel are performing very well. There is also an additional stock option plan which is a long-term retention scheme for the professionals. We also run a profit-sharing scheme which resulted in an 8 per cent annualised payout in 1995. A new UK pension plan, linked to the profits of Intel, is 5 per cent contributory. There is a free healthcare scheme and comprehensive life and business insurance which is also free.'

Contact address

Human Resources Department,
Intel Corporation (UK) Ltd,
Pipers Way, Swindon, Wiltshire SN3 1RJ.
Telephone: 01793 403000.
Fax: 01793 641440.
Information about Intel is available at:
http://www.intel.com

3i Group plc

Τhe world of venture capital houses has many players but only one dominates. This is 3i. It is by far the largest organisation for the provision of capital for growing businesses in the UK. Formerly known as ICFC and latterly Investors in Industry, 3i is a byword for professionalism, astute selection of investment prospects and commitment to emerging businesses. The group has been in the business of providing corporate capital for longer than any other significant operator and remains successful by sticking to the discipline which it knows best. Human resources policy is geared to continuing the impressive commercial track record of the business.

3i at a glance

Employees: 650
Staff attrition rate: up to 8 per cent
Key locations: Central London (HQ), Solihull and major UK and European towns and cities
Average graduate recruitment: 0
Annual intake: 100

An inside view

If there were only one venture capital company in the UK, that company would be 3i. In its specialised sector of the financial services industry, 3i wins all the plaudits. It is the longest lasting, the biggest by a collection of separate measures, it has the most impressive track record and it has the widest network of dedicated offices. The intellectual rigour, its system of advocacy of candidate investment opportunities

and extensive research facilities and experience combine to provide 3i with an act which is hard to challenge.

Since its inception in 1945, 3i has invested more than £8 billion in 12,000 businesses. More than 900 have subsequently floated on the stock market. It states plainly that its core activity is investment and is not tempted to exploit capital in other ventures. Capital investments come in transactions of anything from £100,000 to £25 million. But, through its network of 18 UK and five mainland European offices, it also takes equity stakes in its client businesses and contributes to the development of innovative responses to commercial opportunities. Chief executive Ewen Macpherson reported in March 1996 that the company earned £520.8 million which represents 25 per cent of all shareholder funds. This gives some measure of the 3i hit rate. Management buy-outs and buy-ins command a high share of its investment funds: they represent 56 per cent of all sums and 33 per cent of the numbers of individual investments.

The company has created a demanding environment where professional services personnel and investment executives perform to a high critical standard. 3i has chosen not to recruit graduates straight from university because it believes that they possess insufficient maturity and experience. Caroline Jablonska, HR adviser, says 'There are three groups of qualities which we look for in new recruits to the company – intellectual capacity, drive and resilience, and the ability to build relationships. Most of our clients are directors of businesses and so our people must be capable of establishing and maintaining relationships with people of that level. We are looking for people who have around four to five years' experience post-qualification in industry or the professions.'

This recruitment approach clearly influences the culture, which remains hierarchical and professional in nature. The structure of 3i and the atmosphere within the company is traditional and somewhat formal. This is not a west coast computer company in ethos; 3i is a rigorous, shrewd investment company and its demeanour represents the best of the old school City. It is a standard bearer for the values which appear to have been lost by some companies in the Square Mile: to be commercial and fair; to respect the needs of shareholders, employees and clients; to maintain its integrity and professionalism; and to strive for continual improvement and innovation.

In order to raise the profile of the group, CEO Macpherson committed 3i to its most admired company project. The aim of this initiative was to be included in *Management Today's* assessment of the most admired companies in the UK. Cross-functional groups were set up – and external consultants engaged – to launch a series of steps which will enhance 3i's rating. The company has moved from 119th position to 46th this year and third in athe financial sector.

How does 3i rate?

Pay:	excellent
Benefits:	very good
Communications:	average
Training:	very good
Career development:	very good
Morale:	good

People and personnel policies

3i operates in the highly rewarded financial services industry which means that to attract the best people it needs to provide compelling pay and benefits packages. Its investment stream is the highest paid while its professional services team also command lucrative deals. Pay is partly variable, driven by performance rating in the annual appraisal, partly by status in the company and also by the market rate. Jablonska says that the company runs a wide variety of schemes which are tailored to performance and seniority. In particular, 3i provides an excellent non-contributory pension scheme and subsidised mortgages.

Bonuses are a key component of the pay package throughout the business but their application will vary according to local circumstance. Some 130 frontline investment sales staff command the highest bonuses – up to 90 per cent of salary. The average in the investment stream is 30 per cent of salary which means that many people in that section of the business are extremely well paid. In addition, each head of department has a pool of money to make exceptional awards for individual performance of between £1,000 and £2,000, and to give gifts to recognise employees when they have provided a service beyond the normal demands of their role.

Some designate a certain sum for the benefit of employees and in 1995, for example, a manager took some support staff to a health farm. In a larger sense, where a manager has taken on an important project which is additional to the normal scope of duties and this has been completed successfully, a one-off bonus payment may be made. Jablonska says that examples include the extra work handled by individuals and groups for the company's 1994 flotation, the development of a marketing services database or new client assignments at times of heavy workload. All employees are eligible for an annual profit-sharing scheme which allows for up to a 10 per cent award. Clearly, this depends on the performance of the business but in 1994 3i achieved maximum award.

All staff are recruited, generally, after substantial professional or commercial experience elsewhere. They will then receive further training and development to help them develop their capacities as investment or professional executives. Every year their performance is assessed by their immediate manager and every two years they have a career development discussion with their senior manager. This goes through what the individual wants to achieve in their career and what options are available for them.

In the investment stream, executives spend around five years developing as investors. At which point they may continue as senior investors or become team leaders. None of this is automatic and it is contingent upon high quality performance and the results of a developmental workshop. This takes place around two years before the decision is made and it explores the skills needed for elevation within the company.

Training and development in 3i is based largely on business needs. It falls into the following categories: technical and IT, and management and personal development. A lot of training is done in-house but external programmes are also used. In 1997 the company will issue CD-ROM workstations to every manager, which will enable self-study packages to be used.

Internal communication is an evolving science at 3i. Most high-tech is its *Message of the Day* which covers key business developments and appears on screen every day. It also publishes a company magazine whose editorial mix combines business and social issues. Central commercial themes are disseminated through a series of business conferences and seminars.

Contact address

Ms Caroline Jablonska,
HR Adviser,
3i plc,
90 Waterloo Road,
London SE1 8XP.
Telephone: 0171 928 3131.
Fax: 0171 928 0058.

John Lewis Partnership plc

John Lewis is one of Britain's most famous retailers. Today it combines the John Lewis department stores and the Waitrose supermarket chain. Sales in 1997 from the 23 stores, 115 supermarkets and six other related businesses were £3.2 billion. Preliminary unaudited pre-tax profits reached £217 million. Including 16,300 part-timers, the partnership employs 41,100 people.

John Lewis at a glance

Employees: 41,100
Annual staff attrition rate: 14.5 per cent in John Lewis; 25 per cent in Waitrose
Key locations: London (HQ), mainly southern half of UK plus some in the North and Scotland
Annual graduate recruitment: 45 (25 in John Lewis)
Annual intake: 8,000

An inside view

The retail sector provides some of the most distinctive employers in the UK. It is a discipline which includes some of the country's most respected businesses and others which enjoy a less enviable reputation. John Lewis falls firmly in the former category as a good value, high quality operator where it sees its employees as partners. It is an organisation which can trace its culture back to the earliest days of the business. To some extent the department stores have a utilitarian flavour about them. But nevertheless the managers and employees in the business are alert to modern retailing concepts.

This is a highly democratic organisation where members of the workforce form branch councils. These determine local policy in conjunction with the individual store management. There is also a 180-strong central council which is composed of one-fifth appointees and four-fifths people elected from the workforce. This apparently complicated structure is designed to ensure that employees are fully briefed and involved in the decision-making process.

The partnership believes that it has been successful because of its distinctive style of retailing. Since the 1920s, the company has referred to its permanent employees as partners. This is because they are effectively co-owners of the business and have a direct financial interest in its profitability. Each year every John Lewis partner receives a share of the profits, and that means that many members of the workforce can be extremely well off. The John Lewis philosophy is summed up in its phrase 'Never knowingly undersold'. This commitment is meant to represent a promise of outstanding value for money. It is an assurance that when buying from a

John Lewis department store, people will obtain the best goods at the best prices. But it also underpins the entire John Lewis philosophy. The partnership's chairman, Stuart Hampson, in his recent Tomorrow's Company statement, says that 'This is a statement of our determination never to be out-thought, out-classed or out-performed. In short it is a commitment to think bigger'. He says that none of its expansion in recent years was achieved without challenging its own standards and status quo. 'We are always seeking to review, update and expand both the ranges we stock and the shops that sell them. Existing department stores are regularly refurbished and extended to provide more selling space. Our systems and information technology support are continuously upgraded to meet the developing needs of customers. Furthermore, the number of shops being opened, built or in the pipeline reflects our ambition for continued expansion.'

John Lewis's ambition is to be the most respected and successful retailer in the country. It will not necessarily be the biggest, but it certainly will be a leading contender. It is already one of the most profitable. Throughout the company's literature there is a heavy emphasis on people and the contribution people make to the business. To quote chairman Hampson again 'There is no great secret about the success of John Lewis. It is a direct reflection of the way we respect, encourage and develop our people. We give them ownership of the business and therefore the strongest possible incentive to be committed to its success. True to the spirit of the partnership's founder, we have built our success on certain fundamental business aims: an insistence

on providing unbeatable value; a policy of offering variety; a commitment to excellent service; and above all, a determination to conduct business with the utmost honesty and integrity.'

How does John Lewis rate?

Pay:	very good
Benefits:	excellent
Communications:	very good
Training:	excellent
Career development:	very good
Morale:	very good

People and personnel policies

The John Lewis partnership is an active graduate recruiter. It takes 25 graduates a year into the department store business and another 20 into the Waitrose supermarket chain. The people it recruits must demonstrate a variety of personal, practical and academic skills. But the successful candidates will inevitably be those who can put their intelligence, enthusiasm and drive into practice in very practical conditions. The company looks particularly for hard-working people with flair. And unlike some companies which are looking to give people their first career and then recruit again, John Lewis wishes to recruit people for career-long periods. A plan is set out whereby practical training will be given for the first 18 to 24 months in post, and then early responsibility will be given after the first year and a half. After ten years within John Lewis or Waitrose, the right individuals can expect to be among the top senior management decision makers within the company.

There is a very heavy emphasis within John Lewis on training and development as part of the partnership ethos. It is first and foremost a very commercial organisation. Retail is probably the most commercial of all business activities. Its documentation says 'We are in business to make profit, but it's what we do with the profit that make us so different. Quite apart from competitive salaries we offer financial benefits that are as comprehensive as they are attractive,' says Sally Carruthers, personnel manager. Every March all permanent members of the partnership receive a special cash bonus. This is awarded on a democratic basis with everybody receiving the same percentage of salary. This partnership bonus is an annual recognition of the contribution that each individual makes to the company. The benefits package goes beyond this. Partners take advantage of subsidised dining rooms, free life insurance, non-contributory pensions and substantial shopping discounts on all department store lines and most Waitrose lines.

'The benefits go further. Graduate trainees take a full five weeks' holiday in their first full year in the business. Most organisations have some form of social club and social activity, but John Lewis really does tend to outdo most of them. The company owns five cruising yachts, two mature golf courses and two first-class country clubs. One is Leckford Abbas, which is in the Hampshire countryside, which offers trout fishing on the Test, shooting, tennis, croquet, swimming and golf. At Cookham, on the River Thames, its other country club provides swimming, cricket, boating, tennis and squash. The company has also secured a long lease on Brownsea Castle and 15 acres of Brownsea Island. This is a wildlife sanctuary off Poole Harbour and it's a site where John Lewis partners go on holiday for the weekend or for a longer full-time break. The company also owns Ambleside Park in the Lake District, a former hotel and now a holiday centre on the edge of Lake Windermere.'

The training schemes at John Lewis and Waitrose are extensive. For example, in the Waitrose scheme there are three components to the graduate courses available: retail skills, management skills and personal development. 'It's because of our emphasis on personal development that we attempt to ensure that the programme is constructed and then remodelled to meet personal requirements.' An individual joining John Lewis will be assigned a management trainer who will act as mentor and steer individuals through the challenges on the course. Off-the-job training is equally comprehensive and trainees can expect 40 days a year of diverse opportunities to supplement their work in-store. There will also be residential management development technical training and regular forums where trainees at John Lewis can discuss and compare their experiences with their colleagues.

Contact address

Sally Carruthers, Personnel Manager,
John Lewis Partnership plc,
171 Victoria Street, London SW1.
Telephone: 0171 828 1000.
Fax: 0171 834 5491.

Kwik-Fit Holdings plc

K wik-Fit is Europe's largest independent automotive parts repair and replacement specialist, and the company argues that it is the undisputed market leader. The Kwik-Fit Group operates 845 specialist tyre, exhaust and brake, 123 mobile tyre fitting vehicles and 24 trade distribution outlets in the UK, the Netherlands, Belgium and Ireland. The group's activities have been expanded recently to include insurance services, a customer survey unit and an equity interest in 75 Apples Car Clinics and 90 Hometune Mobile Servicing vehicles. Annual sales exceed £365 million and pre-tax profit is greater than £36 million.

Kwik-Fit at a glance

Employees: 4,000 group, 3,000 UK
Annual staff attrition rate: 28 per cent
Key locations: Edinburgh, Derby, Warrington, Harlow, Wallington, Reading, Glasgow plus 850 Kwik-Fit centres in UK and Europe
Av. annual graduate recruitment: n/a
Annual intake: 800

An inside view

Established in 1971, the Kwik-Fit Group has grown rapidly through a range of acquisitions and the development of new sites. Its product range, competitive pricing, convenient locations and advertising campaign have served to establish the company's brand. Open seven days a week and 363 days a year, Kwik-Fit provides a drive-in-while-you-wait service for motorists. The company's outlets provide basic requirements such as tyres, exhausts, brakes, batteries, suspension, lubrication and in-car child safety products.

Kwik-Fit has a stated central strategic objective to delight its customers. This target underpins all group activities and procedures which are designed to achieve 100 per cent customer satisfaction. Kwik-Fit argues that this core objective is key to its continued growth and success. The company endeavours to set industry standards and is committed to ongoing improvement in every area of the business. Kwik-Fit says that the best example of its success comes with the satisfaction of its customers. The company provides a free telephone helpline where customers can comment on the quality of the products and services received. All customers are handed a questionnaire when they leave Kwik-Fit centres. This invites customers to compare the level of service with the company's code of practice. In addition, the business employs 90 researchers who contact more than 100,000 customers a year within 72 hours of a visit to a Kwik-Fit centre. This enables the company to monitor service quality and to make early improvements.

Since the outset, the company has won a raft of customer service awards. It has been successful in creating an environment where its employees feel positive about the business and want to translate their enthusiasm into commercial achievement. Tom Farmer, chairman and chief executive, has always believed that well-trained and highly motivated people would care about the business and provide customers with a high level of service. In 1990, for example, it won a national training award and in 1993 achieved accreditation under the Investors in People scheme. Kwik-Fit's people also worked diligently to win recognition under the ISO 9002 scheme.

How does Kwik-Fit rate?

Pay:	very good
Benefits:	very good
Communications:	superb
Training:	excellent
Career development:	very good
Morale:	very good

People and personnel policies

Kwik-Fit aims to recruit people who are determined to succeed. This is not an environment for people who want a gentle ride. Kwik-Fit seeks to beat its own customer service best performances on a daily basis. Farmer comments 'Kwik-Fit

people must have a desire to succeed and a genuine commitment to be the best. The company is committed to offering the best training and career opportunities in the sector and we make the resources available to prove it'.

The group operates three purpose-built training centres in the UK and in the Netherlands and six satellite training centres attached to the company's divisional support offices in Edinburgh, Derby, Warrington, Harlow, Croydon and Reading. More than 100 modular training programmes are available to Kwik-Fit people in addition to the standard on-the-job training. The combination gives employees a thorough understanding of customer service, technical skills, administration and management development. In addition, the company sponsors staff through a series of nationally recognised professional and skills qualifications. Some are given the opportunity to work towards a National Vocational Qualification in automotive service and parts replacement. 'All employees have their competency assessed before dealing with customers,' says Farmer. 'The company's structured career ladder means that everyone has an equal opportunity to succeed in the business. We like to promote from within. Every person is given their own training passport which provides a record of achievement and progress.'

Assessment techniques are used to identify Kwik-Fit people who are ready to progress to the next level on the Kwik-Fit career ladder and annual appraisals help to identify personal ambitions within the business. Success in the business leads to an improvement in status to manager or partner. Managers are responsible for the day-to-day operations in Kwik-Fit centres – from sales and marketing to training and career development plans. To become a manager in Kwik-Fit, an individual must demonstrate consistent growth in business for their centre. The company picks its partners from the ranks of its managers. Partners are responsible for groups of three centres. The Kwik-Fit partner development programme prepares candidates for the extra responsibility. Through a series of training modules, partners are tutored on how best to run an efficient partnership. On completion they are recognised as approved partners.

Farmer comments 'Our customers depend on our assurance that they are getting the best advice. Our training programmes are designed to help Kwik-Fit people deliver the level of service that every customer has a right to expect'. Beyond this, further career opportunities exist in divisional management. Regional managers direct operations in up to 30 centres and divisional directors control operations in territories in up to 120 centres.

Pay and benefits packages are performance-driven. A competitive basic salary is paid according to grade. By exceeding group service and performance standards people can boost their earnings and share in the profits which they have helped to create. All employees take part in a profit-related pay plan and anyone who has completed at least three years is allocated free shares through the Kwik-Fit employee share scheme. Managers and partners also benefit from the company's contract of understanding. This agreement gives them enhanced job security by appointing them to their centres for a minimum of three years.

Regular internal communication is a feature of the business. A newsletter is sent weekly to all Kwik-Fit centres and monthly divisional meetings inform all employees of progress in their division and the company.

Farmer argues that Kwik-Fit provides compelling opportunities for many young people. He says that its high speed career progression, comprehensive training and a share in the success of the business are attractive for many people. This is not a graduate culture where people are employed on the quality of their degrees but rather on their willingness to contribute energy, commitment and a determination to succeed. The Kwik-Fit management realised long ago that providing an environment with strong but equal opportunities and high incentives would create a committed workforce. It is a business which clearly values its people and helps them to reach new personal and business achievement.

Contact address

Mr Simon Dawson,
Training and Development Director,
Kwik-Fit (GB) Ltd,
17 Corstorphine Road,
Edinburgh EH12 6DD.
Telephone: 0131 337 9200.
Fax: 0131 337 0062.

Logica plc

Logica is a leading British consultancy, software and systems integration company with a 1996 turnover of almost £285 million, achieving pre-tax profits of £24.7 million. The company provides information technology solutions to meet the business needs of leading organisations worldwide, mainly in the specialist areas of finance, telecommunications, energy and utilities, defence, industry, government, transport, space and aerospace. Logica, with headquarters in central London, employs 4,800 people and has offices in 18 countries throughout Europe, the Middle East, North America and Asia Pacific. Formed in 1969, the company has successfully completed more than 10,000 projects in a total of 50 countries.

Logica at a glance

Employees: 4,800
Annual staff attrition rate: n/a
Key locations: London (HQ) plus ten
   regional offices throughout the UK.
   Its largest overseas subsidiaries are in
   France and the US
Av. annual graduate recruitment:
   200–300
Annual intake: n/a

An inside view

At the time Logica was formed the computer hardware industry made massive mainframes operated by data processing managers and their staff, and visual record computers largely used by sales and accounting departments. The computer industry was dominated by IBM and the so-called seven dwarfs – most of which have either fallen by the wayside or merged. These companies also provided the operating software to run the machines and in so doing tied their customers to a particular manufacturer.

The original founders of Logica, the most well known being Philip Hughes, still a non-executive director and admired for the paintings he continues to create, were among the first to see a niche market for providing custom-designed software which was not only more cost-effective than that supplied by hardware manufacturers, but usually more efficient. The added bonus was that customers were provided with the software they wanted, rather than what was thrust upon them, and very soon a series of healthy business partnerships were established by Logica through hand-holding and guiding its clients through what was becoming an increasingly complex industry.

This same principle has been applied ever since, during the revolution that has taken place with the advent of PCs, networks and advanced international telecommunications. So from starting life as what was then called a software house, Logica is now a world-leader as a creator, integrator and fixer of complex IT systems, increasingly for companies working in a global market. The company recognises that businesses today want to serve more customers more quickly, more cheaply and more effectively, regardless of country or industry. It achieves this by working closely with its clients to bring a total solution to their IT requirements, from strategic consultancy through system design, development, implementation and integration, to training and applications management. It always aims to add value to its clients' businesses.

In a business sector where IT-based projects can cost several millions of pounds, Logica's strengths as a successful independent international company in a fiercely competitive market are embodied in its understanding of the profitable application of leading-edge technologies. This is achieved through the calibre of its staff, its professional integrity and its commitment to developing the most appropriate solutions for its clients.

How does Logica rate?

Pay:	very good
Benefits:	very good
Communications:	excellent
Training:	very good
Career development:	excellent
Morale:	good

People and personnel policies

Jim McKenna, Logica's director of human resources, is a pragmatist. Pointing towards the window of his sixth floor office at the company's imposing headquarters building in the Euston area of London, he says 'My senior colleagues and I are under no illusion. Our business walks out of this, and other of our buildings around the world, every night. If they do not return, we have no business.' He is, of course, referring to the company's employees – of which a staggering 87 per cent are 'extremely bright, talented and ambitious graduates'. It is therefore understandable that when he uses that well-worn and over-exposed cliche, used in numerous annual reports and other corporate publications – 'our staff are our most vital assets' – he really means it.

It comes as no surprise, therefore, that Logica's human resources policy, set against the background of the competitive industry in which it operates, is aimed squarely at attracting the right sort of people and, importantly, keeping them. The average age of Logica's employees is 28. McKenna explains 'We work in partnership with our customers. Relationships are established, based on our long track record, trust and the ability of our people to relate to our customers. Inter-personal skills are a vital ingredient of the people we employ. The fact that 60 per cent of our customers 20 years ago are still customers today is evidence that putting the customer at the heart of everything we do is the right approach.

'We are totally committed to adding value to our customers' businesses; we give them what they want in order for them to succeed. In the process of achieving this customers do not like a procession of different consultants coming and going. That is one very good reason why we like to keep our people and we do everything possible to help them develop their careers to give them greater responsibility, job satisfaction and rewards.' At the core of the company's philosophy is its structure, which is non-hierarchical, and heavily decentralised. Most people work in an open, task-orientated project environment, dealing with one or more clients at any time, led by a project manager, and with or without direct support from colleagues, depending on the size and scope of the project. However, almost all employees at Logica have a so-called staff manager, who operates an open door policy, with whom they can discuss all matters relevant to their current work and future ambitions.

Logica takes on between 200 to 300 graduates a year. Although those with a good technical degree – such as computer sciences, physics or electronic engineering – are in particular demand, graduates with other degrees, for example economics or geography, are also sought. No matter what the qualifications, the company always looks for graduates with strong interpersonal skills.

Successful candidates spend their first year being trained in project management, quality assurances, finance and in the development of interpersonal skills. They start to work as a member of a project team almost immediately and will be given responsibility for smaller projects very early in their careers. Graduates with three to four years' experience currently manage some of the company's most prestigious and challenging assignments. All employees are expected to develop their skills to help develop their careers. The company provides on-going training in strategic and general management, interpersonal skills, team-building, and of course in the ever-changing information technology sector where Logica says it spends 'an enormous amount of money'. Much of the training is in-house, using CBT (computer-based training) techniques. Lunchtime workshops, formal and informal, are also held continuously.

As an international company operating in four geographic regions, the UK, Europe, North America and Asia Pacific, opportunities for working overseas or in various parts of the UK constantly occur, not only in project management but in general management, marketing and finance. Everyone has the opportunity to apply for such appointments as details of them are broadcast on the company's internal *Logica Visual News* – a network of television screens strategically placed in common areas of the company's premises. All employees are set annual objectives and are subject to an annual performance review. There are also more frequent reviews on the progress of particular projects. The company says it pays competitive salaries and operates a profit-sharing scheme. It provides free health insurance and a contributory pension scheme. One novel benefit is the company's house purchase plan through which pension contributions can be paid as part of the mortgage for as long as an employee wishes. This is to assist employees moving to London from other parts of the country to enter the housing market.

Contact address

Ms Margaret Little, Recruitment Manager, Logica plc, Stephenson House, 75 Hampstead Road, London NW1 2PL. Telephone: 0171 637 9111. Fax: 0171 468 7006.

LucasVarity

LucasVarity was formed from the merger of Lucas Industries and Varity Corporation of the US, which was completed in the second half of 1996. The purpose behind the merger was, primarily by combining the Lucas brakes business with Varity's Kelsey–Hayes subsidiary, to create one of the world's top ten automotive components groups. The group is inevitably undergoing a period of uncertainty at present as the two businesses are put together and duplication eliminated, but in the longer term, prospects for LucasVarity are extremely encouraging.

LucasVarity at a glance

Employees: 48,000 worldwide, 26,500 UK*
Annual staff attrition rate: n/a
Key locations: London (HQ),
    West Midlands and various other sites
    in the UK
Av. annual graduate recruitment: 80
Annual intake: n/a
*post-December 1996 restructuring

An inside view

Since the LucasVarity merger was completed in only late 1996, it is too early to draw too many conclusions about life inside the merged organisation. The completion of the merger has been very quickly followed by a substantial restructuring programme, involving the withdrawal from a series of activities in which LucasVarity does not consider it has sufficient critical mass to compete effectively. As part of the shake-out, 13 non-core or underperforming businesses, together employing 5,000 people, have been put up for sale. In addition, a further

3,000 jobs and a third of the senior management are expected to go in a drive to save costs of £120 million in 1997. Therefore, to date, much of the news emanating from the group could be perceived – from the workforce's point of view – to be negative. As with most mergers, however, it is important to recognise that this merely represents a clearing of the decks in order to lay the platform for future growth.

Even at this relatively early stage, it is clear that the new company will be aggressively managed. As well as the streamlining of administrative and operational functions which has already taken place, LucasVarity is adopting a philosophy based on the concept of 'economic value added' (EVA) growth. EVA requires that each business achieves an annual return on assets which exceeds its cost of capital, and a highly demanding EVA target of 20 per cent has been set for all LucasVarity businesses. Through techniques such as these, and the introduction of a much more entrepreneurial culture throughout the company, LucasVarity aims to double annual sales to £10 billion by 2005.

Another initiative which the new management team is encouraging is the delegation of greater operational autonomy to the seven new product-based divisions. The corporate centres (one in London, together with the US headquarters in Buffalo) will be kept as small as possible and their remit limited to strategy and policy issues. The real yardstick for measuring the performance of the underlying business will be whether or not it achieves its EVA target.

In the future LucasVarity will be a more focused, and more enterprising, business. Managers will be encouraged to take advantage of the greater authority on offer to them and will not be punished for making mistakes (provided, of course, that they do not repeat them!). Rid of much of its excess baggage, LucasVarity will adopt much more of a total quality management culture.

How does LucasVarity rate?

Pay:	good
Benefits:	good
Communications:	good
Training:	excellent
Career development:	good
Morale:	good

People and personnel policies

Lucas Industries and Varity had very different attitudes to remuneration and career development issues. As with other areas of the business, the plan is to fuse these into a best of both worlds approach, but this will inevitably take time. It is apparent already, however, that the new organisation will be highly performance-driven. Demanding targets are being set and the rewards for those who can achieve them will be considerable. In tandem with these incentives will be a policy of the company being much more adventurous in making management appointments. One of LucasVarity's key goals is to develop a set of managers who are happy to accept responsibility and enjoy taking risks.

As indicated earlier, remuneration will be increasingly tied to the level of value-added contributed. Accordingly, general pay increases will be phased out. For senior management, LucasVarity has developed an annual bonus scheme based on EVA and there will be no upside cap to the amount of annual bonus that an individual can earn. Furthermore, as part of an attempt to encourage a long-term view within the company, a global share-ownership programme is to be introduced. It is estimated that middle management can expect to earn between 15 and 20 per cent of their annual remuneration by way of incentive payments, and this proportion will rise considerably among senior executives.

In its effort to transform the business, the company is currently focusing a considerable amount of effort on training and development. Although engineering will remain a core competence for the majority of the workforce, LucasVarity will be looking to develop leadership and commercial skills for those employees whom it considers likely to progress further within the organisation. All employees are to have a development plan, as part of which they will be assigned specific projects. Both plans and progress will be reviewed at regular intervals.

One of the most important facets of the new entity, and indeed one of the principal reasons behind the merger, is the extent of its international coverage. Developing a global presence will be a central pillar in the company's development in the next century. Inherent in this strategy is the importance which the group attaches to international expertise in its senior employees. In future, all appointments to the top 100 positions within the group will require experience of working overseas.

Like many engineering groups, the number of women within the upper echelons of LucasVarity is relatively small – there are, for instance, only two women among the top 85 managers in the group. Of course, much of this derives from cultural and sociological factors rather than hostile attitudes to females within the company. On the contrary, Lucas Industries had in place a number of long-standing initiatives, such as a flexible approach to working arrangements for new mothers, which were designed to promote women within the workforce. Such initiatives will continue in LucasVarity. However, conscious of the experience of several companies in the US, LucasVarity is not prepared to introduce any form of quota system to advance either women or those from ethnic backgrounds.

The company is becoming increasingly aware of its role in the community. Prior to the merger, significant amounts of money were pledged by Lucas Industries to a variety of good causes. These generally had either an environmental or educational content. For example, half of the group's community budget is covenanted to universities or other educational establishments, while Lucas' Perkins diesel engines business has been heavily involved in a series of environmental initiatives.

Contact address

Mr Howard Chandler,
Human Resources Director,
LucasVarity plc,
44–46 Park Street,
London W1Y 4DJ.
Telephone: 0171 493 6793.
Fax: 0171 409 0551.

Marks & Spencer plc

Marks & Spencer is probably the single most famous corporate name in Britain. In a recent survey of high profile CEOs across Europe, it emerged as the single most respected business throughout the continent. In the United Kingdom, it is praised for its integrity, reliability and quality merchandise. M&S is a metaphor for a certain style of retailing which is uniquely British but is successful in markets throughout the world. The company employs 65,500 people – 54,900 in the UK. The company has 646 locations around the world delivering £7.2 billion in sales and £993.7 million in pre-tax profits.

Marks & Spencer at a glance

Employees: 65,500
Annual staff attrition rate: 10 per cent
Key locations: 640 worldwide,
    286 in the UK
Av. annual graduate recruitment: 200
Annual intake: n/a

An inside view

It is rare that a store – however large and well regarded – takes on the mantle of a public institution. But Marks & Spencer has transcended the status of popular and patronised retail concern and has entered the folklore of the UK. Many regard the company as a repository of the best qualities of British commercial endeavour and tend to compare other retailers against the standards and conduct of M&S. The company's touchstone is its integrity and reliability. People who shop at Marks and Sparks believe they will be treated fairly, the goods on sale will be value for money and if they are,

perchance, dissatisified they can always take the goods back. In recent years the flagship clothes chain has overcome its rather unadventurous reputation and added some sparkle to its collections. It has also opened top-end food outlets and in the 1980s ventured into customer financial services.

One of the achievements of the current M&S management is that it has remained true to its core traditions while adapting to the challenges of the modern retail environment. The name, which had previously not travelled well outside the British expatriate communities in mainland Europe, is now a global brand. Other British retailers have struggled with the task of modernising their concepts. M&S is an object lesson in how the transformation can be made and how customers can be added through wider and better ranges, improved outlets and targeting new markets. The Marks & Spencer of today has taken a quantum leap forward at the same time as reinforcing its brand image. The result is outstanding commercial success and widespread recognition among the leaders of industry in the UK and the rest of Europe.

The standing of Marks & Spencer among chairmen and chief executives is legendary. The name which the company has created for itself is the envy of many corporate bosses. In the mid-1990s the business has reached what it regards as more or less optimum store numbers in the UK. The format, location and lines run in the stores will change but the community of outlets is at about the right level, its management believes. The real push in coming years will be to extend and develop its UK stores, the further refinement of the quality and vitality of its lines and its expansion overseas. Marks & Spencer is now regarded as chic by the increasingly Anglophile French and its nine French stores are booming. In October 1996 M&S opened its first German outlet which was met by an enthusiastic response by local shoppers in Cologne. It promises to be the forerunner of a select chain. There are also M&S stores in Spain, Ireland, Belgium and the Netherlands.

Outside Western Europe the company has franchised its brand to a broad group of national operators in many countries worldwide. M&S provides store layouts, training and sells stock to franchisees. At present its franchise group includes 86 stores in 20 countries. In the United States it owns Brooks Brothers and Kings Super Markets, and in Canada it has recently sold the D'Allaird chain to concentrate on Marks & Spencer Canada. Real growth is expected to come in Asia where the Hong Kong operation continues to thrive. M&S has opened a representative office in Shanghai to explore retail prospects in China, and has also announced its intention to seek franchise partners in Australia and Korea.

How does Marks & Spencer rate?

Pay:	good
Benefits:	excellent
Communications:	superb
Training:	very good
Career development:	very good
Morale:	very good

People and personnel policies

For many years Marks & Spencer has enjoyed a popular reputation as one of Britain's most generous and thoughtful employers. In the research for the last edition of *The 100 Best Companies To Work For In The UK*, it was regularly cited by company directors as their number one choice for best employer. And it continues to be the leading role model for the retail sector. For shopfloor staff, a combination of reliability, good pay, outstanding benefits, thorough training, informative internal communications and progressive career development makes an attractive package. It is also a distinctive career option for managers who are drawn to M&S because of its commercial reputation and high investment in training.

It was among the first companies to regard its staff as individuals and its primary personnel principal states that all employees must be treated with respect and honesty. Integrity is a hallmark of M&S, underlining every aspect of its business approach. The company's policy on equal opportunities – long established – derives from its overall ethic but in practical terms owes much to the high numbers of women which the business employs. Some 83 per cent of the workforce is female and three-quarters of the store staff are part-time – almost all are women. Two-thirds of management positions in stores are held by women. A three-part initiative to help women who work in stores was launched in the early part of this decade. The extent and flexibility of part-time employment has increased; a child break scheme has been started to allow women to take an extended break but stay in contact with M&S during the early years of having children; and a short maternity package has been introduced to allow female employees to take maternity leave of four months or less. The company is one of the most active users of job-sharing, which it postively encourages in order to allow women with small children to come back to work; this policy extends to managers as much as shopfloor staff.

Half of the managerial posts at head office are held by women; two divisional directors are female and two main board directors including one non-executive are women. Management development in general is a key priority for the company. The primary criterion for filling posts is the suitability of the individual for the job but given this caveat M&S actively promotes its women. As the retail sector becomes more competitive, M&S has chosen to give its managers more authority. It has also made them more responsible for their own career development. A new personal development review system has been initiated which collects data on personal strengths and weaknesses and therefore development needs.

The reward package is geared to the best in industry. Salaries are competitive and include a profit-sharing scheme which normally amounts to 4 per cent of annual salary. All employees take part in a non-contributory pension scheme and permanent staff receive a 20 per cent discount on company merchandise up to £1,500. Medical benefits are an essential feature of the employee package. Doctors, dentists and chiropodists visit stores on a regular basis; cervical cytology testing and breast screening are available to all female staff and wives of male employees; each autumn, flu vaccinations are offered to all staff; and private medical insurance is available to the entire workforce.

Marks & Spencer believes strongly in playing a key role in its communities. The company has stores in most major centres in the UK and therefore enjoys high visibility among the public and business community. It is among the leading businesses to promote shopping as a family experience, and to back plans to revitalise the high street. In 1995–96 M&S spent £8.5 million on community involvement, of which £4.9 million was in donations to a wide range of projects. Some 35 employees are on full-time and another 200 on part-time secondment to charitable and voluntary organisations.

Contact address

Paul Smith,
Manager of Management Recruitment,
Marks & Spencer plc, Baker Street,
London W1A 1DN.
Telephone: 0171 935 4422.
Fax: 0171 487 2679.

The Mars Group

The Mars Group is renowned as one of the great UK employers. It is a standard-setter for pay, benefits, working environment, training, career development and equality. The company demands a high level of commitment and performance from its people and the Mars Group of Companies is not a workplace for those seeking an easy ride. The group embraces world-famous confectionery products, including the Mars bar itself, petfoods, including Pedigree Chum and Whiskas, and a range of other food and electronic businesses.

Mars at a glance

Employees: 28,500 worldwide, 5,500 UK
Annual staff attrition rate: 5 per cent
Key locations: Slough, Melton Mowbray, Peterborough, Kings Lynn, Reading, Leeds, Basingstoke
Av. graduate annual recruitment: 20
Annual intake: 60

An inside view

When human resources professionals discuss the great employers – the companies which have led the field in innovative and thoughtful personnel policy – the Mars Group will inevitably be among the first positive examples to be raised. In the confectionery sector, all three UK market leaders are regarded as strong employers. Cadbury Schweppes used to be a key example of the definitive paternalistic enterprise, founded by altruistic Quakers. Nestle, which now owns Rowntree – another Quaker inspiration – is an entirely different culture, one which is strongly commercial and global in its orientation. The Mars Group stands apart from its competitors as a business with convinced meritocratic values, belief in total integrity and respect for the individual, and an understanding that the company must invest in its people to remain a thriving enterprise.

The growth in the corporation globally has been exceptional and it has opened operations in more than 60 countries worldwide. It is particulary proud of its new ventures in the former Soviet Union, Eastern Europe, Latin America and China. Mars has invested $150 million in Russia alone. The corporation's salesforces now reach markets in more than 150 territories. Mars generates annual sales of around $13 billion. In the UK the business environment has become more combative especially in areas where the group was previously pre-eminent.

The Mars Group is famous for its manufacture of chocolate bars and snack foods. Mars bars, Twix, Snickers, M&Ms, Maltesers, Milky Way, Bounty and Opal Fruits are among its products with the Mars bar being the nation's best-selling single confectionery bar. An equally important section of the business is Pedigree Petfoods which makes Whiskas, Pedigree Chum, Pal, Kitekat, Sheba, Trill and Aquarian. Mars is also engaged in other aspects of food manufacture including Uncle Ben's parboiled rice, Dolmio pasta sauces, and Yeoman potato. In addition, it runs the Four Square dispensed-drinks machine company and features brands like Klix and Flavia. These activities led to a need for a new coin acceptance mechanism which became the foundation of Mars Electronics International. Its IT service function has significant bases across Mars sites in the UK and Europe.

The organisation is underpinned by the five principles of Mars. These are: quality, responsibility, mutuality, efficiency and freedom. They are the bedrock of the company and define the scope of an enterprise which is planned and team-driven, but gives plenty of scope for able and committed individuals. It is a highly focused business. It has achieved outstanding commercial success because the value of its people – both collectively and as individuals – has never been lost. Mars employees are known as associates which signifies the extent to which the company values its people. Customers and employees are equal and integral partners in the Mars equation.

How does Mars rate?

Pay:	superb
Benefits:	excellent
Communications:	very good
Training:	excellent
Career development:	very good
Morale:	excellent

People and personnel policies

Mars in the UK is no longer a collection of discrete national businesses. Mars Confectionery, for example, is now part of Snack Foods Europe, and its electronics company MEI is a global operation. The drinks business, IT, petfoods and confectionery are all worldwide enterprises with significant European regional management. 'Our strategy four to five years ago – in common with many other businesses – was to integrate all of our operations at a European level. I think time and experience has shown us that there are great benefits from working more closely together at a regional level but that there are also legitimate local variations in market conditions or employment policy, for example, which mean that we will still need local focus,' says a senior Mars personnel manager.

Mars is committed to achieving regional economies of scale but at the same time attending to local needs. The principal lines of business within the Mars Group are planned on global and regional lines and the current and future skill requirement is determined on both a national and a regional basis. As in any other multinational company, products for several territories are made at one location and transported to the final markets. The buying of the materials, their preparation and manufacture, and despatch is handled centrally. Marketing is shaped by both regional and national teams, identifying common features but applying them to the exigencies of the local consumer. In this way Mars makes best use of its resources – both its people and its facilities.

In organisational terms the structure of the individual businesses will vary according to operational need. If the local market requires a dedicated team to meet its special demands, then one will be created. But where there is duplication between a regional and a local structure, the company centrally will monitor the situation to ensure that performance is at its most efficient. Fundamentally, Mars is a flat company. It had only seven tiers in the 1960s – long before flat structures became the darling of CEOs and corporate planners. What has changed is the scope of the remit of managers. Managers at the most junior level may have some European responsibility and the most senior will spend much of their time moving from site to site across Europe.

The company is keen to recruit talented and articulate people and has a long tradition of employing graduates. It has a formal graduate entry scheme which annually brings in around 20 individuals direct from university on to the Mars management training programme. Mars sources from colleges and universities all over Europe. It also likes to scoop up another 60 people a year who were recent graduates but who have since had two to five years' experience in industry. The company has become close to a coterie of around 15 universities in the UK which have regularly produced people who have gone on to make successful careers at Mars. It also has summer and industrial placement schemes where prospective candidates for jobs at Mars can get to know the company a little better, and gain real work experience.

In the graduate intake, the company wants people with a good academic background – a 2.1 degree or higher – who can demonstrate motivation, influencing skills and critical thinking. The work requires people who are self-disciplined and enthusiastic and the company wants candidates who can show dedication and enthusiasm. 'We want individuals who are good fun to work with, not just clones,' says a Mars personnel manager. A typical graduate entrant would perform a series of assignments – each around six to nine months – in different functional areas of the business. Then the trainee would take up a full-time managerial position in one of the functional areas. 'We give them responsibilities from day one in the company and each trainee makes a significant contribution to each area of the business in which they work.'

Despite the demands of the business, the culture is very open and honest. Everyone in a particular unit will work in an open-plan office and there are, literally, no doors. Communication is relevant, informative and geared to feedback. Pay and benefits are among the very best in industry – Mars has always believed that if its associates deliver an excellent contribution they deserve outstanding rewards. It also offers an excellent package of benefits, including a superb non-contributory pension plan which is the envy of the sector.

Contact address

Mars Graduate Marketing,
Dundee Road,
Slough SL1 4JX.
Telephone: 01753 514999.
Fax: 01753 215559.

Microsoft Limited

Microsoft Limited is the UK company of the world's largest and most significant software house. Remarkably enough, Microsoft Corporation was founded in Seattle only 22 years ago by Bill Gates and Paul Allen but by 1995 it had reported global revenues of $5.9 billion. The launch of Windows 95 in its twentieth anniversary year further consolidated Microsoft as the defining institution in the industry. Gates always envisaged PC software as a great enabler for businesses, public corporations and individuals and his dream is in the process of being realised. Microsoft – here and around the world – is a highly attractive place to work. Demand among young people for jobs at Microsoft is exceptionally high, especially among creative and software-literate individuals who regard this as the premier applications ideas hothouse in the world.

Microsoft at a glance

Employees: 672 (Microsoft Limited)
+ 110 (global and regional staff based in the UK)
Annual staff attrition rate: 7 per cent, plus another 7 per cent go to other Microsoft companies
Key locations: Winnersh Triangle (HQ), London, Manchester, Edinburgh, Southampton, Dublin
Active graduate recruitment: n/a
Annual intake: 100

An inside view

A little more than 21 years ago a conviction that computer software could create a personal and commercial revolution provided the spark of inspiration to found the greatest postwar American business story. Two young computer nerds growing up on the Pacific north-west coast turned their hobby into a business and founded the Microsoft Corporation. They are now two of the wealthiest individuals in the world. And, as in all great fables, they were the unlikeliest pair to convert a technological vision into a working reality for millions of people across the globe. The company's latest mainstream product *Windows 95* was – on launch – adopted as global standard by virtue of the sheer volume of uptake by businesses.

The culture of the nascent company immediately appealed to young software engineers. The environment in Seattle was similar to a college campus with casually dressed enthusiasts working 36-hour and 72-hour stretches in a driven atmosphere to break the barriers of software capability. Indeed, among the young software designers in the US this atmosphere continues to proliferate but the business is more broadly based today. 'In the early days we had many young and single people who worked very long hours,' says Stephen Harvey, Microsoft Limited's director of FA and HR. 'A decade later many of these people have married and now have families. They are still as enthusiastic about the company and our products, but our work patterns tend to be slightly more conventional.' Nevertheless enthusiasm is the touchstone. Throughout the organisation people are stimulated by what Microsoft is doing. The car park is often packed at 8a.m. with people who stay until 8 or 9p.m.

Harvey recognised that people management skills were as important to the company as its leading technical status. Almost every division within Microsoft requires its people to demonstrate intrapersonal skills and so the directors of the business realised that they would need a director to manage the company's human resources objectives and policy. The company identifies three broad classifications for the skill groups which it uses in its UK operation: sales and marketing, consultants, and product support. Much of the software and systems design is done in the global headquarters in Seattle. In three buildings at Winnersh Triangle, the company created three cultural patterns: sales and marketing has a traditional professional environment, product support is the heartland of the technologists, and consultancy is particularly business-focused.

This is a young and purposeful company which has been governed by enthusiasm and determination to get the job done in the past. Its management has accepted, however, that to sustain its commanding position in its sector and in industry generally Microsoft must complement its product-led methodology with a structure which will enable the company to achieve its broader-based goals.

How does Microsoft rate?

Pay:	good
Benefits:	very good
Communications:	good
Training:	good
Career development:	excellent
Morale:	very good

People and personnel policies

Harvey says that Microsoft has a structured business model which is flexible and adaptable and responds to the needs of its customers, markets and employees. Project imperatives are often best served by a totally fluid environment where individuals can be brought together at a moment's notice but this sometimes conflicts with wider strategic and operational goals for the business. Microsoft is a substantial multinational which is undergoing transformative change. It aims to lose none of its visionary technological prowess but it also plans to strengthen its structure, develop its people skills and enhance its functioning.

'We are one of the market leaders in

terms of the technology. However, there is still room for improvement. People are so keen – and we have grown so fast – that we have concentrated on the outward-facing aspects of Microsoft.' Everyone in the UK operation is becoming more customer-aware. Whether that customer is external – a major corporate client or a personal user – or internal, the focus is on service supplied to the customer. So personal communication abilities are key and these are principal among the skills which the company seeks on recruitment. Foremost among the personal qualities which Microsoft expects in its new people is enthusiasm. 'We want people who are in love with the technology and are so keen that they want to make an impact on the company.'

Recruitment processes at Microsoft are as distinctive as everything else in the company. Harvey explains that the business has not formally recruited graduates on an active basis because the flow of applications is substantial. The company is looking for people who will be adept at customer service as well as technologists. Microsoft Limited has no annual recruitment targets for graduates but it does focus on demand in particular sectors or disciplines. In 1995 the company went on the milk round for the first time but this was largely to achieve a greater understanding of the graduate market rather than any active drive to add numbers.

Few people come to Microsoft expecting a job for life but they will benefit from working at the leading-edge and the company hopes that if they do leave they will go to a Microsoft client. Apart from the corporate credentials and the intellectual stimulation of working for Microsoft,

candidates want to be trained in the most advanced ideas and techniques. Much of the training done within the company until 1996 was of an outstanding nature but was largely ad hoc. The appointment of a training and development manager and the subsequent formulation of a training and development plan has allowed the company to identify a systemised approach to the discipline. Microsoft spends a massive 5 per cent of payroll costs on training and development which indicates the level of commitment which the company has to the discipline. 'Much of the training used to be Go-out-and-get and off-the-shelf, now it will be developed internally in conjunction with leading external consultants.' Some 70 per cent of development is on-the-job, another 20 per cent is coaching and 10 per cent just-in-time training; the emphasis of which is to encourage individual leadership.

The company is a competitive payer. Although Microsoft has participated in many of the major salary surveys, its approach to reward packages has been geared to its worldwide compensation policy. Pay is characterised by three components: base, bonus and stock options. Base pay will vary from country to country and is determined by market conditions. The bonus – and its value – is kicked in twice a year according to the six-monthly performance review. Employees can also take advantage of stock options and some of the people who have been around since the beginning are very wealthy as a result. The company runs what has been described as one of the best group pension schemes in the industry. All employees benefit from permanent and private health insurance and life insurance, 23 to 28 days annual leave, stock purchase scheme and sports facilities. They get discounts on Microsoft products and free access to the MSN on the Internet. Maternity benefits are better than average and Microsoft is flexible about when new mothers return. The headcount is 60 per cent male and 40 per cent female; these statistics are replicated in the manager grades, but the more senior the manager the greater likelihood that an individual manager will be a man. Women are rising rapidly in the company and employees with high intelligence, deep enthusiasm for the technology, a talent for leadership and a capacity to get on with people will prosper in Microsoft.

Contact address

Stephen Harvey,
Director of FA and HR,
Microsoft Limited, Microsoft Place,
Winnersh, Wokingham,
Berkshire RG41 5TP.
Telephone: 01189 270001.
Fax: 01189 270957.
Worldwide web: www.microsoft.com

Milliken Industrials Limited

Milliken & Company, one of the world's largest textile concerns, is financially strong and privately owned. The foundations for the multinational's success were laid in Portland, Maine, US some 130 years ago, but it was not until 1964 that manufacturing operations began outside the United States in Bury, Lancashire. Since then additional manufacturing plants have been established in Belgium, France and Denmark. There is sales back-up in all locations with additional sales offices in London, Paris and Bremen to promote total product offering. Each Milliken location retains the best of a small company while gaining the strength of a world leader in the textile industry.

Milliken at a glance

Employees: 1,000
Annual staff attrition rate: around 2 per cent
Key locations: Wigan, Bury, Stroud
Av. annual graduate recruitment: 10
Annual intake: 50

An inside view

Milliken's European group consists of four individual divisions, supported by the American parent company. In Britain modular carpets are produced at Wigan on a site that comprises the manufacturing facility for European contract carpet design and sales. Wellington Mill at Bury manufactures synthetic textiles for the rubber, tyre and airbag industries. Plants in Stroud and Carn in Gloucestershire produce tennis ball and snooker table products. Specially designed and engineered textile interior trim is made in Burnley for major automotive companies in the UK and Europe.

It is a company whose people, products and philosophies set the standard for quality. Its carpets provide comfort, style and wearability to hotels, business and public areas. Its fabrics keep astronauts safe, soldiers and youngsters warm. It claims, with some justification, that each of its 48,000 products reflects a company-wide commitment to excellence. Quality emanates from a philosophy called the pursuit of excellence – a process which starts at the very top and which became a watchword in 1979. Milliken was already renowned for its high performance products and state-of-the-art technology. But executives wondered why some Japanese competitors achieved higher quality, less waste, greater productivity and fewer customer complaints.

The answer had more to do with management style and people than with machines and automation. So Milliken undertook a new and basic strategy. All employees are called associates, work mainly in self-managed teams and, above all, are empowered with authority and autonomy. An associate in the line can halt any process if they feel that quality or safety is at risk. Collective action teams – teams are the company's hallmark in the pursuit of excellence – address specific manufacturing and business challenges, supplier action teams work to improve supplier relationships, process improvement teams continually analyse and improve products and services. Customer action teams work together to emphasise the partners for profit ethos. And to further maximise quality potential, Milliken makes education – for associates, suppliers and customers – a priority.

The company invests heavily in education each year, and customers and suppliers attend comprehensive seminars in quality. An overriding approach, good housekeeping in business terms, is to reduce costs, improve profits and increase product and service quality. The basis of the company's operation is one of technological leadership with a value system which expects and demands nothing less than integrity, hard work, teamwork and effective communication.

How does Milliken rate?

Pay:	good
Benefits:	good
Communications:	good
Training:	very good
Career development:	very good
Morale:	excellent

People and personnel policies

The main objective at Milliken is simply to ensure that people perform effectively in a motivated and focused environment, at the same time feeling pleased that they are part of a forward-looking organisation. The philosophy is a programme of change: changing people's hearts, minds and performance with the ultimate goal of eliminating non value-added cost. It is set out as harmony between process improvement and people improvement and Milliken believes in only recruiting those of the highest quality.

Human resources manager David Littler says 'We have a fully participatory environment designed to deliver a fast, high quality customer response with a team ethos. Any issues are attacked as a team because that is our culture.' Milliken, like many other companies, sees its associates as front line troops. It demands regular feedback on the business from all its employees. There is, in fact, a requirement for them to speak up, emphasising that the concern is not only a business seeking to make a profit but a complete partnership.

The watchword is simple and straight to the point: OFI. This means opportunity for improvement. Littler comments 'It gets our people involved. No matter how big or small an improvement, we welcome it. The experts in this business are not the management but the people on the shop floor.' That simple and effective principle meant a change of management thinking. There were ten levels, now there are only four, encouraging greater effectiveness. The levels comprise senior management, general management, administrative and shop floor. Graduates enter at management level with clear career patterns established.

And when Milliken recruits the brightest – the company seeks those with skill, capability and a spread of learning – it is determined to get the best. But above all, the company is about involvement, empowering those at the lowest level to contribute to the decision process which will help take the business forward. The company's HR strategy is committed to improving associate contribution and to take Milliken successfully to the year 2000 and beyond. HR is concentrating on working in an integrated manner with associates at all levels and it believes that the quality of service provided by HR should be high and valued by every associate.

It wishes to attract and retain the best graduates to satisfy the company's long-term plans. They spend two months absorbing key issues with a leadership orientation programme in the US, having completed a thorough inter-site UK induction programme. They can expect to be in the middle management population within three years. For newly recruited graduates and ambitious associates the opportunity to be posted overseas to improve their competence is a common occurence.

A main thrust of the Milliken operation is communications, with frequent cascade briefings. This is a two-way operation with a positive accent on feedback. 'We are a highly pro-active concern, taking into account what everybody says or wishes to contribute in the pursuit of excellence.' Milliken is aware of its local responsibilities too with in-house social activities and support and sponsorship for a wide range of local charities and involvement with football and rugby league.

Contact address

Mr David Littler,
Human Resources Manager,
Milliken Industrials Limited,
Hill Plant, Gidlow Lane,
Wigan, Lancashire WN6 8RN.
Telephone: 01942 612745.
Fax: 01942 612739.

Monsanto plc

Monsanto is a multinational chemical company, founded in 1901, with headquarters in St Louis, Missouri. But a vital part of its UK operation since 1949 is production from a 324-acre site in Newport, Gwent. This ultra-modern complex is administered from the UK headquarters at High Wycombe, which also houses the UK sales staff. That, in turn, reports to European headquarters in Brussels. The conglomerate's worldwide sales of $9 billion reflects the importance of the industry's growth and that Newport is an integral part of an aggressive strategy. The £150 million plant employs 250 people, a third of them on round the clock shift working.

Monsanto at a glance

Employees: 250
Annual staff attrition rate: 2 per cent
Key locations: Manufacturing plant at Newport, Gwent. Sales and administration HQ at High Wycombe
Av. annual graduate recruitment: 4
Annual intake: 4

An inside view

Cut-throat competition in the early 1980s in the international chemical industry threatened the survival of parts of Monsanto. Management went back to the drawing board to devise a strategy to ensure continued and growing prosperity. The result was three broad objectives: multi-skilling, a flatter team-based organisational structure and a more open culture. But most important of all was a long-term programme to build the skills of all employees and the introduction of structures and communications so that

the skills could be used effectively. It began by multi-skilling operators and craftsmen in the production and maintenance roles, a move which boosted productivity by 67 per cent in five years.

It meant that instead of having three people doing a job there were two – giving more output for labour costs. The spin off was more motivation and job satisfaction. The strategy also meant structural change by team-based organisation which led in turn to the breaking down of functional barriers. Two layers, those of chargehands and foremen, disappeared, leaving four: plant manager, operations manager, production manager and staff. Another objective was single status working to eliminate the us-and-them attitudes.

A range of services support production activity from maintenance teams and engineering specialists through to analytical laboratory staff. Administration support in finance, human resources and information systems is fully integrated in the site organisation. Some 70,000 tonnes of chemicals are despatched every year to more than 1,000 customers with exports to 90 countries accounting for around 60 per cent of the plant's output. None of the plant's products are sold directly to the public but are used in the manufacture of many items destined for everyday use: from tyres to paints and varnishes; from detergents to heat transfer fluids. The production units are each capable of producing a range of variations and the Newport staff work closely with colleagues in the sales and marketing functions throughout Europe to strive to ensure that the operation meets the changing demands of the marketplace.

The range is wide and impressive. The plant shares the company's approach to environmental concerns in the proper control of operations and transport of waste disposal. It also fully supports the *Responsible Care* programme of the Chemical Industries Association. A team of environmentalists works closely with regulatory bodies to ensure that the activities are carried out within company standards which themselves are well within statutory limits. Recent registration under BS7750 and the European Eco-Management and Audit Scheme reinforce this approach. Monsanto's management is also committed to a safe and healthy workplace for all employees.

How does Monsanto rate?

Pay:	excellent
Benefits:	very good
Communications:	very good
Training:	excellent
Career development:	very good
Morale:	excellent

People and personnel policies

In the early 1980s the workforce stood at 800. And as Bob Ansell, human resources support manager, readily admits 'It was a very unprofessional business'. People were very functionally orientated in compartments in site-wide functions: production, maintenance, engineering and technology. Apart from the structural and cultural changes, sales personnel were concerned purely with servicing customers, and production staff with production. A major reappraisal of the human resource policy shifted the emphasis towards teamwork. That means that customers now regularly go on-site to talk to operational and technical staff with the aim of making everyone feel more involved with the financial aspects of the operation in its totality. Operators are also sent out to visit customers. The organisation was changed internally.

The changes were part of Monsanto's strategic goals, which, according to Ansell, were quite simply a financial reappraisal to seek a 20 per cent return on equity and the company's pledge on the environment. Monsanto had been a traditional organisation with three major unions involved. There were collective agreements with each, although there were no serious industrial relations problems. But it was not an efficient way to run the operation. A new system was agreed on an amicable basis. Hourly pay was scrapped in favour of an annual hour contract with monthly remuneration; overtime payments were eliminated. The basic tenet became trust between the different levels of workforce and management and the system works well. In fact management's age old philosophy of my door is always open is not a sop or a cipher. It is a truism at Monsanto.

Ansell explains 'Problems are there to be resolved. And anyone can take it to the top.' Monsanto involves staff in all of its processes in the pursuit of the all important teamwork, with so-called town hall meetings with a frank and honest two-way dialogue. But equally important are voluntary and anonymous attitude surveys which are conducted by an impartial third party. It is significant that 85 per cent respond because the 18-page questionnaire contains almost 300 questions with five alternative ratings to each – a total of 1,500 options. The comprehensive and worthwhile insight covers issues like training and development, job satisfaction, teamworking, the company, safety, work views, personal well-being and health. There is also an employee forum in which 12 elected representatives meet the management on a quarterly basis to discuss a wide range of issues and to be consulted in the decision-making process.

Monsanto's reward package is so good that few people leave and any recruitment initiative is aimed exclusively at graduates. The target is almost exclusively chemical engineers with the occasional computer expert. At most it recruits up to four a year and Monsanto targets those through a tie up with Oxford, Cambridge, Manchester and Birmingham Universities because of a sponsorship scheme. Training is a two-year induction programme with meaningful jobs from day one in operational areas doing project work.

A basic requirement – apart from academic qualifications – is interpersonal skills in a tightly knit organisation where square pegs do not fit into round holes. Career development is more complicated. There are those who will be quite happy to stay at Newport. But because the organisation is a flat management system, opportunities for promotion can be limited. However, training and development is individual-driven with opportunities for everyone to maximise their skills and grow within their job. Monsanto is one of very few to be awarded Investors in People status on its launch in 1991.

Monsanto aims to be better than average in its reward packages. Basic salaries are very competitive and a merit budget based on personal appraisal can give handsome additional increases, based on performance. Awards are made on the anniversary of a person joining the company. This reinforces the individual nature of the relationship between the company and its employees. A profit bonus calculated on-site and company targets can be up to 143 per cent of basic rates. In addition there is a share option scheme, free private medical cover for staff, with 50 per cent contributions for the immediate family, and a subsidised restaurant with the same prices for everyone.

Contact address

Mr Bob Ansell,
Human Resources Support Manager,
Monsanto plc,
Corporation Road, Newport,
Gwent NP9 0XF.
Telephone: 01633 278221.

JP Morgan

JP Morgan is a global financial services organisation which was formed in 1838 with the opening of a merchant bank in London by American businessman George Peabody. In 1995 the company earned $1.6 billion – an increase of 21 per cent over the previous year. Although headquartered in Wall Street, New York City, the group is truly global with offices or subsidiary companies in more than 30 countries around the world, including more than 12 in North America. Employees number around 15,000, working in the three geographical regions of North America; Europe, Middle East and Africa; and Asia Pacific. Around 300 graduate recruits are taken on each year in Europe and in London alone there are 49 nationalities working together. Almost two-thirds of the 15 top management positions are held by non-US nationals.

JP Morgan at a glance

Employees: 15,000 worldwide
Annual staff attrition rate: n/a
Key locations: New York (HQ) and major global centres in Europe: London, Amsterdam, Brussels, Frankfurt, Geneva, Madrid, Milan, Paris, Prague, Rome, Warsaw, Zurich
Av. annual graduate recruitment: 300 Europe
Annual intake: n/a

An inside view

Precision and quality typify JP Morgan's culture, which is one of efficiency based on the highest standards of personal and professional conduct. To JP Morgan everything is geared to providing the client with work of the highest standard and value. This is perhaps not surprising when clients include governments, multinational companies and central banks plus principals of privately owned companies, wealthy individuals and professional portfolio managers.

Its business sectors are concerned with providing help and expert advice to clients with complex financial needs. There are five such sectors: finance and advisory which helps clients structure and raise capital to support current and future operating plans, and counselling on and helping to execute business strategy; sales and trading helps clients buy and sell a wide variety of securities, currencies, commodities, and derivatives in connection with their investment, risk management, and trade-related activities, asset management and servicing manages portfolios and provides other investment and financial services for institutional and individual clients; the equity investments sector invests and manages a diversified portfolio of private equity for the firm's own account; and the asset and liability management sector manages the interest rate risk and liquidity profile of JP Morgan's assets, liabilities, and off-balance-sheet exposures.

As an indication of the high profile work carried out by the business during 1995, in Britain alone it advised the TSB Group plc on its \$15.3 billion merger with Lloyds Bank; led a 250 million South African rand three-year, 14.75 per cent Eurobond for the London-based European Bank for Reconstruction and Development; and acted as strategic advisor to the board of Forte Plc in its defence strategy against Granada's takeover bid. The firm is one of the top five merger and acquisition advisers worldwide, ranking first in Latin America and second in Europe. The organisation continues to grow in an increasingly competitive and ever-changing financial services sector. The firm still works for clients it served in the nineteenth and early twentieth centuries. Writing of the future for the firm in the latest available annual report, Douglas A Warner III, chairman of the board and CEO, said 'Morgan's edge, we believe, will derive ultimately from its commitment to clients. That commitment implies integrity, a passion to excel, and the integrity to build relationships over long horizons; it engenders trust, the most valuable distinction of all.'

JP Morgan demands much from its employees. It wants the cream of graduate talent, it insists on the highest standards of personal and professional conduct, but does help develop the careers of its employees, rewards them well, and wants them to stay.

How does JP Morgan rate?

Pay:	very good
Benefits:	excellent
Communications:	very good
Training:	excellent
Career development:	very good
Morale:	very good

People and personnel policies

Client-focused teamwork is the bedrock of work at JP Morgan. The company believes that a team-orientated approach gives clients access to the firm's best thinking and the full benefits of all its capabilities, while making the firm a rewarding and professionally supportive place to work. Successful graduates, men and women, are not in general chosen because of the type of degree they have. The academic qualifications held by graduates at the firm's London office, for example, range from forestry to MBAs. What is sought are people who can demonstrate a willingness to work as part of a team – usually comprising no more than six people.

Incoming graduates are hired into one of various business groups, details of which they more than likely will have been given at on-campus presentations. These groups are: investment banking; markets; asset management; private client group; Euroclear operations centre; technology; and operations or corporate resources groups such as financial, audit or human resources. The first week is spent learning about the firm and its work locally and then the graduate starts to work with a team in a specific work group for on-the-job learning. During the first 18 months most graduates spend a period of time – usually two months but it could be as long as six months – at the firm's New York headquarters for extensive global and further on-the-job training. The firm points out that it is globally structured, of necessity, for the benefit of the client, and locally dispersed, again for the benefit of the client. The client is local but the firm's 'product' is global.

As an example, a graduate joining the markets business group, which is a collection of product and businesses engaged in sales, trading and research activities in the world's financial markets, will need to have the ability to be a team player. They would be expected to be proficient with numbers in a fast-paced environment, have an interest in current affairs and their impact on market activity. An assignment would be given in either sales, trading, or research: as a member of the sales force helping to advise clients on investment and risk management opportunities; assisting on a trading team to make markets and proactively take risk in securities and other financial instruments; in a research group conducting business, product, or market analyses. This hands-on experience helps develop an understanding of the markets business and the practical knowledge and experience necessary to derive maximum benefit from the formal training programme in New York.

The firm works in an industry of change and says standing still is not an option. For example, $1 billion of revenue in 1995 was generated by activities that produced little or nothing at the start of the 1990s. Extensive skills-updating training is therefore provided and mobility is encouraged. This means there are many opportunities for working at the firm's offices in other parts of the world. JP Morgan pays competitively in what is a highly paid industry and pay levels are driven by personal performance. This performance is defined using a wide range of criteria spanning from bottom line contributions through effective teamwork. There is a profit-sharing scheme for all employees completing more than two years' service, although those with less than that time with the firm do receive a profit-share at a lower percentage. As one would expect from a firm of this size in a competitive marketplace, other benefits such as pensions and medical insurance are provided.

Communications within the firm are carried out through the use of e-mail, the Internet, magazines, bulletin boards and news releases, both locally and globally. The firm also prides itself on operating a management 'open door' policy. Although there is no formal sports and social club, staff at the London office do participate in sports and organised social activities. They also managed to raise an incredible £1 million for the Macmillan Cancer Relief Fund through a series of imaginative money-raising activities.

Contact address

Human Resources, J.P. Morgan,
60 Victoria Embankment,
London EC4Y 0JP.
Telephone: 0171 600 2300.
Fax: 0171 325 8526/8528

Mulberry Company Limited

Mulberry is an internationally respected lifestyle brand, designing and producing ladies' and mens' leather accessories, clothing and a comprehensive home range. These products are on sale at leading stores throughout the world. Started in 1971, it now exports more than 65 per cent of its output and generates turnover of more than £81 million. It is a business which has always placed great stress on respect for its employees, and one which treats its workforce extremely well.

Mulberry at a glance

Employees: 594 (504 UK)
Staff attrition rate: n/a
Key locations: Somerset, London, mainland Europe and the Far East
Graduate recruitment: n/a
Annual intake: n/a

An inside view

The statistics unfold a remarkable story. In 1969 Roger Saul, an accessories buyer, started making leather chokers and belts from the kitchen table of his London flat. Two years later with initial capital of £500 he formed the Mulberry Company with his mother and designed and made his first collection of belts and bags. Production shifted to an old forge in the garden of his parents' house near Bath. As demand increased, he employed local craftsmen with traditional leather skills, many of whom still work for the company.

In 1997, Mulberry employs 594 people worldwide, 504 in the UK. The company has shops or corners in shops in 22 countries around the globe. There are 51 shops worldwide – nine owned by the company; nine concessions in UK department stores, and 23 franchised outlets. Its products are represented by 536 wholesalers worldwide. It now has a catalogue of 2,700 different products which are divided into 750 in the ready-to-wear collection, 1,000 different accessories and 950 home products. In the last decade Saul and his colleagues have won a wide variety of awards from the Queens Award for Export three times, through Classic Designer of the Year Award and the British Apparel Export Award to Best Consumer Company into Europe Award.

Mulberry's success has been due to the vision and energy of the founders. The company captured the imagination of the fashion buyers and editors in the early 1970s. The mulberry tree logo, designed by Saul's sister Rosemary, was soon a familiar sight in the leading department stores and clothes shops of the early 1970s. Mulberry's designs often combined high quality craftsmanship with an amusing idea. One commentator summarises the essence of the achievement in that 'he created an instant classic'.

Mulberry Company Limited

Key points in the early history of the company were: Saul's first large overseas order in Paris in 1972 for 1,000 belts, the opening of the Mulberry factory in Chilcompton in 1973, the creation of agencies in France and Germany in 1974 and joining the London designer collections in 1975. The following year was a big one – Mulberry presented its legendary hunting, shooting, fishing collection, the company opened showrooms in London and New York, and Saul designed belt collections for Ralph Lauren and Enrico Coveri. In the next decade the company established itself throughout the world, with the UK as its biggest export market. By 1988, it was the largest manufacturer of designer leather accessories in the UK.

How does Mulberry rate?

Pay:	good
Benefits:	good
Communications:	superb
Training:	excellent
Career development:	good
Morale:	superb

People and personnel policies

The apparently unquenchable growth of Mulberry resulted in the opening of the new Mulberry headquarters in March 1996 by the Princess Royal. Monty Saul, people director of Mulberry, says that much of the success of the company should be credited to its employees. She says that from the outset Roger Saul took the view that people were central to the success of the enterprise and he wanted to run a business which would treat its employees with care, understanding and respect.

From the early days he attracted people who wanted to work with him because of the company's approach, which combines pride in its quality products with a sense of challenge in achieving the impossible. As the business grew – both in the UK and internationally – and the reputation of Mulberry spread, finding good people was not an issue, only sorting through the applications. The company employs 303 people in the headquarters in Somerset and it has made extensive use of local people to staff the enterprise. Many of them have been with Mulberry since the early days and few show an inclination to work elsewhere. Although there are not many high volume employers in the country, Mulberry commands extraordinary loyalty from its people and it is not lack of opportunity elsewhere which binds them to the business. Part of the Mulberry mission statement emphasises the creation of a work environment which is committed to developing, training and caring for its team at all levels.

A substantial step for the business was the accreditation in 1994 of the Investors in People scheme. Monty Saul, as people – not personnel or human resources – director, says that the company has gained a great deal from its involvement with IIP. She told *Somerset Business News* 'We were growing fast and we were worried that the spirit of the company – so important to its success in its first two decades – would be more and more difficult to sustain as it became more widely spread. We looked to IIP and it seemed to mesh beautifully with everything we believed in – developing individuals' skills, building a thorough understanding of company goals and generating in staff the kind of commitment that we felt ourselves.'

She says that continuous improvement had already been a way of life for the company, and directors relished the idea. The process took 18 months and involved, among other tasks, an assessment of Mulberry' strengths and weaknesses. 'Happily in our case the strengths were many and the weaknesses few.' But she comments that the structure provided by the accreditation process was extremely valuable.

As for training during 1996, 917 employees attended 128 assorted courses from induction to recruitment and appraisal to team building skills. All courses are vetted by Monty Saul and if necessary tailor-made to suit the Mulberry future. She is now assembling a package of courses which will cover the majority of the training needs of Mulberry's managers.

The structure, which IIP and the related training initiatives have provided, has allowed Mulberry to continue its dramatic growth but not at the expense of losing its intimate culture. It has given the company a stronger organisational pattern and codified its people policies in ways which are distinctively Mulberry. From a certain perspective, the Mulberry people approach is not unlike its products – durable, well crafted and with a sense of humanity.

Contact address

Monty Saul,
People Director,
The Mulberry Company Limited,
Kilver Court,
Shepton Mallet,
Somerset BA4 5NE.
Telephone: 01749 340500.
Fax: 01749 345532.

3M

3M is one of the world's great companies. It is the personification of the great innovator in industry. The company introduces more than 500 new products every year in a wide range of different industrial and commercial sectors. It is famed for its Post It Notes, the repositionable yellow notepapers with the adhesive strip on the back. But it also works in fields as diverse as reflective materials, healthcare, adhesives, and computer disk storage. 3M places great store by its capacity to generate original new products and markets.

3M at a glance

Employees: 3,900 UK
Staff attrition: 5 per cent
Key locations: Bracknell, HQ; plus 16 sites across the UK
Annual graduate recruitment: n/a
Annual intake: 150

An inside view

3M, the Minnesota Mining and Manufacturing company, started in 1902, is the benchmark business for entrepreneurs and innovators. It is a cri de coeur of 3M that it consistently breaks fresh ground in every aspect of its business. High emphasis is placed on the will and the talent to innovate – and not only in the commercial market. It launches around 500 new product lines every year, some completely new ideas, others refinements of existing successes. But, also, the structure and systems of the company are regularly updated and as recently as 1994 3M went through a major restructuring to organise new business centres and disciplinary functions.

This company has won the widespread respect of business leaders throughout the world for its dedicated approach to the creation of new products and the development of existing lines. The time to innovate on a daily or weekly basis is built into the work schedule of every employee. Also the decision-making process is a rapid and alert one. For people used to the more sluggish and bureaucratic companies, 3M comes as a revelation. Although traditionally teamwork-biased, it is low on structures and remarkably quick on getting ideas to market. But 3M does its research and no product will be launched without active and detailed analysis of marker possibilities.

The culture at 3M is one which encourages individuals and teams to work effectively but it is rather low key in comparison to many other US-owned corporations. While the company is driven by values, these underscore its activities. Many multinationals focus overtly on their missions, values or company statements as a method of getting their message across.

It is perhaps revealing that 3M does not need to employ such devices. It expects commitment, high quality and original work, speed of thought and action, and fresh thinking. In return it is in the upper echelons for pay and benefits, giving its people remarkable latitude and freedom to make a contribution, and total integrity.

Both worldwide and in the UK, 3M is viewed as a blue chip business against which to benchmark. Its approach to quality, process systems, ability to innovate and attitude towards its people are all seen as among the best in industry.

How does 3M rate?

Pay:	excellent
Benefits:	superb
Communications:	very good
Training:	excellent
Career development:	good
Morale:	very good

People and personnel policies

There is a group of US multinationals based in the UK which operate in the vanguard of excellent human resources policy. Among them are Mars, IBM, Xerox, Hewlett-Packard and 3M. These are the standard-setters for a wide range of HR issues, offering superb working conditions. From the launch of its UK operation, 3M has striven to be an innovator not only in products but also in its attitude towards its people.

It has taken the view that in order for its people to be at their best they must have freedom and flexibility of operation and be remunerated well for the application of their talents. It is an arrangement which appears to have worked well. 3M's people consistently beat competitors to market with completely new ideas or substantial refinements on existing lines.

The company is heavily geared towards effective communications. Open, frank and honest communication is often difficult in multinationals but it is a priority in 3M. Unlike many businesses it is good with words and has an apparently innate capacity for simple and direct expression. Even the most complex industrial processes are documented clearly and precisely. Also, all major policy decisions are communicated quickly and effectively to the workforce. The business encourages feedback which will assist managers and directors in the improvement of ideas, systems and output.

The approach to pay and benefits is a typically direct one. Pay is pitched at a high standard point with an increasingly variable element according to grade within the company. Benefits are broadly based with strong pension, life and health cover and generous holiday and sick pay entitlements.

The training regime within 3M is one which attracts considerable praise. For many years training has been seen as an important element of its human resources policy. The business has invested heavily in both on-the-job training and courses which extend the knowledge and skills of its managers and general employees.

There is a high graduate intake at 3M as the company sees this as a coherent way to ensure that it draws intelligent and able people into the company. Once within

3M people join one of the streams of business but today there is active cross-disciplinary working and there are many opportunities to move to different areas of the business. The appraisal programme ensures that skills and development needs are assessed and that training is provided which will meet the skills demands of future assignments.

There is low attrition in 3M. It is a company which has consistently retained its talented people – indeed people clamour to join the organisation. It is one of the favourite choices of undergraduates, particularly those with scientific backgrounds. Since applied research is a major feature of what 3M does, the opportunities within the organisation for developing new product ideas are legion. Undergraduates are also attracted to its reputation for personal headroom.

Candidates for employment within 3M are also expected to have strong commercial instincts. As well as creating new products the company often establishes completely new markets, and a capacity to identify new markets and ways to sell to them is highly prized. 3M looks for people with a range of skills – the capacity to communicate well, the ability to work as an individual and as a team player, and an understanding of markets.

As technology changes, 3M's need for people of different academic and technological backgrounds will expand. In the last decade the company has established a series of new market sectors and has drawn in people to exploit the commercial and research opportunities in these areas. However, strong emphasis is placed too on growing and developing its own people.

Contact address

Human Resources Department,
3M,
Bracknell,
Berkshire .
Telephone: 01344 858000.
Fax: 01344 858278.

Nationwide Building Society

The Nationwide is the most successful building society to remain committed to the principle of customer ownership. A product of one of the largest building society mergers ever to take place in Britain, it has a sustained record of efficiency gains, innovation and sound financial performance. One of the key goals of the society is to be a place where its employees want to work. To this end, it has adopted the most modern employment practices, with a particular emphasis on project teamwork and customer care. It also has an outstanding approach to equal opportunities.

Nationwide at a glance

Employees: 10,724
Annual staff attrition rate: 9 per cent
Key locations: Swindon (HQ),
    Northampton (admin centre), plus
    689 branches across the country
Av. annual graduate recruitment: 20
Annual intake: 900

An inside view

It is a rare commercial organisation that deliberately aims to cut its income and profits, but this policy is at the heart of the business strategy of the Nationwide Building Society. The society wants to offer its customers highly competitive rates and services, and so pass on to them in the most direct way possible the benefits of their ownership of the society.

At a time when many building societies have chosen to become quoted companies to raise enough capital for continuing growth, as the largest remaining society it faces little difficulty

on that score. It is not drawn to the added opportunities for takeover and mergers afforded by a stock market listing – there have been enough expensive and unsuccessful acquisitions in financial services for it to view this mode of expansion with caution. Nor does it feel that shareholders are the only party that can discipline and hold management to account – its customers as members of the society can do just as good a job.

Instead, the Nationwide has emphasised its differences with shareholder-owned companies by adopting new measures of performance in the area of customer satisfaction and business efficiency, to replace the traditional measures of profit and the cost: income ratio. While keeping a careful eye on traditional performance indicators to ensure stability, it aims to restrict its profits to a level no greater than is necessary to sustain the business.

Like other financial institutions Nationwide is broadening its range of services, taking in areas such as life insurance, unit trusts, a specialist loan service for the self-employed and health insurance. But unlike some others it concentrates on offering added benefits to all its loyal customers rather than special rates for newcomers. It is also particularly keen on new technology. It was among the first financial companies to host an Internet site and won an award for installing a multimedia information service for customers in its branches, with the option of video-conferencing with a member of staff for hard-to-answer questions.

How does Nationwide rate?

Pay:	very good
Benefits:	excellent
Communications:	very good
Training:	excellent
Career development:	very good
Morale:	good

People and personnel policies

The Nationwide became the largest financial institution to gain accreditation to the Investors in People initiative in the early 1990s. In so doing, it committed itself to the highest standards in practices such as the communication of company objectives to employees, the setting of individual training and development plans and the holding of regular performance reviews for all staff.

The society has put a lot of effort into making sure that all employees know what the organisation's objectives are and how their individual goals relate to them. The

work of managers in this sphere is complemented by posters, papers and videos. The directors also regularly convene separate groups of employees and managers to hear their views on how the business is being run. Everybody who works for Nationwide has a performance agreement, outlining clearly what they are required to do, and there are formal annual reviews of performance. Training tends to be on-the-job through coaching, computerised courses and other methods, with a bias against off-site courses.

Like other organisations, Nationwide is replacing the tall, narrow pyramid of traditional hierarchies with a wider, flatter organisational structure which gives employees more broadly defined roles. This change is offering employees greater opportunities for work in cross-disciplinary project teams and it is quite possible now for staff to be working for several different managers on more than one project at a time. As a result, interpersonal skills are at a premium.

The public has traditionally looked on building societies with greater warmth than other financial institutions and this attitude is matched by employees of Nationwide, according to human resources director Jeremy del Strother. 'There does seem to be a warmth of feeling among employees who feel the organisation has one sole objective: customer satisfaction. We pursue this for its own sake rather than as a means to another end, that of earning profits for shareholders,' he says.

An ability to relate to all kinds of people is the most important attribute Nationwide looks for in prospective recruits. 'They have to have a proper understanding of the customer. They have to have a degree of initiative beyond the ordinary. They also have to have a balance between creative, innovating, and enterprising qualities and a set of skills involving control and quality,' del Strother says. Most recruits join as customer advisers working in small front-line teams but there is a graduate training programme and the society likes to have around 60 people passing through this at any one time. Graduates are taken on for a two-year period and exposed to all areas of retail financial services. By the end of this training period, they will have passed the first stage in the Institute of Banking exams and, if they have achieved their performance targets, will have secured an opening in the society.

Graduates are expected to be able to deal effectively with people, work in a team and be action-oriented, just as much as any other recruit. 'On the whole, we are not looking for people straight out of college,' says del Strother. 'We would prefer that they had gained some experience of life and spent a year backpacking in Australia or taken a year out between school and college and worked as a labourer,' he says.

The society encourages cross-functional career moves, and a broad portfolio of experience, together with an understanding of people across the business are essential for any employee who wants to enter senior management. Pay is linked to performance through bonus schemes with the objective being to reward the employee's contribution to the society through their achievement rather than their status or the effort and skills they have brought to bear. The Nationwide aims for pay rates to be in the upper quartile of a comparison group of companies. 'Upper quartile pay for upper quartile performance,' is the description given to this policy by del Strother.

In its commitment to equal opportunities, the society provides a model that many other companies would do well to follow. The Nationwide is an active member of the Opportunity 2000 Group, which promotes the prospects of women at work. It is also a founder member of the Employers' Forum on Age, which promotes the benefits of a mixed-age workforce, and a member of the Employers' Forum on Disability. Women make up half of the society's branch managers. Flexible working arrangements such as part-time, job-share and term-time contracts are open to men and women and more than 85 per cent of women employees return to the society after maternity leave.

Contact address

Mr Jeremy del Strother,
Human Resources Director,
Nationwide Building Society,
Nationwide House,
Pipers Way,
Swindon SN38 1NW.
Telephone: 01793 513513.
Fax: 01793 455341.

NatWest Group

Natwest Group is one of the largest financial services organisations in the UK and is active in many markets across the world. Its UK retail arm, NatWest UK, lies at the heart of the operation. The group's other principal businesses are NatWest Markets, the corporate and investment banking arm, Coutts & Co, Ulster Bank and Lombard, the UK's largest financial house. In 1996, NatWest Group reported income of £7.27 billion and a pre-tax profit of £1.12 billion.

NatWest at a glance

Employees: 71,000
Staff attrition: n/a
Key locations: London (HQ), and
    locations in every sizeable town or city
    in the UK. Many overseas offices
Annual graduate recruitment: up to 250
Annual intake: n/a

An inside view

The financial services community is one of the great industries of the UK. It generates substantial external revenues for the British economy and provides a financial backbone for industry. Every company and the vast majority of individuals in the land operate bank accounts and run insurance policies. The banks are the dominant forces in the financial sector and the four English high street banks – NatWest, Barclays, Midland (HSBC Group) and Lloyds – are the key players.

In the 1980s – in common with banking institutions worldwide – British banks wanted to be global operators,

providing a broad range of services to a wide portfolio of clients. But only a handful of financial services organisations had the strength and expertise to be profitable in all markets. Coupled with the incidence of problem country debt and the effects of the recession, many of the adventures, did not prove fruitful and, for a variety of reasons, the early 1990s saw British banks reporting substantially reduced profits.

NatWest was among the first to realise that it needed to restructure and to become more proficient at those areas where it had or could have a profound market advantage. The appointment of Derek Wanless in 1992 as group chief executive was symbolic and he – and his principal colleagues – have refocused NatWest into a more purposeful, integrated and profitable business relevant to the 1990s and beyond.

1996 was a year of considerable achievement for the group. Management effort is now firmly directed on businesses where the group can deliver improved shareholder value from a leading, sustainable and profitable presence. During 1996, the group sold its US retail operation, Bancorp, as well as its Spanish retail business. In the same period, it bought Gartmore, the highly regarded UK fund manager, as well as Greenwich Capital Holdings and Hambro Magan to strengthen its expertise in fixed income sales and trading, and corporate advisory. The group's strategy is now clearly focused on three key areas: commercial banking and retail financial services in the UK and Ireland; global investment banking; and wealth management. This refocusing of its strategy is already paying dividends as the strong underlying performance reported in the group's 1996 results clearly shows.

NatWest UK has changed in concert with the needs of customers and will continue to adapt as the market environment evolves. Ulster Bank has a distinctly different profile – its branches are found throughout the province and in the Republic even in relatively small communities. Its profile is somewhat more relaxed than the busiest of the NatWest branches and Ulster Bank emphasises the personal banking philosophy which was commonplace here.

NatWest Markets is experiencing one of its most successful periods, and the three acquisitions made during the course of the year as well as that of Gleacher at the end of 1995 have added considerably to the scale of its operations. Lombard is the UK's largest finance house with more than three million personal and commercial customers. A new business grouping comprising Gartmore, NatWest Life & Investment Services, NatWest Ventures and, with effect from January 1997, Coutts, has been established to develop further the group's strategic ambitions in the markets for private banking, long-term savings and investments.

How does NatWest rate?

Pay:	good
Benefits:	very good
Communications:	very good
Training:	excellent
Career development:	very good
Morale:	good

People and personnel policies

The five businesses of the NatWest Group run their own personnel policies, to a large degree. The centre is committed to certain principles, such as open and honest communications, well-structured training and fair reward packages, but the operational aspects of human resources are down to the individual businesses. Chris Wathen, director, group human resources, says 'The market conditions in each of our businesses are very different. In NatWest Markets, for example, the remuneration packages are higher but that is because investment banking requires a higher proportion of specialist skills which are in particular demand in that type of business. In the retail business we seek different people to fulfil differing functions and the package will reflect market circumstances.'

Wathen says that establishing a groupwide HR policy on many personnel issues would be inappropriate. The managers of the five core businesses are alert to the people issues which impact on their operations. One initiative which has come from the group is the creation of a worldwide staff council, which meets regularly. Elected members of the workforce and trade union representatives form this council where management puts forward issues and the council members are invited to make their own contributions to the agenda. The establishment of the council is a major step towards improving communication and dialogue with the employees.

Another area where the group influences thinking is in the creation of a performance culture. Derek Wanless says 'A performance culture is vital in our highly competitive markets. I am determined that we measure performance in a way that is truly about the long-term interest of the group. That is why we have used a balanced business scorecard and why the focus must not be purely on short-term financial measures. Performance must be measured against the broader long-term health of the group. That is why there is not one single model for remuneration policies.'

NatWest has stepped up its commitment to the training and development of its employees throughout the group to respond to more challenging market conditions. Again the operational aspects of training are administered by managers in the business areas. The training needs of a securities trader in NatWest Markets will be clearly different from a branch manager in Ulster Bank. Nevertheless, the group has emphasised its objective to make training relevant to the needs of the individual and business. As the strategic reshaping of the group is almost complete, the scope of ambitions within individual businesses can be assessed and appropriate training offered.

Graduates joining NatWest can expect to be recruited into a specific role, but during their first couple of years will see something of the rest of the group. Prospective managers will look for career opportunities throughout the group and not only in the stream into which they have been inducted. Traditionally banking was very compartmentalised but this has been breaking down and now there is greater cross-functional exposure.

NatWest's involvement in the Investors in People initiative has been a major step in its human resources policy. Wanless told *Agenda*, the NatWest staff magazine 'Investors in People provides a formal structure linked to our business objectives, to ensure that our training and development programmes provide the opportunity for staff to develop their full potential within the business.

'We have publicly stated our intention that all UK units will achieve IIP accreditation by mid-1997. Some units have already achieved accreditation; others are well on the way to reaching that goal. But for me the most important thing about IIP is not the achievement of accreditation but the spirit and the processes which lead to accreditation. That means positive developments like the involvement of staff in the business and the creation of teams.'

Contact address

Mary Locke,
Recruitment Manager,
NatWest Group,
Level 27 Drapess Gardens,
12 Throgmorton Avenue,
London EC2N 2DL.
Telephone: 0171 920 5555.
Fax: 0171 920 5923.

Nestlé UK Limited

Nestlé is one of the world's largest and most respected corporations in the food and drink industry. Its traditional focus has been on confectionery and beverage products but it also makes baby foods, petfoods, fruit juices, breakfast cereals, pasta, and chilled and frozen meals. In the UK it acquired the York-based Quaker confectioner Rowntree Macintosh in 1988 and since then it has gradually integrated the Nestlé and Rowntree management structures. Globally the Nestlé corporation reported sales of £28.5 billion in 1995. Its British operation employs more than 14,000 people in four divisions – Grocery, Rowntree, Food (including Nestlé Lyons Maid) and Food Services.

Nestlé at a glance

Employees: 220,000 - globally; 14,500 in the UK (approx. 1,600 managers)
Staff attrition rate: 16 per cent
Key locations: 24 factories, depots and sales offices. Group HQ is in Croydon, Nestlé Rowntree operates from York
Active graduate recruitment: 40
Annual intake: 120 managers

An inside view

When Henri Nestlé started manufacturing the first powdered baby milk in 1867 in the small Swiss town of Vevey on the banks of Lake Geneva, he probably had little appreciation of the size to which his company would grow. In 1996 Nestlé was one of the world's top two coffee and confectionery companies with a broad sweep of brand leaders in other food and drink sectors. The company operates 489 factories in 73 countries worldwide. In the UK its brands include Nescafe, Kit Kat, Carnation milk, Aero, Crosse and Blackwell (including Branston pickle), Findus, Libby's, Buitoni pasta, Lyons Maid ice-cream, Dairy Box chocolates, Quality Street, Sarsons vinegar, Rowntree's jelly, and Sun Pat peanut butter.

The company was founded on children's and dietetic foods and has spread by acquisition and organic growth into its current range. According to Nestlé SA, the parent company, the real thrust for brand diversity began in 1960 with the purchase of Crosse & Blackwell which was followed by a string of acquisitions including Findus, Vittel, Libby's, L'Oreal, Chambourcy, Carnation, Herta, Buitoni, Rowntree and Perrier. Nestlé has stamped its imprint on each of these businesses as it has brought them into the group fold. Inherently the personality of this outstandingly successful company is at once a strongly professional, hierarchical, instinctively private and well-ordered management culture. It ranks with Shell, ABB, Mercedes Benz and other global businesses which started on mainland Europe. It is a reputable and highly structured world class company. Continental market leaders often owe a great deal of their success to the efficiency of their management systems, the concentrated focus of their products and the quality of their production and marketing skills. So it is with Nestlé. In recent months Nestlé UK has completed an exhaustive exercise to identify and promulgate common values and goals.

For graduates Nestlé is an excellent company to begin a career with. Its sharply honed commercial instincts are channelled into effective training and thorough development procedures. Graduate recruits go straight into a full-time position while launching a personal two-year training programme. Nestlé has operated a graduate recruitment initiative for many years. It has developed through various stages of sophistication and is today among the leaders in European industry. 'We are looking for a mixture of individuals, many of whom show a capacity for assuming high-flying management positions but some will prefer to work in more technical disciplines. We look for certain characteristics beyond, obviously, educational ability. These qualities include a capacity to communicate with other people, openness, honesty, objectivity and a preference for teamworking over a solo operation,' says Nestlé UK's group personnel director John Reid. 'We hire people at graduate level whom we believe are capable of moving quickly and a long way up the management tree.'

How does Nestlé rate?

Pay:	very good
Benefits:	very good
Communications:	very good
Training:	excellent
Career development:	very good
Staff morale:	good

People and personnel policies

The company is similar to that other pre-eminent advocate of brand leadership, Procter & Gamble. Like P&G, Nestlé relies heavily on first appointment recruitment and promotion thereafter from within. 'Nestlé worldwide does this. And we either develop within markets or around markets to a great extent. We do some external recruitment but not for the higher levels of management. We tend to develop people from within and concentrate on the qualities and characteristics which we are looking for.'

Graduates typically move twice or three times during their first two years. They are employed by the company centrally but work in one of the divisions in a real job. The rationale behind this approach is to give potentially high-flying managers an early overview of the company and a chance to experience work in different divisions. The company, however, is flexible and does not insist that people with a marketing inclination work in production or vice versa.

'One of the virtues of Nestlé is that it is a truly international company which means that its 1,600 UK managers can expect to enjoy assignments on any continent and in most countries. In particular Nestlé is active in almost all of the developing countries where some of the most exciting work is emerging. Other companies are perhaps not investing as much in these markets. We have been in China and India for years, and we are hiring people locally. Management is often brought in from the developed world. In the last couple of years we have exported 50 plus managers a year to the international structure.'

Nestlé aims to give its managers early and varied experience. As these individuals rise in the company, this wide-ranging appreciation of the extent of the company and its operations will assist in the quality of decision making. 'In companies of our maturity, there will inevitably be a certain degree of rationalisation. So anyone who moves on will be equipped with some of the best skills currently available in industry.'

The company aims to be upper quartile in terms of pay for higher management and median in the lower levels. The Nestlé pension scheme is among the best in UK industry with a good investment performance. Private health insurance is widely available in the company but a remarkably generous scheme which extended into retirement has been capped. It also operates staff shops which are open in many locations where employees can buy Nestlé products at discounted rates. The company provides what it calls an early years database. This gives new mothers information on child care facilities and contact names in their area.

Although Nestlé does not measure its annual attrition rate – or at least if it does, then it does not make it known – the company believes that it is good at keeping people. A large majority of the UK group's employees are long-term staff. Many have served 20, 25 or 30 years; there are even some who have been with the enterprise for 40 years. This, says Nestlé, is testimony to the loyalty that the company has earned from its people.

'Our focus is to recruit efficiently and well, not on how many we lose. Typically the reward structure, say, for one of our secretaries will be more attractive than for most employers. So the emphasis among staff is generally on staying with and growing in the company. We tend to treat employees as individuals rather than collectively. If someone leaves, we ask if there is an issue here we can do something about.'

Nestlé is an active communicator with its staff. Although some information passes through the channel of trade unions – there are 10,000 union members in the company – most comes through a package of initiatives which is produced by the business. Regular programmes include cascade briefings which are disseminated through direct reports from the management team to the shop floor. These happen six times a year. In addition there are two company-wide results presentations at half and full year.

Contact address

For recruitment enquiries:
Nestlé UK Limited,
St Georges House,
Croydon CR9 1NR.
Telephone: 0181 686 3333.
Fax: 0181 681 1218.

Nissan Motor Manufacturing

Nissan chose the location for the company's British manufacturing operation in 1984 and the story since then has been one of unmitigated and unqualified success. It negotiated a trailblazing single union no strike agreement to bring peace to what had been a notoriously troubled industry in the dark days of industrial relations. The Sunderland plant opened in the summer of 1986, and less than nine months later the year's millionth vehicle rolled off the assembly line. In September 1995 Nissan invested an additional £250 million to increase the UK commitment to £1.25 billion.

Nissan at a glance

Employees: 4,200
Annual staff attrition rate: 4 per cent
Key locations: Sunderland, Cranfield, Rickmansworth
Av. annual graduate recruitment: 12
Annual intake: 150

An inside view

As the research for this book reached its culmination, Nissan announced yet another milestone in its 11-year history of ever-increasing success. The company planned to create several hundred new jobs in Tyneside as part of its deepening commitment to the region. Production of a third model was announced to start in the year 2000. Nissan's achievement is not only to have created a vibrant company in an area of economic decline but to have pulled off this coup against the tradition which said that workers and management

must be at loggerheads in this part of the world. The death of the staple industries of the North East was, in fact, a significant element in persuading Nissan to set up its operation on the former Sunderland airport. But Nissan was shrewd enough to recognise that there were government grants available and it took full advantage of them. The pits had closed, the shipyards shut, the steelworks phased out and there was a pool of skilled workers who wanted to make a living.

Nissan dragged the old restrictive practices into the modern age with a system which may have seemed alien but is now second nature. It is a showcase European plant which aims to build, profitably, the highest quality car sold in Europe. Some 5 per cent of all cars sold in this country are Nissan, but the company's commitment runs much deeper than that. It also has extensive technical facilities which enable British engineers to design and build cars especially for the European market. Nissan's philosophy at the Sunderland plant is to develop a high degree of teamwork with complete mutual trust and cooperation between all staff. Everyone is encouraged to work together towards the common goal of high quality and profitable production. Advanced management techniques ensure there are no costly buffer stocks on components because parts are delivered as and when required and Nissan rightly insists that Sunderland is far more than only an assembly plant. It manufactures engines and axles, presses body parts and produces aluminium castings and major plastics components, such as fuel tanks and bumpers.

Total quality is a core philosophy which runs through every aspect of the business: the way in which the plant is run and the way in which the cars it produces are built. Quality is not something left to people called quality controllers. It is the responsibility of every single person in the organisation from receptionists to employees working on the production line, and all administrative staff including the managing director.

The company's main thrust is in the North East where the vehicles are made with a 80 per cent plus European content. Nissan's technology and design centre at Cranfield, Bedfordshire and the marketing and sales section based at Rickmansworth, Herts are ancillaries to the all-important production operation. No motor manufacturer since the early days of this century has grown with the speed that Nissan has developed its Sunderland plant. The company is now producing two models – the Primera, which has won 21 major European motoring awards, and the Micra. The supermini is the first Japanese badged vehicle to win the coveted European car of the year award. Equally impressive is the speed with which a network of more than 200 European component suppliers has been found to satisfy nearly all of Nissan's requirements. The only major components to be imported from Japan for production of the Primera and Micra are the transmission system and the engine block.

How does Nissan rate?

Pay:	excellent
Benefits:	superb
Communications:	good
Training:	very good
Career development:	very good
Morale:	superb

People and personnel policies

The tripod was not invented by Nissan, but the company has adapted the principle of three legged stability to found the basis of a firm and stable operation. All legs are equal: flexibility which means expanding a person's capability to his or her limits; quality consciousness; and teamwork. The selection of staff has a crucial impact on the success of this approach and this process, which gives equal weight to its three core components, is regarded as all-important. All prospective employees are interviewed by those under whom they would work. The Nissan guidelines are simple to the point of expediency: a team of between 15 and 20 people make up the core activity under a supervisor who is pivotal to the well- being of the organisation. Within that framework they are free to range within the whole area and width of their responsibilities. The plant's philosophy is to develop a high degree of teamwork with complete trust and cooperation between all staff.

Culturally, Nissan tries to embody the best of all traditions. Some of the people management techniques appeared somewhat unorthodox when introduced into the plain-speaking North East. But after initial reservations they were absorbed and applied highly effectively. Central to the company's thinking is the concept of *kaizen* which means continuous improvement. It works like a spiral staircase with four basic principles: plan, do, check, action and improvement, and then plan again, and the system works well. The foundation for Nissan's regard and involvement for its employees is laid down in a comprehensive 34-page booklet of terms and conditions. There is no big brother in a wide-ranging ethic which determines that no one is sacked for a first offence against company discipline, apart from gross industrial misconduct.

As Philip Ashmore, personnel director explains 'We believe we are a special company. We spend a lot of time talking about teamworking and flexibility. We have leadership courses, communication courses, workshop technique courses and all are geared to improving performance in the workplace.' Nissan does most of its own training from the inside because it regards itself as a big family concern. Trainers from outside could easily be unfamiliar with the nuances of the Nissan culture and ethos.

Ashmore says of graduate recruits 'We take around a dozen a year. In the early days of our operation it was twice as many for obvious start up reasons.' Those who are hired take around 30 months to reach the engineer controller or supervisory level and there is no shortage of applications to join the company. 'We have a good reputation for the quality of training we give. We try to get them into decision-making roles as early as possible because they are high quality people. We attempt to give them an up front job and support them when they need support, but they are not regarded as an elite. They have to earn respect.'

In fact Nissan regards all of its workforce as an elite and sings the praises of all the people who work for the company. It targeted the North East when setting up after extensive market research into attitudes throughout most regions of the UK. But Nissan spotted the inherent work ethic and generations of craftsmen and capitalised on that talent. The reward package is the envy of the area: competitive basic salaries with extra money based on an annual appraisal – typically 2 per cent in addition to an annual all-round basic increase. In the last five years the basic rate has been 10 per cent over and above inflation in real terms. Free health insurance means private healthcare for employees and their immediate family.

Contact address

Mr Philip Ashmore,
Director – Personnel,
Nissan Motor Manufacturing (UK) Ltd,
Washington Road,
Sunderland,
Tyne and Wear SR5 3NS.
Telephone: 0191 415 0000.
Fax: 0191 415 2741.

Nortel

A century ago, Northern Telecom, or Nortel as it is now known, was established as a small Canadian telephone system manufacturer in Montreal. In the 1960s, it became a significant force in the United States marketplace, and 20 years later had extended its operations into Europe, Asia and South America. Its European presence gathered further force in 1991 with the acquisition of one of Britain's foremost telecommunications companies, STC; and in 1992, it launched joint ventures with Matra in France and in 1995 with Daimler Benz in Germany, making Nortel a leader in European and, indeed, global telecommunications.

Nortel at a glance

Employees: 7,000 UK
Annual staff attrition rate: 4 per cent
Key locations: Maidenhead (HQ), New Southgate, Harlow, Moulestown, Paignton, Cwmcam
Av. annual graduate recruitment: 100–200
Annual intake: 500

An inside view

Explaining what Nortel is not is sometimes easier than stating what it actually is. Nortel is not a telephone operator, so the company does not compete with its customers. Instead, it provides the transmission and switching technology which enables private and public telecommunications companies to run their own networks and deliver advanced services to their customers.

Half of the European telephone companies and major public network operators around the world have chosen Nortel, for everything from small switches to handle local lines to giant gateway switches connecting customers to international networks. Established operators such as British Telecom and Mercury, and new entrants in the field such as Energis and Konica, all base some or all of their business on Nortel's technology.

The company designs, develops and manufactures digital phone systems for businesses, with more than 700,000 installed in businesses of all shapes and sizes worldwide, including 95,000 in the UK. Nortel is at the forefront of the latest developments in telecommunications, both multimedia and cellular, and today is deploying full interactive broadband technologies for its customers worldwide.

Nortel has become strong in Europe, and particularly the United Kingdom, because the country is at the heart of East-West trade routes. The company believes that this country has the twin advantages of geographical position and the English language. More than 130 licences have been granted in the UK and competition has stimulated a great deal of innovation, giving Nortel the opportunity to provide new technology to new players.'

The company's commitment to the United Kingdom is clear through the spread of its workforce. It is one of the largest industrial employers in Northern Ireland with its specialist research and development laboratory; and has one of Europe's most advanced manufacturing plants at Cwmcam in Wales, as well as employing more than 2,000 people producing fixed radio access Optoelectronic products in Devon. This workforce will increase by more than 1,000 over the next five years.

How does Nortel rate ?

Pay:	very good
Benefits:	very good
Communications:	good
Training:	excellent
Careers:	very good
Staff morale:	good

People and personnel policies

Nortel is highly regarded for locating in areas that have suffered severe industrial deprivation, bringing new life and jobs into societies that have not known economic well-being for long periods of time. When it took over the Cwmcam factory from BT and STC, the company spent £2 million upgrading the building, £6 million on new plant and equipment

and another large amount of money on improving the riverbank adjacent to the site. From exporter to multinational, from multinational to global company, Nortel is ever expanding with as many as 500 open job vacancies at any one time in the UK. Latest turnover sits at $1 billion in the UK, $1 billion in continental Europe and a worldwide corporate total of $10.67 billion in 1996.

In an industry that has undergone as much change as technology itself, this company has remained one of the few stable and consistent performers. One of the largest employers of engineering graduates in the UK, it employs twice as many female engineers than the national average. It hires top talent through its university recruitment programmes. In 1995, it hired more than 100 of the country's graduates, masters and PhDs in computer science and engineering.

Its total commitment to quality hiring and training is renowned. More than $30 million a year alone is spent on training. 'Training is our life blood,' says John Cartland, vice-president of human resources for Nortel in Europe. Nortel's HR policy has gone through significant cultural change because Nortel has grown itself through acquisition, and there have been major alterations in the past five years.

'We have to be very flexible,' says Cartland. 'We have to be comfortable working with ambiguity. Clearly we want to be the employer of choice. Nortel has to be a company that someone automatically wants to work for. We are very focused on our business, so we meet the needs of the employee.' Nortel's key quality driver is putting the customer first. David Ball, chief executive of Nortel Ltd, puts it like this 'We aim to achieve this by attaining business excellence, delivered through the skills and abilities of the people who make up the company. As a knowledge-based organisation, our employees are fundamental to our success, and because of this, the underlying philosophy, *Our people are our strength*, is one of our core values. All of our people management policies, processes and systems, aim to recognise this, and strengthen our people.'

Ball emphasises that the rate of change in the industry is rapid, and combined with the volatile climate means that nobody, whether employer or employee, can afford to become complacent. The universal issues of Nortel's human resources policy cover leadership, performance management, operational excellence, and strategic recruitment and selection. There is almost continuous assessment of quality levels, and the company uses the London Business School as an independent assessor. 'This keeps us out of jail,' says Cartland. 'We need someone to do a reality check.'

On career development, Nortel puts the responsibility basically in the hands of the employees, giving them the right tools and processes to complete their aims. But he emphasises that no one has to be a manager to be successful. 'This is a knowledge-based organisation, and the power for anyone is in the knowledge. We emphasise the role of the individual contributor, and we don't want that person to be an also-ran.' The company defines rewards as being more than pay. In particular, it wants every individual to look at ways the company does things and pass on their conclusions. Internal communication is achieved by a series of networking structures where corporate

policies, standards, and programmes on environmental health and safety are disseminated through safety advisers or senior managers. 'Talking to our employees and giving them the chance to talk to us are vital parts of our people management activities,' says Ball. 'They are reflected in our communication strategy. We encourage *management by walking about.*'

However, there are also structured programmes aimed at improving communications overall. Employee satisfaction surveys are used as a basic test of company morale and satisfaction results have improved from 53 per cent to 61 per cent through a programme put in place in 1995. Nortel is particularly concerned about the perception of the organisation among society at large. Since 1991, it has wholly sponsored a programme designed to investigate the relationship between information technology, business organisation and the impact upon society in Europe. To date, more than 170 European CEOs, public policy makers, academics and educationalists have been through this unique programme.

Contact address

Mr John Cartland,
Human Resources Director,
Nortel,
Stafferton Way,
Maidenhead, Berkshire.
Telephone: 01628 813000.
Fax: 01628 432586.

The Oracle Corporation

The Oracle Corporation is a relative newcomer to the US corporate scene but its status is undiminished for all that. Its hard-driving and results-orientated culture has paid handsome dividends for its shareholders and it is increasingly viewed as a trendsetter and preferred partner for many other blue chips. Despite its emphasis on technical expertise and intellectual rigour, there is enormous personal scope for individuals to make a contribution to the business.

Oracle at a glance

Employees: 3,000
Staff attrition rate: 14 per cent
Key locations: Reading (HQ), Bracknell and other sites in the Thames Valley plus the City of London, Bristol, Manchester, Edinburgh, Aberdeen
Active graduate recruitment: 110
Annual intake: 300

An inside view

One of the fascinations of Oracle is that it does not stay still for very long. Up to 80 per cent of jobs in the corporation are linked to the customer and so the unending drive to find new solutions means that the business is continually refining its product and service portfolio. The benefits of this approach are seen in its financial results which have grown – by many measures – by around 30 to 40 per cent annually, across the world. Oracle's distinctive technology is the leading commercial force in the company. In the past it has tended to compete with the primary software vendors but successful experience has emboldened the company and it is facing up to the IBMs and Microsofts to influence the world's information industry.

Oracle started in the 1970s in California providing database products for UNIX machines and has enjoyed heady expansion ever since in relational databases, applications, tools and consultancy. In recent years it has allied with Sun Microsystems to promote the network computer – a replacement for the dumb terminal – but it is encountering stiff competition from the Intel and Microsoft combination. Nevertheless its core applications and databases business is thriving. Clients are generally large enterprises which have bought from several manufacturers and operate open systems. Oracle provides means by which these systems can talk to each other. It recognises that its most significant competition comes from Microsoft whose focus has been the personal computer whereas Oracle concentrates on the World Wide Web and on servers.

The business is split into four main divisions: licenced sales, consultancy, sales and customer support. The biggest area is consultancy where it does not rank with the largest IT consultancy companies but sees itself as a technology supplier in partnership with companies like Coopers & Lybrand and Andersen Consulting.

Since graduates are a large source of new personnel, the company has begun to establish relationships with certain technology-driven universities such as Staffordshire and Southampton. It will focus increasingly on a tight group of high education establishments with a technological orientation to locate graduates with potential and in return the company will engage in its version of inward investment. Certain projects, at those colleges, related to the longer term business objectives of Oracle will be funded by the company.

How does Oracle rate?

Pay:	good
Benefits:	very good
Communications:	very good
Training:	excellent
Career development:	good
Morale:	very good

People and personnel policies

Allan Miller, human resource manager, says 'We have refined our selection processes in recent years. A high intellectual aptitude towards technology is a pre-requisite. Following that we are looking for people who take responsibility for themselves, their development and the projects which they work on. There is far more concentration on interpersonal

skills, client handling and empathy. We need self-starters – people who will take responsibility for the delivery of effective solutions to client issues and will not need to be led. This is – and always has been – a flat structure where up to 80 per cent of the roles are active in client relationships.'

Graduates come into Oracle and serve a two-month period of induction. This is largely given over to technical and corporate skill training. Then they enter a project team at assistant consultant level. They will work to a given manager and will be mentored by a senior manager – often a project leader – and members of the previous year's graduate intake. The vast majority of graduates come into the consultancy where they will be dealing directly with clients. In their first year Oracle expects its graduate entrants to bed into their assignments but from the second year onwards they can apply for posts anywhere in the company.

Miller says that Oracle is an advocate of the 360 degree appraisal. Corporate staff appraisal occurs annually, and twice a year in the consultancy. The process is led by the individual being appraised and his or her manager. But the project leader and other managers in the company who deal with the individual will make comments.

In keeping with Oracle's overall philosophy of flexibility, it defines the skills and capabilities which it needs as a business but tries to adapt any specific training or development to the needs of particular individual employees. Psychometric profiling is conducted to locate personal talents and abilities and to point to areas which need to be developed. Any training then fits to personal requirements. 'This is quite challenging because we are dealing with a moving feast of individual needs. A manager, for example, might have assembled a new team and may discover that they are not taking the initiative enough. We will hold a meeting to identify the issues and then relate the findings to the work situation. We will try work up actions that they can take back.'

Miller says that there are a lot of talented people in Oracle and there is a degree of personal risk involved in this process. 'It can be quite awesome to join Oracle, partly because of the quality of the internal competition. It is a difficult company in which to get up to speed and to be seen as competent. In that context there are many easier companies to join than Oracle. There are people I would advise not to join us because it will be too difficult for them to make headway. But there is also risk in an industry which is uncertain about where it is going to be in the future. Can our outstanding growth continue at the same pace? The extent of our ambitions is clear but individuals should be sure about where they would see themselves in the business.'

There's a lot of pressure in the company to perform and candidates should be able to cope with stress. The Wall Street share price for the company is one of the key indicators of success which means Oracle must perform regularly and consistently. 'We cannot wait for the big deal to come in and save us each quarter. We are working more with partners and we are aiming for better market coverage, which means everyone must contribute.' For self-starters who perform well, internal recruitment is packed with opportunities. The 40 per cent annual growth rate creates scores of opportunities and the real challenge for successful individuals is to interpret what the changing technical and work environment means for individual careers.

Pay – a significant proportion of which is variable – is in the upper quartile. There is also a bonus scheme and a contributory pension plan. All employees, plus spouses and children, are covered in the corporate healthcare scheme. Cars are available to many grades. Oracle also believes in keeping its employees well informed. There is a staff magazine called *Oragram* and weekly *Oraflash* business and technical bulletins. The workforce meets annually and six-monthly for briefing meetings, and Kick-Offs combine a business review and entertainment at the beginning of each year. As a business with a highly flexible approach to human resources, promotion and career development for women should be easier here than in some other companies. But the industry is inherently male-dominated. Oracle makes an effort for women returning from maternity leave but no diversity programmes currently exist in the UK.

Contact address

Vance Kearney,
Human Resources Director,
The Oracle Corporation,
Oracle Parkway, Reading Business Park,
Reading RG2 1DL.
Telephone: 011892 40000.
Fax: 011892 43882.
Worldwide web: http://www.uk.oracle.com

Panasonic Europe

In the 78 years since its founding in Osaka, the Matsushita Electric Industrial Company (MEI) has grown from a small electrical housewares manufacturer into one of the world's largest producers of quality electric and electronic products for the consumer, business and industry. In Europe, MEI is known as Panasonic, the most famous of the company's trademark names. Its products are sold in some 160 countries, with Panasonic, National, Technics and Quasar as the prominent brand names. There are 265,000 employees worldwide, with 10,000 in Europe and 4,390 in the United Kingdom. Panasonic's success in the UK is testament to the ability of management to create a unique work ethic from British and Japanese cultures.

Panasonic at a glance

Employees: 10,000 Europe, 4,390 UK
Annual staff attrition rate: 7 per cent
Key locations: Uxbridge (HQ), Bracknell, Newbury and five factories in Wales
Av. annual graduate recruitment: 30
Annual intake: 300

An inside view

In April 1994, Matsushita launched a worldwide, three-year revitalisation plan aimed at restoring profitability, which it has always considered to be the yardstick against which to measure the company's overall contribution to society. Structural innovations and improvement in management efficiency have been the bedrock of this programme. It sold a controlling interest in the US entertainment company MCA. This strategic move resulted in overall lower net sales and earnings in 1996. Excluding MCA's previous revenue impact, 1996 consolidated sales would have shown a 5 per cent increase. Instead, its overall sales edged down 2 per cent to $64.1 billion. Domestic sales grew and also remained solid in Asia, while slowing in the United States and Europe. The company ranks second on the *Fortune 500 Electronics and Electrical Equipment Index*.

Panasonic in Europe embraces 32 companies, 15 in sales, 15 in manufacturing, and three in research and development. In the UK, there are seven manufacturing and one sales company, and two devoted to R&D. The European operation, launched in 1962, accounts for approximately seven per cent of MEI's global turnover. Many of the company's most successful products are manufactured inside Europe, including television sets, microwave ovens, vacuum cleaners, VCRs and mobile phones. MEI's year 2000 plan targets European and other foreign-sector growth to bring a better balance to the company as a whole, aiming for a sales structure in which 50 per cent of revenues are generated in Japan and 50 per cent abroad.

The human resources policy of MEI has developed its European identity over the last 24 years. It is constantly evolving, has changed considerably in the past five years, but is still inspired by the company mission of the founder, Konosuke Matsushita, who told one of his young employees more than 70 years ago 'If you are asked by one of your customers what Matsushita Electric makes, you should answer that at Matsushita we make people first and, in addition, we make electrical products'. In a more modern idiom, it could be said that the employees are treated in a way that the company believes its customers must be treated. One rubs off on the other.

If the philosophy of company founder Matsushita is taken along a literal line, the success of its attitude and policy towards personnel is essential to the success of its commercial activity. In other words, as the human resource mission statement says 'Only by helping each and everyone to reach their full potential will the company as a whole grow and prosper'.

How does Panasonic rate?

Pay:	good
Benefits:	excellent
Communications:	good
Training:	very good
Career development:	very good
Morale:	good

People and personnel policies

The overseas training centre of MEI has expanded on the Making People First philosophy, by emphasising that while the company's business operations are guided by high ideals and goals, 'it should be noted that whether such high ideals and goals are achieved depends on people, on all of the employees working in the Matsushita organisations. So, in order to better achieve these sublime goals, each individual has to develop their personal and professional capabilities through day-to-day devotion to their respective jobs and open-minded reflection on their performance, in the light of the company's mission. We indeed have to make people before products. As a prerequisite for us to contribute better benefits to society, individual growth is critically important.'

Danny Kalman, personnel and general affairs manager for Panasonic Europe, sums it up like this 'Electronics may be our business but the end product is the improvement of society. Profit is only there to improve the ability of the company to improve society.' In the European operations, the best of UK and Japanese practices have been blended. 'There are two distinct cultures and we have put them together as a human resource marriage.' As a result, the workforce has become far more focused on the long-term aims of the company as they relate to achieving the objectives of the business plan. And having a business plan, to which there is commitment, ensures a common employee commitment, and gives them a greater confidence about the future. 'We think long-term, not the next three months. Looking at a five-year plan gives employees a sense of security. We all have a vision which extends out a distance.'

While there is a very small percentage of Japanese people in the Panasonic workforce in the UK (258), the influence is clear. Management and employees have become proactive rather than reactive. Japanese concepts centre on flexibility of mind and action, non-demarcation, the knocking down of workforce barriers. This has been mixed with the innate talents of the British worker which lay dormant under less imaginative management. In particular, as Kalman and his senior colleagues at Panasonic put it, there is a willingness to listen to new ideas. The workforce is creative and innovative, and willing to change, accepting the challenge to do better. At the same time, it is admitted that the influx of American and Japanese industry into this country has itself changed management.

The key philosophy at Panasonic is collective wisdom, which means developing a human network that encourages everyone to talk to each other, permeating ideas and actually participating in the management of the company. Panasonic has a flattening hierarchy.

'As far as communications is concerned, this company does not have a rigid structure; there's an open-door policy with a human network that breaks down divisional barriers. While expressing the determination to get everyone to think European, the sales companies of Panasonic occasionally send their people to Japan for a year to bring back a better understanding of the company's culture and the way Matsushita works in Japan.'

The biggest problem that the company has had to confront is the classic glass ceiling – but this ceiling has nothing to do with the gender gap. Back in 1989 only 20 per cent of board members were European. Management then formulated a ten-year plan to bring the percentage of Europeans on the Panasonic board up to 50 per cent by the year 2000 – with a division of 70 per cent in sales and 30 per cent in manufacturing. Each director was asked to identify key people (Europeans) who had the potential to become board members. A training programme was designed to turn managers into directors. There were originally 162 on the list; there are now 193, and the company expects to meet its Millennium target. This should not be seen as reverse discrimination. 'The objective is to have the best person in the job, regardless of their nationality,' says Kalman.

Contact address

Mr Danny Kalman,
Personnel and General Affairs Manager,
Panasonic Europe (Headquarters) Ltd,
3 Furzeground Way,
Stockley Park,
Uxbridge, Middx UB11 1DD.
Telephone: 0181 899 2208.
Fax: 0181 899 2214.

Pearson plc

Pearson has experienced major changes since 1993. Originally a model of the diversified conglomerate, it has transformed itself into a focused media and entertainment business which is increasingly international in scope. Its brands include the *Financial Times*, Addison Wesley Longman, Penguin, Les Echos, Mindscape and the Tussauds Group. The new management team wants to promote greater synergies between some of its divisions. The group reported 1995 sales of £1.83 billion with pre-tax profits of £365 million. Its most homogenous division is education where it is the world's third largest publisher of educational material. Pearson's other divisions are information which includes the *FT*, and entertainment which embraces film and television, Penguin, the Mindscape software business, Tussauds and the Future Publishing magazine publishers.

Pearson at a glance

Employees: 19,400 worldwide, 10,600 UK
Staff attrition rate: 2–10 per cent
Key locations: London, New York, Reading (Massachusetts), Harlow, Bath, Paris, Madrid
Active graduate recruitment: 20
Annual intake: 1,000

An inside view

These are changing times at Pearson. As recently as 1993, the group decided to move away from its role as a traditional diversified conglomerate and concentrate wholly on its media and entertainment interests. The process is on-going and senior executives say that there are no sacred cows in the group. Every part of the new business will be reviewed by the new chairman and chief executive in 1997 and any part which does not fit the new model will be either reformed or removed from the group. In the old days, Pearson's group board had the lightest of touches, leaving the managing directors of the operating companies to fly their own flags. Now, while it still believes in giving divisional directors and operating company executives room for creative manoeuvre, the centre takes a more positive role in shaping a more coherent enterprise.

Peter Cabrelli, director of human resources, says the pace of change within Pearson is undiminished and the group is likely to evolve still further over time. The group is now based on three divisions: education, information and entertainment. Education centres on Addison Wesley Longman which, following the acquisition of HarperCollins' North American educational publishing interests, has become a significant force in global education publishing. Information is a collection of companies including the *FT*, FT Information, Extel, Pearson Professional, the French newspaper and magazine organisation Les Echos, and Recoletos, the Spanish newspaper and magazine company. The third of the divisions is the least integrated because Pearson's interests here are so diverse. Entertainment includes television and film (including Thames Television, and Grundy Worldwide), Penguin (which with the acquisition of Putnam Berkley has become an even more significant player in consumer publishing worldwide), Mindscape (computer games), Tussauds (which includes the Chessington, Alton Towers and Port Aventura theme parks) and Pearson New Entertainment, whose products are primarily specialised magazines and videos.

'I would characterise the Pearson approach which has been espoused over the years as integrity, respect for the individual and quality,' says Cabrelli. 'Pearson takes the view that the proprietor must not interfere in the day-to-day operations of the individual businesses.' Cabrelli points to the decision by *FT* editors to endorse the Labour Party at the 1992 general election despite the fact that Pearson was a donor to the Conservative Party at the time. There is emphatically no headquarters interference in editorial judgement.

'Our approach when we acquire businesses is to retain the top management. We do not believe in removing people as a matter of policy. I believe we are well known for the fact that we want to acquire well-run businesses. Addison Wesley is an example. The board of that company approached us because

they saw us as a beneficial owner which would respect their contribution and let them get on with their business. This does not mean that we would hesitate to remove poor performers.'

How does Pearson rate?

Pay:	very good
Benefits:	very good
Communications:	excellent
Training:	excellent
Career development:	very good
Morale:	very good

People and personnel policies

The focus of the business is currently on the further refinement of the group as a focused international player in the media and entertainment markets. Already some 30 per cent of profits are generated in the US and it also has substantial holdings in France and Spain. A stated aim is to improve the potential synergies within the group and at a personal level this means that anyone in the group has the opportunity to apply for any other post. Journalists, for example, can move into management or advertising, or sales people can apply for posts in production or human resources. 'We have started to move people around between operating companies. We have a Pearson Intranet where we advertise job vacancies throughout the group. And anyone with access to a computer will be able to see all of these positions,' says Cabrelli.

The group is also moving towards greater cross-functional working through highly focused groups in key areas such as human resources, IT and intellectual property rights. 'The intellectual rights group looks at innovative ways in which we can exploit our rights. For example, we hold the book rights to the Beatrix Potter collection and we have gone on to stage an ice show with the characters and Mindscape has developed a computer game based on Peter Rabbit and other personalities in the series.'

Pay is determined at the operating company level except for the packages of the most senior executives. Policy is determined at the centre for people reporting directly to the chief executives of the businesses and is above market average for excellent performance. There is a bonus scheme which will enable individuals – in a good year – to reach the top quartile. The market conditions of Pearson companies vary so radically that fixing the most basic guidelines on pay is as much as the centre can realistically achieve. These basic guidelines are: performance of the individual, cost of living price increases and that individual rises should not be out of kilter with the overall level of rises in the company. The Pearson pension plans have been through various stages of development. In the early 1980s the operating companies ran their own schemes but a decision was taken to bring them together. In 1988 and 1995 further stages towards harmonisation were realised and the latest moves have made movement within the group much easier in terms of pension rights.

One area where Pearson can claim that it has made substantial progress is in equal opportunities. The group has recently appointed the first woman chief executive in the FT-SE 100. Human resources executives, who are largely women, decided not to introduce positive discrimination for female employees. A representative of Opportunity 2000 visited Pearson to ask that it should have a target of 50 per cent women board members and it was able to point to the Penguin UK board which had already achieved that status and Longman which at the time had a female CEO. Ann Stradwick, head of management development, says that the maternity benefits in the company are very generous even by the standards of many top class companies. 'Our emphasis is on dealing with individual arrangements in the operating companies for particular employees and in each case we will work out a package which is appropriate to the circumstances of the employee concerned.'

Personal creativity and individual performance within the structure of the operating companies is the touchstone of the Pearson approach. The central personnel executives are conscious of the fact that the success of this group – perhaps more than many others – is conditional on the contribution of talented people.

Contact address

Mr Peter Cabrelli,
Human Resources Director,
Pearson plc, 3 Burlington Gardens,
London W1X 1LE.
Telephone: 0171 411 2000.
Fax: 0171 411 2329.

Although this is the address for the holding company, recruitment is dealt with locally by the group's subsidiary companies and communications should be sent to these businesses directly.

PepsiCo Inc.

Formed only 30 years ago, PepsiCo is now one of the largest consumer products companies in the world, with annual sales of more than $30 billion. In addition to Pepsi-Cola, the group incorporates a host of world-leading household name businesses including 7-Up, Frito-Lay, Pizza Hut, Taco Bell, KFC and Walkers Snack Foods. In a highly competitive marketplace, the company's success has been built on nurturing an entrepreneurial spirit among its workforce. Employees are encouraged to be innovative and are rewarded with authority and responsibility at an early stage in their careers.

PepsiCo at a glance

Employees: 500,000 (worldwide), 15,000 (UK)
Annual staff attrition rate: 10 per cent*
Key locations: SW London (HQ)
Active graduate recruitment: 30*
Active non-graduate recruitment: 120*
*excluding restaurant employees

An inside view

PepsiCo was created in 1965 by the merger of Pepsi-Cola of New York and Frito-Lay of Texas. Since then, it has grown rapidly, with sales and profits doubling roughly every five years. Pepsi-Cola soft drinks are now on sale in more than 180 countries, and Pepsi is the leading cola in nearly 50 of the world's markets. Courtesy of companies such as Frito-Lay, Walkers and Sabritas, the group is also by far the world's largest snack chip producer while more than 22,000 franchised and company-owned Pizza Hut,

Taco Bell and KFC restaurants make it the world's biggest restaurant system.

PepsiCo has a very well-defined corporate strategy – to be the best in everything it does. This necessarily requires a heavy investment in the image, quality and value of its brands. It also means striving for excellence in its customer relationships. The company believes that not only will this approach persuade customers that PepsiCo's brands are their favourites, but it will also help potential recruits to think of the company as the employer of choice. PepsiCo is also very results-oriented; its philosophy is that both the company and its employees thrive on being set challenging goals. In a competitive marketplace, constantly upgrading the value of its products and the quality of customer service is essential. Employees are therefore encouraged to think creatively about how they can improve the business. This makes PepsiCo an energetic and innovative environment.

Another essential element of the company's success is its focus on teamwork.

PepsiCo Inc.

PepsiCo regards as vital that all its employees work together to offer the highest levels of customer service. Related to this issue is another one of its core values – integrity. Roger Enrico, PepsiCo's CEO, defines integrity as 'the glue that binds us together in the fast-moving, entrepreneurial and informal work environment we prefer'. Integrity means more than honesty and fairness, it also means having the courage and freedom to speak your mind to anyone in the company at any time. Only by encouraging such open debate can the company generate the best ideas and arrive at the right decisions.

PepsiCo remains a company dedicated unambiguously to aggressive growth. Its workforce is encouraged to think early on that they can make a difference to the way the firm operates. Its team-driven and informal structure necessarily makes it an exciting and rewarding place to be and its most successful people are those who see this fast-moving, fluid environment as an opportunity for both personal and professional growth.

How does PepsiCo rate?

Pay:	very good
Benefits:	very good
Communications:	excellent
Training:	excellent
Career development:	excellent
Morale:	very good

People and personnel policies

An inherent factor in PepsiCo's strategy is that it should recruit and retain the best employees in the industry. This means not only locating the most promising candidates – whether at graduate level or among experienced professional staff – but also providing them with a continuous training and development programme. PepsiCo considers that it is both a right and an obligation that all individuals have the skill, know-how, resources and freedom to do their job.

The majority of the company's training is performed on-the-job. Its philosophy is that the most effective training is provided by giving people difficult assignments, and thereby providing them with first-hand business experience. This approach is supplemented by formal training initiatives. These are generally managed and run internally and fall into three main categories: functional and technical skills, leadership, and understanding the business.

Employee development is very closely monitored. Although there is a formal appraisal process which is conducted annually, informal reviews will take place more regularly. Assessments focus in particular on four main objectives: financial targets, long-term contribution, people development skills and personal development. In common with many other companies, PepsiCo is trying to move towards a much more performance-based culture with a large variable element in the reward package, and this means almost constant feedback on how individuals are performing. Finding talent within PepsiCo is a strategic imperative.

Given the company's global reach and ambitions, the movement of staff both internationally and across functions can be easily facilitated. Indeed, it is increasingly common for senior management to have experienced at least one overseas posting during their career with the company. However, there is no single designated route to the top: the company's founder started as a salesman, its CEO as an accountant and its vice-chairman as a personnel clerk. So, anyone in the company located in any function can make progress to senior positions within PepsiCo.

In order to maintain its position at the leading edge of industry, PepsiCo recognises that it must pay competitively. Its overall benchmark is to set salaries in the top quartile, which are then supplemented with performance-related bonuses. A particularly innovative development is the company's *Sharepower* stock option scheme, which extends stock options to every employee in the world. There are also further incentive bonus schemes at management levels and long-term incentive programmes.

With a total workforce of more than half a million worldwide, communication can obviously be a problem area, especially since a significant proportion of employees do not speak English. The company attempts to address this through a variety of channels. As well as using company newsletters and e-mail, PepsiCo organises regular conferences and focus groups both to brief employees on the latest company developments and to receive feedback about conditions and feelings on the shop floor. There is also an annual *Sharepower* rally, which is traditionally addressed by the company president.

PepsiCo's global presence demands that it takes a positive attitude to encouraging diversity in the workforce. Its behaviour is reinforced by the company's emphasis on team-working: individuals must be able to work with different types of people. In addition, managers are required to demonstrate a commitment to diversity in their recruitment. The success of this approach is shown in the increasing number of women in the senior ranks of the company. PepsiCo's involvement in the community is largely determined at the local level. However, given that the company is frequently a major employer, most of its businesses have strong links with the local community: for example, Walkers Snack Foods is currently the sponsor of the Premiership's Leicester City Football Club. Involvement with local businesses, charities and arts groups is also encouraged.

Contact address

Jan Nuttall,
Vice-President,
Organization Capability,
Frito-Lay, 2 Sheen Road,
Richmond,
Surrey TW9 1AE.
Telephone: 0181 334 1000.
Fax: 0181 334 1010.

Peugeot Motor Company PLC

The Peugeot Motor Company is among the top five car makers in the UK. In 1995 it achieved sales of £1.8 billion and improved its share of the diesel and fleet markets. In diesel cars it is the UK market leader with more than 20 per cent of a fragmented sector. The company is based predominately in Coventry, where it employs 4,500 people on three sites. The vast bulk of its workforce is located at Ryton in the 306 assembly plant, but other Peugeot people are based at Stoke and Tile Hill, as well as in its network of 25 wholly owned distributors.

Peugeot at a glance

Employees: 4,500
Annual staff attrition rate: 2.3 per cent
Key locations: three in Coventry plus 25 distributors nationwide
Av. annual graduate recruitment: 20
Annual intake: 80

An inside view

The British car industry has changed out of all recognition in the last 20 years. From an over-populated sector with appalling industrial relations, the sector has slimmed down into an increasingly efficient business area employing substantially fewer people. The Peugeot Motor Company is a prime example of this transformation. In the 1960s it was Rootes, one of the hallmarks of the motor trade in Coventry, which metamorphasised into Chrysler. Chrysler sold out to Peugeot Talbot and this emerged as the Peugeot Motor Company. The style of management and the culture of the business shifted radically with each change in ownership.

Peugeot UK is a secure and settled business which plays an increasingly influential role in the entire Peugeot group. This is a far cry from the Chrysler days when, according to current personnel director Michael Judge, 'Long-term planning then was the day after tomorrow. If you asked me when the last dispute was I would have looked at my watch. We had 800 disputes in a year. Now we have a role in the planning stages of the next new car and the car after that. We have never been in that position before. Our visibility within the group and within the industry has never been higher. Now we are consulted and drawn into the development process.

The level of morale in Peugeot is outstandingly high. Contrasting the level of enthusiasm for the company and its management in 1996 with 1966 among the workforce is comparing two ends of a spectrum. Peugeot was one of the first of the slimmed down car companies to achieve a high degree of enthusiasm from its staff. It is personified by a range of initiatives led by and involving employees, such as the huge gala day in 1995, the launch of a Peugeot employee rally team and even a staff-organised fun run at Ryton.

Judge says that the workforce is treated with a high degree of respect. The most tangible manifestation of this is the company charter, which identifies the business's commitment to its people and leads to a series of communications initiatives when its people are informed about key indicators within the UK company, the group and the industry. 'The focus for this is the internal team briefing. We send out red and green communications bulletins. The red are for urgent releases and are normally briefed on the day of issue. The green are for less time-sensitive issues. Management at local level brief staff regularly and at the start of 1996 senior management briefed the entire workforce on the plans for the year.' Communications also include an employee newspaper and annual employee reports, which have been running for many years.

The company also works with the trade unions on an assisted development programme where employees can attend non-vocational training courses at the company's expense – to a maximum of £250 each. Around 20 per cent of the workforce take up this option each year. The aim of the exercise is to build tighter bonds in the relationship between the company and the employees.

There is a deeper reasoning behind this apparent largesse. The motor industry, in common with many other sectors, demands a degree of individual flexibility which its workforce has never experienced before. Certainly its reputation until the late 1980s was one of rigid and entrenched attitudes. In order to cope with increasingly high quality competition and the changing demands of a more discriminating customer, Peugeot needs its people to be inherently flexible. Hence the value of the assisted development programme.

How does Peugeot rate?

Pay:	good
Benefits:	excellent
Communications:	superb
Training:	very good
Career development:	very good
Morale:	very good

People and personnel policies

The willingness to attend courses in new disciplines shows a determination to participate in the future of the company and its industry. 'The idea is to switch people on to learning again. At Ryton today on the track something new happened. A new process, a new colour, a new adhesive. We are asking our employees to do something new every day. So we asked ourselves how could we encourage the process of lifetime learning among our people. These courses show an individual's personal flexibility and capacity to adapt. The French view is a manager is a manager is a manager. You do not need a technical discipline to be a manager. But you rarely get to the top of the company without an understanding of, and experience in, people management.'

Judge says that a company cannot work without the active cooperation of its people. He scorns the concept of human resources management and says that his department is personnel, dealing with people. 'The only constant in business is change and our role is to prepare our people for that change.' People issues are top of the agenda within the UK enterprise and pivotal in decision-making within the group. The company is an average payer for this industry and it comments that more of its salary comes from basic pay than perhaps elsewhere in the industry. It has a profit-related pay scheme but this has not kicked in since 1992. However its pension scheme is commendable.

Employees can buy the company's product at discount prices of up to 25 per cent on run-out models and are offered reductions on spare parts which make them highly attractive over high street suppliers. Employees with ten years' service can own a new Ryton-built car for around £100 a month (including insurance, tax and servicing). The company has a large sports and social club where it stages a variety of entertainment for the staff. It is the only large company which still has its own cricket pitch and is among the few which still runs an internal radio service. Like others in the motor industry, Peugeot has instituted in-house video and computer bulletin board facilities. The company is highly active in its community. It encourages employees to become involved in community projects and activities while giving 35p for every car sold to the industry's charity BEN. It was also the first business in the motor trade to create employee giving from the payroll, which has now spread to other companies in the sector. In summer 1996 it was applying for planning permission to set up a day care centre at the bottom end of one of its car parks. This would be for elderly or distressed relatives of Peugeot employees.

For 15 years the company has conducted employee satisfaction surveys. The most recent staff survey shows that more than two-thirds of the workforce is very satisfied with Peugeot as an employer. Another 17 per cent were satisfied. The combined effect of these initiatives is to create a dialogue between employees and company, and to build a bond between them. Judge says that the demands on the employee today are much greater than they were 20 or 30 years ago. 'In those days our industrial relations were average. We were not the worst or the best but everyone was bad. It was a terrible time. In 1979 Chrysler sold us for one dollar and one year later we lost £110 million. Today many of those same employees have produced a business with sales of £1.8 billion. We now rank with the best quality production in the group. Our paint shop – set up in 1969 – now turns out some of the best paint in Europe. We have taken Peugeot from 1.5 per cent of the total market to 8 per cent. Our record shows a very long period of industrial relations stability. The level of pride in the business among workers is very high.'

Contact address

Mr Michael Judge,
Director of Personnel and Industrial Relations,
The Peugeot Motor Company PLC,
Aldermoor House, Aldermoor Lane,
Coventry CV3 1LT.
Telephone: 01203 884035.
Fax: 01203 884288.

Pilkington plc

Pilkington is a world leader in glass products for the building, transport and electronic markets. The worldwide group boasts sales of more than £2.9 billion, in excess of 39,000 employees and operations in more than 20 countries. The float process, invented by Pilkington, is used by manufacturers throughout the world in the manufacture of high quality flat and safety glass. Pilkington enjoys a superlative reputation for commercial innovation and production quality, but equal to this is its standing as a highly esteemed employer.

Pilkington at a glance

Employees: 39,100 worldwide, 7,000 UK
Annual staff attrition rate: 1 per cent
Key locations: St Helens, Lancashire (HQ) plus locations in the UK and around the world
Active graduate recruitment: 20–35
Annual recruitment: n/a

An inside view

Pilkington is a blue chip company with a global reputation for quality and innovation. About half of the company's business is transacted in Europe but South America, and the Asian/Pacific markets are being developed and exploited. And the North American presence accounts a quarter of trade. Financial results show that 1996's turnover stood at £2.8 billion with an operating profit – before exceptional items – of £214 million. This was in spite of a pause in economic growth in Europe and North America. But chairman Sir Nigel Rudd is confident of further steady progress.

Pilkington is a household name: its technology and advancement is taken for granted by almost everyone who looks through a window or drives a car. Its watchword is to add value through innovation. The group's products help make buildings and cars comfortable and safe. It is a high tech business and the company successfully applies its expertise in compositions and coatings to the manufacture of products which keep heat either in or out. Advances in thin float glass manufacture are bringing new opportunities to the electronics market. A revolutionary process has been developed for continuous manufacture of mirrors.

Pilkington invests more than £50 million a year in research and development in the United Kingdom, US, Germany and Italy. The group also has strong technical links with Nippon Sheet Glass Ltd, a leading Japanese glass manufacturer. More than half the group's sales are in glass products for building. Pilkington is a market leader in many countries with coated and tinted products which save energy, laminated and wired glasses which resist fire, and structural systems which allow large continuous areas of glazing. It is the world's largest supplier of toughened safety glass for cars. In fact, one in four of the world's vehicles contains its products. So do aircraft, high speed locomotives, buses and trucks.

The company was founded in St Helens in 1826 and remained in family ownership until 1970. Since then the business has grown and expanded as a result of organic and acquisitional growth. Its float glass process revolutionised the manufacture of high quality flat glass and is recognised as one of the major industrial inventions of the twentieth century. The process is licensed to 42 manufacturers in 30 countries and there are more than 170 worldwide float plants with a combined output of 3,000 miles of glass a day.

How does Pilkington rate?

Pay:	very good
Benefits:	very good
Communications:	very good
Training:	superb
Career development:	very good
Morale:	very good

People and personnel policies

Merseyside can be and has been a hotbed of industrial relations problems. Pilkington had more than a smattering of militant activity in the early and mid-1970s. It led to the short-lived foundation of an alternative union to the still recognised and heavily involved GMB. Both the company and the union have taken the view that prosperity for the company is beneficial to both owners and employees. So the two work together to pursue corporate objectives rather than take the narrow view.

The group's overall HR policy is designed to create a working environment in which all employees can fully develop their potential and be motivated to maximise their contribution to business aims. The creation of effective dialogue between employees at all levels is seen as an effective method of enhancing cooperation, teamwork, integrity and mutual trust. The company pledges to provide challenging and interesting jobs – using skills and initiative, talent and experience. In addition there are regular, frank and honest personal appraisals which help employees to understand the value of their contribution, to improve performance, fulfil potential and identify career opportunities and needs.

People matter at Pilks, as the company is known locally with affection and pride. And the company's policy is geared towards compatibility and profitability – ably succeeding in both ultimate aims. Its traditional approach to management was paternalistic in former days and it still is to a certain extent. But now it is on a more sound business footing with little or no room for excess fat. Non-core businesses have gone and there is a growing emphasis on research and development. But a major development has been to push decision making down the line to the most effective working group. And employees now have to have more than one responsibility, more than one skill. The days of demarcation and strict thou-shalt-not guidelines have gone.

John Benson, group director of human resources, says 'Every employee now has to cope with more than one task, more than one skill. We are trying to get people more multi-faceted in what they do and this fits into what we are trying to do as a group. The key point in our employment development policy is the fact that our people have a lot to do with their own development. They have to generate quality and commitment. We are also looking at managerial competencies and we are using those in selection training.' A check sheet for recruitment is geared to a requirement for specific technical qualifications coupled with an analytical and rational thought process. Benson comments that he looks for people who can demonstrate precision and clarity of thought. 'We need people who have a clear objective vision of what they are trying to achieve. Quality plays a key role in our business. We are consistently working to improve our performance and we need people who always have a forceful urge to get better in terms of customer support and customer awareness.'

Pilkington is profoundly aware of the globalisation of industry and is working hard to refine its thinking on commercial strategy. 'We are achieving a clear and global strategy which features a decentralised network. People are given clear targets but allowed sufficient operational freedom to make a personal and team contribution to the business.' Assessment methods are tied firmly to management competency and the managers of the future are recruited from the ranks of dedicated graduates. One of the early tasks for new entrants is to work out a career development plan which takes them to a two-year watershed. There is an appraisal every six months during this significant and formative process.

Benson comments 'We try to ensure that in addition to practical experience there is some intellectual input'. To this end there are part-time modular courses at Lancaster University. But there are no what he terms Cooks Tours of the business, which means graduates are no longer brassed off with listening and doing nothing of real value. He says 'They are now part of a European management team and that has major ramifications. We have peeled away management layers, there are excellent periods of training and people are confident about taking decisions.'

It is all a matter of mutual respect and trust; and coupled to a reward package which ensures that few people want to leave the company. There is a minimum and maximum band for every job and progression through those grades depends on ability and a willingness to progress. A bonus scheme and share option facilities, and a contributory pension scheme operate and there is free health insurance for management with a discounted rate for the shop floor.

Contact address

Mr John Benson, Group HR Director,
Pilkington plc,
Group HQ, Prescot Road,
St Helens WA10 3TT.
Telephone: 01744 28882.
Fax: 01744 692660.

Procter & Gamble Limited

Procter & Gamble is a global detergents, household cleaning, health and beauty care, chemicals, pharmaceuticals and foodstuffs manufacturer. Started in the 1830s in Cincinnati, US, the company sells its products in 140 countries worldwide, marketing more than 300 brands. P&G has a formidable reputation as a marketeer and also as a centre of excellence in business in the UK. It employs 5,500 people in the UK, drawing heavily on an annual intake of graduates to provide the foundation for its middle and senior management of the future. The company doubles its size every 10 years and so the demand for talented people is significant.

Procter & Gamble at a glance

Employees: 100,000 worldwide, 5,500 UK
   (2,000 laundry and cleaning products,
   3,500 cosmetics, pharmaceuticals, etc)
Annual staff attrition rate: 4 per cent
Key locations: 12 (7 manufacturing),
   Gosforth (HQ), Weybridge, Staines
Av. annual graduate recruitment: 130
Annual intake: 200

An inside view

Every household in Britain probably has at least one Procter & Gamble product. Every decade since its inception in 1837, P&G has doubled its size. Today, it generates $33 billion in global revenues; it is also a repository of the highest business and management expertise. P&G commands market leadership in a whole range of product sectors. It makes the UK's best selling detergent Ariel, its number one washing-up liquid Fairy, the top household cleaner Flash and the leading disposable nappies Pampers. Other top rank P&G brands include Daz, Head & Shoulders, Oil of Ulay, Max Factor, Giorgio, Clearasil, Vicks Vapour Rub, Bold and Crest Toothpaste.

P&G has grown by acquisition as well as organic improvements. Worldwide some 31 per cent of its income derives from laundry and cleaning products, 28 per cent from paper products (nappies and sanitary towels), 19 per cent from beauty care, 12 per cent from food and 9 per cent from healthcare. A further 1 per cent comes from corporate sales. The UK operation sources the largest part of its income from detergents and in recent years has expanded its activities in chemicals, pharmaceuticals, household cleaning and cosmetics. Geographically, P&G has northern British operations which are largely manufacturing and household cleaning, and southern businesses which are mainly marketing operations.

This is a highly structured business which is profoundly data and markets driven. P&G operates according to defined principles laid down at the centre. The first and most important of its key tenets is that the consumer is king within Procter & Gamble. The company reaches its customer through market-leading brands which are as famous – or even more famous – than P&G itself.

How does Procter & Gamble rate?

Pay:	very good
Benefits:	excellent
Communications:	very good
Training:	excellent
Career development:	excellent
Morale:	very good

People and personnel policies

Procter & Gamble was founded by an Englishman and an Irishman who emigrated to Cincinnati in 1837. Part of the reason for its success is the professional management of the business, which led to high retention of qualified people. The result is a global company with operations in 40 countries. It can no longer be described accurately as a US multinational, since four of its six senior directors are non-American.

P&G employs 100,000 people worldwide and 5,500 in the UK. The policy of first level recruitment and then almost exclusively internal promotion is a cornerstone of the operation. People do tend to stay with Procter & Gamble – there have been only nine CEOs since the inception of the company. Unlike many businesses, P&G aims to recruit for lifetime – or at least long-term – careers. 'We recruit only at first stage. We are looking for top level graduates with a rounded profile. The five key attributes are: intelligence, ambition, leadership, energy and creativity. This is a challenging environment and we need people who are up to the task. Some of the recruitment is done on the milk round but increasingly we are looking to recruit from internships and vocational business courses,' says Dennis Shuler, director of human resources. The internships generally last two to three months and will cover the summer vacation from university. Vocational business courses last a week and every area of P&G operates these exercises. 'Increasingly, we want to draw all of our intake from these sources. They give us a better idea of the calibre and quality of the candidates and it gives a real impression of what it is like to work for us.'

Procter & Gamble is keen on an early contribution by newcomers. 'It sounds like a cliché but we employ people because we want them to contribute. The sooner they can contribute, the more they can contribute and the highest level at which they can contribute means that we all win. Entrants are given a job at start date and are encouraged to perform, under supervision.' The degree of supervision is relaxed as early as possible to allow each individual to play a full creative role and to fly solo.

'When you have grown as much as Procter & Gamble there is always demand

and opportunities for good people,' says Dick Johnson, director of corporate affairs. 'When you start opening up China, India, Pakistan and all the Pacific Rim countries. When you continue to grow in South America and you have the whole of Africa, which is almost untouched territory, the demand for top quality people is larger than that which you can meet.' The company believes very much in goals. The global corporation sets universal targets for the business, European level management establishes its own goals within the framework of the international picture and the UK business devises its gameplan to make its contribution to global and regional targets. Each division and department will fashion its objectives in keeping with British national goals.

The internal communications system is focused heavily on the cascade of information within the business to demonstrate to each employee and department their role in the corporate story. Twice a year the UK general managers brief the entire establishment on new national goals and progress in meeting existing targets. Each quarter, every department will hold a briefing meeting. The core of this gathering will be a video produced by the top executives in Cincinnati where the state of the company will be discussed. Local managers will also discuss progress in meeting departmental targets. Each individual creates a computerised work and development plan with their manager. The employee is fully responsible for the operation of the plan and for identifying the people who should contribute to their evaluation. The purpose of the plan is to assess what results the individual has achieved against the targets which were set. 'The individual is very much the focus of this process. Opinions will be requested from that person's manager, the people to whom they supply work and their people. And the evaluation is the starting point for next year's plan,' comments Dennis Shuler.

The work and development plan will inevitably recommend some training which will add to the personal skillbase. Most training in P&G is on-the-job, although there is some corporate training to teach some managerial skills such as project management, effective report writing and running a meeting, and some functional training to boost specific capabilities. 'There is no training for the sake of training. Our approach is "You need some training to deliver a particular job. Good. Then, we'll get it for you",' says Dennis Shuler. 'This means that people go into training understanding its relevance. More than 90 per cent of training is done by line managers, not by external trainers.' Reward, like training, is based on the work and development plan, is specific to the individual and there are no across the board settlements. 'We believe that we should be paying at the leading edge for people who do comparable work to us.'

Contact address

Mr Dennis Shuler,
Director of Human Resources,
Procter & Gamble Limited,
P O Box 1EE, Gosforth,
Newcastle upon Tyne NE99 1EE.
Telephone: 0191 279 2000.
Fax: 0191 279 2282.

RAC Motoring Services

RAC Mortoring Services was the UK's first motoring organisation and this year is celebrating its first hundred years. In 1995, the latest year for which figures are available, the company generated an income the £262.8 million in subscriptions from the 5.6 million members of both the motoring organisation and its two clubs, one in London's Pall Mall and the other, a country club at Woodcote Park in Surrey. An increasing amount of income is also derived from its insurance-broking activities – £27 million in 1995.

The RAC at a glance

Employees: 3,800 (1,700 field-based roadside assistance personnel, engineers and salespersons).

Annual staff attrition rate: 6 per cent

Key locations: Small corporate HQ in London; sites in strategic geographic locations: Bristol, Glasgow, north-west of England (2), Walsall, Belfast, London, Lyon (France) and the Irish Republic.

Av. annual graduate recruitment: approx.10

Annual intake: 6 per cent

An inside view

The RAC is concerned with the promotion of mobility, because it believes motoring enhances the quality of life. This translates into providing high-quality services to its members through the provision of a wide range of services, from roadside assistance for a member's malfunctioning vehicle (there were some 3 million calls for help in 1995) to conducting in-depth research into car usage and its effect upon the environment. The RAC, not surprisingly, is a champion of promoting road safety and also lobbies the government on high levels of motoring taxation.

The organisation is also the governing body of British motor sport. In 1995 the RAC Motor Sports Association issued 30,975 competition licences and oversaw the running of 15 British championships – in rallying, racing, hillclimbs, sprints, trails, autocross, rallycross, drag-racing, autotests, cross-country, kart racing – and over 3,750 events in 22 disciplines.

Her Majesty the Queen is Patron of the RAC which is governed by a committee comprising sixteen members, only three of whom are executive directors of the company. The committee, which approves the appointment of directors to the boards of the various RAC companies, sees as its primary duty and responsibility the maintenance and reinforcement of providing a quality service to members.

The RAC, however, is not resting on the laurels it has gained in its 100-year history of almost continuous growth. In 1995, after recording a surplus of £5.4 million, it is currently restructuring at a cost of £16.8 million. Explaining this, Neil Johnson, the company's chief executive officer and general secretary, says it is necessary to reshape the business to better meet the challenge of highly competitive and rapidly changing markets.

Much of this expenditure is being directed at investment in new technology. An early example of this is that all roadside assistance patrols are now equipped with CD-ROMs which provide instant access to more technical information than has been possible before. The RAC is proud that its patrols fixed 82 per cent of breakdowns at the roadside in 1995.

Says Johnson 'This is one of the ways in which traditional motoring assistance is changing. "Intelligent Transport Systems" using advanced information, communication and control systems are only a few years away. The RAC will be at the forefront of these developments.' These developments will provide challenging opportunities for the RAC's current and future employees.

How does the RAC rate?

Pay:	very good
Benefits:	excellent
Communications:	excellent
Training:	very good
Career development:	good
Morale:	very good

People and personnel policies

By definition, the RAC is heavily customer-focused and because it provides a country-wide service the company operates on a distributed basis. It has a network of strategically placed sites for specific functions, such as telephone selling operations, marketing and customer services (non-roadside, such as legal), roadside assistance services, and assistance services dedicated to the company's growing number of corporate members – fleet operators.

The view of Diana Palmer, director of human resources at the RAC, is that almost without exception, its employees feel their job to be worthwhile and that this attitude is manifested in enthusiasm for the work, and this results in quality products and services. Every year employees are asked to take part in an opinion survey through which they are questioned on topics such as what they think of the business generally, and specific aspects of it, communications procedures, and working relationships.

Explains Palmer 'Ours is a people-orientated business. To succeed you need to be adaptive, and ally to the philosophy of providing an outstanding service. You have to have an affinity with what the customer wants and then deliver it.'

'A key ingredient of this is working openly, and cooperating with colleagues in a friendly atmosphere. We actively encourage people to acquire skills, knowledge and attributes across a range of disciplines. A simple example of this is that people working in our telecentres dealing with our members and customers have a wide knowledge of our services and because of this will know what the person at the other end of the line wants and how best to service those needs.'

The RAC is heavily committed to training. Every new employee is required to spend up to 30 days on a structured induction programme that provides an insight into all the company's activities. This is combines with on-the-job experience and includes the completion of a project.

Following this a running programme of training is provided in many disciplines to enable personnel to gain new technical skills, customer-relations techniques, and management styles. This is achieved in-house and through the use of external consultants. The RAC, in a consortium of other companies, also runs management courses at the Cranfield Business School for its high-flying management.

Career development is up to the individual. The company is committed to a multi-skilling approach and provides opportunities for employees to learn new skills. Every employee is given a challenging personal development plan each year, the achievement of which can lead to promotion vertically or through cross-functional movement.

Women continue to make progress within the RAC, with several women occupying senior management positions in marketing, human resources, finance and customer services. There is also one woman member on the executive board. Palmer says all these appointments have been made on the basis of merit. The company operates maternity leave schemes and says many women return to work following such leave.

Employee communications is an important and active part of the company's HR policy. Apart from a bi-monthly newsletter, there is a staff magazine and dynamic programme through which 'news flashes' and company briefings are distributed quickly when important news needs to be communicated. There are also dedicated publications covering various disciplines, such as sales and technical services, and all employees receive 'Callsign', an audio cassette produced each month.

The RAC's remuneration package is geared to recognising the skills and ability of each employee, or groups of employees (the company is heavily unionised). Apart from the salary, which is subject to annual review, the company provides a non-contributory pension and permanent sickness scheme. The company says the remuneration package is under constant review and compares favourably in the marketplace.

Contact address

Ms Diana Palmer,
Director of Human Resources,
RAC Motoring Services,
PO Box 700,
Bristol BS99 1RB.
Telephone: 01454 208000.
Fax: 01454 208388.

The Document Company, Rank Xerox

Rank Xerox was formed in 1956 as a joint venture of the Xerox Corporation of the US and the Rank Organisation in the UK. It has since adopted The Document Company as a trading name. It manufactures copiers, duplicators, electronic printers, optical scanners, fax machines, digital publishing machines, software and supplies. It is based in Marlow, Buckinghamshire. Sales in 1995 reached £3.6 billion with profits before restructuring up 80 per cent to £616 million. The parent group, which is based in Stamford, Connecticut, reports annual turnover of $17 billion and owns 80 per cent of the financial interest in Rank Xerox.

Rank Xerox at a glance

Employees: 7,000 UK (4,500 in field sales and marketing, 1,000 engineering, 1,350 manufacturing, 150 HQ)
Annual staff attrition rate: 5 per cent
Key locations: HQ at Marlow, Bucks; manufacturing at Mitcheldean, Gloucestershire; technology centre at Welwyn Garden City; research centre at Cambridge, customer support offices in major centres in the UK
Annual graduate recruitment: 50
Annual intake: 350

An inside view

Rank Xerox has experienced a transformation in the last five years. The company has undergone a radical reconfiguration of the business and a substantial reorganisation of the way in which it is structured. The benefits are legion and each year since the early part of the decade it has improved its performance by the measures which Rank Xerox regards as key. It tests itself on four principal criteria. The combination of a strong track record in customer satisfaction, market share growth and improved employee standing have flowed through to excellent financial results. Sales and profits in each business area have flourished year-on-year in the 1990s, peaking in 1995 with an overall rise in profits of 80 per cent.

Executive director, group resources and quality, Ralph Orrico puts down the resurgence of Rank Xerox to several factors. 'We have now established first-rate technology in all our products and a worldwide engineering and manufacturing capability. We have excellent people in place to sell our products and services.' It has also broadened the scope of its operations, invested heavily in technology and emphasised its commitment to quality, its customers and its people.

Since 1990 when Rank Xerox adopted the name The Document Company, it has focused its business approach on commercial documents rather than solely selling photocopiers. Orrico comments that 90 per cent of all corporate information is stored in documents of one sort or another. Some 60 per cent of employee time is spent in document production; after payroll costs, documents are the largest single item of expenditure in the company budget. Five billion documents are created every day in Europe alone and a growing proportion of these will be in electronic formats. This represents a major shift from only a few years ago when paper was the principal vehicle for documents, and prompted Rank Xerox to become the premier document specialist.

'We realised that to meet and anticipate market changes and to become more effective and profitable, we had to make changes ourselves. We had to restructure our entire organisation from top to bottom and become customer-focused and market -led. We had to communicate to the business world that no one understands the business document better,' Orrico says. Rank Xerox's outstanding technological expertise in this field needed to be broadened to be world leader in document production through emerging digital systems. In addition the company wanted to demonstrate to customers its capacity to provide solutions to customer issues in a dizzying array of market conditions and circumstances. Some 800 staff at its technical centre in Welwyn Garden City grapple with scores of customer problems such as efficient document production through networks which are composed of systems originated by different manufacturers.

How does Rank Xerox rate?

Pay:	very good
Benefits:	excellent
Communications:	superb
Training:	very good
Career development:	very good
Morale:	very good

People and personnel policies

The Rank Xerox approach to employee management is underpinned by eight basic principles: honesty, trust, respect, openness, professionalism, teamwork, initiative and humour. It has also defined nine cultural dimensions in which each employee is expected to perform. These range from customer focus to team orientation. The company has equally assembled a set of 23 leadership attributes against which management competency is rated. These attributes form the basis of a series of personal, manager and direct report assessments to evaluate performance and provide a structure for personal development.

Each individual employee is responsible for their own career and personal development which is linked into business requirements. Graduates are enlisted into an organised recruitment programme. Rank Xerox aims for at least a 2.1 result at first degree level. 'We look for candidates who can demonstrate high energy, a capacity to integrate with others, a good leadership style, respect for others, and a results-orientated approach,' says human resources manager Lis Barnes.

The company encourages entrants to gain experience across the company and in the longer term to enter the management development programme. 'The aim is to bring in high calibre people and take them through the organisation quite quickly,' she says. Orrico remarks that the restructuring created a much flatter structure and now the managing director has 25 direct reports. People are much closer to the decision-making process and its extensive communications programme is geared to high quality dialogue and feedback. As well as formal printed material and cascade briefings, it also holds regular cross-functional breakfast meetings to ensure that a wide group is aware of current business issues. 'This allows employees to get to know the directors better and we can take the pulse of the organisation,' says Orrico.

Each job is part of a job family and is graded according to the skills and competencies required for that post. Individuals are then encouraged to compare their own performance against those required for the putative assignment. 'At a higher level we are able to roll these competencies up to see what skills we need across the company,' says Orrico. Nearly all employees experience a variable element to their pay. The further up the organisation, the greater the element which is variable. This part of the remuneration is conditioned by performance at a personal, team and corporate level. Sales people are on a high variable (60 per cent variable, 40 per cent fixed). The benefits package is excellent:

an excellent pension scheme, health insurance for all employees, profit-related pay, life insurance and subsidised high quality restaurants.

In 1996, Rank Xerox launched its X-teams initiative which focuses on high achievement teamwork. Around 500 teams have registered for the process which will direct them towards personal and collective growth through working together to push back the boundaries of their assignments. Orrico says that as well as sharpening their commercial edge, it brings a dash of fun into the workplace. Rank Xerox is also in the forefront of the learning culture approach and has 28 learning resource centres where employees can go to boost their understanding of a wide range of disciplines. The centres are networked so that what is available in one centre can be shared throughout the company. Diversity is another major area of focus for Rank Xerox. 'We have looked at it in two ways,' says Barnes. 'The Document Company had established policies, goals and frameworks for equal opportunities and we broadened these to encompass diversity. We also examined the way we work and took an educational approach. We want to be active in encouraging diverse opinion, as well as background, in the company.'

Contact address

HR department,
Rank Xerox Limited,
Parkway,
Marlow,
Buckinghamshire SL7 1YL.
Telephone: 01628 890000.
Fax: 01628 892001.

Reader's Digest Limited

Reader's Digest is a US multinational with substantial activities in the UK. It publishes the largest-read monthly magazine in this country – *Reader's Digest* – which sells around 1.6 million copies a month. The company is highly active in condensed books, high quality family publications, CD/cassette collections, videos and related forms of publishing. It enjoys a reputation as the leading direct marketing publisher in the world and combines excellent quality products with highly aggressive marketing approaches. Its worldwide sales amount to $3 billion, of which the UK generates £200 million. Reader's Digest employs highly educated and talented staff in a range of disciplines but largely in editorial, design, promotion, marketing and IT.

Reader's Digest at a glance

Employees: 800 in the UK, 700 for the British operation and 100 for the European
Annual staff attrition rate: 5 per cent
Key locations: Canary Wharf and Swindon
Graduate intake: none
Annual intake: 40

An inside view

The world is changing at the Reader's Digest. An enormously successful US direct marketing publisher, it is evolving to face the challenges of rapidly expanding and developing markets. In 1990, this traditionally conservative enterprise took a decisive step to become a public company and so began a series of initiatives which would profoundly alter the culture of its business. This single step has given a sharper commercial and marketing edge to a company which was known in the industry as the University of Direct Mail. It has sustained and enhanced its profitability, broadened its range of products, entered new markets and extended the profile of its customers.

UK managing director Neil McRae explains that the conversion from private to public company was the catalyst for a programme of changes in the global business. 'Since 1990 we have increased our turnover by 50 per cent and introduced major improvements into the company. But we recognised that the market was changing rapidly and we needed to adapt with it.' The foundation stone of the company is its brand name magazine. It has achieved this position by sharp editorial coverage of contemporary issues and sophisticated marketing. Renewal rates are extremely high, providing the company with a loyal customer base to which it can supply other published products. A wide range of fiction and non-fiction books, CD/cassette collections, videos and other magazines have all been introduced successfully to the Reader's Digest subscription base.

McRae says that there are two key principles which underpin its achievements in these areas: the outstanding editorial and design quality of its products which provide superb value for money, and the no commitment basis on which the products are sold, which differentiates RD from almost every other direct marketer. A key example of its success in the UK is the launch of *MoneyWise* which is the country's largest personal finance magazine. With a subscriber base of 130,000 it is leagues ahead of its nearest competitor which has 30,000. The company has grown almost entirely organically by extending its reach, products, disciplines and the performance of existing titles. However, it recognised that it needed to change to stay ahead. One factor was the age profile of its customers. 'Our audience by definition is middle Britain, middle aged, usually in established family units. As people do business with us over an extended period we tend to attract and retain older rather than younger people. We need to keep bringing younger customers on board and so we have rejuvenated our core product line.'

The company has not been afraid to try new methods to reach potential customers. In the US, its mainstream *Family Handyman* series added 750,000 readers by direct response television advertising in six months. Importantly, the publication, which generally has an older readership garnered 150,000 younger people as subscribers. Plans are underway to introduce strategic alliances with specialist

businesses. In the US the parent company has already concluded deals with Microsoft, Meredith and Avon. 'We are riding on America's coat-tails to a certain extent in the UK but we hope to conclude similar relationships here in the future.' A move to Canary Wharf in Spring 1997 will also alter the pattern of working within the UK company. Traditionally, RD has grouped people together according to discipline whereas in the new open-plan environment people from different disciplines will be brought together to work on specific projects.

How does Reader's Digest rate?

Pay:	excellent
Benefits:	very good
Communications:	good
Training:	very good
Career development:	very good
Employee morale:	very good

People and personnel policies

Despite operating in sectors which have historically experienced high staff turnover – marketing and journalism – Reader's Digest has minimal attrition rates. The loyalty which the company builds with its customers is replicated in its relationship with its employees. It pays extraordinarily well for a publisher and marketeer and compares strongly with other blue chips in London. Benefits are good, especially the company's pension scheme. But the reward system is only a reflection of the genuine respect which the management has for the workforce and RD has placed great emphasis on multi-level internal communications and dialogue with its people. HR director Frank Ross says that as the business runs several sites, communications have emerged as a key priority. It is an enthusiastic publisher of internal newsletters and bulletins, and seeks to encourage internal discussion through monthly manager meetings with staff. A briefing sheet is issued to all managers to provide subjects for debate and useful comments are fed back up the line. Its Swindon site has a much greater natural unity than its premises in the capital because everyone sees each other on a daily basis. The move to Canary Wharf will bring the London workforce together in the open-plan setting. Also RD's management aims to create informal meeting areas where less formal gatherings can take place and the bonds between team members developed.

As a multinational with a commanding reputation, Reader's Digest is able to provide its employees with a secure career path and many opt to stay for long periods of time. There is also a significant degree of job assignment and permanent placings internationally. The deputy editor of the UK edition of Reader's Digest recently went to be the editor of the Canadian edition. Marketing and promotions managers have gone on assignment to Poland and the US. A French manager came to the UK to learn about new promotional techniques. 'We can provide a variety of overseas assignments and permanent placings which may be attractive to people wanting to add greater experience.'

The company also offers a degree of flexible working for women who have returned from maternity leave. Some jobs in London are shared and the human resources department of the business is investigating ways in which it can be more flexible. The maternity benefits package is one of the best in the UK which is not surprising since the company employs a large number of women in senior positions. The UK company is not a glass ceiling company and two women have recently been promoted to the UK board.

In the early 1990s, Reader's Digest took a landmark decision to terminate its graduate recruitment scheme. The decision, which may seem strange at first glance for a graduate culture, was taken because some of the entrants would spend a relatively short time with the business. McRae says that they saw RD as an excellent first assignment in their careers but failed to stay long enough to give the company a return on training costs. 'We chose actively to recruit at second assignment stage. Inevitably we still brought in graduates but they also had work experience, often in blue chip companies.' The company places great emphasis on long term commitment in jobs that are professionally rewarding and stimulating.

Contact address

Mr Frank Ross,
Human Resources Director,
Reader's Digest Association Limited,
11 Westferry Circus,
Canary Wharf,
London E14 4HE.
Telephone: 0171 715 8000.
Fax: 0171 715 8181.

Rentokil Initial plc

Rentokil Initial claims to be the world's largest business services company. It supplies a range of cleaning and hygiene, distribution and plant, personnel, pest control, property, and security services to more than 1.5 million customers in over 40 countries, including all the major economies of Europe, North America and Asia Pacific. It has a pro-forma annual turnover of approximately £3 billion and profits of approximately £370 million. It is capitalised at approximately £6.5 billion and has a staff totalling some 150,000 worldwide. The group's objective is to provide for its shareholders growth of at least 20 per cent a year in profits and earnings per share. Over the last 10 years these have grown on average by 23.5 per cent and 24.4 per cent respectively. It was voted Britain's Most Admired Company by *Management Today* magazine in 1994, one of many accolades bestowed by the media over recent years.

Rentokil Initial at a glance

Employees: 150,000 worldwide, 60,000 UK
Staff attrition rate: variable across the group
Key locations: East Grinstead, East Sussex (HQ); more than 500 branch offices through the UK. Main overseas offices: Antwerp, Sydney, Cape Town and throughout the North American and Asia Pacific regions
Av. annual graduate recruitment: n/a
Annual intake: n/a

An inside view

Forget the image you may have of Rentokil Initial as a company staffed by uniformed men who turn up in a distinctive van and do a professional job of getting rid of woodworm and other pests in your home. Nothing could be further from the truth, although this is how the company began business some 70 years ago. Today the company, through a series of acquisitions over recent years to support its corporate development plan, provides a growing number of services to businesses rather than householders. Too numerous to enumerate fully here, they extend from the familiar pest control and timber-preserving services to the provision and care of tropical plants, and from office machine maintenance to textile services. In between there are more than a dozen other services encompassing facilities maintenance, catering, cleaning, security and personnel.

The company is committed to growth through acquisition. In 1995, for example, it acquired 20 businesses in North America, Scandinavia, Australia, Portugal and

Belgium. Its largest acquisition to date was British Electric Traction (BET) bought for £2.2 billion in April 1996. At a stroke this added 100,000 employees to the payroll, almost £2 billion to the turnover and a range of complementary products and services. Rentokil Initial is headquartered in a country house, called Felcourt, in 13 acres of countryside at East Grinstead, in West Sussex. It is from here that a handful of directors, regional managing directors and senior management control and guide the company's global business. Few disciplines are centralised, apart from finance, corporate affairs, management development and one or two others. Personnel services are very much de-centralised.

The day-to-day action at Rentokil Initial takes place in the company's branch offices. There are more than 1,000 worldwide, around half of which are in the United Kingdom. The branch manager is a key player in the management structure of the company. Each branch has a geographical area of operation, a range of services to sell, targets to meet, a financial reporting system, promotional budgets and a personnel, or human resources, responsibility. It is through the branch that almost all the company's employees enter the business.

How does Rentokil Initial rate?

Pay:	good
Benefits:	very good
Communications:	good
Training:	excellent
Career development:	excellent
Morale:	very good

People and personnel policies

Rentokil Initial has an ongoing recruitment requirement. It is not primarily concerned with previous academic achievements and stresses that anyone, whether a graduate or non-graduate, can apply to join the company, which operates a policy of meritocracy. The point of entry is invariably at branch level where a new recruit intent on a career in management joins a close-knit team in one of the specialist service areas offered by the branch, such as pest control, office cleaning, facilities maintenance or medical services. A branch has on average a staff of between 40 and 60, including salespeople.

As each branch is responsible for its own service, sales and administration operations at local area level, the performance of every employee will be recognised. This results in those people with ability being spotted early in their careers and given extra responsibilities and promotion. For example, for a person recruited to the service, rather than sales, side of the business the first promotion will be to supervisor directing a team and managing contracts. This can lead to an appointment as service manager with responsibility for a number of supervisors.

After a spell in service, the structure exists for a move into selling with responsibilities for developing existing business and acquiring new contracts. Successful salespeople become sales managers and then, possibly within three to five years, branch managers.

Such promotion opportunities are not restricted to a particular division, or indeed country, within the company. Rentokil Initial businesses are run along similar lines worldwide and management skills are largely transferable from one business to another. The company positively encourages movement within the organisation and sees this as a key to its success. The average age of branch managers is mid-to-late twenties and 30-plus for area managers.

Comments Ken Bowman, group management development director 'With our meritocracy policy, the most senior positions in the company are open to those people who demonstrate ability and we attach great importance to developing the careers of those people showing talent.

'We do this through ongoing management development and training. All development programmes are held at our own group training headquarters at East Grinstead, with the exception of our international senior managers' programme which is held at Sundridge Park Management School in Bromley, Kent.

'Delegates discover key learning points for themselves by participative discussion, case study exercises and the use of CCTV where appropriate. All courses and programmes are multidivisional and multi-functional, allowing delegates to exchange ideas and experiences with colleagues from other divisions and functions within the group,' he says.

Among the subjects covered are interpersonal skills; people skills; optimising resources; team leadership; team building; recruitment and selection skills; time management; and public speaking and presentation skills. A much-coveted Rentokil Diploma in Management is presented to successful delegates.

Says Bowman 'We have a saying within the company "If you stay around for 18 months you will stay for life".' The rewards offered by Rentokil Initial include competitive salaries, an on-target bonus, a profit-sharing scheme (after two years' service) for all employees, a share option for middle to senior management, a company car where necessary for the position held (such as branch manager), selective free healthcare, and a contracted out pension scheme. Among the methods of communication within the company are a corporate worldwide magazine and several in-house publications covering local and divisional matters.

Contact address

Mr Ken Bowman,
Group Management Development Director,
Rentokil Initial plc,
Felcourt,
East Grinstead,
West Sussex RH19 2JY.
Telephone: 01342 833022.
Fax: 01342 326229.

Reuters Holdings plc

R euters is renowned throughout the world as one of the greatest news-gathering enterprises. Its fame derives from its function as a news agency but it has long since broadened out beyond its original operation and now supplies information and information systems to a variety of organisations. It aims to be number one supplier of information to the global financial community and intends to remain the top news and information service to newspapers and broadcasters. In the last 10 years it has enjoyed outstanding sales and profits growth and is among the top five FTSE 100 companies in terms of increase in turnover. In 1996 the company reported sales of £2.9 billion and profits of £701 million. It employs 15,478 people in 91 countries but distributes its services in more than 161 countries.

Reuters at a glance

Employees: 15,478
Annual staff attrition rate: 4 per cent
Key locations: Reuters HQ is located in Fleet Street, London. The company has major centres in New York, Washington DC, Tokyo, Singapore and Geneva
Av. annual graduate recruitment: 30
Annual intake: 300

An inside view

Reuters established its commanding reputation as a news agency. Guided by principles of speed, truth and accuracy, it is respected worldwide. 'When we visit universities we need to explain that Reuters is more than a news agency with an outstanding international reputation. Nearly 50 per cent of our people today are technical working on leading edge software and systems. We have also recruited large numbers of sales, marketing and support personnel to look after our customers,' says Irene Dibben, personnel manager UK & Ireland. 'Our heritage is journalism and we still adhere to the values which made Reuters famous. These include independence, impartiality, speed and accuracy.'

The key part of the business is its information products division which accounts for 69 per cent of revenues. This is the provision of real time and historical information, datafeeds and software tools to analyse data to almost all of the large financial services institutions across the world. This includes currencies, stocks, bonds, and futures and options. The second largest part of the company is transaction products which enable traders to deal from screen in such markets as foreign exchange, futures and options, and securities. Its third business is media products which historically is the core of the old Reuters operation – in text, televisual images, still pictures, sound and graphics. Its employees fall into three major blocks: technical, working on systems maintenance, software and strategic systems; sales and marketing based around the world; and editorial staff engaged in news gathering, image and text preparation and dissemination. It has one of the largest private leased communications networks in the world.

John Freeman, head of personnel for UK & Ireland, says that its intake direct from further education is relatively low. This is because the company recruits experts. In its editorial operations, Reuters has a justified reputation for authority and expertise. This is regularly achieved by identifying the leading specialists in specified fields and inviting them to join. This policy stretches to its information systems products. 'Our systems and software people are consistently pushing back the barriers. They are often so far ahead of the field that they are the only operators in their area of expertise. This colours the nature of the people who want to work for Reuters. They are innovative and courageous individuals, unafraid to speak their minds,' says Freeman.

The company employs an unusual mix of personalities. Culturally, journalists, technicians and sales and marketing people operate to different rules but within Reuters they all sign up to the central values of the business. 'This is an organisation which is prepared to change its structure and its business approach as the market demands. So we are looking for people who are adaptable. This may be seen as unconventional but our recruits enjoy meeting new challenges. The traditional journalistic enthusiasm for working up against a deadline is prevalent throughout Reuters,' Dibben comments.

How does Reuters rate?

Pay:	very good
Benefits:	very good
Communications:	superb
Training:	good
Career development:	very good
Morale:	very good

People and personnel policies

Freeman says that personnnel policy in Reuters has been constructed in various ways. 'Originally, the operation in Fleet Street was the core of the company. Most of the people were based here or controlled from London. So policy was run from London. As the structure spread to other territories and we established separate management in other continents, so the approach to human resources became more fragmented.

'Recently we have decided to centralise certain basic approaches and we formed an HR group which represents the geographical regions of the company – Europe, Middle East and Africa; Asia; and the Americas,' he says. 'This group meets three times a year to coordinate those parts of human resources policy which need to be common. Also the group spends the majority of its time planning a development programme for managers across the world. This is designed to extend the skill base of existing senior managers and to prepare the next generation for the assignments which lie ahead,' he remarks. The issues which this group deals with regularly concern a common approach to pay and benefits, training and career development. Freeman says that in the UK Reuters pay is considered by HR professionals to be median – or average – while benefits are exceptional. For example, all employees have six weeks' holidays a year. Around 40 per cent of staff receive car allowances rather than just cars as part of their package. Reuters encourages its staff to be shareholders and many have bought Reuters shares through its Save As You Earn scheme. The maternity benefits scheme is considerably better than statutory provision and the company provides a child care allowance for newly returned mothers of £150 a month. Paternity leave has also been introduced.

Internal communication is cogent, well expressed and pertinent, as one might expect from the market leader in information distribution. It reflects the true conviction for honesty and clarity within the business. But this is not a nanny company. Career development is largely in the hands of the individual. The personnel function will stimulate the process by providing detailed information on jobs available within the group but chasing those opportunities lies in the hands of the individual employee. The company draws its new managers from the ranks of those who, given a task, will produce something extra. Freeman says that the company is heavily accented on project management which means that those individuals who have evident and

effective influencing skills will win through.

The editorial division of the company continues to be highly attractive for entrants. Reuters is the world market leader – it is faster and more reliable than many of its competitors. In professional terms it is a highly satisfying place to work. The company aims to continue to grow in the market sectors where it is already the leader and to expand aggressively in other business areas. It aims to expand its coverage geographically and to add to its thriving client list. Opportunities, therefore, for experts in particular disciplines will be particularly promising.

The biggest demand in the next few years will be for articulate financial market people. This is where the real growth in the company will come from. And Reuters has invested heavily in a range of technical and corporate initiatives to ensure that it remains ahead of the field. Its recent Armstrong programme which led to the 3000 product series cost the company £100 million. On the product side, Dealing 2000 and Instinet are prime examples of its commitment to the development of leading edge systems. Reuters is a company which has embraced the future.

Contact address

Mr John Freeman,
Head of Personnel UK & Ireland,
Reuters Limited,
85 Fleet Street,
London EC4P 4AJ.
Telephone: 0171 250 1122.
Fax: 0171 542 6704.

Rolls-Royce plc

Now focused on the aerospace and industrial power systems markets, Rolls-Royce is one of the UK's leading engineering groups. The group is increasingly developing an international presence and more than 75 per cent of its sales are exported. Roll-Royce has an ethos of quality and technical excellence and attaches the highest priority to management and employee development, recognising that it needs a high calibre workforce to remain competitive in demanding market conditions. With many of the company's activities at the leading edge of technology, Rolls-Royce represents an exciting and challenging place to work.

Rolls-Royce at a glance

Employees: 42,500 worldwide, 31,500 UK
Staff attrition rate: 3 per cent
Key locations: London, Virginia (US), Derby, Bristol, Indianapolis, Newcastle-upon-Tyne, Coventry, Derby, Gateshead, Toronto
Av. annual graduate recruitment: 170
Annual intake: 500

An inside view

Rolls-Royce is a leading company in the power systems industry. It currently operates through two main businesses: the Aerospace Group, which specialises in gas turbines for civil and military aircraft; and the Industrial Power Group, which designs, constructs and installs power generation systems for marine propulsion, oil and gas pumping, offshore materials handling and defence markets. The company is extremely well represented internationally, with more than 70 operating companies worldwide and 77 per cent of its turnover earned overseas.

In common with other companies in the aerospace and power industries, recent trading conditions have been difficult, in particular as the defence market has contracted substantially following the fall of the Eastern bloc. Rolls-Royce has responded to these pressures by enhancing its global presence, undertaking new product development and entering into various alliances and collaborations with a series of partners. It has also carried out a wide-ranging business restructuring as part of which it withdrew from activities in which it did not see itself as having a clear competitive advantage.

The company is founded around a culture of technical excellence and achievement. This is manifested in the importance which it attaches currently to new product launches as being critical to the future success of the business. For many of those hoping to work in Rolls' highly regarded research and development programmes, a rigorous academic background is essential. Around 70 per cent of those recruited will have some sort of engineering background – a proportion which has stayed remarkably constant over time. Nonetheless, strong interpersonal skills, an ability to work well in teams and a grasp of commercial matters are becoming increasingly important qualities in recruits.

In terms of management structure, Rolls-Royce is much more streamlined than it used to be. However, since many of the company's activities have vital safety and security implications, a hierarchy of approvals and controls in inevitable. As a result, therefore, the company is much more traditionally structured than companies in, for example, the service sector.

How does Rolls-Royce rate?

Pay:	good
Benefits:	good
Communications:	good
Training:	excellent
Career development:	very good
Morale:	good

People and personnel policies

Given the highly competitive nature of the power and aerospace industries worldwide, Rolls-Royce has placed a strong emphasis on the importance of recruiting and developing a high calibre workforce. The company aims to establish an environment in which continuous learning can take place, and is placing a much greater responsibility on the individual to specify the type of training they wish to receive.

In 1995, Rolls-Royce undertook a major review of training and its role within the group. As a consequence of this review, significant new training and development initiatives were launched. One of these was the Rolls-Royce business manager programme, a suite of technical programmes in support of a major investment in electronic product definition and multi-skilling programmes. In addition, learning centres have been established to provide computer training for employees to upgrade their skills, both through work-based projects and study in their own time.

In recognition of the quality of the group's training for young people, one Rolls-Royce employee recently won the New Graduate Engineering Prize from the Royal Academy of Engineering. Another former graduate trainee represented the Industrial Power Group at the World Energy Council Youth Energy Symposium 1995. Training also plays an important part in support of sales and marketing internationally. Various long-term training initiatives have been established with governments and institutions in a number of developing countries.

The group's remuneration policy is to set salaries based on market rates. However, Rolls-Royce is increasingly keen to reward employees based on their performance and see the workforce share in the success of the company by introducing a variety of incentive schemes. Building on the success of its Sharesave scheme (which has been in existence since 1987), the company has recently introduced a performance-related pay scheme for all employees, in order to align their interests more closely to the group's performance. The company is also examining ways to create a closer identity of interest between shareholders and senior management by developing a long-term incentive plan.

One of the major benefits of the company's wider international representation is that offers much greater opportunities for developing its management team through overseas postings. Similar opportunities are offered by the number of joint ventures and alliances in which the company is entering. International experience is increasingly seen as a pre-requisite for a senior management position.

Traditionally, engineering has been a male-dominated profession, and to a large extent it remains so, not least through the general reluctance of females to take engineering and other scientific disciplines at university. Both through its recruitment policy, and by offering flexible working arrangements such as career breaks, Rolls-Royce is trying to retain and promote women within engineering. There are a handful of senior women within the organisation, who can act as role models, but progress is slower than the company would like.

The company employs a variety of techniques to communicate information through the organisation. As well as the standard written forms of communication such as employee newspapers, there are also briefing and focus groups which are designed to communicate change to lower levels. Management and employee representatives hold regular meetings at each location to discuss problems and opportunities. For graduates, there is also an annual conference, while all executive directors meet younger members of the management team at regular lunches.

The company acknowledges its social responsibilities, especially in areas where it has a strong local presence. For example, it operates youth training programmes for unemployed school leavers. In 1995, the Industrial Power Group recruited 100 young people – making a total of 243 receiving training of this kind – and it is hoped that the majority will find work with local employers. In another initiative, the Aerospace Group supported two schools in Derby in their successful bids to become technology colleges.

Contact address

Mr D'Arcy Payne,
Human Resources Director,
Rolls-Royce plc,
65 Buckingham Gate,
London SW1E 6AT.
Telephone: 0171 222 9020.
Fax: 0171 227 9178.

Rover Group Limited

The Rover Group is one of the standard-setters of the British motor industry. Ownership by the German industrial giant BMW has guaranteed the company a long-term future signified by the investment of £30 million in a state-of-the-art design centre in Gaydon, Warwickshire and some £500 million a year in capital projects over a six-year period. Rover made a commitment to its workforce in its New Deal in 1992 which stops short of a jobs for life promise but which goes a great deal further than many other manufacturers. In effect no worker can expect compulsory redundancy provided they are willing to accept any reasonable retraining, reskilling or move within the company. Rover currently employs 37,000 people.

Rover at a glance

Employees: 37,000
Annual staff attrition rate: 2 per cent
Key locations: Warwick (HQ),
    Birmingham, Solihull, Oxford,
    Swindon and Gaydon
Av. annual graduate recruitment: 100–130
Annual intake: n/a

An inside view

For anyone who feels passionate about cars, Rover is a wonderful place to work. Even if you enjoy business and would sign up with any great company, Rover is still exciting. No one could deny that the UK motor industry has had an eventful career during the last three decades and there have been times when industrial relations were so bad that many distinguished commentators doubted that it had a future at all. Much of the mutual antagonism between employers and employed has vanished, and there has been a recognition by everyone concerned in the industry that the future lies in cooperation and teamwork.

Nowhere is the transformation more evident than at Rover. The relatively recent takeover by BMW was greeted with howls of disquiet but, in practice, it has served to give the company a future. The Germans are renowned for their commitment to the long-term vision and providing investment to ensure that their products are durable, commercial successes. Translated into the Rover scenario, such staying power coupled with Rover's innate design flair should create a pattern for sustained and long-lasting business success. Four manufacturing sites in the UK are turning out a wide range of Rover, MG, Mini and Land Rover vehicles, panels and tools, and the company is convinced that it has sufficient design ingenuity, feel for the market, production integrity and superb sales potential to achieve long-term profitability.

The heartland of Rover is the Midlands – unsurprising since this has long been the home of the UK motor industry. Headquarters are at a purpose-built site on the outskirts of leafy Warwick and its £30 million design centre lies further out into the South Warwickshire countryside at Gaydon. At Longbridge in Birmingham, Rover makes the Mini, the Rover 100, 200 and 400 and the MGF, and most of the engines and gearboxes for use in the group. In Solihull it turns out the Discovery, the Land Rover Defender, the Range Rover and some dedicated engines and gearboxes for use in these cars. The site at Cowley, Oxford produces the Rover 600 and 800, and at Swindon it designs and manufactures the tools for the big body presses, and presses these panels for use in Rover and Honda cars.

Personnel director David Bower says that Rover is not a passive place, it is an environment for people who wish to achieve. 'In our managers, we look for good intellectual ability but, in particular, people who are personally resilient, and teamworking orientated. These are individuals who, on the one hand, are capable of sharp intellectual focus on particular issues but, on the other, can see those issues in the general context of a business. This is a culture which appreciates people with personal drive and who are results-focused, but at the same time work well in teams and are good at interpersonal skills.'

How does Rover rate?

Pay:	very good
Benefits:	excellent
Communications:	very good
Training:	superb
Career development:	very good
Morale:	very good

People and personnel policies

Rover normally takes up to 130 graduates into its entry scheme each year (in 1996, it was 133). Milk round recruitment has scaled down because, Bower argues, the company is well known among the universities, where its reputation is high. At the end of the penultimate student year a group of potential recruits join Rover for a period of four to ten weeks to familiarise themselves with the business.

'When they join they spend approximately three months in manufacturing. We have to prepare them in advance for what will be a shock to the system. It means working on assembly lines and shift working, but we are absolutely convinced that there is no better way of understanding the overall manner in which the business works. On the assembly line or in a direct manufacturing job you see the culmination of everybody's efforts to plan, to specify, to organise material, to create a working environment and to organise an appropriate management process. They begin to appreciate the very complex process of design, engineering, logistics supply and manufacture, prior to delivery to the customer. We aim to provide every graduate we recruit with direct experience of dealing with the customer, either in the service department where they are listening to customer calls seeking help and assistance, or working in a dealership or with a distributor. It helps to create a greater sensitivity to the customer,' says Bower.

The highest level statement of Rover's commitment to its people came in the Rover Tomorrow – New Deal agreement, which was signed in 1992. 'The *Sun* newspaper claimed that this was a jobs for life deal. It was not, but what it said was that if you were willing to retrain or reskill during the course of your career and carry out any reasonable request as regard to work within the company, then there would be no compulsory redundancy. It was a high level, very straightforward commitment. Making that work is a major challenge. We have honoured it for nearly five years. We believed that in order to change the nature of relationships and attitudes inside the business, it was a necessary step. It has created a much more positive set of employment relationships. In 1994, BMW purchased Rover and people asked if the new owner would continue to honour that pledge. The answer was yes.'

Bower suggests that birth is easier than resurrection, and that renewing an on-going concern is harder than creating a greenfield company. As a result, Rover has launched initiatives which are designed to boost relationships inside the business and breed confidence and trust. 'We needed to move away from a conflict-centred relationship with the trades unions which we did with the New Deal. We established a set of processes and procedures for more genuine communication and we aimed to win

commitment from the unions to provide a responsible contribution. We have done some worldwide benchmarking with the trades unions in a programme called The Way Ahead. This is an active programme to open people's eyes and minds.'

The real focus for employees in delivering the New Deal has been in learning, training and education. 'We have created inside the company a unit called the Rover Learning Business. We offer everyone within the company each year a sum of money to pursue their own learning programme. It need not be anything to do with their job – it could be a foreign language. The extremes which illustrate the flexibility of the programme include sheep husbandry and inshore navigation. The basic notion is to open up eyes and minds to the learning experience. Additionally, it brought with it a sense that the company is not only a hard input-output style of operation, we are prepared to give – reasonably – to individuals' personal development. The nature of work is changing. The scope of intellectual, professional, managerial and project management skills will be redefined in the future and our role is to create the environment for these skills to be developed.'

Contact address

Mr David Bower,
Personnel Director,
Rover Group Limited,
International Headquarters,
Warwick Technology Park,
Warwick CV34 6RG.
Telephone: 01926 482000.
Fax: 01926 482001.

The Royal Bank of Scotland plc

The Royal Bank of Scotland is one of the UK's leading - and most respected - financial services companies. It is engaged in a wide range of banking, insurance and financial sector activities in Britain and overseas. By assets, it is the UK's sixth largest commercial bank, and for each of the last three years it has been independently assessed as the top UK bank for customer service. Its Direct Line insurance subsidiary has revolutionised the UK's general insurance industry.

Royal Bank of Scotland at a glance

Employees: 19,500
Annual staff attrition rate: 10 per cent
Key locations: Edinburgh (HQ), with regional headquarters in London and Manchester. More than 700 high street branches throughout England, Scotland and Wales
Av. annual graduate recruitment: to 100
Annual intake: 2,300

An inside view

The Royal Bank of Scotland's chief executive Dr George Mathewson sees a clear vision for his business: to be the best performing financial services group in Britain by the end of 1997. This challenging target will be achieved, he argues, by building on the strong reputation which the bank has already created for itself. Inside the group, there is a continual comparison of underlying growth in earnings per share and dividends which provides an effective yardstick to measure progress towards his vision. In 1993, the bank became the largest company headquartered in Scotland. But today's RBS took shape in 1985 following the successful merger with Williams and Glyn's. Earlier it had become the first UK bank to have all its branches connected on line to a central computer. It played a leading role in the launch of the switch debit card and in 1991 RBS became the first to introduce laser-etched photographs of customers on plastic cards – cutting fraud by 99 per cent.

Its approach of corporate and product innovation has served the Royal Bank well. UK banking remains the largest part of the group's business. The march towards even greater ambition has meant mergers and acquisitions in the US and the strengthening of an alliance with the Banco Santander in Spain. The customer base has been increased with more product sales, with continued diversification within related areas which has reduced the sensitivity of earnings to bad debts. Organic growth is expected to improve earning still further.

Group diversification means the RBS provides personal customer service including banking and savings accounts, credit cards and mortgages, life assurance, innovative investment products, motor and home insurance. Business customers range from small concerns to large corporates. In addition to lending, leasing, structured finance and development capital, also on offer are money market, foreign exchange and derivative products. Foresight means a wide range of opportunities are on offer for those who are judged to have drive and ability to take advantage of them. UK financial services are going through a period of change. The RBS believes that the changes it has made in its own organisation enable it to face the future with confidence, more focused on meeting the needs of customers. Bureaucracy has been stripped to minimum levels and the accent is on the recognition and reward of achievement.

How does Royal Bank of Scotland rate?

Pay:	very good
Benefits:	very good
Communications:	good
Training:	very good
Career development:	good
Morale:	good

People and personnel policies

To become the best in a daunting sector, the Royal Bank's managers seek to employ the best people: those with ability, initiative and ambition. Training is designed to release individual potential and success is rewarded accordingly. Investment in business also means investment in people: and that is why the Royal Bank of Scotland aims to attract high calibre staff who can rise to the very top. Changes to banking in recent years have meant diversification: the retail sector serving small business and the single customer, and a corporate arm serving middle and large organisations.

Its principal employee groups are customer service personnel, process staff, sales staff, relationship managers and the lending function, with a career structure for each. Human resources director Dr Mike Mosson explains 'Each needs different types of skills, deployed in focused jobs instead of general jobs. And our HR policy is designed to drive the business forward, meeting every need.' To that end he has recruited human resources professionals to operate throughout the organisation. He frankly maintains that most banks are inward looking in what he regards as an essential prerequisite to success. The Royal Bank is anything but. That is why the HR strategy has a strong focus on designing, developing and implementing policies designed to equip the bank for up to the next 15 years. It is geared to one over-riding principle: the need to maintain, hone and improve a competitive edge. Technology and lower cost structures cannot alone do that. The answer lies in what the strategy defines as the quality and effectiveness of a highly motivated workforce.

A substantial number of roles within the organisation have been redesigned.

More than 1,000 managers have been trained in staff selection techniques with a greater focus of achieving results. Training and development are aligned to business needs, and more reliable resource and skills planning tools. The bank attaches major significance to the phasing out of outdated reward structures, replacing them with packages which reflect individual and business performance. The next phase of the plan has seven advanced bases: encouragement of and reward for creativity and innovation; the respect and value of individuals; skills and aspirations to be matched with roles and business needs; teamwork and collaboration to be regarded as critical to success; the realisation of potential by continuous development and training; the recognition of achievement, contribution and success by reward; and all dealings with customers and each other to be of the highest ethical standards.

It is an impressive shopping list. But it is one which has been designed with care and thought. Banking traditionally had a high staff turnover, because most front line employees were women who left to bring up families. The bank actively encourages female advancement for those who see it as a career. One senior executive is female, two non-executive directors are women, more are in senior management and numbers are rapidly growing in management. Dr Mosson comments 'We are trying to create a climate in which people can achieve success on the basis of ability and competence. There are no barriers and the proportion is changing quite quickly.' Most new staff are recruited either straight from school with GCSEs and A

levels or from other clerical and sales positions. Up to 100 are graduates who undertake a series of learning roles over a period of 18 months and then enter the internal jobs market. Dr Mosson says 'We provide job opportunities, we provide training, and we provide development opportunities. But individuals choose one of the various streams in the organisation and the direction in which they wish to go. I do not think a fast-changing organisation can sensibly set out a long-term career plan. We concentrate on building skills, knowledge and developing competency in specially focused roles.'

To get the best staff the RBS has made its reward packages a priority. It has been reshaped over the past two years from a single structure to more than 20 different structures with an ultimate target of about 40. There is a competitive basic salary for all grades and job descriptions plus a variable bonus or incentive element depending on achievement. A profit-related element – 8.4 per cent of basic salary in 1995 – adds a top up. Retirement is at 60 with a non-contributory pension. There are loans – including mortgages – at special staff rates and free private health-care for management staff.

Contact address

Dr Mike Mosson,
Director of Human Resources,
The Royal Bank of Scotland plc,
PO Box 31,
42 St Andrew Square,
Edinburgh EH2 2YE.
Telephone: 0131 556 8555.
Fax: 0131 557 3084.

Safeway Stores plc

Safeway Stores is one of Britain's largest and most innovative supermarket chains. In 1996 it reported sales of £6.5 billion and pre-tax profits of £401 million. The company employs more than 69,000 people in 420 stores. Safeway has placed heavy emphasis – for many years – on its role as a good employer and this has been further developed by its Safeway 2000 initiative, which has completely reorganised and strengthened the business. A key element of the fresh direction is its approach to customer service supported by its Make A Difference and Mystery Shopper programmes.

Safeway at a glance

Employees: 69,000 (64,000 non-management, 5,000 management)
Annual staff attrition rate: 30 per cent
Key locations: 420 stores plus head office facilities in Hayes, Middlesex. These stores (Safeway and Presto) include Isle of Man, Channel Isles and Gibraltar
Annual graduate recruitment: 100–150
Annual intake: 25,000

An inside view

Few industries in the UK economy have changed so radically as food retailing. In the last 10 years, according to industry market research, there has been a massive switch to supermarket shopping. The large chains now account for 80 per cent of all food sales whereas a decade ago the balance with other outlets was more even. Safeway – along with Tesco and Sainsbury – has been a primary force in making the change. Its management believes that sponsorship of this process

has brought countless benefits for customers. It has equally created a highly competitive environment among the major players where continuous improvement in service, quality of outlets, diversity in stock and accessibility have been crucial components in the battle for brand loyalty and market share.

The business approaches of these key operators have come under constant review and refreshment. Safeway has made decisive changes, building on its existing substantial reputation for innovation, service and quality. 'We took a fundamental, long and hard look at our business two to three years ago and as a result reshaped and repositioned it,' says CEO Colin Smith. 'It was inevitable because of the competitive pressures in the market and we came back to the same starting point, which must always be the customer.' The review led to a new focus – under the banner of Safeway 2000 – on three core goals: customer choice, dynamism and innovation, and value for shareholders. 'Our function is to make shopping easier, especially for families.' Its recent Harry and Molly advertising campaign is regarded as the most successful in food retailing history. In 40 stores the company has installed creches with trained nursery nurses. It aims to be the most innovative and dynamic of the three large groups. Safeway is the world market leader, for example, in self scanning. 'We are half the size of either Tesco or Sainsbury in terms of annual sales so we must punch above our weight and be quicker to market with new products or service innovation. We must be seen as the most creative force in the industry,' says Smith.

Safeway has always been the most astutely financially managed supermarket chain and the third element of the new direction is to translate its skill here into results for its shareholders. In 1995 Smith set a target of increasing sales per square foot to £15 within three years. In fact the business was more than half way to this goal inside a year. The company is advancing – sales were up 11 per cent, pre-tax profits by 7 per cent, and dividends and EPS by 6 per cent each. Significantly, the group is more focused than at any stage in its recent past. It has moved away from discounting which it had done through its now divested Lo-Cost division

The balance between the corporate centre and the store manager and staff is now more directly attuned to the needs of the market. Safeway's management has taken an industry lead in technology which is directed centrally but empowers managers to be more effective with customers. The existing culture in the Safeway stores is the least formal of any of the major retailers and this approach has been extended and supported by professional systems and training. A series of initiatives to improve service such as

Make A Difference! which encourages everyone in the business as individuals to contribute in their own way to excellent service for customers, and Mystery Shopper, where employee shoppers pen reports rating the quality of specific stores, have been launched.

How does Safeway rate?

Pay:	good
Benefits:	good
Communications:	excellent
Training:	excellent
Career development:	good
Morale:	very good

People and personnel policies

'The big change for us was the move to a new customer proposition which says that we want to make shopping easier for today's families. Having decided that was what Safeway was all about, in order to deliver something uniquely different we needed to think of a new way to manage our people,' says Gordon MacDonald, Safeway's director of human resource development. 'Customer service requires us to be much more responsive, much more flexible at the point where we meet the customer. To do that from the centre is impossible. So we took out several layers in a long hierarchical structure. We had 25 grades which we compressed to ten in total, from CEO to checkout operator, so decision making is much quicker and more effective.'

MacDonald says that the company then widened individual spans of control thereby giving managers more accountability. The training programme was also overhauled to reflect the shift to a greater customer focus. And it placed much greater emphasis on the quality of its internal communications to ensure that employees were fully briefed about strategic and operational issues. A manager for in-store customer service has been appointed in each outlet. This individual is backed up by a body of regional and national expertise. Also the reward and benefit system was reorganised to create incentives for quality service. A recognition system was introduced to make awards to individuals who show exemplary service. 'This represented a major change in management philosophy by rewarding someone for doing something well rather than catching them doing something wrong,' says Kathie Collins, employment policy manager. Managers can make an instant award of perhaps flowers to an employee who delivers some exemplary act of service. 'This is food retailing – it is supposed to be exciting, it is supposed be fun. Let's work hard but enjoy ourselves as well,' she says.

In April 1995 Safeway introduced profit-related pay and employees have seen their income increase by around 7 per cent, including the standard pay rise. It has also introduced a three year savings-related share option scheme for all staff which is unusual. Safeway also offers pensions, life assurance and accident assurance for both full-timers and part-timers. Healthcare insurance is free for managers and available at a highly discounted rate for non-managers.

Employees can also buy house mortgages at reduced rates from leading building societies.

Retail by its nature has a high staff turnover in comparison with other sectors – due to its high proportion of part-time engagements – but Safeway is at the lower end of annual attrition. It recruits between 100 and 150 graduates each year and has strengthened its management development programme. Previously these recruits have been taken on for specific disciplines but Smith is keen that they are moved around the organisation. 'We pay a premium for graduates and to get a return on that investment we need to move them around the organisation,' he says. Recently, Safeway commissioned detailed research on all graduates who have been recruited, those who left the company and those who turned down an offer to work for the company. A key issue for these individuals was the need to secure a real job rather than enter another period of education. As a result Safeway has created a new development scheme where a distinctive group – the class of 96 or 97, for example – is formed which come together for training and development but who spend the bulk of their time in increasingly demanding roles.

'We were the first retailer to introduce behavioural assessment and development centres – more than 15 years ago,' says MacDonald. This has been modified and adapted to suit changing demands. In 1994, Safeway identified a bias-free framework of 21 competences which it regards as essential for the effective development of its managers. In the case of each job nine such competences are drawn out as the most pivotal. The reports from these centres on these core competences give individuals a focus to identify the path which they want their careers to take. 'There is a high emphasis on mutuality,' says Collins. 'The company does not dictate the pattern of careers, they are agreed, with the employee taking an equal level of responsibility for the direction of their careers.' Safeway is an active member of Opportunity 2000 and has won praise for its flexible approach to the hours of working women. It also offers career breaks for certain employees and gives better than average maternity benefits. The company is considering the most appropriate way of helping with child care. There has been a rapid increase in the number of women senior executives within Safeway.

Contact address

Mr Gordon MacDonald,
Director of HR Development,
Safeway Stores plc,
6 Millington Road,
Hayes, Middlesex UB3 4AY.
Telephone: 0181 756 2005.
Fax: 0181 573 5101.

The Sage Group plc

The Sage Group is one of the most respected software houses in the UK. The company has dazzled industry with its high selling and high performance applications. In recent years it has begun to expand internationally and commentators say that the company has a bright future. It publishes branded accounting software in the UK, France and US. Turnover in 1995 doubled to reach £102.2 million and operating profits expanded by 71 per cent to £24 million. It is expected to report sales of £135 million for 1996.

Sage at a glance

Employees: 1,700
Staff attrition: 5 per cent
Key locations: Newcastle upon Tyne plus companies in France and the US
Average graduate recruitment: 5
Annual intake: 50–100

An inside view

Sage is a class act in the growth companies market. It is often cited as a primary example of a business which has grown from scratch in a comparatively short period to be a market leader. The group derives 44 per cent of its income from primary software sales, a division of the business which grew by 94 per cent in 1995. A further 47 per cent of sales comes from support, upgrades and training services sold to existing software clients, and 9 per cent is derived from pre-printed stationary sales.

Chairman David Goldham says 'We expect the proportion of group sales derived from existing customers to rise progressively in the future as the number of software users increases'. In September 1995, the company announced that it had more than three-quarters of a million users and that would rise to more than 800,000 users when it had integrated its acquisition of the French software house Sybel in early 1996. A further corporate purchase – the US software developer Saari – helped to create a balance of income. Group sales since the takeover derive 40 per cent from the UK, 40 per cent from mainland Europe and 20 per cent from the US.

'The inclusion in the group of Multisoft in the UK and Sybel in France means that we now have access to client – server technology, essential to cater for the needs of larger companies. As hardware prices fall, we expect that client – server technology will extend its reach downwards to medium-sized companies.'

Goldman was running a Tyneside printing business in the late 1970s when he was intrigued by a government announcement of incentives to sell microprocessors. At the same time, technical director Graham Wylie discovered that there was no package on the market to estimate printing products, so he created some suitable software. Goldman says that Sage sold this software and suitable hardware as a package to the print market, taking advantage of the government's incentives. Within two years it had moved 80 systems. This was followed by a basic bookkeeping package for small business, introduced in 1983.

These products did extremely well and Sage sold its printing software business. The capital which the sales realised was put on deposit and eventually released into massive advertising campaigns to increase customer awareness. Goldman says that the company spent as much as 40 per cent of sales on advertising at one point. A big step forward for Sage came when Goldman visited a computer show in October 1985 where Amstrad launched its PCW – a low-cost word processor. It was the break that Sage had been waiting for. The company repackaged an old CPM accounting package which it sold at £100 a unit. By January 1986, Sage was moving 6,000 units a month. In 1989 the company was listed on the London stock exchange.

How does Sage rate?

Pay:	good
Benefits:	good
Communications:	good
Training:	very good
Career development:	excellent
Morale:	superb

People and personnel policies

When a company is doing well commercially and it has positive policies towards its people, its run of success is likely to continue. Sage has grown both by acquisition and organically but its directors have also been extremely adept at getting the best out of their employees. The company is warmly regarded by undergraduates and it has no trouble attracting talented software engineers.

The process of acquisition has meant that Sage Group has brought into the organisation a series of companies which have distinctive and individual cultures. Goldman says that the aim of the group is to preserve the particular identities of the acquired businesses and to build on their existing dialogues with their markets.

Sage places emphasis on the quality and efficiency of operations but it is also keen to give its people freedom to achieve their assignment in their own way. Its objective with its original purchases was to integrate all acquisitions into a single entity under the Sage banner. In recent years the policy has changed and each new business which is bought by the group will operate under its own logo. For employees in the group this means that they can retain their existing market relationships.

Sage employs people in a range of disciplines: software development, support, product upgrades, sales and marketing, distribution, and professional and administration. The bulk of people in the company work closely with the company's clients and so Sage recruits articulate and intelligent individuals with an aptitude for technology. It employs technologists in research and development but its customer service and support personnel are often people with proven communication skills rather than technical specialists.

The company believes in promoting from within and this policy extends to anyone in any role inside the company. Sage regularly asks people who are not in the management levels to put themselves forward for management assessment. In addition, managers are asked to look out for people with potential to go further. Goldman mentions one man who was a software packer and without a substantial formal education. His manager realised that he had potential to rise further in the company. The company paid for the employee to be trained on management courses and he is now a successful manager in the business. The company is serious about people succeeding on merit and is keen to develop its own management culture.

In terms of its reward packages, Sage aims to reflect market conditions. Its UK operations are based in the north east which is one of the lowest paid regions in the country, but the company is active in high quality software which can be one of the highest paid industries. So Sage employees certainly do well financially for Tyneside and are paid comparably with the sector. Benefits are good for the region but not remarkable for the software industry.

Sales and marketing people, managers and directors are on variable incomes and these will expand to a wider reach within the company. Reward packages in the French and US businesses are different from the UK operation and respond to local circumstances.

Contact address

Human resources department,
The Sage Group plc,
Sage House,
Benton Park Road,
Newcastle-upon-Tyne NE7 7LZ.
Telephone: 0191 255 3000.
Fax: 0191 255 0308.

Schlumberger plc

Schlumberger is a US oil industry multinational which operates in more than 100 countries worldwide, generating more than £7 billion a year in income. It employs more than 56,000 people globally at 930 facilities and is a world leader in two distinct sectors: oilfield services, and measurement and systems. The company has a formidable reputation for production and service quality, but also for the care and understanding with which it manages its people. At the core of its personnel policy is its concept of 'borderless careers' which means that anyone with talent has the opportunity to take any assignment within the company. Schlumberger recruits heavily among engineers and applied scientists for demanding and challenging assignments.

Schlumberger at a glance

Employees: 56,000 worldwide (60 per cent oil services, 40 per cent measurement & systems). UK, 7,200 (43 per cent oil services, 57 per cent measurement & systems)

Annual staff attrition rate: 4 per cent

Key locations: Some 930 in 100 countries. UK, 11 onshore sites plus various offshore. Oilfield services at London, Aberdeen, Great Yarmouth, Shetlands, Gatwick and Cambridge. Measurement and systems are at Felixstowe, Port Glasgow, Manchester, Blackburn, Dundee and Ferndown.

Annual graduate recruitment: 200

Annual intake: 150–200

An inside view

Schlumberger's distinctive origins as an entrepreneurial oil industry pioneer continue to imprint the company's culture today. Seventy years after Conrad and Marcel Schlumberger made a discovery which revolutionised the global oil industry, the business now employs 56,000 but remains true to the basic business principles of the two founding brothers. Bruce Christie, the UK company's recruiting coordinator, explains that in the early days without a series of separate drillings oil company exploration managers had no idea of the extent of oil deposits. The Schlumbergers discovered an electrical technique for accurately estimating and measuring the size of potential hydro-carbon layers. This discovery was quickly deployed by the oil majors and Schlumberger's reputation was made.

'Our engineers would typically go out into the desert or the jungle to take measurements in potential oilfields. The technique, called 'logging', was in demand throughout the world, often in the most remote and inhospitable locations. So our people were used to making autonomous decisions in the field. This capacity for independent decision making and autonomous operation has stayed with us and remains an essential part of our culture. Clearly, since we started business in Alsace in 1927, the company has evolved but it is a relatively young business to be employing 53,000 people and the original approach still significantly influences how we do business.' The company's growth is testimony to the creativity and enterprise of the founders and their successors. The business now has two distinct divisions with a total of 12 principal product lines. Its oilfield services activities account for around 60 per cent of revenues worldwide and include seismic data gathering and evaluation, operation of the world's largest fleet of oil rigs, sophisticated drilling processes, fluid engineering and well stimulation, evaluation of oil and gas formations, high level computing to interpret field data, and integrated project management for any combination of these services.

Measurement and systems operates in a range of sectors: design and manufacture of domestic and industrial meters, similar services for the gas and water industries, the design of test solutions for printed circuit board and semiconductor manufacturers, and the provision of transaction systems such as smart cards, telecoms systems and retail petrol distribution systems.

Schlumberger is a graduate employer, recruiting mainly engineers and applied scientists from the top universities. The requirements of the individual businesses are particular and so the numbers of

annual intake will vary. In 1994 the company recruited 90 graduates whereas in 1995 the intake increased to 175. The commercial prospects for the UK businesses are strong and so in 1996, 1997 and 1998, total graduate employment is expected to build upon these levels.

'Our policy is to recruit recent graduates from every country where we are based and to develop them as technical experts,' says Christie. Any individual recruited can make it to the top of the company. The current chairman and CEO Euan Baird is a primary example. 'He joined us straight from Cambridge University with a degree in geology and engineering.'

How does Schlumberger rate?

Pay:	excellent
Benefits:	very good
Communications:	good
Training:	superb
Career development:	excellent
Morale:	very good

People and personnel policies

Many companies argue that people are their greatest asset. So the critical reader will want more evidence than a simple assertion that a business is people-orientated. In the case of Schlumberger, the history alone is compelling. The company was built on individual achievement and has lost none of its respect for personal contribution. Especially in the oilfield services division it needs individuals who may work occasionally long, hard hours in sometimes difficult environments conducting work which will be crucially important to its clients. As well as technical skills, personal qualities of resilience, communication and adaptability are critical.

As long ago as the 1950s Schlumberger realised that to be an effective supplier to multinationals across the world, it needed to change its composition in favour of people from diverse localities, backgrounds and cultural groups. That decision was inherently forward-looking as many other international businesses at the time were largely populated by white Anglo-Saxon males. It remains an issue for the company today and in 1994 Schlumberger appointed a diversity manager to further enhance the company's approach in this area. Diversity is a key factor in the company's personnel policy which can be summarised as: people, technology, profit. Schlumberger aims to be the leading edge, low cost innovator in the sector. The company is also profoundly keen on profitability. It cherishes its independence and refuses to affiliate itself with any government or government agency, other than as a supplier. 'Among the people we recruit in the UK this year probably 30 per cent will be immediately based overseas. So we are looking for adaptable people, they should also possess good communication skills, have strong technical abilities and be resilient.' Some field engineers spend large sections of their careers abroad. This, therefore, may not be suitable for individuals with family commitments who need to remain in one area. Christie cites Port Harcourt in Nigeria as an example

where the engineers live on a compound and space may prove limited.

Training is very specific to the individual business areas. In wireline and testing, the founding business, the first month is spent at a well site in a 'preschool' to familiarise the candidate with the nature of the work and the culture of the company. Then there is a three-month programme at a training centre – up to 11 hours a day, six days a week – where trainees are taught and tested on the operation of specific tools, how to repair them and how to explain to clients what findings the tools reveal. Candidates must succeed in both programmes to stay with Schlumberger and around 90 per cent of those that enter make it through the preschool. There is, however, a much higher drop out rate – around 25 per cent – after the preschool. Christie said the introduction of the preschool has benefited candidates and the company, because it gives a chance for both to see how well suited they are. Then there will be an intensive period of working on assignment with another engineer and the client. 'It is a very responsible job because the client may decide to close a well based on the engineers' recommendations.' In measurement and systems, the environment is less dynamic and has greater stability. Joiners go through an induction process and then take training courses over a period of time.

The company describes its personnel approach as 'borderless careers' which means there are no limits to where an individual can go within the company provided that they perform. 'Employees can start as a field engineer in oilfield services but end up as marketing manager for our automatic test business.' As a matter of policy Schlumberger fills vacant posts internally. It relies heavily on the outstanding quality of its training and field experience. 'We pay our recruits very well indeed and we provide a competitive collection of benefits. Combined with the intensive training and experience, this provides an excellent platform for senior management.' During the last few years, the company has set a series of targets, especially in the area of diversity and training, to consistently improve its performance. At one stage there were few women engineers, but Schlumberger is in the forefront of attracting women engineers into the sector. It works in tandem with AWISE (Association of Women in Science and Engineering) and runs seminars for potential female entrants. Now the company is hitting its global targets for 15 per cent women in field engineering recruits and it is backing a series of initiatives to attract more women into technical disciplines and into the company. But, with its big company structure, Schlumberger has not lost its personal touch or its sense of humour.

Contact address

Mr Bruce Christie,
Schlumberger UK recruiting co-ordinator,
High Cross, Madingley Road,
Cambridge CB3 0EL.
Telephone: 01223 325281.
Fax: 01223 311523.
Worldwide web: http://www.slb.com

Schroders

There are few investment banks operating in London – the European capital of financial services – which enjoy the same reputation among colleagues as Schroders. In a market sector which is unlikely to win awards for the quality of internal management, Schroders stands head and shoulders above the pack for its efficiency, quality, profitability and talented personnel. The scope of its UK operation is broadly based on its Cheapside offices in the City but it also runs a range of overseas offices, the largest being in New York. In the Far East its operations are centred on Japan, Hong Kong, Singapore and there is also an office in Australia. As well as being a highly attractive option for graduates, Schroders also offers outstanding opportunities for experienced people looking for a longer career.

Schroders at a glance

Employees: 5,000 worldwide, 2,600 UK
Annual staff attrition rate: 10 per cent (UK)
Key locations: Several offices in
  Cheapside in the City of London (HQ),
  Harrow, Milan, Madrid, Paris, New
  York, Tokyo, Hong Kong, Singapore,
  Sydney, Jakarta, Kuala Lumpur
Annual graduate recruitment: 30 (UK)
Annual intake: 125 (UK)

An inside view

Merchant banks regularly feature in the list of attractive employers for undergraduates – some of them are included in this book. An exciting and demanding lifestyle on the equities trading floor can exert a magnetic pull for bright and highly motivated graduates. Others are drawn to the mergers,

acquisitions, disposals and flotations handled by the aggressive corporate finance departments, where relatively junior employees can come into contact with major players in the industrial and commercial worlds. This environment as well as being challenging also offers excellent financial packages but it is a very volatile climate where long-term careers are never certain. In the first few years after leaving university many graduates spend an exacting but rewarding spell in City offices at the heart of the European financial services industry.

Schroders stands among the most reputable and respected City institutions. It has earned this status as one of the best-run investment banks in London through able and dexterous management. Its executive appears to be one of only a handful in this sector which understands effective management of profit in banking. Schroders has replicated capable corporate management approaches and focused on market sectors where it can make a difference. Through this philosophy it has achieved excellent financial results through its specialist expertise. Most UK employees are engaged in the key sectors of corporate finance and securities, investment management, financial markets, and banking. The British operation also has leasing and venture capital operations. The principal market sectors are backed by a full range of support services including financial control, compliance, IT and personnel. Schroders' directors point to the bank's continued independence after 200 years as a principal reason why it remains consistently stable and high performing. It is well placed to choose from the cream of the crop in terms of its graduate intake. Sue Cox, group personnel director, says 'In the UK we take undergraduates who move quickly into the business. They tend to work extremely hard and benefit from a great deal of experience. We consider our UK graduate intake as equivalent to us MBA graduates.'

Many of the people who accept offers from Schroders will have a handful of other offers from investment banks. These are the highest quality people of their year from throughout Europe. Personality plays a key role in deciding in which parts of the business to place new entrants. The qualities needed to be successful in corporate finance are profoundly different from those required in research or as a trader on the dealing floor.

How does Schroders rate?

Pay: excellent

Benefits: good
Communications: good
Training: good
Career development: excellent
Morale: very good

People and personnel policies

When graduates join Schroders they immediately start a three-month induction course which is arranged by the centre. Regardless of which division they go to ultimately, each new employee takes this course, which covers most of the basics. This is a generic course which introduces them to Schroders and the City, some of the key products and core skills such as IT. They then go on to specific assignments where more dedicated training is provided.

Although the business does not generally use a mentoring programme, new people are – self-evidently – supervised and encouraged by more experienced colleagues. In corporate finance, for example, a new recruit will be given some small projects to work on, reporting to a senior manager. Over at securities, they would sit next to an experienced analyst who will provide both formal and informal guidance and in the first month they will be required to qualify with the SFA, for which formal training is provided. If it were banking, the new recruit would start with credit reviews. 'Each of the product areas has a different way of approaching the process of bringing new people into their teams.'

The overall human resources policy is led by the application of the company's values. It sees itself as a high quality, committed, client-focused, collegiate and risk-averse operator. 'To foster and reinforce that culture, the HR policy aims to get the best people we can for the task that we have. So, for example, in our selection process we are constantly reviewing to ensure that we really do get the right people.' This means that Schroders regularly benchmarks against the best in the market, it uses only highly trained recruiters and selectors and that it analyses data on all the candidates who apply to the company.

Using articulate and trained interviewers has another crucial benefit – it communicates a positive and committed impression of the business to the candidates. 'Many of our graduate recruits have told me that one of the key reasons why they chose Schroders was the impression of the company that they gained at the interview. They liked the Schroders people they met, who seemed motivated, switched on, they understood their company and they were very committed to Schroders. Two other factors are also important: this is a successful business and operating internationally, it is British.'

Cox sets the HR policy for the company globally, together with the senior management, but personnel managers, who report to the functional director and the head of territory, interpret this according to relevant local circumstances. In practical terms this operates as a network since Schroders is structured as a matrix. There is some migration between countries. The current country head in Japan comes from the investment management business in London. The joint managing director of financial markets, based in Asia, came out of the Australian business.

There is little cross-functional traffic because the skills needed for one discipline will be distinctly different from another. Capital markets people rarely make – or want to be – good stockbrokers. A venture capitalist is unlikely to perform as a derivatives specialist. Cox has a clear appreciation of what the individual businesses need in terms of individual professional and academic backgrounds and the personality traits of the people who could be successful in such roles. Her job is to help find the best people available according to this brief.

The organisation rates revenue earners highly, as opposed to managers, and the focus of the vast majority of the training and development is therefore on product. In the future, this focus will be changed to some degree because as the company grows there will be a need for greater management expertise. Training objectives form part of an annual appraisal process for all employees and the onus will be placed on the individual to achieve their training objectives. 'In the same way that we would measure the performance against an employee's financial targets, we would examine how much progress had been made in realising last year's training targets.' Most people are assessed by their immediate manager, and in corporate finance, they work on several teams and so several people would input.

Contact address

Ms Sue Cox,
Group Personnel Director,
Schroders plc,
120 Cheapside, London EC2V 6DS.
Telephone: 0171 382 6000.

Shell Transport and Trading Company plc

The Shell Transport and Trading Company, a publicly quoted UK company which, together with Royal Dutch Petroleum, owns (in proportions of 40–60 respectively) the Royal Dutch/Shell Group of Companies, is one of the world's largest and most successful oil companies, operating in more than 120 countries worldwide. Notwithstanding recent setbacks over the Brent Spar and its operations in Nigeria, the group has a long-standing reputation for professionalism and achievement. Earlier this year, Shell completed an internal reorganisation of its activities to improve its responsiveness and business focus. The company believes in taking a long-term view of both its markets and its workforce, and the diversity of its operations still offers significant career opportunities.

Shell at a glance

Employees: 104,000 worldwide, 10,500 UK
Annual staff attrition rate: n/a
Key locations: London (HQ),
   and many others around the UK
Av. annual graduate recruitment: 250*
Annual intake: n/a
*further graduate recruitment is conducted by operating companies

An inside view

Shell is one of the major players in the world oil and gas market, earning net income of over $4 billion in 1995. Despite the strength of its market position, however, its operating performance in recent years has been somewhat mixed. Partly in response to criticisms of its record, Shell has undertaken a major reorganisation of its business activities which was completed in early 1996.

The purpose of the reorganisation was to introduce greater responsiveness and accountability into the group, as well as to eliminate unnecessary costs. Shell is now divided into four basic business areas – exploration and production, oil products (covering refining, trading, shipping and marketing), chemicals, and gas and coal. Each of these business areas incorporates a series of underlying operating companies and is also responsible for performing its own research (whereas previously research was carried out centrally). It is the operating companies which remain the principal entities through which business is conducted. Shell's philosophy is that managers should have as much autonomy as possible and that decisions should be made close to the customer interface. Supporting the entire business structure are a series of central, service companies, but the general rule is that bureaucracy should be reduced wherever possible.

Shell's core values are professionalism and integrity. In addition, it attempts to engender in its workforce a sense of pride in working for Shell and, increasingly, a respect for colleagues, other people and the environment. Within this framework, however, the company is also trying to foster a more entrepreneurial spirit which it hopes will more successfully exploit the innate talents of its workforce. In return, Shell is introducing a much greater element of recognition and reward for individual performance.

Another characteristic which distinguishes Shell is that it attempts to take a long-term view of its business and people. While the company can no longer be considered as providing jobs for life – given the current trends in the labour market no sensible company can offer this, and Shell have actually been reducing their headcount over the last five years – it does at least take career development issues more seriously than most companies and makes a conscious effort, where possible, to satisfy employee aspirations.

How does Shell rate?

Pay:	very good
Benefits:	good
Communications:	good
Training:	very good
Career development:	excellent
Morale:	good

People and personnel policies

Shell looks for a series of qualities in its employees, three of the most important of which are intellectual capacity, a record of achievement and strong interpersonal skills. By ranking its employees against each of these criteria, the company is able to assess the ultimate potential of all members of its workforce. Information on the high-fliers within Shell is held on a central database, allowing them to be easily matched against opportunities within the group. Increasingly, it is an individual's performance and personal skills – their ability to work within a team, their initiative and flexibility and whether they have leadership potential – which is seen as critical to their development and ultimate success within the Shell organisation.

Training and development is primarily the responsibility of the underlying business units. While there has always been a high technical content to the training which Shell provides – and the quality of such training is one of the main reasons why Shell has long been such a highly regarded employer – personal development training is now increasingly on offer. To foster entrepreneurship, the company also offers greater amounts of marketing and commercial skills training. At a central level, Shell has set up a Learning Centre based in the UK and the Netherlands where employees from across the group can come together and solve real-life business problems. It is hoped that this Learning Centre will also prove to be a successful way of improving communication and developing leadership skills within the organisation. Through a variety of initiatives, Shell is trying to place a greater onus on the individual to take responsibility for their own training and development.

A further key element of the recent reorganisation was the formation of value creation teams, whose function it is to drive change through the organisation. The company is determined to unleash the potential inherent in its people and sees one of the principal ways of doing this as delegating authority down to the lowest possible level. Another increasingly common feature is the movement of individuals between different parts of the company and around the world, both to create multi-disciplinary skills and give them a wider appreciation of the business as a whole and cross-cultural experiences.

Shell's policy is that its levels of remuneration should be in the top quartile. While this basic philosophy has remained unchanged, its approach to the way in which employees are remunerated has done so significantly. In particular, the variable pay element of the overall package has become much more important relative to salary. Bonuses are being introduced throughout the company based on business performance. At higher levels, executives are being rewarded through stock option schemes. Where necessary, Shell recognises that it must pay very competitively to attract and retain the best people.

Given that the group operates in more than 120 countries, there is a rich diversity to Shell's workforce at lower levels. More importantly, however, this is now also being reflected at more senior levels in the organisation. One area where the company acknowledges it is weak, and on which it is focusing attention, however, is in the number of women holding senior jobs within the workforce. Shell tries to encourage women to remain in the workforce by offering flexible working arrangements wherever possible.

Probably more so than most large companies, Shell is painfully aware of its responsibilities within the community. One of the key lessons of both Brent Spar and events in Nigeria was that the company needs to be much more effective in communicating reasons for its behaviour to people outside the company. For example, although ensuring that products and operations are safe and environmentally acceptable is now an integral part of all research programmes, this is not always widely appreciated. In a further attempt to improve its profile, various members of the group are also heavily involved in arts and educational initiatives and sponsorship.

Contact address

Ms Elaine Chubb,
Recruitment Services (HSL/3),
Shell International Limited,
Shell Centre, London SE1 7NA.
Telephone: 0171 934 2947.
Fax: 0171 934 7606.

Siemens plc

Siemens is one of the largest electrical and electronics companies in the world. Around the globe it employs more than 379,000 people and in recent years it has consolidated its activities into a group of major business segments: energy, industry, communications, information, transportation, healthcare, components, lighting and household. In the UK Siemens reports annual sales of £1.5 billion. It has a staff of 11,000 working through a full series of group businesses. Real growth has come recently in automation, network systems, automotive systems and information systems.

Siemens at a glance

Employees: 379,000 worldwide, 11,000 UK
Annual staff attrition rate: 7 per cent
Key locations: Bracknell (HQ), Manchester, Poole, Cowes, Eynsham, North Tyneside
Av. annual graduate recruitment: 80
Annual intake: 500

An inside view

Many people who are familiar with Siemens tend to think of it as a German company. And they would be right, except for the fact that Siemens has a long history of involvement in the United Kingdom. William Siemens arrived in Britain in 1843 to translate his scientific discoveries into working practice. His initiative created the first street lighting and his broader role in the industry won him a knighthood. The principles of quality and innovation which characterised his work still guide the company today. Two world wars led to the removal of the company from the UK but in the 1960s it returned and in the decades that followed became involved in a series of joint ventures which brought Siemens back to the heart of the electrical sector here.

The strategy of the group is to focus on the global electrical and electronic market which it estimates will grow significantly faster than the world economy. This market is currently rated as worth more than £1,000 billion worldwide, and Siemens aims to take a sizeable chunk. The growth in its international presence means that 62 per cent of its income is now sourced from outside Germany. Its commitment to research and development is heavy. The group spent £2.6 billion worldwide – and £134 million in the UK – on new R&D and innovation programmes in 1996. The company now has 12 manufacturing sites in Britain, which account collectively for around a quarter of the UK workforce. The largest site is at Cowes on the Isle of Wight, where it makes leading edge air traffic management equipment. Then there is Congleton the global production centre for variable speed drives, Siemens Measurements in Oldham which creates electricity and gas meters, and Oxford Magnet Technology which produces magnets for body scanners. The latest site is a £1.1 billion semiconductor wafer factory in North Tyneside which will be completed in summer 1997.

The UK company's strategy resembles that of its parent. It aims to focus on its core markets – where it has a competitive advantage and can consolidate its businesses to most profitable effect. Siemens' target is to increase its market share in each of these key sectors for the company, and to raise productivity and profitability across all of its operations. The company intends to extend the range of its services to expand its operation in the total value chain for each sector. Having achieved market leadership positions in core markets, the group's objective is to increase its work up and down the chain, building closer relationships with its customers.

Siemens' traditional business approach, described by some observers as a classical model of an engineering multinational run from Munich, has given way recently to a decentralised approach. The aim has been to shift responsibility down the line to the individual companies of the group. Coupled with this trend is the top-fit programme which comprises a series of initiatives to make a leaner, fitter organisation. The top-fit plan was devised by Siemens centrally and has been rolled out through all the UK operations. It focuses on quality, technological innovation and, increasingly, efficiency and productivity.

How does Siemens rate?

Pay:	superb
Benefits:	excellent
Communications:	good
Training:	good
Career development:	very good
Morale:	very good

People and personnel policies

The human resources policy of the group is in transition. The company has shed its protective, conservative and somewhat paternalistic attitude towards its employees. It was a good example of a traditional continental European company – extremely well managed, thoughtful and hierarchical – with most of the decision making done in Munich. Recognising the global nature of the market and the intensity of the competition, Siemens is going through a process of relaxing the reins.

Step by step, subsidiary national and regional businesses are winning a great share of authority on their commercial futures. This has re-energised the group while losing none of its focus. One of the benefits is to increase the role played by managers and staff outside Germany. UK personnel director Trevor Bromelow says 'We still have a long way to go to complete decentralisation but we are making significant progress. Our aim is to free up our individual businesses to compete in their own markets. Our chief executive often says that we want a fleet of speedboats rather than one supertanker.'

Bromelow is nervous about using the word federal too often but he says that it best describes the relationships between the centre and the operating companies. Some activities and the basic values of the enterprise remain core for the whole group while specific policies will vary according to market circumstance.

As Siemens is an engineering and electronics company, it is a technology-led business. 'The majority of our people have an engineering qualification of some description. Among our graduate intake we look for people with a 2.1 or above in one of the higher technology disciplines and, because our emphasis is on career development of engineers into management, we aim to find graduate engineers who have the talent to progress into senior managerial roles. We locate our graduate entrants from a preferred group of 12 universities which are the primary source of our intake. We also sponsor 35 to 40 people a year through four-year sandwich course degrees.'

Bromelow comments that the reward package is composed of pay which is between median and upper quartile and benefits which are very good. 'On benefits – for our sector – we are above average. Our pension plan is independently rated as one of the top 10 in the country. It is philosophically geared to people spending a long time with the company. It is not cradle-to-grave like the Japanese, or hire-and-fire like the Americans, but somewhere in between.' The company offers contributory health insurance for all employees, generous holidays and subsidised meals. The group's core values are not specific about individual benefits – these are left to the personnel teams in the operating companies to work out but

the group is highly regarded in its sector for the integrity of its intentions and the thoroughness which goes into working out the individual deals.

The group is an active communicator. Team briefing is a core policy so every aspect of the group organises regular team briefings but the base content will change according to which companies it is presenting to its people. A newspaper is issued by Siemens UK, covering national and international business issues. But companies within the group can have their own slip editions where local pages are inserted covering events within that business.

Graduates have a mentor for their first three years in the company. 'These are expensive people and so we do whatever we can to bring them up to speed quickly.' Other staff who join are given a minder for the first three months. Appraisals are out at Siemens. They have been replaced by a process called 'staff dialogue' where individuals prepare the first draft of what their objectives should be. It inevitably builds into a training plan, which would be both pragmatic in meeting immediate job needs but also lay the foundation for the future.

Contact address

Mr Trevor Bromelow,
Personnel Director,
Siemens plc, Siemens House,
Oldbury, Bracknell, Berks RG12 8FZ.
Telephone: 01344 396210.
Fax: 01344 396239.

W H Smith Group plc

The W H Smith Group is the UK'S largest retail newsagent, distributor of newspapers and magazines and vendor of recorded music and books. Its history can be traced directly back to the late-eighteenth century and its reputation as a household brand stems from its status as operator of railway newsagents and booksellers. In the twentieth century, the company established its leading position on the high street and today is a familiar feature of many town centres and shopping malls.

W H Smith at a glance

Employees: 33,625
Annual staff attrition: n/a
Key locations: London (HQ), Swindon, throughout the UK and US plus some outlets in mainland Europe
Annual graduate recruitment: 50
Annual intake: 2,000

An inside view

W H Smith is a group in transition. Throughout the 1990s the company has sought to refine its market image while retaining and building on considerable customer loyalty. The public perception of the group is through the flagship newsagent, stationer, bookseller and recorded music outlets. Most high streets have a branch of W H Smith and it ranks alongside the banks, supermarkets and Boots as a familiar feature of modern shopping.

However, the group's interests are much wider and it embraces Waterstones, Our Price and the Virgin music shops. In addition, its news distribution business is complemented by a highly successful retailing operation in the US. The group, which reported sales of £2.7 billion in 1995, has come under fierce criticism from parts of the City and the financial press in the last two years. A decline in profits in 1995 led analysts and reporters to conclude that the company, which has always been a bellwether stock, was losing its touch.

Straightforward investigation shows that Waterstones, Virgin, Our Price, its news distribution arm, and US operations are doing well. The principal focus of the doubters was the flagship chain. They argued that the WH Smith-branded stores were slipping and that an out-of-date policy towards retailing in the core brand was symptomatic of a wider malaise. The debate led the editors of this book to question the validity of the inclusion of W H Smith. Our view at the end of that process was that the group is intrinsically strong – and in the middle of a long distance reassessment of its approach and values.

Several of its leading activities are thriving and the flagship chain is taking some time to realign itself for the market challenges of the next decade. Former Royal Mail CEO Bill Cockburn has made some major changes since taking over at the beginning of 1996. There have been job losses but these appear to have been handled reasonably well and there have been significant refinements of the cost-effectiveness of certain product lines.

How does W H Smith rate?

Pay:	good
Benefits:	very good
Communications:	very good
Training:	very good
Career development:	good
Morale:	good

People and personnel policies

For many years W H Smith has been regarded as one of the better UK employers, especially in the field of employee and management training. The company has access to its own training facilities in Oxfordshire where it runs a wide variety of courses all the year round. In our last book, the company was selected as one of the best trainers in UK industry, and this standing is in no way diminished.

Since there has been a much higher emphasis on customer-facing activities and enhancing levels of service to the shopper, many employees attend customer services courses and there is extensive on-the-job tuition in relationships with the buying public. Cockburn speaks about the enhancement of the experience of shopping for the customer which means more knowledgeable and helpful staff. This is already the case in Waterstones, which is a book-lover's paradise, and in the music shops where the sheer range and diversity of stock goes a long way to meeting the music enthusiast's tastes.

He says that there will be greater focus on the flagship stores to find better ways to meet the needs of the general buyer of publications, books, stationery and music. Better quality service is the first step, but in the longer term the company is aiming to match the needs of the shopper in a more complete way. Everything on sale in W H Smith is a discretionary buy. So the shop has to try harder to win and keep its customers.

Staff motivation is the key player in this objective. It has taken rather a knock due to the reshaping which has been taking place, and the gainsaying in the press. However, the group has sharpened its already well-managed internal communications strategy. Cockburn comments 'We operate an open and participative style of management. This encourages communication and provides the opportunity for staff to take part in the decision-making process.'

'As directors we meet informally with employees to discuss matters of concern to the group. We also meet regularly with staff associations and trade unions so that their views can be taken into consideration when we are making decisions about matters which affect their members.' The group is a vigorous communicator through team briefing and listening sessions, reports on annual and interim results and stages meetings to discuss key issues as they emerge. As might be expected from a news vendor and distributor, the company also likes the printed word. It issues various publications and newsletters for the group and individual businesses.

The company is strongly wedded to feedback and it has put in place a variety of mechanisms for employees to comment on issues of the day. These range from routine business meetings, through team briefings to employee attitude surveys.

The group believes that employee commitment is strengthened when staff are given the opportunity to hold shares in the business. It operates three Inland Revenue-approved schemes where around 22,000 past and present employees have taken up the option to buy shares. The largest is the Profitshare scheme which has some 16,700 subscribers. The Sharesave scheme has around 5,000 members and the Executive Option scheme has 75.

The reward package has traditionally been a good one for its sector and the company, until now, has adopted a mildly paternalistic approach to employee benefits. In the new leaner, fitter and more cost-focused group, a more selective and value-driven approach may take shape. Certainly Cockburn wants to improve the utilisation of the subsidiary businesses, the individual outlets and the employees. There will be much greater stress on performance in the future, which may not be always be to the taste of long-standing W H Smith employees. But for those individuals with talent, drive and ambition the new revamped W H Smith may well be a company of the future.

Contact address

John Aincey,
Group Human Resources Director,
WH Smith plc,
Greenbridge Road,
Swindon SN3 3LD.
Telephone: 01793 562885.
Fax: 01793 562999.

SmithKline Beecham plc

SmithKline Beecham is one of the world's largest, most active and successful healthcare companies. It was created from the 1989 merger of the UK giant SmithKline Beckman and the UK pharmaceuticals company well known for its Beechams Powders. In 1996, the company reported an annual turnover of £7.9 billion and pre-tax profits of £1.35 billion. SB employs around 50,000 people worldwide. It produces more than 300 healthcare products in more than 160 countries.

SmithKline Beecham at a glance

Employees: 50,000 +
Staff attrition: n/a
Key locations: London, Philadelphia
Average graduate recruitment: n/a
Annual intake: n/a

An inside view

SmithKline Beecham's 1997 started well. *The Sunday Times* announced that the international pharmaceuticals giant had climbed one place to number three in its annual table of companies which provide market value added. MVA is a method of rating companies according to their performance – often over many years – stripped of accounting anomalies and other corporate devices. Many commentators see MVA as a way to see the true worth of businesses. *The Sunday Times* commented 'It has been a good year for the drugs giant, moving up one place in our rankings and adding £7 billion to its MVA. With plenty of new

products, SmithKline should be near the top of the list for years to come.'

CEO Jan Leschly told shareholders in 1996 that it was the goal of SmithKline Beecham to become the world's leading healthcare company. Through processes of organic growth and acquisition of businesses, SB is establishing market leadership positions in key areas of the healthcare spectrum. SB operates in three key sectors: pharmaceuticals, consumer healthcare and healthcare services. The largest contributor to sales is pharmaceuticals which brought in £4.8 billion of the company's £7.9 billion revenue in 1996. Pharma sales rose 14 per cent year on year, with new products accounting for 36 per cent of all sales. In 1996, the company invested £764 million in research and development, an increase of 17 per cent over the previous year. These high levels of investment appear to be paying off – the SB pipeline has produced products which in 1995 generated £1.54 billion in sales. The company is also world market leader in DNA research. Consumer healthcare deals with over-the-counter products which represent £2.3 billion of the company's sales. The 1996 figure was an increase of 16 per cent on 1995 and also contained a rise in international sales of 18 per cent. Its brands such as Panadol, Lucozade and Ribena are well known in the UK market. Clinical laboratories is more than holding its own in difficult markets and provides testing in a wide range of clinical settings.

The company's strategic direction has been carefully orchestrated to ensure that everyone hears the same voice and the same message. The global healthcare market is fiercely competitive and only the best will survive. So Leschly and his colleagues devised the Simply Better Way. He says that it means creating a working environment which motivates and provides the means for personal and professional growth. It is a process of continuous improvement grounded in strongly supported company beliefs.' SB's values – customer, innovation, integrity, people, performance – are translated into everyday behaviour. The Simply Better Way incorporates the systems and processes by which work in the company is organised, and the methods and tools which it uses to achieve its goals.

How does SmithKline Beecham rate?

Pay:	excellent
Benefits:	very good
Communications:	good
Training:	excellent
Career development:	very good
Morale:	superb

People and personnel policies

SmithKline Beecham has achieved a great deal since its founding merger in 1989. It has taken two significant players and forged a major force in the global healthcare industry. It is an uncompromising marketplace where products need to be excellent, the distribution channels and marketing skills have to be top notch and the investment and foresight in the long pipeline of research and development must be at a peak. Against that, a well-managed business must seek to be increasingly more effective and to get the best out of its people.

Leschly and his team have set their people three challenges: to create a world-class, customer-driven company, to develop pioneer products and services, and to continuously align its cost structure to the competitive environment. Responsibility lies with each employee to help the company reach these targets. And this is no empty piece of corporate speechmaking. More than many companies in this book, SmithKline Beecham is its people. The healthcare sector is one of the toughest commercial environments in the world. All its people – in every part of the business – need to be functioning at peak levels to transcend the efforts of the competition.

'The daily involvement of SmithKline Beecham people in their jobs is the way in which we can enhance team and individual performance and unleash the enormous power and energy of our organisation. Through this effort we will learn to think of our work as processes to be owned, understood, standardised and improved, rather than functions or activities to be managed,' he says.

This vigorous climate requires people with energy, vitality of thought, spirit, determination and the capacity to get on with others. This company seeks out the best for roles in research, sales and marketing, production and professional functions. SB recruits from the top performers at universities across the world and it runs a graduate recruitment scheme. The management access programme allows graduates to join a two-year development initiative. It includes assignments in different business functions and locations worldwide. Graduates can also join different departments directly.

Pay and benefits at SB are among the highest in the UK. Leschly says 'We offer highly competitive pay and benefit packages that are, as much as possible, tied to performance. Most employees are also members of plans which build ownership of SB shares. In the US 80 per cent of employees own shares; in the UK 65 per cent. We also believe in a free flow of information to employees, and from them to management. Global communication systems, including newsletters, bulletins and televised and video coverage of major events builds identification with other SB employees.'

Education and training is a major strategic issue for SmithKline Beecham, and one where it places a high degree of investment. The company provides a wide range of courses to its employees with the ultimate objective of getting them to work more effectively. Working Smarter in SB parlance is the phrase applied to a whole raft of training initiatives which are designed to change the approach to work

of the entire workforce. The Simply Better Way which underscores the strategic direction of the business also underpins the objective of this retraining exercise. By approaching education and training in a carefully planned and managed way, SB aims to introduce process improvement throughout the company with every manager and ultimately every employee taking ownership. The Company says 'It represents an enormous commitment of time, money, effort and human resources. It will lay the foundation of a daily management system where every employee practises process improvements as part of their daily work.'

Contact address

Human resources,
SmithKline Beecham plc,
New Horizons Court,
Brentford,
Middlesex TW8 9EP.
Telephone: 0181 975 2000.
Fax: 0181 975 2001.

Sony United Kingdom Limited

Sony is the one of the world's largest electronics companies – and perhaps its most famous. Sony is one of the great postwar success stories, founded by the legendary Akio Morita, and active in broadcast, audio, visual, music, television and film production. Many of the world's leading television and radio stations operate predominately on Sony equipment, a high proportion of homes use Sony televisions, Walkman personal stereos, VCRs and camcorders, and many arena and stadiums depend on Sony's display screens. The company is also a major supplier of computer monitors, computer peripherals, semi-conductors, electronic storage devices and other electronic components. In 1996 Sony reported global sales of $43.3 billion and profits of $1.3 billion. Worldwide it employs 151,000 people.

Sony at a glance

Employees: 151,000 worldwide, 4,700 UK
Annual staff attrition rate: 5 per cent
Key locations: Three in the UK. HQ at Weybridge, Surrey; manufacturing of television sets, display monitors, cathode ray tubes and key components at Bridgend and Pencoed, South Wales; broadcast at Basingstoke, Hants
Av. annual graduate recruitment: no specific corporate programme
Annual intake: 300

An inside view

In 1955 Sony introduced the first transistor radio. Shortly afterwards the company launched the portable, transistorised television. By 1971 it brought the first colour VCR to the market and eight years later announced the first Walkman personal stereo. Three years on, Sony presented the first CD player and in 1985 a personal handheld camcorder. In the 1990s the business has refined its Trinitron television sets, announced the first fully digitised television studio and offered digital audio tape (DAT) players to the consumer market. A career of innovation characterises the history of Sony. As competitors struggle to match current product portfolios, Sony is anticipating the market demands of the future and devising engineering solutions to meet expectations of the new age.

To many Sony is also the quintessential Japanese multinational – it combines expertise in production and marketing, it is highly alert to the nuances of a vigorously competitive sector, it has developed original and thoughtful people policies and it consistently outstrips its rivals at home and throughout the world.

The scope of Sony's vision in its sector is breathtaking. There is no other electronics company which has become brand leader in so many disciplines within its markets as Sony. While Sony itself is one of the best-known commercial brands in the world, its products such as Walkman, MiniDisc and Handicam have also entered the popular and professional lexicon. Its production processes are among the most progressive and efficient in the electronics industry.

A common misconception of Japanese subsidiary companies is that they are rigidly structured, highly controlled by Tokyo, and that all they do is assemble kits manufactured in Japan. Sony was the first major Japanese company to set up shop in the UK and it has enjoyed increasing autonomy, over the years, from the centre. The UK business is a component of the European region of the company, which is a fully fledged division of the global corporation, and to a large extent sets its own agenda in consultation with the rest of the Sony world. Increasingly, the British operation has provided its employees with remarkable freedom to rise within the business and to take on fresh areas of responsibility. The company genuinely has no barriers to ability. Regardless of gender, culture or background, people can make their mark on the business.

In the mid 1980s Sony's state-of-the-art Bridgend manufacturing facility was one of the leading exponents of quality circles. This is a process where groups of employees assemble to elevate the quality of the production or development techniques in use. The quality circle concept became so successful that it spread throughout the site and was quickly adopted by other leading Japanese blue-chip businesses. Like that other famous name in quality management, Black & Decker, Sony rapidly extended the idea into its relationships with clients.

Quality circles have long since been superceded. Now the line is the quality team. Everyone on the line is respected equally. Ideas are shared and a new concept which saves time or money or which enhances the quality of the operation is a team victory. Typically a line is 20 plus people strong and the level of interest in the work is outstanding. Sony line leaders are often highly articulate people who can explain and demonstrate highly complex processes in direct and simple language. It pays testimony to the company's recruitment and training approaches.

How does Sony rate?

Pay:	excellent
Benefits:	very good
Communications:	superb
Training:	excellent
Career development:	very good
Morale:	very good

People and personnel policies

Many Japanese employers are perceived, falsely, to be ritualistic in their approach to personnel management. Newspapers and magazines delighted – in the early days of major Japanese inward investment – in painting a picture of employees conducting a variety of unfamiliar work practices and unusual team-building exercises. Some approaches to human resources management were different from what British employees had been used to. But most served to empower the employee and to give greater freedom in the job. At the core of the majority of Japanese-owned businesses lies a substantial respect for their staff. Wherever they have been based Japanese businesses have served to revitalise local economies and they have, in the main, earned the respect of local workforces.

Sony was the first substantial Japanese-owned company to arrive in the United Kingdom, building its first factory at Bridgend, South Wales in 1974, and it has contributed heavily to the renaissance of the locality. In 1993 the company built an additional facility in Pencoed and now employs 4,000 people at its two manufacturing sites. Not only has Sony directly employed several thousand people but it has also given work to more than 70 smaller businesses which supply the company. Such is the fairness with which Sony has treated its people, they have repaid their employer with a high degree of personal loyalty. As matter of core policy, Sony reflects the national culture of its local operations wherever it sets up shop. The social structure of the parent is not evident in the daily operation of the British company. Sony UK is a British enterprise which gives its people remarkable freedom to make a creative contribution to the management and operation of the organisation. Sony's respect for the individual employee is genuine and the absence of restriction on personal mobility within the business is remarkable. The company wants its employees to achieve and it allows

remarkable scope for any individual to make a contribution to the success of the enterprise.

One senior personnel executive told the editorial team 'Sony's approach to HR is unusual. There are few companies which give their staff such room for individual expression and responsibility. The company gives managers as much scope for personal contribution as they can carry. As long as the individual is able to perform to a high and improving standard, responsibilities will be added.' This policy is conducted in an organisational environment which promotes and encourages teamwork and is project-based. The British business is a key component in Sony Europe and many of the daily management issues which emerge are settled at a European rather than a corporate level. Contact with headquarters in Tokyo are substantially less now than they were before a regional operational framework was created. Despite its global scope, the company remains an entrepreneurial business and encourages 'The Sony Spirit' among all its employees. This is the essence of the commercial and creative pioneer who seeks to push back the boundaries of what is possible both technically and in business. It is an extremely positive organisation, which, while being shaped by an overriding commitment to quality and excellent performance in every sphere of its activities, also sees into the future of customer demand. Each individual who works for the business is part of The Sony Family, which may seem somewhat coy to British observers but indicates the strength of company teamworking and fellow feeling.

Sony is among the best payers in

industry and employees enjoy a comprehensive set of benefits. They gain access to all Sony products at discounted rates and its locations in South Wales and the Thames Valley have company shops. Sony's video and recorded music releases are also available at preferential rates even though the music and film companies are not part of Sony UK. Training within the company is among the best in industry, and much of it is on-the-job and teamwork-focused.

Contact address

Stephen Barrett,
General Manager,
Human Resources,
Sony UK Sales Company,
Sony United Kingdom Limited,
The Heights, Brooklands, Weybridge,
Surrey KT13 0XW.
Telephone: 01932 816000.
Fax: 01932 817000.

Sun Microsystems Limited

Sun Microsystems is one of the most innovative and far-seeing computer companies operating in the UK today. At the heart of the Sun business is the principle – the network is the computer, which the company foresaw more than a decade ago. The company dominates the technical workstation market and provides the hardware and a whole range of software tools and applications for network computing. It is effectively a one-stop shop for any business which runs computer networks. Sun is highly successful. Around the world it generated $8 billion in turnover in 1996.

Sun Microsystems at a glance

Employees: 1,600
Staff attrition rate: 5 per cent
Key locations: Bagshot, Surrey (HQ), Linlithgow (manufacturing) and other sites in the Thames Valley plus the City of London, Cambridge, Manchester, Bristol and Coventry
Active graduate recruitment: 30–40
Annual intake: 300

An inside view

As long ago as the early 1980s Sun Microsystems developed a remarkable vision of the future of information technology. Its directors realised, ahead of most other IT businesses, that open computing platforms would become standard and that they would be the only technologies capable of ensuring the commercial success of major businesses. So with this focus in mind Sun made network computing its focus. Today it has converted its vision of open computing systems into its own success story. It is

world market leader in open systems for certain vertical markets and its influence is spreading to a wider range of commercial sectors. Sun's history lies in business information and software applications based on UNIX systems and it is a true pioneer of open and distributed computing in UNIX environments.

In 1985 when the network computing concept was beginning to emerge Sun produced global revenues of $115 million. By 1996 its sales had exploded to $8 billion – around half from the US and a quarter from Europe. The extent of its growth, around 45 per cent year-on-year for a decade, is vindication of the early inspiration of its directors. By almost every conventional measure of profitability, Sun has experienced rapid and sustained growth. In terms of employee productivity, for example, it has quadrupled the contribution of each member of the workforce in 10 years and enjoys productivity rates which are the envy of the industry.

The company's original specialism lay in technical workstations and it can claim

50 per cent of the entire worldwide market in heavy duty workstations. But this is a limited market and Sun has exported its ideas and expertise into other sectors. Sun is essentially several companies under one roof, the biggest being systems – a hardware operation for commercial application rather than the technical environment. Systems has concentrated on selling network computing and its service company provides software support, hardware support, professional services and education. Sun's software strategy has been the opposite of the proprietary approach which dominated the industry in the 1980s. Sun has offered many technologies to other companies at peppercorn rates to ensure their establishment as industry standards. Its *Solaris* package accounts for 50 per cent of all UNIX operating system sales. Its biggest development recently has been the creation of *Java*, an entirely new computer language which allows users to write programs for the Internet. *Java* is a completely new approach and represents a technical leap forward.

How does Sun Microsystems rate?

Pay:	very good
Benefits:	excellent
Communications:	excellent
Training:	excellent
Career development:	very good
Morale:	superb

People and personnel policies

Sun's dramatic rate of growth means that, despite having a relatively small workforce in the UK, it is recruiting as many as 300 people a year – a trend which is likely to continue. As a matter of corporate policy it believes in keeping locations small and manageable and so the bigger offices rarely amount to more than 150 people. As a proportion of Sun's total annual intake, its direct recruitment of graduates from university is small and is largely technical in nature. As a general rule Sun is very attractive to graduates but the company has drawn more on people with some industrial and commercial experience rather than take many recruits direct from higher education.

The Sun corporate style is informal but committed. 'We put a lot of emphasis on management as a discipline. What a lot of people tell us is that we appear quite relaxed, even though we are deadly serious about winning in the marketplace. Our managers always seem very friendly and approachable. Beneath that they are organised and dedicated to what they do. We do not have many people with massive egos, which can be commonplace in the IT industry. We have an approach which says everyone here works very hard but we will respect the role that you play and we will empower you to do that to the best of your ability. If we can get every individual in the company to perform their role to the peak capacity, then we will beat the competition,' says Northern European human resources director Paul Harrison.

One of the more compelling aspects of

the Sun culture is that policy is conducted subtly. The company has a mission statement and values but these are not forced on employees. They are used as guidelines. When a manager is appointed, they will attend a five-day training course which outlines precisely and practically what Sun expects from someone in that role. 'Management means creating a shared vision in each team so everyone is clear what they have to do. Then setting objectives, review progress and initiate a programme of on-going improvement. A Sun manager must also relate to other teams in the business and take a whole company view about the targets of their group.' Sun managers speak of the values as the DNA in the business – unseen but definitive in ordering the way the organisation works.

This is an understated, warm, positive and good-humoured company. Its team ethos is a natural and spontaneous expression of the company's approach to business. Sun has not adopted flat structures because they are currently fashionable but rather because this is the way the company has always operated. It retains this intimate but disciplined style by choosing its managers extremely carefully. 'It is the number one area of failure for many companies. They say because someone is good at sales, for example, they must be made a manager. Management is a completely different skill. It is a specific competence and we profile what we need in our managers. Candidates for management positions are assessed for their capacities in defined skills. They will be confident and good communicators.'

Interaction is a great theme with Sun. Every July the company takes 1,000 people at a time for a full day of presentations and fun activities. 'There can't be many companies which spend as much as we do on employee interaction.' It also runs half-day business issues brainstorming sessions with the directors of the business divisions. 'We then take 20 high potential managers away each year for a week and bring in lecturers from leading business schools to discuss the issues which have emerged at the brainstorming meeting. Specific business issues are then discussed by teams using the business school lecturers as mentors and resources. Then the group continues working on the project for three to six months after the week away and they have to present their recommendations to our virtual country management team.'

Sun conducts regular business assessments in terms of the skills which it will need to move forward into the next period. This is also extended to the level of the team and individual employees. In a typical team of seven to ten people, a manager and an employee would look at how well the employee had performed against objectives and also reassess the competencies needed in a particular role. The reward package is tied into the annual assessment and is fixed at the highest levels in the industry. Benefits include a comprehensive pension plan, health insurance for all employees and a free medical.

Contact address

Paul Harrison,
Human Resources Director,
Sun Microsystems, Bagshot Manor,
Green Lane, Bagshot, Surrey GU19 5NL.
Telephone: 01276 451440.
Fax: 01276 451287.

Tesco plc

Tesco has recently surpassed Sainbury's as the UK's largest and most profitable food retailer. Its success has been built on offering high levels of customer service and consistent value for money, as exemplified by its ground-breaking Clubcard initiative. The company continues to pursue a vigorous store opening and refurbishment programme, and is expanding increasingly into Europe. The contribution of the workforce has been instrumental in Tesco's success, and they have been rewarded with one of the best pay and benefits packages in the retail sector.

Tesco at a glance

Employees: 147,000 worldwide, 142,000 UK
Annual staff attrition rate: 20 per cent
Key locations: 550 stores in the UK, 108 France and 100 in Eastern Europe (Hungary, Poland, the Czech Republic and Slovakia)
Av. annual graduate recruitment: 150–200
Annual intake: n/a

An inside view

In 1996, Tesco finally overtook arch-rival Sainsbury to become the UK's leading food retailing group. Following its 1995 acquisition of Scottish supermarket chain William Low, Tesco now operates 550 stores throughout England, Scotland and Wales and has an annual turnover in excess of £12 billion. The company also owns 108 stores in France (which are operated by Catteau), and has a growing presence in Eastern Europe where, in sharp contrast with Sainsbury, it is focusing on countries with a relatively underdeveloped retailing sector. In the UK, its store opening programme is continuing apace, with an increasing emphasis on new formats – such as compact and Metro stores – to access new markets.

Tesco's strong trading performance in recent years has been based on a series of factors. Firstly, the company believes strongly in offering customers value for money through aggressive pricing initiatives. Secondly, Tesco is committed to customer service. It was, for example, the first food retailer in the UK to provide 5,000 customer assistants dedicated to service. Thirdly, Tesco believes in providing as wide a choice as possible. In the first half of 1996, the company introduced 1,000 new products, adding particularly to its *Items* clothing range. Finally, the company has generated intense customer loyalty with the launch of its Clubcard programme. Over the last two years, Clubcard has grown into the UK's most popular loyalty card, with more than 8 million cards now in issue.

Tesco has achieved its success in a food retailing market which remains intensely competitive and in which the pace of change continues to grow. One of the principal ways in which the company has differentiated itself from its competitors is in its willingness to listen to its employees and allow them the freedom to act on their own initiative. A trend towards greater local responsibility and autonomy has been complemented by the movement towards a much flatter management structure within the group as a whole.

In these circumstances, flexibility and innovation are an integral part of the company's culture. Tesco is determined to end the perception that food retailing is inevitably a poorly paid and high staff turnover industry. On the contrary, the company's philosophy is that a high quality of customer service can only be provided successfully in the long-term by a high quality workforce.

How does Tesco rate ?

Pay:	very good
Benefits:	good
Communications:	good
Training:	good
Career development:	very good
Morale:	good

People and personnel policies

In order to realise its ambitions, Tesco has recognised it must treat its employees with the same respect as its customers. This means that issues such as training

and career development, which have traditionally been relegated in importance in food retailing, are now much higher up the corporate agenda. Furthermore, while the majority of the company's workforce is likely to remain part-time (partially due to the increase in opening hours), Tesco is putting greater resources into the recruitment of experienced full-time employees. Tesco in the UK employs 47,000 full-time and 95,000 part-time employees.

The company's training and development programme is underpinned by its commitment to improving levels of customer service. As well as the technical training which is provided, there are now many more personal development and management skills training courses on offer for those who wish to progress within the organisation. Tesco's graduate recruits are initially placed on a 24-month training programme which will typically include specific projects and key tasks which they will be asked to complete. After this has been successfully completed, they can then expect to be appointed to a management position in the company. However, it should be noted that similar opportunities exist within the group for those without an academic qualification. Another constant is that some experience of life on the shop floor is mandatory.

As identified earlier, Tesco is currently trying to address the perception that retailing is a poorly paid profession. In order to attract candidates of a sufficient calibre, remuneration levels have improved markedly in recent years. The company is now acknowledged as being the second-best paying company in the retail sector – after Marks & Spencer – and has introduced a series of benefits which are generally available to all staff (including those who are employed on a part-time basis). For example, everybody with more than two years' service qualifies for profit sharing; in 1996, the company paid out £29 million to more than 80,000 staff.

Tesco also maintains a very generous pension scheme, and was one of the first companies in the UK to make this available to part-time staff. More than 30,000 of the workforce participate in Save As You Earn schemes, which allow them to buy Tesco shares. Another highly prized benefit is the range of discounts which it offers to staff. Tesco believes that its attractive remuneration package is one of the primary reasons why it enjoys a significantly below-average staff turnover rate.

Tesco has also taken pains to improve the quality of its communications with the workforce. This is manifested by the annual staff attitude surveys which the company organises. Presentations to the workforce by senior management on issues such as strategy and current trading are also held. In addition, line managers are encouraged to communicate regularly with their employees and the success of these efforts is recorded in attitude surveys.

Retailing has traditionally been an industry with a high level of female involvement and this remains the case today – more than 90,000 of Tesco's UK employees are women. Unlike many other leading companies, however, Tesco has managed to translate this into a relatively high female representation at senior levels.

Involvement in the community is another area in which Tesco has improved considerably. Its best-known initiative is Computers for Schools which is now in its fifth year and has so far provided more than 21,000 computers to 12,000 schools. In addition, store managers are encouraged to become involved in various local community projects. Both at a local and a corporate level, Tesco makes substantial charitable contributions – in 1995/96, for instance, the Riding for the Disabled Association received £850,000 as Tesco Charity of the Year.

Contact address

Mr Roger Roberts,
Personnel Policy Director,
Tesco Stores Limited,
Tesco House, PO Box 18,
Delamere Road, Cheshunt,
Waltham Cross,
Herts EN8 9SL.
Telephone: 01992 644146.
Fax: 01992 644695.

Texas Instruments

D igital technologies are changing everything, connecting people and information in new and productive ways and creating a global networked society. Texas Instruments is a multinational digital technology operation based in Dallas. However, it has had a major presence in the United Kingdom since 1959 and is placing an increased emphasis on the company's role in Britain. The global business is making great strides as shown by its latest profit figures which have risen to $1.6 billion. It has a formidable reputation for its quality procedures, winning the highly respected European Quality Award.

Texas Instruments at a glance

Employees: 500
Annual staff attrition rate: n/a
Key locations: Northampton and
    Sunbury-on-Thames
Av. annual graduate recruitment: 30
Annual intake: n/a

An inside view

The basic philosophy and tenet of Texas Instruments is to pay close attention to how people live their everyday lives at both personal and business levels. The company creates components, systems and technologies just because it believes that every day matters. And that philosophy benefits both consumers and shareholders, for most recent figures show a global 47 per cent annual increase in profits to $1,594,000,000. The company's Northampton-based UK operation makes a significant contribution to the operation's overall turnover and profitability.

By any yardstick its standard of efficiency and overall return is outstanding following capitalisation on strong semiconductor operating performance and robust worldwide market semiconductor growth. Productivity improved by more than 25 per cent and there has been significant recognition for operational excellence, including the European Quality Award, and the Singapore Quality Award, with similar accolades from the company's home territory. But perhaps the most significant development is what TI describes as the goals and roadmaps which will lead it into the next century.

There is no doubt that the semiconductor revolution is changing the way that people live, learn and – most importantly of all – work. The pace of that revolution is accelerating on a daily basis and TI is gearing itself up for nothing short of world leadership because the company believes it has only begun to tap its true potential, with an increased emphasis on the network society, including semiconductors, signal processing, wireless communications, networking and digital imaging. The ultimate objective is to be a single company with multiple businesses focused on a common objective.

It is a determined outlook in an increasingly competitive market. And TI's British base has a significant part and role to play in those determined objectives which see Europe as an important and integral part of those growth programmes. The game plan is to develop a superior marketing culture – a commitment to go beyond giving customers what they want in order to build entirely new markets around a deep understanding of end users' current and future needs.

But above all, the company plans to almost double capital expenditure to $2.5 billion. Research and development spending is projected to rise to $1.1 billion to support targeted opportunities in digital signal processing solutions, advanced memory and micro processors, digital imaging technology and wireless transmission of video, voice and data. The plan is aimed at the long term and to strengthen TI's position, building on gains made over the past three years.

How does Texas Instruments rate?

Pay:	very good
Benefits:	very good
Communications:	excellent
Training:	very good
Career development:	very good
Morale:	good

People and personnel policies

The company's UK headquarters is a brand new office complex within easy reach of road, rail and air links. And that is seen as of paramount importance where speed of essential communications can be vital. It has two main functions: semiconductor marketing and sales, and the design group. Sunbury-on-Thames is TI's European software centre. Other key European locations, each responsible for a different aspect of the company's business within the European Union, are located in Munich, Nice, Almelo (the Netherlands) and Rome. But the guiding HR philosophy and principle in all of the company's centres is one of informality with a steel-backed resolve to enhance TI's reputation and profits.

It is not an inward-looking culture: but there is a strong policy of recruiting from within, with internal job bidding for vacancies which occur. And they are few and far between, because, with a worldwide operation, those who are seen as the senior executives of tomorrow are allowed worldwide opportunities. Peter Stirling, vice president of human resources (Europe), says 'There is a heavy emphasis on personal development and career management.' This, in effect, means recruiting the right people and sticking with them. TI insists on getting it right first time. The HR philosophy concentrates on giving recruits skills to take advantage of opportunities when they come along. The same applies to those who have been with the company for some time: the ethos is a total learning curve with the emphasis on teamwork. Some teams may have a limited life cycle for a particular project which may be put together for a specific purpose. But, nonetheless, the ability to work as a member of a team is seen as of paramount importance.

Stirling comments 'One of the most important things about our HR policy is that it is not isolated or idealistic. But it has to match the requirements of the company; it is an enabling strategy. It is easy and tempting for HR practice to be attracted to particular causes which do not serve the business. He insists 'We try not to be seduced into types and cloning. There has to be a mix. We look for those with high levels of energy, intellectual capability, good technical knowledge. And they must keep their skills up to date.

'Texas Instruments is a company of continuous learning. We demand from our people the capacity to accept change and to operate effectively when all the answers are not there: to make decisions without complete data.' These demands can be extensive. But so are the rewards with a comprehensive and attractive package which ensures that TI vacancies are at a premium. Basic salaries provide a foundation: variable incentives depend on the company's financial results and pre-set goals on an individual or team basis. All employees are entitled to shares which can be translated into cash – but again depending on the company's global financial results. There is free medical insurance, company pension scheme and in-house subsidised restaurant facilities.

'The individual employee must maintain their value in the marketplace and we have the environment for people to do just that, and there is security of employment under those circumstances because you are valuable to another employer. We have developed quality of leadership to enable people to maximise their abilities: directive management has gone.' TI, in common with most forward-looking companies, has sliced and pared down management layers. It relies on the people it employs to make on-line decisions and backs them to the hilt. Another attraction of the TI ethos are opportunities in all parts of the world.

Stirling adds 'If a person is totally mobile and willing to work in other countries, seize the opportunity and gain experience, they will find a higher visibility.' That means early career opportunities to switch skills. This is especially true of graduates who seek out TI and are sought by TI: they have to test various options and are then focused into particular business areas. He adds 'We tend to give opportunities at an earlier stage in peoples' careers than most other companies. There are internal opportunities for those who are mobile and willing.'

Contact address

Mr Peter Stirling,
Vice President Human Resources (Europe),
Texas Instruments,
800 Pavillion Drive,
Northampton Business Park,
Northampton NN4 7YL.
Telephone: 01604 663024.
Fax: 01604 663025.

TNT UK Limited

Winner of the European Quality Prize for business excellence in 1995 and 1996, TNT UK is also a highly respected employer which has gone from strength to strength in terms of both business and innovative personnel policies. Started as recently as 1978, the UK business is a key part of the global enterprise. Sales have grown from £6 million annually to around £8 million a week. It is the UK market leader in express delivery, providing national same-day and overnight carriage of urgent documents and parcels. It commands around 70 per cent of the newspaper and magazine transport market and employs 8,500 people in 300 British locations.

TNT United Kingdom at a glance

Employees: 8,500
Staff attrition rate: 5 per cent
Key locations: Atherstone (HQ), Bury
plus around 300 depots nationwide
Active graduate recruitment: n/a*
Annual intake: 1,000
*most new management employees are graduates

An inside view

TNT UK is a passionate business which thrives on personal energy and team ambition. The company wins national and international awards for its structured but highly personalised approach to quality and service, and, in increasingly tough markets, its people have a talent for transcending their own highwater marks. These are straightforward people who want to be the best. A zeal for continuous improvement fires TNT UK. It believes confidently in its own capacity to exceed any commercial and service goals and to translate its enthusiasm into substantial returns. This is not arrogance but good-humoured hard work and application. Customer service is the number one priority in the business; the current which drives the entire workforce.

A system of internal competition lies at the heart of TNT UK and is one of the great themes of managing director Alan Jones. The impact of the vitality and commitment of TNT's people is evident in its financial results. The company has grown from an annual turnover of £6 million in the late 1970s to around £8 million a week in 1996 with profits to match. The organisation consistently outperforms its competitors. Against stiff competition, it has captured market leadership positions in a range of key industrial sectors and is dominant in the same-day and overnight parcels delivery markets.

TNT UK continues to win external recognition for its innovative and high quality approach, and is now seen as a role model by organisations as diverse as the European Foundation for Quality Management, Investors in People and the Duke of Edinburgh's Award Scheme. TNT was the first UK company in its sector to be certified with the BS 5750 quality standard. It majors on service, refined on an hourly and daily basis, as the company's teams beat new personal bests. Jones says that the company believes that teamwork and a positive attitude can surmount even the most demanding challenges. But it is the extent of the competitive enthusiasm generated among TNT's staff which is its biggest achievement and which has defined the company in the UK as a world class business. Jones says that the enterprise prospers through a shared determination to succeed. The magazine *European Quality* described TNT UK's drive for quality as 'intrinsic and instinctive' and a central element of the culture.

Every employee is involved in internal competitions to beat past best performances. The company's publications are regularly filled with the names and photographs of individuals in its workforce who have made excellent contributions. League tables are present throughout the business. If a depot manager moves up from regional or national number four to number one, that takes effort and conviction. We praise the personal achievements of our people.' Whereas some businesses focus on correction of personal weaknesses, TNT UK takes great pleasure in applauding people who get things right. The management of the company is genuine in wanting everyone to be successful. From personal and team achievement comes corporate prosperity.

How does TNT United Kingdom rate?

Pay:	very good
Benefits:	strong
Communications:	superb
Training:	excellent
Career development:	very good
Morale:	excellent

People and personnel policies

'We are looking for people with the right make it happen attitude; staff who are enthusiastic and prepared to learn about our products and services; practical teamplayers who are ready to commit themselves to getting the job done right first time,' says Jones. 'We want the best people and to attract and keep them we have to pay competitive rates. Our pay packages are among the best in the sector. Some of it is basic pay and the rest is performance-related.' The pension scheme, open to all employees, has been improved in recent years. A free healthcare plan is also available. Relationships between TNT UK and its unions are positive. 'This is because we listen and talk to union representatives. The Post Office lost 62,000 working days due to strikes last year. We cannot afford to lose a single day. We have never had a strike at TNT UK.'

Personnel director David Hanley says 'We put new graduate management trainees through an 18-month course to see various different operations. Their expectation at the end of the course is very high and we give early responsibility. In recent years we have also been filling some key junior positions with graduates. What we do is to give all of our people an opportunity to succeed. If our people are successful in lower level positions, then they can apply for more senior appointments. All such posts are advertised internally. We base some of our graduates at major contract locations initially to show them what it is like to work directly for a client. And we then give them experience in our business development teams proposing logistics solutions to our customers. We try to give our recruits early responsibility whether they start in operational or business development positions.'

Hanley says the TNT 'home grown timber' policy has been a cornerstone of the company's success over many years. 'Our career progression policies have enabled the really talented people to shine through. We were recognised as Investors in People in 1994 and our appraisal system and training needs analysis have helped us to develop our people throughout the business. Our people are enthusiastic and everyone receives annual customer care training within our total quality management environment. We were recognised with the UK Award and Northern Ireland Award for Quality Management in 1994 and The European Quality Award Prize in 1995 and 1996.

'In contracts operated by TNT Logistics our people work very closely with clients. Here, you are trying to make things work, think problems through and take remedial action. Our business development team on the other hand assembles data to shape a best practice model which will help us jointly decide

with a client how an operation should be organised. We then need operations staff to put the plans into practice. What we look for in our people is drive and energy. Our successful "promotion from within" policies have enabled numerous men and women to rise from jobs such as drivers to director positions.'

Transport has traditionally been a male preserve but women run many of the TNT UK depots and have made their way steadily through the company to director levels. TNT UK is one of the most positive examples of a vigorous and competitive culture which is extending its expertise to other organisations in its communities. Alan Jones is one of Investors In People's champions and he advises other organisations on how to improve the quality of their service. The business is also active in a range of charitable and voluntary organisations at both a corporate and a personal level. John Major said when he presented the 1994 UK Quality Award to the company, 'TNT UK is a success story of the very first order and provides a clear example for other companies to emulate.'

Contact address

Mr Alan Jones, Managing Director,
TNT UK Limited,
Atherstone,
Warwickshire.
Telephone: 01827 303030.
Fax: 01827 713746.

Ulster Carpet Mills

Ulster Carpet Mills is an old, established Northern Ireland company which exports its high quality carpets throughout the world. Local commentators say that the company is a caring and considerate employer which builds lasting relationships with its people. The company reports annual sales of £45 million.

Ulster Carpet Mills at a glance

Employees: 1,200
Staff attrition: 5 per cent
Key locations: Portadown, Kidderminster, London, Atlanta, Paris, Germany
Average graduate recruitment: 6
Annual intake: 100

An inside view

Ulster Carpet Mills was established in 1938 in Portadown by the late George Wilson. His sons, Chairman Walter, John and Edward are the current owners of the business. The company employs around 1,200 people engaged in the production of high quality woven Axminster and Wilton carpets. It is the second largest producer of Axminster in the world, using the fleece from more than two million sheep. It is a vertically integrated company handling every stage in the production process, from purchase of raw wool through to sales and marketing of the finished product.

The company operates from three manufacturing sites in Portadown with 52 Axminster and Wilton looms and a computer-controlled warehouse with some 300 different designs and colourways in stock. It has a direct sales staff in the UK and Ireland with marketing subsidiaries in France, the US and Germany. Ulster Carpet Mills cover other markets with a sales manager and mobile sales executives. The company is fully committed to design and has 40 designers located in four inter-linked offices in Portadown, Kidderminster, London and Atlanta, Georgia. It is also seen as an innovator in carpet design and production. Its Uniweave concept, which has been registered, allows the weaving of long and complex designs in one continuous carpet.

The company has issued a mission statement which is customer-focussed but which also mentions the harmony of its people. This is particularly important in a business which draws from both religious communities in a sensitive part of the province.

This is a professionally managed business with a strong commitment to quality. All the factories have been registered under the ISO 9001 quality standard. Its achievements in this field won the company the Northern Ireland Award for Quality for 1991, the UK Quality award for business excellence in 1996, and made it finalist for the European Quality Award, also in 1996. A total quality master plan has been integrated into the company's five-year business plan. Until 1992, the company ran a quality department but in that year it applied its philosophy that every employee is responsible for quality, and closed the function.

Ulster Carpet Mills is a great enthusiast for technological improvement and enhancement, and it has invested £15 million in new systems. The carpet weaving industry is traditional in its approach and it is rich with opportunities for the application of modern engineering and electronics. Ulster Carpet Mills is in the vanguard of this activity and its engineering research and development department, staffed with young and articulate individuals, is at the heart of this innovation.

How does Ulster Carpets rate?

Pay:	good
Benefits:	good
Communications:	very good
Training:	excellent
Career development:	very good
Morale:	good

People and personnel policies

Ulster Carpet Mills' personnel policies are a mixture of leading-edge human resources management theory and the personal – even intimate – approach of this growth business. Part of this particular cultural mix derives from its history as a family-owned operation which historically adopted a mildly paternalistic attitude towards its people. Today the flavour of former times remains with the business as it translates into a highly efficient, quality-driven international enterprise.

Since the outset in the late 1930s, Ulster Carpet Mills has been characterised by respect for the individual. Edward Wilson says 'care for our people forms one of our four principal objectives from the company's mission statement. We have a strongly supportive workforce prepared to adjust to new and changing technologies. We enjoy a reputation in the trade for the integrity, openness and friendliness of our staff.'

The company is much flatter structurally than in former days. There are few levels between the managing director and the shop floor worker. One of the reasons is to allow ideas to circulate freely and to recognise everyone's contribution to the business. Another slightly old-fashioned way in which the company acknowledges the impact of its people is by making an award to the employee of the month.

Ulster Carpet Mills has no problems in recruitment. The company is well known in its region and indeed it is respected throughout Northern Ireland. In addition, people in the carpet weaving commercial sector are familiar with its reputation as a technological and design innovator. This is a highly attractive company for people wanting to join the industry since its growth in sales and market share during the next decade are expected to be high.

The company pays well for the province and offers strong benefits. Its pension scheme is excellent, healthcare insurance is available for all, and profit-related pay has been introduced in recent years. Communications are a key priority. There is already a remarkable dialogue between employees and managers, but Ulster Carpet Mills also runs team briefings and a whole series of internal communications publications.

Training and development is a major strategic theme at Ulster Carpet Mills. It has an active employee and management development programme and it makes extensive use of internal and external training courses. For all employees there will be at least three days a year doing on-the-job training, and a personal performance review which will identify training needs.

The company's directors are keen on building managers of the future, so they have created an extensive leadership course which is available for all managers. It involves 29 key training modules including business strategy themes. Some of the tuition is delivered internally, but candidates also go away to residential sessions. The aim is to complete the programme in 18 months.

Ulster Carpet Mills is deeply committed to equal opportunities and it has actively encouraged its female employees to take roles in management. In two years there has been a 30 per cent rise in female group leaders in the company. Mike Mills, managing director, says 'The keys to Ulster Carpets continuing to be a successful company – developing our people for progressively more interesting and more rewarding jobs – lie in our hands. The responsibility for achieving excellence rests with us all – the team.'

In recent years the company has expanded its employee feedback mechanisms to include opinion surveys, personal development plans and Investors in People interviews.

Contact address

Personnel department,
Ulster Carpet Mills,
Portadown,
Craigavon,
Northern Ireland.
Telephone: 01762 334433.
Fax: 01762 333142.

Unilever plc

The component brands and companies within the Unilever group are some of the world's best-known names. The business, as it is presently constituted, came together in the early 1930s and has developed into a highly polished and respected multinational. Around 50 per cent of the company's income is derived from foods – frozen items, ice-cream and dairy products. It also produces: detergents; personal products – cosmetics, toothpaste, shampoo and conditioners; and speciality chemicals. Expansion will come mainly in developing countries which are the focus of the group's strategy. Unilever has long been regarded as one of the finest employers in the UK. Its graduate entry scheme is widely praised and places on it are keenly sought. Despite its size and influence as a global product and marketing force, Unilever is a friendly place to work and positively encourages individual initiative and creativity.

Unilever at a glance

Employees: 308,000 worldwide; UK, 20,000
Annual staff attrition rate: not recorded
Key locations: 80 worldwide
Av. annual graduate recruitment: 150
Annual intake: 1,000

An inside view

Throughout UK industry, the Unilever graduate training scheme has emerged as an excellent role model. Since the late 1940s, other businesses have based their graduate entry programmes on those which have been evolved at Unilever. In many ways, this is hardly surprising since Unilever is a company which enjoys a global reputation for quality, innovation and good stewardship. Its expanding portfolio of brands include Magnum, Persil, Ponds, Elizabeth Arden, Omo, Lipton's Teas, Flora and I Can't Believe It's Not Butter.

In January 1930, the washing powder manufacturer Lever Brothers and the Dutch Margarine Union combined to make Unilever. The scope of the new formation was widespread both geographically and in product terms. The Union and Lever Brothers shared a common customer in the housewife and both owed their success to the growing prosperity of the European working man. Two separate companies, Unilever PLC and Unilever NV, operate effectively as an integrated business and are managed by a common management team. British graduate trainees will normally spend their first five years in the UK before being considered for international assignments: nearly all senior managers have worked abroad at some stage in their careers. The focus of attention within the group is on the developing markets – Asia, Africa, Latin America – and its management believes that the potential for business growth here is substantial.

Despite its acknowledged status as one of the largest and most successful global multinationals, Unilever in the UK is one of the most friendly and personable organisations in the British commercial sector. The company places great reliance on the talents of individuals and so gives employees – and especially managers – considerable personal freedom in the conduct of their assignments. Although the business has a clearly and centrally defined corporate strategy, individuals are much less bound to a company directive on building business and relationships with clients than some competing businesses.

John Bulpitt, head of management recruitment and training, says that individual initiative and creativity is positively encouraged at Unilever. This is not a culture where edicts are issued from the centre and managers must perform within established strictures. 'We believe strongly in working hard to locate the most suitable people – inevitably some of the top performers at university – to join the company and granting them the freedom to operate.' They come from a wide span of academic backgrounds but they tend to be self-starters who enjoy working both in teams and solo. The Unilever system throws new recruits in at the deep end by putting them straight to work in one of the many product divisions. Unilever managers enjoy remarkable latitude in comparison with many of the leading multinationals but this personal contribution is a major facet of the Unilever approach.

How does Unilever rate?

Pay:	excellent
Benefits:	very good
Communications:	superb
Training:	excellent
Career development:	good
Morale:	very good

People and personnel policies

Among personnel professionals, Unilever is regarded as one of the top performers. This is partly historic because Unilever was the first of the UK's major businesses to establish a management training facility and a graduate trainee scheme. Throughout the decades since those developments, the company's reputation as a trainer has, if anything, been further enhanced. Its trainee scheme was the template for many in British industry and has been adapted to take account of changing conditions and demands in the company's development.

The company currently styles itself the multi-local multinational which emphasises the local and brand orientation of the business. Although there are certain guiding principles in place in personnel policy – upper quartile pay and benefits, high commitment to training, teamworking and room for personal contribution – the stress lies in local management responding to local customer demand. Like Hewlett-Packard in the computer sector, Unilever managers enjoy the support of the centre and the strength of the international brands, but also remarkable freedom to manoeuvre. Each year Unilever introduces more than 1,000 graduates worldwide. Traditionally, these individuals would have worked mainly in the national businesses but with added commitment to learning from other territories they can in the future be expected to take up managerial positions anywhere in the world.

The company places increasing importance on international project teams. Employees in one country will link with experienced people in other territories. It is one of the most obvious examples of the skill and knowledge interchange which is taking place at all levels to revitalise the culture. A Unilever university has been set up in central Europe where people from all over the world come to attend courses on the latest events in product development and marketing.

John Bulpitt explains that graduates will move from role to role roughly every 18 months to two years. The individuals who are starred for senior management will certainly take assignments overseas. As the company is an Anglo-Dutch combine, it is likely that people who will assume senior positions will experience a spell in Rotterdam.

Unilever is focusing much of its energy on the developing markets around the world – China, Latin America, Africa and Asia. High profile graduate trainees are being given the opportunity to contribute to the territories where Unilever is placing its greatest efforts. Managers who take placements in these regions will be at the forefront of the development of the global business.

The rules for Unilever managers are clear: the company will provide

opportunity, good rewards and room for creativity. It demands – as it always has – total integrity. This is the ultimate bottom line. If there is a problem, people are there to help and the culture supports managers who, when experiencing difficulties, are totally open. This is normally a friendly and informal atmosphere in which to operate but managers who conceal their difficulties will quickly lose the sympathies of their colleagues.

Beyond the managerial grades, Unilever has a strong if somewhat paternalistic reputation for looking after its shopfloor staff. Pay is excellent and employees report that they enjoy good working conditions and a positive environment. Despite local variations in approach, Unilever facilities are standard-setters within their industries. But the decentralised culture of the Unilever group gives local management the opportunity to develop the quality and depth of their own personnel.

Contact address

Mr John Bulpitt,
Head of Management Recruitment and Training,
Unilever PLC, Blackfriars,
London EC4P 4BQ.
Telephone: 0171 822 5252.
Fax: 0171 822 5951.

Unipart Group of Companies

The Unipart Group of Companies (UGC) is Europe's leading independent logistics, automotive parts and accessories business. Grown from a management buyout from British Leyland in 1987, it has become one of the established beacons of new British industry through its innovative treatment of employee and customer. Its chief executive, John Neill, is a lightning rod for change, first introducing the notion of stakeholding long before any political party thought it was a good idea. The company employs 3,700 people and reports rapid financial growth.

Unipart at a glance

Employees: 3,700
Annual staff attrition rate: 4 per cent
Key locations: Oxford (HQ, manufacturing and university), with nine other sites in the UK and Europe
Av. annual graduate recruitment: 20
Annual intake: 150

An inside view

Unipart is a classic success story of privatisation, albeit through the management buyout process. Known mostly for its provision of a full spectrum demand chain management service for UK vehicle manufacturers, it produces a complete range of parts under the Unipart brand for all makes of cars on European roads. It has also created a cellular telephone service supplier, an information technology company and a creative communications agency.

Since its management buyout, the company has gone from rags to riches,
showing consistent growth every year. In the last financial year (1995), turnover increased to £864 million with profits before interest and tax at more than £31 million – up 13 per cent on 1994. The stakeholder philosophy, which Neill has raised from dusty textbooks to active workplace, is an economic theory which mixes partnerships and social responsibility with specified investment policy. It is not widely appreciated, partly because Unipart is not a quoted company and Neill is not that well known outside industry, which treats him with great respect tinged with a little wonderment at what he has achieved. Part of the stakeholder partnership is connected to the shareholder, and in 1995 the large rise in profits translated into dividends worth £6.5 million, more than double the £3.1 million paid in 1993. Share value has risen 46,000 per cent since 1987.

The way that Unipart has risen from the broken bits of Leyland is assuming the aspect of legend; but the success is very much founded on an employer-employee culture, and the personality of Neill who some observers say is the best businessman in Britain. Dan Jones, a professor at Cardiff Business School, believes that Neill has turned Unipart into 'one of the most efficient and demanding companies in the world' by seeking more and still more in service and production efficiency, and giving back exactly the same to those who produce the goods for the consumer and the shareholder

His message is clear: if the UK is to survive the potentially awesome challenge from the very low-cost economies of the Far East, then business has to adopt radical, new working practices. And Unipart has done precisely that – particularly as change relates to the employee.

In terms of employee qualifications, the UK has, for a long while, ranked in the lower half of the OECD's list of 22; and no government since the Second World War has really made training an absolute priority. Unipart has responded positively to the problem. The heart of its human resource philosophy is on the ground floor of the company's headquarters at Cowley where a training university was created in 1992. Neill believes that training and inspiring employees to learn is essential to survival. That is how the UK can confront the new era of global competition.

How does Unipart rate?

Pay:	good
Benefits:	excellent
Communications:	excellent
Training:	superb
Career development:	strong
Morale:	good

People and personnel policies

'Three billion people in China, Korea, Vietnam and elsewhere are entering the global economy. They are paid between a tenth and a hundredth of the wage of people in Europe and these countries do not have our welfare burden. In Europe, we have the highest work costs. These 3 billion people have a hunger for the Western lifestyle and they know that to get it, they must forge well into Western markets. And they also have a hunger for learning – it is part of their culture. Human resources are always the most important part of any business in any part of the world,' says Neill. There are 180 courses on offer at the Unipart University, and every employee takes ten basic courses, adding up to ten days every year. These are run mainly by line managers who have themselves been taught how to teach and encourage employee involvement in continuous improvement, customer service and the elimination of waste.

The group's corporate goal – to make the UGC logo the mark of outstanding personal customer service – is mainlined through the Unipart U Programmes such as 'Our Contribution Counts Circles' (OCC Circles), which is the Unipart approach to the so-called Quality Circles, providing a framework for team problem solving using techniques taught in the University. These continuing improvement principles encourage employees to improve quality and reduce cost – the only way that Neill believes companies like Unipart will survive and prosper.

OCC Circles were first launched in the Unipart Group in 1991, being developed from the successful best practice experience of industry in Japan and North America. The programme has been designed to reflect the culture of Unipart, and is designed to give power to the employee, allowing them to solve challenges faced at the workplace. There are hundreds of circles operating at Unipart currently involving almost a third of the company's workforce. It is estimated that more than £5 million in costs has been saved through this initiative.

The company's £2.5 million investment in the Unipart U reflects its commitment to put continuous learning at the core of the company's strategy for competitiveness. Frank Nigriello, group communications director, says that 'the question is whether we can deliver continuous learning and upskilling. Learning is the way we do business; it is not a bolt-on activity.' The human resource philosophy was developed in such an all-embracing fashion that in the first years after the buyout from British Leyland, the traditional unions became virtually irrelevant. In 1992, they were de-recognised. 'We put so many working practices into place that the unions no longer had a strong role to play. The company puts tremendous effort into direct communication with the employees, both upwards and downwards, and it became clear that there was no role for an intermediary,' says Nigriello. 'Unipart has created a culture built on teamwork across all traditional boundaries. People are motivated by their high level of personal involvement in aspects of the business that make a real difference to the customer,' he says.

The second outstanding element of its people policy is a £1 million investment in an employee club called The Lean Machine. While the University focuses on the mind, The Lean Machine – the company's unique health and fitness centre – provides a focus for the body. Opened in 1992, it is basically a private club for employees and their families, centred right in the middle of the Oxford headquarters.

Chief executive Neill, always at the centre of change in the company, is well aware of the pressures that change bring. 'We are told that change in this decade will be ten times faster than in the past. Consider what this means for employees who must adapt quickly and welcome change. This rapid pace of changes means that employees are facing more and more stress which can manifest itself in physical and mental problems. In the Lean Machine, they can not only get fit so that they can cope with stress, and receive treatment to deal with some of the problems created by stress, they can also learn how to manage stress ...'

Contact address

Mr Frank Nigriello,
Group Communications Director,
Unipart House,
Cowley,
Oxford OX4 2PG.
Telephone: 01865 383339.
Fax: 01865 383047.

Virgin Group

S ince its formation by Richard Branson in 1970, Virgin has grown into one of the largest private groups in the UK. Various Virgin companies and their joint ventures now employ more than 15,000 people worldwide and operate in 22 countries in a mix of media, entertainment, retailing, publishing, merchandising and travel activities. The group is characterised by an informal and iconoclastic style, and is ideally suited to those who are seeking freedom and early responsibility in an invigorating environment.

Virgin at a glance

Employees: 15,000 worldwide, 11,000 UK
Annual staff attrition rate: 5 per cent
Key locations: Mostly central London and Crawley
Av. graduate intake: none
Av. annual recruitment: 1,500 (esp. heavy recruitment for Virgin Atlantic)

An inside view

Virgin is synonymous with Richard Branson. He has emerged as one of the few business leaders of his generation to have a real dialogue with the young and through his energy and distinctive vision to have carved out a commercial concept which embraces a wide span of cultural interests. If one word were to be applied to the Branson federation of businesses, perhaps eclectic – a good 1960s rock and roll adjective – would fit the bill. After starting in records mail order, Branson's remit has spread to his own music label, record shops through airlines, cola and vodka to life assurance. As much as his

instinct for business, it is Branson's personal gift for imaginative marketing and capacity to translate a sense of fun into his enterprises which has captured the public imagination.

Although the term Virgin Group represents a convenient label to use, it is, strictly speaking, a misnomer. There is actually no such legal entity and nowhere are the financial results of the underlying operating companies consolidated centrally. It is more correct to think of the Virgin empire as being a loose federation of businesses, which are bound together by the strength of the brand name, a set of core values and the personality of the seemingly ubiquitous Richard Branson. In this respect, Virgin is styled on a Japanese *keiretsu* (society of businesses) such as Mitsubishi.

When taken together, Virgin's businesses now have a combined turnover in excess of £1.5 billion. These operate in eight main divisions: Virgin Communications (including its publishing arm); Virgin Radio; Virgin Retail Group (including its worldwide chain of megastores and the Our Price record shops); Virgin Travel (including Virgin

Atlantic Airways, Virgin Holidays and the group's burgeoning rail interests); Voyager Investments (which effectively consists of a range of stand-alone investments); Virgin Hotels; Virgin Direct Personal Financial Services; and Virgin Cinemas.

Despite the diversity of its operations, all Virgin businesses are bound together by a series of four core values. These are quality, competitiveness, innovation and fun. The first three of these values define the attributes with which the name Virgin should be associated in the minds of customers, and lie at the heart of the group's objective of creating a global brand name. The last characteristic derives from Branson's desire to create a sense of enjoyment both in working for Virgin and from using its products and services. The importance which Virgin attaches to fun is one of the principal ways in which the group differentiates itself from its rivals.

Virgin's strategy is to focus on businesses which generate above-average growth potential. Having identified suitable opportunities, it frequently works through alliance or with joint venture partners to exploit them, hence minimising its capital outlay and reducing its risks. Virgin's management style is to delegate as much autonomy as possible to the business areas. The group prides itself on its lean management structure and a capacity to respond more quickly than its rivals to potential business opportunities. Within business areas, employees are organised into small, manageable units in order to maximise their effectiveness.

Virgin is quite unlike most other UK companies. Many employees have an almost evangelical fervour about working for the group and a strong devotion to its charismatic founder. But its unconventional style does not suit everyone. According to Will Whitehorn, Virgin's corporate affairs director, 'People either leave after six months or stay for a lifetime'. For those who relish an informal and fast-moving environment, Virgin can offer unparalleled opportunities – as well as fun!

How does Virgin rate?

Pay:	average
Benefits:	good
Communications:	excellent
Training:	good
Career development:	very good
Morale:	excellent

People and personnel policies

Consistent with its philosophy of keeping bureaucracy to a minimum, Virgin does not have group-wide personnel policies. Recruitment, terms and conditions are all determined at an individual operating company level. Furthermore, the group does not have a graduate recruitment programme. As a matter of policy, it prefers to recruit individuals who have had some business experience after leaving university. In addition to espousing its core values, Virgin employees will also be expected to demonstrate creative flair and be willing to accept responsibility early. While the company may have a reputation for being unconventional – hardly anyone wears a suit at Virgin – it is also strongly entrepreneurial.

In terms of remuneration, salary levels tend to be set around the industry average. Salaries are supplemented in most operating companies by profit-share or bonus schemes which can typically be worth around 10–15 per cent of base salary. Virgin has also recently introduced a shadow share ownership scheme for senior employees. Moreover, since one of Virgin's preferred methods of growth is by joint venture, many executives have an equity stake in the fortunes of the business concerned. This accords with the group's policy of empowering the individuals within the business as much as possible. It is an acknowledged fact that the Virgin Group has created a significant number of millionaires. Another attraction of working for the Virgin group of companies is the wide range of perks that are on offer.

Traditionally, the disparate nature of the Virgin organisation has meant that there has been relatively little movement of individuals between various companies in the group. This attitude is slowly changing, however, as the group expands and skills become more easily transferable. One example of this is that an employee who has been working in the marketing function at Virgin Atlantic Airways has recently been transferred to develop new marketing initiatives for the Eurostar cross-Channel rail service. Perhaps not surprisingly given the personality of Richard Branson, communication within the group is considered to be a priority and is something into which the group puts substantial effort, especially in the larger companies. As well as the standard, formal methods of communication such as newsletters, Virgin organises employee get-togethers – such as a recent trip by a group of employees to DisneyLand Paris – to improve communication and morale.

Virgin has been very successful in fostering the promotion and development of women within the workforce. Uniquely among leading UK companies, it is estimated that 40 per cent of the most senior executives within the Virgin group of companies are female. Virgin Atlantic, in particular, has a strong female involvement. Much of the reason for this success lies in the informal working style within the group and the flexible working arrangements which are on offer. Virgin also offers men paternity leave. The group takes its social responsibilities seriously. It has established its own charitable foundation and currently works with 25 charities in the UK. As well as the financial support which the group provides, the involvement of Virgin employees in charity work is also encouraged. Virgin – and Branson in particular – is also well known for funding innovative and sometimes apparently eccentric small business ventures. He believes, probably correctly, that some of these wacky ideas would not receive funding through conventional sources but a proportion may have commercial merit and he enjoys seeing them succeed.

Contact address

Ms Lily Lu,
Group Personnel Manager,
Virgin Management,
120 Campden Hill Road,
London W8 7AR
Telephone: 0171 229 1282.
Fax: 0171 229 3234.

Western Provident Association

The basic philosophy and aim of the Western Provident Association is quite simple and straightforward: to become the most professional and highest quality provider of health insurance services. And it insists this can only be achieved by offering customers the widest choice and greatest value in health insurance and to exceed their expectations through unrivalled personal service. It all began in 1901 with the Reading District Working Men's Hospital Fund which enabled people to save for the contributions they would need to make if they or their families were admitted to hospital. In 1945, following the merger with the Bristol Hospitals Fund, the Western Provident Association was formed.

WPA at a glance

Employees: 260
Annual staff attrition rate: 11 per cent
Key locations: Taunton (HQ)
Av. annual graduate recruitment: 6–8
Annual intake: 30

An inside view

Provident associations are completely non-profit-making and all their funds are used for the benefit of subscribers. Today WPA insures more than 500,000 individuals and more than 5,000 companies in a fiercely competitive market: a figure which represents approximately one in every 100 people in the United Kingdom. Each year 200,000 claims are processed. A key factor in the company's growth has been the recognition of insurance brokers of the value and quality of WPA which remains committed to independent

intermediaries. It is always aware of their role in the future development of the health insurance market.

Business expansion triggered a move from Bristol to a purpose built headquarters in Taunton in 1992. A highly sophisticated fourth generation computer system provides instant access to all subscriber information. An innovative feature of that system is the world's leading use of integrated image technology, giving instant access not only to members on-site, but to any WPA person anywhere in the world equipped with a lap top computer. The challenge, as WPA saw it – a move which proved both practical and effective – was to convert information to knowledge.

That could only be done by having all the information, including original application forms and correspondence, available on screen. WPA standards of business operation and customer service are not mere claims. It has been accredited with the ISO 9001 quality standard for the totality of its operations and TickIT for its software development by the British Standards Institute. It was recognised by the Department of Trade and Industry and the Confederation of British Industry as a top 100 company in 1994. The company, realistically, recognises that computer technology in itself resolves nothing and certainly does not provide service to customers. What makes the difference is staff of a special calibre and WPA has set rigorous standards of recruitment and staff training at all levels and for all departments. That emphasis has been recognised by Investors in People since 1993.

WPA has always been to the fore of the campaign to hold down medical inflation by reducing charges and preventing the overcharging particularly prevalent where patients are known to have private health insurance. It insists that this vigilance will always be necessary and procedures to monitor and contain the costs of private treatment will be rigidly maintained. WPA is one of the few health insurers which negotiates contracts with all major private and NHS hospitals.

Hospital accommodation costs form a major part of most claims. Although patient care should always be a priority, there are cases where hospital stays are unnecessarily prolonged. WPA actively discourages this in negotiations with hospitals. All bills for private treatment are scrutinised to ensure that charges for treatment, accommodation, drugs and other services are both correct and reasonable. Patients are also encouraged to check the bills before claiming on their policy. WPA maintains expensive errors and overcharging are avoided, making a major contribution to holding down the costs of claims and therefore future premium increases.

How does WPA rate?

Pay:	good
Benefits:	very good
Communications:	excellent
Training:	good
Career development:	good
Morale:	very good

People and personnel policies

In 1992, WPA was reconstructed from the top down, or the bottom upwards, whichever way one cares to examine the then situation. Now it is run as six semiautonomous business units with self-managed teams. Responsibility has been pushed downwards so that decision making is effected quickly and positively in the customers' best interests. There is an overt policy that respect and gratitude for effort and achievement is worth far more than a kick when things go wrong, as they sometimes do.

Before the catalytic move to Taunton a staff of 450 serviced a customer base of under 400,000. Now, in its new purpose-built offices in Taunton, and with significant investment in the latest IT, the 260 employees serve the needs of more than 500,000 customers. As well as this marked improvement in overall efficiency, WPA continues its drive to excellent customer service, which is inspired by its motto 'Always A Little Further'. To deliver world class service, WPA's managers are aware that they must recruit high quality staff and then train and motivate them. The company does not specifically seek graduates when recruiting, but nevertheless many do apply for positions within the company. All training – for entrants or otherwise – is on-the-job. Newcomers complete a modular series of multi-skilling projects in the first three months.

WPA has only one reserved car park space, which is indicative of its approach to employee management. The slot next to the reception is retained for the employee of the month. If the chief executive, Julian Stainton, were to leave his vehicle there, he would be politely asked to remove it. A conservatory straddles two wings of the building and houses the staff restaurant where everyone eats.

The overriding and significant driving force is simple, as head of best practice Adrian Schuler points out 'We live up to the values we have set ourselves and we are deeply proud of the fact that we are recognised as Investors in People. We believe that if we look after our employees, our employees will look after our customers.' That, in turn, means more output with an added professionalism and attention to detail. But above all, he insists, new recruits must have the right attitude and be prepared to play a team game.

'The world of private medicine is not rocket science. But our people must have initiative, enthusiasm and take responsibility for their actions. If you want to get on, we provide the environment. But it is up to the individual to seize the initiative.' This is reflected in the first employees' question in the bi-annual appraisal which asks 'What have you added to your cv during the period of appraisal?' But the fact that they are responsible for their own progress is the basic underpinning of the company's philosophy. That, in turn, means that those with ambition and the dedicated high fliers tend to move on. Not because their worth is not a valuable asset. The size of the company, and the fact that managers are of extremely high calibre, means that opportunities can be limited.

A basic pay banding structure is common to all, with appraisal-based increases and bonuses. There is, naturally, free medical insurance and a pension scheme. Communications are important and all relevant information is on everyone's screen through an internal e-mail message system. Company meetings – easy to arrange with a small workforce – encourage a two-directional feedback.

Contact address

Mr Adrian Schuler,
Head of Best Practice,
Western Provident Association Ltd,
Rivergate House,
Blackbrook Park,
Taunton TA1 2PE.
Telephone: 01823 623238.
Fax: 01823 623588.

WPP Group plc

WPP is the world's largest advertising and marketing services group. Consisting of 40 individual companies, it operates in more than 80 countries and numbers more than 300 of the *Fortune 500* companies among its clients. Although the operating companies have retained a considerable amount of autonomy and distinctive cultures, there is a commitment to excellence running throughout the group. WPP is acutely, and constantly, aware of the need to recruit and retain talented individuals to satisfy increasingly demanding client requirements.

WPP at a glance

Employees: 21,000 worldwide, 3,500 UK
Annual staff attrition rate: 15 per cent*
Key locations: 784 offices worldwide, 270 offices in Western Europe including UK
Av. annual graduate recruitment: 100–150
Annual intake: 850
* industry average

An inside view

WPP was formed a little over ten years ago and has grown rapidly, both organically and by acquisition, to become the world's largest advertising and marketing services group. The group is split into four separate operating sectors – media advertising, market research, public relations and specialist communications – and its stable of businesses includes a number of household names such as J Walter Thompson, Ogilvy & Mather, BMRB International, Hill & Knowlton and The Henley Centre.

Initially, after its formation, WPP acted as little more than an investment holding company. It remains true that the operating subsidiaries enjoy a considerable amount of autonomy, but nevertheless a group culture is now starting to emerge. In particular, all companies in the WPP Group share a commitment to intellectual rigour, and a clarity and integrity of thought. The best employees are those who can make an intellectual contribution to the business. As a service business, WPP recognises that it is the talent of its workforce which represents its critical source of competitive advantage and differentiation, and its attitude to the remuneration and development of its workforce reflects this.

WPP is a highly results-oriented group. The parent company only intervenes in the activities of its subsidiaries if it can be clearly demonstrated that it will add value by doing so. Otherwise, the role of head office is purely to set a framework of standards and monitor progress. All operating companies are encouraged to build their own brands and develop their own specialist skills and expertise.

Although the image of a creative person as a pony-tailed prima donna might be a rather tired stereotype, it is true that the temperament of many people involved in the advertising and marketing services industry is better suited to smaller, discrete units than to large corporations. WPP is keen to maintain this informal and flexible atmosphere.

As in many industries, life for media companies continues to be intensely competitive, particularly as clients become more demanding in their service requirements. WPP will maintain its leading position only if it continues to provide clients with a high quality service, and this is itself largely a function of recruiting the best and the brightest in the industry.

How does WPP rate?

Pay:	good
Benefits:	good
Communications:	good
Training:	excellent
Career development:	excellent
Morale:	very good

People and personnel policies

According to Brian Brooks, WPP's group human resources director, the group's human resources strategy is 'to develop and manage talent, to apply that talent throughout the world for the benefit of clients, to do this in partnership (with the operating company), and to do this

profitably'. While there has been concern elsewhere in the industry about the calibre of entry-level recruits, WPP is determined that this will not apply to the group. Its philosophy is that all its recruits should be 'best in class'.

Although most career development continues to be performed at an individual company level – J Walter Thompson, for example, has long been regarded as the 'University of Advertising' – there is an increasing focus on group-wide training initiatives. For example, the group has developed a management programme in association with the London Business School. It has also instituted a Marketing Fellowship programme, as part of which selected graduates rotate through group companies as part of the process of building multi-disciplinary managers. There are week-long brand leadership workshops, designed to bring together rising stars from different parts of the group. Also at higher levels within the group, there are the 100 and 300 Clubs. These consist of the respective number of most senior executives within the group and are designed to act as a training ground for future leaders.

The creation of a more distinct WPP culture means that careers are no longer limited by the company which the individual joins, and moves within the business are now increasingly common. To aid this, an electronic employment exchange showing opportunities within the group is being developed. There is also a database maintained of potential future company leaders around the world. Its people undergo an annual appraisal process – which includes 360 degree feedback – which is highly focused in the personal development of the individual.

Clearly another important factor in attracting and retaining staff is remuneration. As benefits a results-oriented organisation, the professional targets and personal rewards of an increasing number of people within the group are linked to agreed company and group financial objectives. WPP has developed a policy of incentivising senior members of its workforce through generous share ownership schemes. This approach will be cascaded down through the organisation in the near future. A belief in the value of share ownership programmes is unique in the advertising and marketing services industry. The group's key principles in terms of remuneration are that employees should be paid competitively and that this should be closely aligned to performance, with the intention that this results in the retention of critical talent. In virtually all companies, the emphasis is moving towards a total package as opposed to base salary.

As a matter of policy, WPP takes the issue of the diversity of its workforce very seriously and, to this end, it has adopted a strong equal opportunities statement. It also attempts to be as flexible as possible in its working arrangements. The group is assisted in its objective of promoting women within the workforce by the fact that the media industry is one, courtesy of its high creative content, which tends to be attractive to females anyway. A number of businesses, including Ogilvy & Mather, are currently headed up by women. Indeed, diversity of the workforce – be it by gender, racially or by social-economic background – is a quality which is highly valued by WPP. It believes it achieves the best results for its clients by fostering a

diversity of opinion and thought among its employees.

Communication within the organisation is primarily a matter for the individual operating companies. However, the group's policy is one of openness and the effective communication of group strategy and progress by the operating heads is encouraged. Similarly encouraged is an involvement by employees in their local community. This tends to take the form of individuals giving their time, rather than money, to a deserving cause. Both advertising agencies within the group have long-standing policies of undertaking *pro bono* work, for example on behalf on AIDS-related charities.

Contact address

Mr Brian J Brooks,
Group Human Resources Director,
WPP Group plc,
27 Farm Street,
London W1X 6RD.
Telephone: 0171 408 2204.
Fax: 0171 493 6819.

Company Suitability

Best for non-graduates

Allied Dunbar
Asda
The Body Shop
Boots
Federal Express
Finelist
Green Flag
John Lewis
Marks & Spencer
Nissan
Safeway
TNT
Virgin

Graduate favourites

ABB
Andersen Consulting
Esso
Glaxo-Wellcome
Hewlett-Packard
ICI
Mercury Asset Management
JP Morgan
Schroders
Unilever

Great companies for women

The Body Shop
Hewlett-Packard
Eli Lilly
Pearson
Rank Xerox
Reader's Digest
Safeway
Schlumberger
TNT
Virgin

Great trainers

British Steel
Allied Dunbar
Hewlett-Packard
Procter & Gamble
WH Smith
Unilever
PepsiCo

Companies included in the 1989 edition

The following companies were included in the previous edition.

Abbey National
Allied Colloids
Allied-Lyons (now Allied Domecq)
Amersham International
Apple Computer
Baxter Healthcare
Blackwood Hodge
Blue Arrow (no longer independent)
British Aerospace
HP Bulmer
Cala
James Capel
Charterhouse
C & J Clark
Compaq
Continental Can
Dana
Digital
Du Pont
Fitch & Co
Glynwed
Hallmark
Horsell Graphics
Jewellers Guild (no longer trading)
Johnson Wax
Kodak
Komatsu
Littlewoods
LWT (now part of Granada)
Lowe, Howard-Spink & Bell
Meridian
Metal Box
MFI

Motor Panels
National Freight Corporation
Norsk Hydro
Parker Knoll
Paterson Jenks
Petrofina UK
Philips
Phillips & Drew (now part of UBS)
Polaroid
Prudential Corporation
Raychem
Robertson Research
Saatchi & Saatchi
J Sainsbury
Christian Salvesen
Scottish & Newcatle Breweries
Thomson Holidays
United Biscuits
Vickers Defence Systems
Waddington
Weetabix
Whitbread